D0025763

Nonverbal Communication

To our friend Maureen O'Sullivan,
whose underappreciated scientific contributions were always
informed by the real world, and whom we miss dearly.

Nonverbal Communication
Science and Applications

EDITORS

David Matsumoto
San Francisco State University and Humintell, LLC

Mark G. Frank
University at Buffalo, State University of New York

Hyi Sung Hwang
San Francisco State University and Humintell, LLC

Los Angeles | London | New Delhi
Singapore | Washington DC

Los Angeles | London | New Delhi
Singapore | Washington DC

FOR INFORMATION:

SAGE Publications, Inc.
2455 Teller Road
Thousand Oaks, California 91320
E-mail: order@sagepub.com

SAGE Publications Ltd.
1 Oliver's Yard
55 City Road
London EC1Y 1SP
United Kingdom

SAGE Publications India Pvt. Ltd.
B 1/I 1 Mohan Cooperative Industrial Area
Mathura Road, New Delhi 110 044
India

SAGE Publications Asia-Pacific Pte. Ltd.
3 Church Street
#10-04 Samsung Hub
Singapore 049483

Acquisitions Editor: Reid Hester
Editorial Assistant: Sarita Sarak
Production Editor: Cassandra Margaret
                          Seibel
Copy Editor: Mark Bast
Typesetter: C&M Digitals (P) Ltd.
Proofreader: Charlotte J. Waisner
Indexer: Jeanne R. Busemeyer
Cover Designer: Anupama Krishnan
Marketing Manager: Kelley McAllister
Permissions Editor: Karen Ehrmann

Copyright © 2013 by SAGE Publications, Inc.

All rights reserved. No part of this book may be reproduced or utilized in any form or by any means, electronic or mechanical, including photocopying, recording, or by any information storage and retrieval system, without permission in writing from the publisher.

Printed in the United States of America

Library of Congress Cataloging-in-Publication Data

Nonverbal communication : science and applications / editors, David R. Matsumoto, Mark G. Frank, Hyi Sung Hwang.

p. cm.
Includes bibliographical references and index.

ISBN 978-1-4129-9930-4 (pbk. : acid-free paper)

1. Body language. 2. Facial expression. 3. Nonverbal communication. I. Matsumoto, David Ricky. II. Frank, Mark G. III. Hwang, Hyi Sung.

BF637.N66N657 2013 302.2′22—dc23 2011041108

This book is printed on acid-free paper.

MIX
Paper from
responsible sources
FSC® C014174
www.fsc.org

12 13 14 15 16 10 9 8 7 6 5 4 3 2

Contents

Preface

Goals

Who doesn't want to be able to read people better in order to understand their motivations and intentions, gain insight about an individual's personality or credibility, or get a glimpse at their mental and emotional states? Understanding nonverbal communication well can be one of the keys to gaining this edge. This is why scientists, practitioners, and laypersons have been interested in nonverbal communication for centuries. Recent years have especially witnessed a flurry of interest in the topic. Practitioners in fields as wide and varied as business, health care, the legal system, law enforcement, and intelligence and national security are interested in leveraging scientific knowledge about human behavior generated over the past several decades and transforming that knowledge into practical and concrete skills that can improve proficiency and performance in the office, clinic, interview room, or field. Recognizing the importance of nonverbal communication and being able to decipher nonverbal behaviors quickly, accurately, and reliably can make the difference in any interview, negotiation, interrogation, or surveillance—in short, any situation involving people.

Because of the great interest in this topic, over the years a number of books about nonverbal behaviors and communication have emerged. They have tended to fall into one of two categories. One consists of books written or edited by scientists for scientists. These tend to be scholarly précis of the field, written in academic jargon, and based heavily on scientific research. The other includes those written by practitioners—former law enforcement officers, businesspersons, or just interested individuals—who used nonverbal communication heavily in their professional careers. These "body language experts" provide readers with valuable tips on how to read people learned through their experience.

We saw that there was a gap between these two types of books. On the one hand, books based in science were excellent for their reviews of the scientific literature in summarizing research and for providing an agenda for future research. After all, much of the knowledge driving increased awareness of the importance of nonverbal communication comes from scientific research on nonverbal behavior during human interactions. Indeed, there is great value in providing the science to those in the applied world whose goals include accurate appraisals of other people's behavior. Books exclusively presenting science, however, were not good at answering the "so what?" question so often asked of basic research, and scientific findings were often left on the shelves of libraries in publications that did not often reach practitioner audiences who could actually use the information in their professional lives. Moreover, these scientific books usually consisted of reporting the results of research studies derived from controlled laboratory settings that were often too artificial to be considered relevant or useful to many practitioners.

On the other hand, books by practitioners were great because they were based in actual experience, so readers got a sense of what actually worked "out there in the real world." But these books were not very good at bringing the vast research literature on nonverbal communication to bear on their experiences. Although they all wave their hands to the science, none of the books do justice to nor are they based in the considerable amount of scientific knowledge generated by empirical research over the past half century. Some outright misrepresent the science. Thus many in the academic community have been concerned that so-called knowledge of nonverbal communication has been applied too simplistically, erroneously, or even irresponsibly, and readers could never be sure of the degree to which the knowledge presented in these books was generalizable beyond the case examples presented.

This book's goal is to set the record straight by informing readers what is known and unknown so that practice can be appropriately evidence-based. The book cautions readers about glib overreading of nonverbal cues, thereby establishing the limits of what is currently known and can be applied with confidence. The book makes it clear that nonverbal cues mostly do not come with a dictionary and that context is extremely important in knowing what cues mean. Although academics are often, but not always, aware of these issues, the lay community and professional practitioners may not be, and clarifying this is one goal of the book.

This book bridges the gap between science and application by presenting chapters relevant to both and is the first of its kind in the literature. In Part I we provide five state-of-the-art reviews of the scientific knowledge in the literature concerning facial expressions, voice, body and gesture, cultural influences on nonverbal behavior, and deception. These reviews summarize years of research in these areas and bring to bear the most relevant information from these areas. Because the three of us are scientists actively engaged in scholarly research on these topics, the reviews are current and scientifically accurate. In Part II practitioners from a variety of fields—law enforcement, business, the courts and legal system, and health care professionals—describe how they have used nonverbal communication in their lines of work in order to improve their accuracy and proficiency. They describe not only how the knowledge has been used in practical, concrete terms; they also discuss the advantages and disadvantages of the approach. Some of them offer suggestions or describe how they came around to understanding the power of nonverbal communication. Many describe specific case studies in which their knowledge, or lack of knowledge, of nonverbal communication helped or hindered their professional work. Additionally, most of the authors of the chapters in Part II were trained by us or our colleagues in learning to read nonverbal behavior in programs based on scientific research findings; thus they are particularly well positioned to speak about the utility of nonverbal communication science to applied settings.

This book is relevant to both scientists and practitioners. Scientists will resonate with the chapters in Part I and in Part II will be able to see how knowledge generated from scientific research is put into practice by people in widely divergent fields, answering the "so what?" question so often asked of academic researchers. Practitioners should enjoy seeing how knowledge of nonverbal behaviors is applied in so many areas in Part II, including case studies, but should also appreciate the summaries of the scientific literature presented in Part I so that they know which knowledge about nonverbal behaviors has been vetted scientifically. Both scientists and practitioners will enjoy seeing how the knowledge from scientific laboratory research has been vetted by real-world observations, particularly made by the sorts of experienced professionals who wrote chapters for Part II. This is directly consistent with our own personal scientific philosophy: we strongly believe that any research results observed in the controlled setting of a laboratory are not "real" insights into human beings unless we can see them in the uncontrolled, wild and wooly world outside the laboratory. Thus, this book is truly unique in bridging the gap between science and application, and it is the first to truly highlight the strength of evidence-based training—training that is based in cutting-edge behavioral science research but also vetted in the field.

Markets

Given the goals of the book just described, there are two primary markets for the book. One is for scientists—beginning and experienced—and students interested in the areas of nonverbal communication. They will learn state-of-the-art research relevant to the most important aspects of nonverbal communication and behavior in Part I and see how the knowledge is put to work by the practitioners in Part II. For students, the ability to see how academic research can have an impact in everyday life is an especially important message that is missing in much of contemporary academic curricula. The book is especially relevant for courses on nonverbal communication that exist in many universities today. Moreover, many of the situations or case studies in Part II can serve as an impetus to conduct research studies, to trigger new ideas, or to test or elaborate on the observations made by these experienced professionals.

The second market is for practitioners who want to leverage evidence-based information about nonverbal behaviors based on scientific research. These are individuals from any and all walks of life for whom observation of human behavior and face-to-face interactions is an important part of their professional activities. This could include physicians; therapists; counselors and others in the health care profession; law enforcement officers; individuals involved in intelligence or national security; lawyers, judges, and negotiators; and businesspersons. We hope they find the issues, case studies, and applications informative and useful, either through helping "speed up" their acquisition of knowledge, to suggest new approaches to old or new problems faced on the job, or also to know the limits of what this advanced knowledge of nonverbal communication can do. Moreover, it may also provide them with the foundation upon which to critically evaluate any new "secret" technology or approach based on nonverbal communication, to more quickly know if they are dealing with a legitimate scientist or a huckster.

We sincerely hope that by bridging the gap between science and application this book provides the platform by which scientists and practitioners have greater dialogues that can inform each other symbiotically. This will lead to better science concerning topics with real-world relevance and better practice that is informed by the available science.

Acknowledgments

There are so many people to thank who made this book possible. First of all we would like to extend our deep appreciation and gratitude to the contributors who gave their time and effort outside of their busy professional and personal lives to provide us with chapters. Their expertise gave this book a special meaning that readers will not find anywhere else, and the authors all went above and beyond the call of duty in not only drafting their chapters but working with us through a very detailed editing process that required revisions, sometimes multiple times, to get to the format that readers will enjoy. We also appreciate the courage they showed to describe sensitive topics, including their occasional failures, so that others can learn. We truly hope that readers will recognize the great insights and experiences the authors bring to the work, which certainly inspire us to do better science.

We also would like to thank all of the staff at SAGE, starting with Chris Cardone, the editor who acquired the work and has encouraged us throughout the process. Sarita Sarak provided excellent editorial assistance throughout the project, guiding us from the start to the finish. Mark Bast did a superlative job of copyediting our manuscripts.

Although there are many in our lives who contributed to the creation of our ideas and the conduct of our research, any mistakes that are in the book are only ours.

DM

MGF

HSH

August 2011

PART I

The Science of Nonverbal Behavior

1

Reading People

Introduction to the World of Nonverbal Behavior

David Matsumoto
San Francisco State University and Humintell, LLC

Mark G. Frank
University at Buffalo, State University of New York

Hyi Sung Hwang
San Francisco State University and Humintell, LLC

You are walking home late at night. You notice a man is walking toward you. He suddenly quickens his pace, body leaning forward, hands out in fists moving rhythmically with his stride. His eyebrows are drawn down in the middle. His eyes are wide. His lips are tight. He looks right at you.

How did this story make you feel? What did you think was going to happen? Notice that whatever assessment you made was based exclusively on the nonverbal behavior of this man. You did not need to hear a single word spoken; yet you likely got a clear and distinct impression from his behaviors.

This book is about nonverbal communication. We hope to explain the current science of nonverbal communication but also show how it is used in the real world, with perspectives written by professionals from the legal, security, police, medical, marketing, negotiation, and people skills–training worlds. We hope to identify why the man in the vignette would display those behaviors, and why you would have the reaction you did.

This introductory chapter describes some overarching aspects of nonverbal communication that will help us better comprehend the science and experiences spelled out in this book. We will identify where nonverbal communication fits in with science, provide some history of the study, and show how it relates to verbal communication.

What Is Nonverbal Communication?

Although "language" often comes to mind first when considering communication, no discussion of communication is complete without the inclusion of nonverbal communication. Nonverbal communication has been referred to as "body language" in popular culture since the publication of Julius Fast's book of the same name in 1970. Researchers, however, have defined nonverbal communication as encompassing almost all of human communication except the spoken or written word (Knapp, 1972). We also define nonverbal communication as *the transfer and exchange of messages in any and all modalities that do not involve words*. As we discuss shortly, one of the major ways by which nonverbal communication occurs is through *nonverbal behaviors*, which are behaviors that occur during communication that do *not* include verbal language. But our definition of nonverbal communication implies that it is more than body language. It can be in the distance people stand when they converse. It can be in the sweat stains in their armpits. It can be in the design of the room. Nonverbal communication is a broader category than nonverbal behaviors, encompassing the way you dress, the placement of your office within a larger building, the use of time, the bumper stickers you place on your car, or the arrangement, lighting, or color of your room (Henley, 1977). The exact boundary of nonverbal communication, as part of communication, is a point of contention.

One source of messages in nonverbal communication is the *environment* or *context*. Different houses send different messages about their occupants. This is accomplished through the use of color, lighting, heat, fabric textures, photos, and so forth. Restaurants will capitalize on the messages sent by these environmental factors to influence the behaviors and impressions of diners. Fast-food restaurants use active, bright colors like orange, yellow, and red, in a well-lit environment with hard plastic seating. These messages subtly urge diners to eat more food more quickly and to not feel comfortable lounging around afterward so that the fast-food restaurants can get a quick turnover in order to maximize their profits. In contrast, elegant restaurants use dimmer lighting, softer and darker colors, and more comfortable chairs to communicate a more intimate impression, subtly urging diners to feel comfortable and stay around for dessert and coffee; this will cause diners to spend more per visit, as well as ensure repeat business through positive word of mouth. Designers of gambling casinos also know well about the power of creating an environment to send a message. And people can make relatively accurate judgments of the occupant's personalities just by viewing a room (Gosling, Ko, Mannarelli, & Morris, 2002). Thus the nonverbal messages sent by the environment can help guide the behaviors that occur within that environment.

Another source of nonverbal messages is one's *physical characteristics* or *appearance*. By physical characteristics, we mean the static physical appearance or smell of a person, including one's height and weight, skin color, hair, eyebrows, cheeks, chin, proportion of eyes, nose, and chin size, as well as odors. Sheldon (1940) believed that different body types were predictive of personality; endomorphs (heavier, obese, rounder, softer looking) were sociable and pleasant, mesomorphs (angular, muscular, harder looking) were leaders and strong-willed, and ectomorphs (thin, frail, brittle looking) were withdrawn, smart, and nervous. The media capitalizes on this association by casting actors and actresses accordingly; notice how the leading man is almost always a dynamic mesomorph, the comic relief is almost always the sociable, chubby endomorph, and the smart person is almost always the nerdy, skinny ectomorph. Although these beliefs persist, there is no strong evidence that body types predict personality.

Moreover, people have historically made the same judgments of personality based upon facial appearance. Chinese face reading, for example, is based on observations of the structure of a person's face. The ancient Chinese were not the only ones to do this; in the late 1800s, Europeans led by Caesar Lombroso felt they could characterize criminal personalities based upon the heaviness of one's eyebrows and jaw (Gould, 1981). As with the body research, there has been no evidence that one can pick accurately criminals by their facial appearance. Research in the 1980s by other scientists found that adult humans with more babyish-looking faces—defined by a higher forehead, proportionally larger eyes, and smaller nose—are seen as more naïve, honest, and less likely to be picked as a leader (Berry & McArthur, 1986). However, research in the 1950s still best sums up the findings in this area: although people have reliably assigned personalities to particular faces, their assignments were not accurate (Secord, Dukes, & Bevan, 1954).

Odors also send messages, both at a conscious and unconscious level. At a conscious level, perfumes and aftershaves and lack of body odor send messages about hygiene in North America, but such messages are not so clear in other cultures. At a subconscious level, males send pheromones that, when placed under the nose of a woman, make her judge a man as more attractive, and men's testosterone levels will rise when they are exposed to the scent of an ovulating woman (Miller & Maner, 2010). Infants can also recognize the smell of their mothers and will show strong preferences for items that smell of Mom. Many adults will also note how they are comforted by the smell of loved ones (reviewed in Knapp & Hall, 2006).

Physical appearance clues also include what are called artifactual clues, such as jewelry, clothes, glasses, and so forth. People wearing glasses are seen as being smarter. Jewelry sends messages about one's socioeconomic or marital status. For example, North Americans signal their married status by wearing a band on their left "ring" finger, whereas Europeans often wear this signal on the right ring finger. Clothing also sends messages about income, group membership, and even respect for others. The person who wears a T-shirt and jeans to a formal occasion sends a message about how he or she feels about that occasion, although, as in the previous instances, this message can be inaccurate.

Nonverbal communication also occurs in the *dynamic actions* of the face, voice, and body. These are known as *nonverbal behaviors*. Nonverbal behavior intrigues us. We see the way a person looks, the way he or she moves, and how he or she sounds. Nonverbal messages are transmitted through multiple nonverbal *channels*, which include facial expressions, vocal cues, gestures, body postures, interpersonal distance, touching, and gaze. We call these *channels* because, like channels on a television, they are each capable of sending their own distinct message. Our biology, learning, and culture influence these actions. This book will focus on these dynamic expressive elements of nonverbal communication, and we will limit our description of the static elements. We will address these dynamic nonverbal behaviors in more detail in Chapters 2, 3, 4, 5, and 6.

What Are the Functions of Nonverbal Communication?

Nonverbal communication serves a number of functions (Harrison, 1973). For example, nonverbal communication can *define* communication by providing the backdrop for communication—quiet, dimly lit rooms suggest to people that the communication that occurs within that environment should also be quiet and hushed (like in a religious venue). Brightly lit rooms, with active colors like yellow and orange, communicate active, upbeat activities. It could also be the behavior or dress of others in the room. If others are moving calmly, or crying, and/or wearing formal clothes, that sends a message quite distinct from a room full of people moving with a bounce in their step, laughing, and wearing Hawaiian shirts.

Nonverbal communication can also *regulate* our verbal communication. Much of our conversations are regulated by nonverbal cues so subtle that the average person does not notice them. For example, people nod and smile at particular moments during a face-to-face conversation. This signals to the talker that the listener understands and that the talker should continue talking. When the talker is finished, he or she will drop his or her voice tone and loudness to let the listener know. If the talker wishes to continue talking, he or she will fill the pauses that occur with a louder voice, and with many "umms, ahhs" and so forth. These subtle nonverbal signals are called "back channel" communication, because they are not the main focus of communication. Instead they function at the periphery of communication. We will describe in more detail in Chapter 3, The Voice, how we can converse without constantly speaking over each other.

Nonverbal communication can *be the message* itself. A smile indicates joy. A frown indicates unhappiness. A wrinkled nose, accompanied by the phrase "I love it" may indicate deception. A wave of the hand signifies "good-bye." A quiver in the voice signifies distress. Raising your index finger to your lips signifies "shhh" or "be quiet," yet raising the index finger into the air in a thrusting manner may mean "We're number one!" (Raising other fingers has entirely different meanings too!) No words are needed to send these messages. Note that most of these meanings are culturally determined, but some of them are not. We will address these in more detail in Chapters 2, 3, 4, 5, and 6 on the face, voice, body, culture, and deception, respectively.

What Are the Structures and Properties of Nonverbal Communication?

Scholars have suggested that nonverbal messages conform to many of the same properties as verbal communication—properties such as structured rules, intentionality, awareness, how much of it is covert or overt, control, and how private or public it is—but in slightly different ways (Andersen, 1999; Burgoon, Buller, & Woodall, 1996). In order to communicate meaning, nonverbal messages must be rule bound, like speech. For example, the sentence, "Floats otter the on sea the" does not make much sense because it does not conform to certain rules applying to word order. "The otter floats on the sea" does follow those rules and, thus, makes sense. Nonverbal communication has similar properties, and rule violations change their meanings. In North America, there are often unspoken rules that guide where we can touch people and when we can do it. We may not hug our students, but we might give a congratulatory hug when they successfully defend their thesis. Male teachers might at some point touch a female student on her forearm, likely not touch her on the small of her back, and definitely not touch her on her backside. They would apply the same touch rules to a male student. However, under very narrow circumstances, they might be able to touch a male student on the rear end—if they were playing on the same intramural basketball team, and this male student made a great play, he might get a congratulatory slap on the butt. But that same student would not receive that congratulatory slap on the butt when he turned in his term paper two days early. So again culture and situation conspire to set some rules—and if they are violated, we might cause resentment, or even a lawsuit. As we'll see in Chapter 5, situation and culture drive a lot of these differences.

We assume that the vast majority of spoken communication is *intentional*; we choose the words we speak. Likewise, most nonverbal communication is intentional. We deliberately wave to people or give them an insulting finger gesture. Scientists have argued, however, that a greater proportion of nonverbal communication is unintentional (Ekman, 1985). For example, some people may intend to communicate calmness and maturity about the death of their cat, and yet they often unintentionally communicate sadness through their voice tone and facial expression.

Similarly, people are also less *aware* of their nonverbal communication compared to their verbal communication. Except for unusual circumstances, people can hear all that they speak. People are mostly aware of some of their nonverbal communication, for example, the clothes they wear, the gestures they use, and the expressions they show—but not always. For example, when lying, a person may feel afraid and yet feel he or she was able to hide that fear. Despite their beliefs, liars are often unaware that in fact they are expressing clear signs of fear in their face, posture, or speech (Hurley & Frank, 2011). More on this in Chapter 6.

Verbal communication is also more *overt,* and nonverbal behavior is more *covert.* People are formally trained in their verbal behavior in the schools. Nonverbal communication is less obvious, as in subtle facial expressions and barely perceptible changes in voice tone, and people are not typically formally trained in their nonverbal communication. For example, children are not as often given lessons on how close to stand to others when talking or how to express anger in a facial expression. Studies of blind and sighted people show that their spontaneous expressions look similar, but their deliberately posed expressions are much easier to tell apart (see Matsumoto & Willingham, 2009, for a review).

Nonverbal communication is also less *controllable* than verbal communication. Verbal communication is easy to suppress, or to express, and people choose the words they use. Although much of nonverbal communication follows the same pattern, e.g., people choose to display a hand gesture, nonverbal communication is much more likely to have an unbidden quality to it. This is the smile that creeps onto one's face when one knows he or she should not be laughing (Frank, 2003). This is the person who is instructed to not smile when being interrogated but still smiles, even though the person admits trying to conceal his or her smile (Hurley & Frank, 2011).

Finally, verbal communication is more *public* than nonverbal communication. Speaking typically requires an audible or visible message that is available for others to hear or see, not just the intended target of the communication. Once public, this communication is also fodder for public discussion. In contrast, nonverbal communication tends to be fodder for private conversation. When political candidates spoke in the past, people publicly discussed and debated their policies, not their shoes or their gestures. This trend has changed in recent times, where it seems there is now as much focus on how the candidate delivers a message as the message he or she delivers. This has gotten to the point that every 24-hour news channel will have on at some point some alleged expert to analyze the nonverbal behaviors of people of interest, such as politicians, criminal suspects, athletes, and so forth.

What Is the Relationship Between Verbal and Nonverbal Communication?

Ekman & Friesen proposed that there are six ways in which verbal and nonverbal communication relate (Ekman & Friesen, 1969). They suggested that nonverbal communication can *substitute* for verbal communication, as well as *repeat, contradict, complement, accent,* and *regulate* verbal communication.

Substitution refers to the idea that nonverbal communication can be substituted for verbal communication. If asked whether we want another helping of our mother's wonderful pasta, we can nod our heads up and down to signify "yes," rather than attempting to utter the word "yes" through a mouthful of spaghetti.

Nonverbal communication can also *repeat* verbal communication. People can simultaneously speak the word "no" and shake their heads side to side. Repeating and substitution seem like the same idea, but *substitute* means someone doesn't speak the word or phrase represented by the nonverbal gesture, whereas *repeat* means he or she does speak the word or phrase.

But sometimes these verbal and nonverbal signals will *contradict* each other. Someone might utter the phrase, "This will be fun" and yet display a facial expression of disgust as he or she speaks those words. This is sarcasm; the words seem positive, yet the facial expression is negative.

Nonverbal communication can also *complement* verbal communication. People might say, "I've had a tough day," and at the same time their shoulders are slumped, and they drag their feet. Note that slumped shoulders and dragging feet can express a number of things (sadness, fatigue, injury, daydreaming), but in conjunction with the verbal message of "I've had a tough day" they enrich and focus the message.

Sometimes nonverbal communication will simply *accent* a particular part of a spoken verbal communication. Someone might speak the phrase, "It is important to punctuate your speech with nonverbal gestures" while rhythmically moving one hand up and down whilst pronouncing each syllable in the word "punctuate." In this instance, the moving hand gestures for the word "punctuate" will accent that word, thus letting the listener know that this concept is important.

Finally, nonverbal communication can *regulate* verbal communication. As discussed earlier, there are various unspoken rules regulating conversations that are displayed nonverbally, with what is called backchannel communication. This helps to keep the verbal communication organized and the conversation efficient.

Who Studies Nonverbal Communication?

Nonverbal communication is an area of study that straddles many disciplines—sociology, psychology, anthropology, communication, and even art, computer science, and criminal justice. Each of these fields tends to focus on a slightly different aspect of nonverbal communication. For example, psychology might focus on the nonverbal expression of emotions; anthropology might focus on the use of interpersonal space in different cultures; computer science may focus on making realistic looking and acting human agents or avatars; and communication might focus on the content of the message. But there is more overlap amongst these fields than divergence.

Regardless of modern science in nonverbal communication, it appears that all cultures have had for centuries written or oral traditions expressing the importance of nonverbal communication to their basic understanding of human beings. For example, over thousands of years Chinese culture has developed a set of rules on how to judge the character and personality of an individual by observing the size, shape, and relative positions of the nose, eyes, eyebrows, chin, cheeks, and forehead (known as Chinese face reading). Someone with wide-set eyes would be a "broadminded" person, or someone with a high forehead would be a "smart" person. Although there does not seem to be much scientific evidence that facial characteristics predict personality, modern people still believe this to be valid.

Ancient Greek culture also relied upon nonverbal communication to understand people. The playwright Theophrastus created a list of "31 types of men" that he made available to other playwrights to assist them in the creation of characters for their plays. Theophrastus relied upon insights gleaned from nonverbal communication to describe these personalities; for example, the penurious man doesn't wear his sandals until noon; or the sanguine man has slumped shoulders. We still rely upon nonverbal insights like these to judge people's personalities and emotions.

In India, the sacred Hindu texts called the *Veda,* written approximately 1,000 years BCE, described the nonverbal characteristics of a liar as someone who, when questioned, rubs his big toe along the ground, looks down, and doesn't make eye contact. Late twentieth-century research based on North Americans shows that people still concur with the *Veda* on this description of a liar.

Research into African history has shown that one of the characteristics of an effective chief was his ability to move his subjects with the power of his speeches, made particularly potent by the heavy use of nonverbal communication. This legacy is apparent in the traditions of the predominantly African American churches in America. These same principles of strong body language and voice tone accompanying speeches have now been adopted in various forms by the rest of American society and politics because of their ability to persuade above and beyond well-crafted words. We will discuss in Chapter 5 the role of culture in shaping nonverbal communication.

What Is the Importance of Nonverbal Communication in Everyday Life?

What are you missing in face-to-face interactions? Given the wealth of information that nonverbal behaviors communicate, it is no wonder that studies that have compared the relative contributions of verbal versus nonverbal behaviors in conveying messages report that the vast majority of the messages communicated are nonverbal (Friedman, 1978). Depending on the study, the estimated amount of information communicated nonverbally ranges between 65% and 95% of the total messages conveyed. This is ironic, especially because people most consciously attend to the verbal language when interacting with and judging others (Ekman, Friesen, O'Sullivan, & Scherer, 1980; O'Sullivan, Ekman, Friesen, & Scherer, 1985). Nonverbal behaviors are part of the "hidden dimension" of communication, a silent language (Hall, 1966, 1973). If you do *not* pay attention to the nonverbal behavior there is a great chance that you are missing much of what is actually being communicated by the other person. Thus, while active listening is always good, active observation is also necessary.

We all have a bias to pay attention too exclusively to the words being spoken, and there's a reason for this bias in our person perception. From the time we are very young we learn to communicate very precisely with words. We go to school and learn about grammar, punctuation, vocabulary, spelling, reading, and writing. In the US we learn to judge others by the words they use, and we are told that we need to be effective communicators via the words we choose to use.

Contrarily, there are no schools or classes on nonverbal behavior. Despite the obvious importance of nonverbal behavior in communication, all of our training in this important aspect of communication is done on the job. We learn how to manage our nonverbal displays from our parents, families, teachers, bosses, and friends. But all of this is done informally, often implicitly.

This bias is even more pronounced if we are in a situation where we are evaluating the credibility of what someone else is saying, evaluating truthfulness, or detecting deception. In these situations, we attend even more strongly to the words being spoken—the stories being told—in order to find some evidence of an inconsistency in what is being said (Ekman et al., 1980; O'Sullivan et al., 1985). This is especially unfortunate because these are precisely the times when nonverbal behavior can be so important, and so telling.[1]

Goal and Outline of the Remainder of the Book: Science and Application

This book brings together for the first time a blending of the science and practice of nonverbal behaviors. The book is divided into two parts. In Part I, we will present the state of the art in scientific research literature regarding nonverbal behaviors. These chapters will describe what we have learned through the years through scientific research and the current state of knowledge in the field. Chapter 2 deals with facial expressions; Chapter 3 deals with voice; Chapter 4 with body and gestures; Chapter 5 with culture. In Chapter 6 we bring all of these together and summarize the research on nonverbal behaviors associated with deception and lying, as this is a topic and concern for all practitioners.

Part II of this book puts nonverbal communication back front and center into everyday life—a world where nonverbal communication affects interpersonal encounters ranging from police interviews, first dates, doctor visits, job interviews, negotiation, airline travel, and advertising. In Part II we bring together chapters from a number of practitioners in a wide variety of professions who use the power of nonverbal behaviors as an active and important part of their professional work. We will hear from practitioners who work in the real world and learn how they have used nonverbal communication in their jobs, how it has helped them, and what they found about some of the limits in using it in the real world. This part of the book is loosely arranged around major categories of professions, including law enforcement and national security, officers of the court (lawyers and judges), negotiators, human skills trainers, and members of the health care profession.

In Chapter 18 we end this book by reapplying the eye of the scientist to these real-world accounts put forth by our practitioners, who are all considered amongst the best people in their fields, to see what principles we can derive from their experience and expertise. We believe that any of our scientific research findings in nonverbal communication, be they from the controlled laboratory conditions or otherwise, really don't count until we can see them in the real world, through the wild and wooly contexts that we face every single day.

Note

1. This is not to imply that paying attention to the words is not important. Of course it is extremely important. But what we are saying is that if you don't pay attention to the nonverbal behaviors as well you will be missing a large amount of the messages being conveyed.

References

Andersen, P. A. (1999). *Nonverbal communication: Forms and functions.* Mountain View, CA: Mayfield.

Berry, D. S., & McArthur, L. Z. (1986). Perceiving character in faces: The impact of age-related craniofacial changes on social perception. *Psychological Bulletin, 100,* 3–18.

Burgoon, J. K., Buller, D. B., & Woodall, W. G. (1996). *Nonverbal communication: The unspoken dialogue.* New York: Harper & Row.

Ekman, P. (1985). *Telling lies: Clues to deceit in the marketplace, politics, and marriage* (1st ed.). New York: Norton.

Ekman, P., & Friesen, W. V. (1969). The repertoire of nonverbal behavior: Categories, origins, usage, and coding. *Semiotica, 1,* 49–98.

Ekman, P., Friesen, W. V., O'Sullivan, M., & Scherer, K. (1980). Relative importance of face, body, and speech in judgments of personality and affect. *Journal of Personality and Social Psychology, 38,* 270–277.

Frank, M. G. (2003). Smiles, lies, and emotion. In M. Abel (Ed.), *The smile: Forms, functions, and consequences* (pp. 15–43). New York: The Edwin Mellen Press.

Friedman, H. S. (1978). The relative strength of verbal versus nonverbal cues. *Personality and Social Psychology Bulletin, 4,* 147–150.

Gosling, S. D., Ko, S. J., Mannarelli, T., & Morris, M. E. (2002). A room with a cue: Personality judgments based on offices and bedrooms. *Journal of Personality and Social Psychology, 82*(3), 379–398.

Gould, S. J. (1981). *The mismeasure of man.* New York: Norton.

Hall, E. T. (1966). *The hidden dimension.* New York: Doubleday.

Hall, E. T. (1973). *The silent language.* New York: Anchor.

Harrison, R. P. (1973). Nonverbal communication. In I. S. Pool, W. Schramm, N. Maccoby, F. Fry, E. Parker, & J. L. Fern (Eds.), *Handbook of communication* (pp. 93–115). Chicago: Rand McNally.

Henley, N. (1977). *Body politics: Power, sex, and nonverbal communication.* Englewood Cliffs, NJ: Prentice-Hall.

Hurley, C. M., & Frank, M. G. (2011). Executing facial control during deception situations. *Journal of Nonverbal Behavior, 35,* 119–131.

Knapp, M. L. (1972). *Nonverbal communication in human interaction.* New York: Holt, Rinehart, and Winston.

Knapp, M. L., & Hall, J. A. (2006). *Nonverbal communication in human interaction* (6th ed.). New York: Harcourt Brace.

Matsumoto, D., & Willingham, B. (2009). Spontaneous facial expressions of emotion of congenitally and non-congenitally blind individuals. *Journal of Personality and Social Psychology, 96*(1), 1–10.

Miller, S. L., & Maner, J. K. (2010). Scent of a woman: Male testosterone responses to female olfactory ovulation cues. *Psychological Science, 21,* 276–283.

O'Sullivan, M., Ekman, P., Friesen, W. V., & Scherer, K. R. (1985). What you say and how you say it: The contribution of speech content and voice quality to judgments of others. *Journal of Personality & Social Psychology, 48*(1), 54–62.

Secord, P. F., Dukes, W. G., & Bevan, W. (1954). Personalities in faces I: An experiment in social perceiving. *Genetic Psychology Monographs, 41,* 231–279.

Sheldon, W. H. (1940). *The varieties of human physique: An introduction to constitutional psychology.* New York: Harper & Brothers.

2

Facial Expressions

David Matsumoto and Hyi Sung Hwang

San Francisco State University and Humintell, LLC

The face is arguably the most prominent nonverbal channel, and for good reason. Of all the channels of nonverbal behavior, the face is the most intricate. It is the most complex signaling system in our body. It is the channel of nonverbal behavior most studied by scientists. It is a channel that can reflect involuntary reactions and produce voluntary gestures. And arguably it is the seat of the greatest amount of information that is conveyed nonverbally. That's why we have "face-to-face" interactions. Sometimes we need to get "in people's faces." When we have meetings with others this is "face time," and sometimes we need to "face off." When talking with others we need to "face the facts" or "face the consequences."

One of the most important signals the face displays is emotion. Being able to read the emotional states of the person you are talking to is an incredible skill that can help anyone whose profession requires face-to-face interaction. Being able to read others' emotions can give you insights not only to their emotional states but their intentions, motivations, personalities, trustworthiness, and credibility. Emotions can inform us of malicious intent, hidden information, or downright deception.

Emotions do this because they are immediate, automatic, involuntary, and unconscious reactions to events that are important to us. If people have emotions and you read them on their faces you know something just happened that they are interpreting as important to them in their lives. And knowing what emotion you are seeing gives you ideas of why that event was important to them. You can gain this knowledge without their knowing about it because people don't usually know what they are doing on their own faces (Barr & Kleck, 1995). This can give anyone whose profession requires interaction an edge, whether it is a patient intake, deposition, hiring interview, or police interrogation.

Moreover, as we will see shortly, facial expressions of emotion are universal. That is, the ability to read facial expressions of emotion can help you in interactions with anyone regardless of his or her race, culture, ethnicity, nationality, sex, religion, or age. It doesn't matter what languages are spoken either; even if you work through an interpreter, you can read the emotional expressions of the person you are talking to.

Emotions prepare us for behavior. For many individuals whose jobs put them in harm's way the ability to read facial expressions of emotion can give them that added edge in knowing if a person is about to attack, run, or shut down psychologically. Knowing the differences between these potential future actions can mean the difference between life or death for some. Being able to read faces may give someone the extra few seconds to take evasive action and even prevent violence and aggression.

Emotions facilitate or block the giving of information. If your job requires you to obtain information from others, then reading their emotions can be an invaluable tool. When people do not give information readily there is usually an emotional reason why. Getting people to give up that information requires you to be able to address those emotional needs of the person, which requires you to read his or her emotions in the first place.

Reading emotions in others can help you to gain insights about a person's personality, motivations, and intentions. It can help you build rapport and establish relationships. It can help you get the person's whole story, reliably and accurately. It can help you vet individuals, establish credibility, and evaluate truthfulness. It can help in any situation involving negotiation, persuasion, and influence.

That is why we start this book discussing facial expressions of emotion. In this chapter we describe the scientific basis for our focus on facial expressions of emotion. We hope to convince you that what we know about faces is not voodoo, witchcraft, magic, or something we just dreamed up. Instead what we present is based on solid scientific evidence accumulated in psychology and the social sciences over the past half century. We bring that collective evidence to bear here.

We begin our presentation by discussing emotion and its characteristics, which gives you a platform with which to understand the scientific basis and importance of facial expressions of emotion.

Emotions

Defining Emotion

Humans experience a wide range of affective phenomena, and much of it is called "emotion" by researchers and laypersons alike. Emotion is an aspect of our lives that all have a lifetime of access to, and we contemplate about the proper words to describe its nuances. Thus it is difficult to arrive at a consensual definition of emotion that encompasses all possible types of emotion and yet distinguishes it from other affective phenomena. At the same time researchers and practitioners who leverage emotion need to make explicit their working definitions so they and others can understand what part of the affective world they call emotion. We do so here.

We define emotion as *transient, bio-psycho-social reactions to events that have consequences for our welfare and potentially require immediate action*. Emotions are biological because they involve physiological responses from the central and autonomic nervous systems. They are psychological because they involve specific mental processes required for elicitation and regulation of response, direct mental activities, and motivate behavior. They are social because they are often elicited by social factors and have social meaning when elicited.[1]

Emotions are rapid information processing systems that help us act with minimal conscious deliberation (Tooby & Cosmides, 2008). Problems associated with birth, battle, death, and seduction have occurred throughout our evolutionary history, and emotions aided in adapting to those problems rapidly and with minimal conscious cognitive intervention. If humans didn't have emotions they could not make rapid decisions concerning whether to attack, defend, flee, care for others, reject food, or approach something useful. For instance, drinking spoiled milk or eating rotten eggs has negative consequences for our welfare. The emotion of disgust, however, helps us immediately take action by not ingesting them in the first place or vomiting them out. This response is adaptive because it aids in our ultimate survival and allows us to take action immediately without much thinking. In some instances taking the time to think about what to do is a luxury that might cost someone his or her life.

Emotions are elicited as we scan our environments and evaluate (appraise) them for consequences to our welfare (Ekman, 2003; Ellsworth

& Scherer, 2003; Frijda, Kuipers, & ter Schure, 1989; Roseman, 1984; Roseman, Dhawan, Rettek, & Naidu, 1995; Scherer, Schorr, & Johnstone, 2001). If events do not have such consequences, we continue scanning; if they do, they trigger emotion in order to prime action and motivate behavior (Frijda et al., 1989; Tomkins, 1962, 1963). When triggered, emotions orchestrate other systems such as perception, attention, inference, learning, memory, goal choice, motivational priorities, physiological reactions, motor behaviors, and behavioral decision making (Cosmides & Tooby, 2000; Tooby & Cosmides, 2008). They simultaneously activate certain systems and deactivate others in order to prevent the chaos of competing systems operating at the same time, allowing for coordinated responses to environmental stimuli (Levenson, 1999). Thus, fear will prepare us to flee and, in the process, shut down temporarily unneeded digestive processes, resulting in saliva reduction (a dry mouth). Emotions initiate a system of components that includes subjective experience (feelings), expressive behaviors, physiological reactions, action tendencies, and cognition; the term "emotion" is a metaphor for these reactions.

The Difference Among Emotion, Moods, and Personality Traits

We distinguish emotions from other affective phenomena such as moods, personality traits, and some psychopathologies. The key characteristics of emotion to us are that it is a state not a trait; a mental condition, not just physiological or cognitive; a reaction that results from an appraisal process; and it involves multiple components including affect, physiological response, mental changes, and expressive behavior. Our understanding of emotion is supported by studies that distinguished emotions from other affective phenomena (Clore & Ortony, 1988, 1991; Clore, Ortony, & Foss, 1987). These studies showed that emotions refer to internal, mental conditions as opposed to external (e.g., abandoned) or physical conditions (e.g., aroused); are states (i.e., transient) and not dispositions, other nonstates, or borderline examples of states; and have affect (subjective experiences or feelings) as their predominant referential focus as opposed to behavior (e.g., careful) or cognition (e.g., certain). They concluded that although all words in the affective lexicon concern affect in some way, emotions are a subset of those with a predominant rather than a peripheral focus on the experience of affect, with an emphasis on a state and not a disposition.

Moods differ from emotions in that moods refer to longer-lasting affective states. Moods dispose people to have certain emotions more frequently. They can last for hours, days, or even longer; emotions last for only a few seconds or minutes. Emotions are triggered by specific events, but moods can be triggered by nonspecific events or even by lack of sleep, hunger, ruminating, or a string of previous emotions. When people are in a blue mood, that does not mean that they are sad all the time; rather they are more likely to become sad more often because they are in a state that disposes them to become sad, and they may have some of the sad affect or feelings.

Emotions also differ from affect-related personality traits. All individuals are born with a certain personality trait that predisposes them to have certain emotions (McCrae & Costa, 1999). Some people are hostile individuals; some are shy; some are happy-go-lucky and optimistic. These traits likely come from a combination of genes and environmental learning. But these personality traits are not emotions; they are predispositions to have emotions. A person who has a hostile personality is not necessarily angry all the time. In fact, it would be impossible for a person to be in an emotional state all the time because the physiological consequences of emotions are too toxic to the body. Instead, a person with a hostile personality is predisposed to become angry more often. But that doesn't mean that that person doesn't feel other emotions as well.

Some psychopathologies also have emotion as a central feature. But the difference between normal emotion and psychopathology is large. As mentioned earlier, emotions are transient; psychopathology, however, involves a more chronic state. When emotions are involved it is as if the individual is "stuck" in some part of the process of emotion and cannot get out. Phobias or panic disorder, for example, involve recurrent and strong reactions of fear; depression involves being stuck in intense sadness. Table 2.1 lists some emotions and their corresponding moods, personality traits, and

Table 2.1   Emotions Are Different From Moods, Personality Traits, and Psychopathologies

Emotions	Moods	Personality Traits	Psychopathology
Anger	Irritable	Hostile	Chronic impulsivity
Fear	Apprehensive	Shy	Panic anxiety, phobias
Sadness	Blue	Melancholy	Depression
Joy	Euphoria	Optimistic	Mania
Disgust	Disdainful	Arrogance	Anorexia

psychopathologies that feature them; but it is clear that the latter are not emotions. Many researchers and laypersons alike conflate any affective phenomenon with emotion probably because our awareness of emotion is represented in affect or feelings.[2] But clearly not all affective phenomena are emotions. Being tired, hungry, or in pain, for example, produces a feeling state; but we do not believe they are emotions.

Biological Versus Nonbiological Emotions

Even within the world of emotion all emotions are not the same. Humans experience a wide range of emotions including anger, disgust, fear, shame, guilt, jealousy, pride, triumph, love, etc. Researchers have proposed different categories of emotions, including basic emotions (Ekman, 1992, 1999; Izard, 2007), self-conscious emotions (Keltner & Buswell, 1997; Tangney, 2003; Tracy & Robins, 2004), positive emotions (Fredrickson, 2001; Fredrickson & Losada, 2005), prosocial emotions (McCullough, Bono, & Root, 2007), and moral emotions (Haidt, 2001). For our purposes we make a very gross distinction between emotions that evidence indicates are biologically innate (reviewed in more detail shortly; Buck, 1999; Ekman, 1992, 1999; Izard, 2007; LeDoux & Phelps, 2008; Panksepp, 2007, 2008) and those for which there is no or insufficient evidence. We call the former group *biological emotions* (Matsumoto & Hwang, in press-a).

Characteristics of Biological Emotions

There is strong evidence for emotions of anger, disgust, fear, joy, sadness, and surprise to be classified as biological emotions (Buck, 1999; Ekman, 1999; Izard, 2007).[3] Over the years research has demonstrated that this set of emotions shares certain distinct characteristics that differentiate it from other emotions. Here we review the major characteristics of this category of emotions that has been documented by scientific research.

Universality in emotion antecedents (triggers). An important aspect of emotion is the events that trigger them in the first place. *Emotion antecedents* are the events or situations that trigger or elicit an emotion. For example, losing a loved one may be an antecedent of sadness; getting an "A" in a class in which you wanted to do well may elicit happiness or joy. In the scientific literature, emotion antecedents are also known as emotion *elicitors or triggers.*

A considerable number of studies have supported the universality of emotion antecedents (Boucher & Brandt, 1981; Brandt & Boucher, 1985). The most prominent work has been that of Scherer and his colleagues, who have conducted a number of studies using questionnaires designed to assess the quality and nature of emotional experiences in many different cultures. Their largest study involved approximately 3,000 participants in 37 countries on five continents (Scherer, 1997a, 1997b; Scherer & Wallbott, 1994). Respondents wrote about the event that last triggered each of seven emotions. These situations were then coded into general categories such as good news and bad news, temporary and permanent separation, and success and failure in achievement situations. The findings indicated that no culture-specific antecedent category was necessary to code the data, indicating that all categories of events generally occurred in all cultures to produce each of the seven emotions studied. In addition, Scherer and his colleagues found many similarities across cultures in the relative frequency with which each of the antecedent events elicited emotions. For example, the most frequent elicitors of happiness across cultures were "relationships with friends," "temporary meetings with friends," and "achievement situations." The most frequent elicitors of anger were "relationships" and "injustice." The most frequent elicitors of sadness were "relationships" and "death." These findings supported the view that emotion antecedents are universal across cultures.

Universality in emotion appraisal processes. Just as important as the event that triggers an emotion are the cognitive processes that occur to evaluate this event in order to know whether to trigger an emotion in the first place. This process is known as *appraisal,* which can be loosely defined as the process by which people evaluate the events, situations, or occurrences that lead to their having emotions. The largest cross-cultural study on emotion appraisal processes is that of Scherer and colleagues just described. In that study respondents not only described the events that brought about their emotions; they were also asked about how they appraised or evaluated those events. For example, respondents were asked to rate whether the antecedent helped them achieve their goals or blocked their goals; was expected or not; or was fair or unfair. There was a very a high degree of cross-cultural similarity in emotion appraisal processes. Other researchers have replicated this cross-cultural agreement in appraisal as well (Mauro, Sato, & Tucker, 1992; Roseman et al., 1995). Thus biological emotions are triggered by the same psychological themes in all cultures (Lazarus, 1991). Table 2.2 summarizes the universal psychological themes that trigger each of the universal biological emotions.

Table 2.2   The Triggers and Functions of Biological Emotions

Emotion	Universal Underlying Psychological Theme (Trigger)	Function
Happiness	Goal attainment or accomplishment	Future motivation
Anger	Goal obstruction, injustice, perceived norm violations	Remove the obstacle
Sadness	Loss of loved one or object	Recoup resources; call for help
Disgust	Contamination; offensive, rotten objects	Repulsion or elimination of the contaminated object
Fear	Threat to physical or psychological well-being	Avoid threat; reduce harm
Surprise	Sudden novel objects	Orient and obtain more information
Contempt	Immoral actions	Assert one's superiority

Universality in physiological responses. For years there were debates concerning whether different emotions are associated with specific and unique physiological response profiles. Early research in this area was inconclusive. The first definitive evidence for this came from a study that used the universal facial expressions as markers to signal when to examine physiological reactions. This study demonstrated that each of the universal emotions, when signaled by the universal facial expressions, had a distinct and discrete physiological signature in the autonomic nervous system (Ekman, Levenson, & Friesen, 1983). Subsequent research has replicated these findings and shown how there are specific patterns in central nervous system activity (the brain) as well (Davidson, Scherer, & Goldsmith, 2003; Ekman, Davidson, & Friesen, 1990; Levenson & Ekman, 2002; Levenson, Ekman, & Friesen, 1990; Mauss, Levenson, McCarter, Wilhelm, & Gross, 2005). These findings have been also replicated in cross-cultural samples including Chinese and European Americans (Tsai & Levenson, 1997) and the Minangkabau of West Sumatra, Indonesia (Levenson, Ekman, Heider, & Friesen, 1992).

Different emotions produce unique physiological signatures because emotions help individuals respond to emotional stimuli by preparing the body to engage in activity. When we're angry, our heart rates increase and blood rushes to the upper parts of our bodies and toward our extremities in our arms and hands, preparing us to fight. When afraid, our heart rates increase, but the blood flows to the lower parts of our bodies and to our legs, preparing us to run. When afraid, our digestive system shuts down because there is no need to digest food if our well-being is threatened. Each emotion prepares us to engage in specific behaviors to adapt to the event that elicited the emotion.[4]

Universality in cognitive processes. Each of the biological emotions produces universal cognitive processes in a form known as *cognitive gating* (Levenson, 1999, 2003). Cognitive gating refers to the channeling of mental activities and attention. For example, surprise and fear produce increases in our visual field so that we can scan the environment more broadly and thereby be attentive to novel stimuli that may have consequences to our welfare. Anger, however, narrows our vision as we focus and burrow in on the target of our anger; in anger we have tunnel vision. Disgust turns off sensors in our olfactory system so that we do not become overwhelmed with the contaminated object that elicited the disgust in the first place (Susskind et al., 2008).

Moreover, emotions channel our thought processes. When we are sad it's easier to think about other sad thoughts, to remember previous sad experiences, and to have a gloomy prospect of the future. When we are happy it's the opposite. We can remember previous emotional experiences (we liked that movie; we didn't like that restaurant), but we may not remember exactly why. Emotions are the cognitive glue in our brains that ties our memories together (Bower, 1981; Bower et al., 1994); they open the cognitive gates to similar emotionally tagged memories and thoughts.

Universality in subjective emotional experience. Emotions produce specific feelings, which are also known as affect or subjective experience. Each of the biological emotions produces a specific feeling state, and these feeling states are universal. The feeling of anger is the same all around the world as is the feeling of sadness or fear. The most prominent study to examine subjective experiences across cultures is the work by Scherer and his colleagues, described earlier (Scherer & Wallbott, 1994). They asked respondents to rate their subjective feelings, physiological sensations, motor behaviors, and expressions when they felt anger, disgust, fear, joy, and sadness. For all response domains, the emotions differed significantly and strongly among each other. Geographical and sociocultural factors were much smaller within any given emotion than those for differences between the emotions. Thus the researchers concluded that there are strong and consistent differences between the reaction patterns for the emotions and that these are independent of the country studied. In other words, there were many more similarities in the responses across the cultures than there were differences, providing evidence for universal, psychobiological emotional patterning in subjective response.

Universality in expressive behavior. Emotions produce specific and unique nonverbal behaviors, including facial expressions, voice, body postures, and gestures, and these expressive behaviors are universal. In fact, most of the research done on emotions has occurred in the last 40 years or so in psychology, and much of it gained its impetus from studies that documented the universality of facial expressions of emotion (described in more detail shortly). Indeed, the study of the face opened the door for scientists to study emotions more accurately and precisely.

Facial expressions are more than simple readouts of internal states; they coordinate social interactions through their informative, evocative, and motivating functions (Keltner & Kring, 1998). They provide information to perceivers about the individual's emotional state (Ekman, 1993; Scherer, 1986), behavioral intentions (Fridlund, 1994), relational status vis-à-vis the target of the expression (Keltner, 1995; Tiedens, Ellsworth, & Mesquita, 2000), and objects and events in the social environment (Mineka & Cook, 1993). This view of facial expression emerged in developmental studies of emotional exchanges between parents and children (Hertenstein & Campos, 2004; Klinnert, Campos, & Sorce, 1983; Klinnert, Emde, Butterfield, & Campos, 1986) as well as ethological studies of social behaviors like flirting, reconciliation, aggression, and play and is consistent with claims regarding the coevolution of signal and perceiver response to displays (Eibl-Eibesfeldt, 1989). Thus, an individual's emotional expression serves as a "social affordance" that evokes "prepared" responses in others (Esteves, Dimberg, & Ohman, 1994). Anger, for example, evolved to elicit fear-related responses and the inhibition of inappropriate action (Dimberg & Ohman, 1996), and many people label another person's angry expression as "scary" (Matsumoto, 2006). Distress calls might have evolved to elicit sympathetic responses in observers (Eisenberg et al., 1989). Through these reciprocal processes, emotional communication helps individuals in relationships—parent and child, mates, boss and subordinates—respond to the demands and opportunities of their social environment. They are basic elements of social interaction, from flirtatious exchanges to greeting rituals. This is why people are reliable judges of emotional displays, which is supported by many studies (more to follow).

Universality in the coherence among emotion response systems. Not only is there universality in the various responses of emotion—antecedent events, appraisals, physiology, cognition, subjective experience, and expressive behavior—there is also coherence among them. *Emotion response system coherence* refers to the idea that the various response components—face, voice, physiology, etc.—are related to each other in a meaningful way.

Coherence refers to the fact that the responses are coordinated, organized, and orchestrated so that they allow individuals to adapt to the emotion-eliciting stimuli immediately and with minimal conscious deliberation. It wouldn't make sense for our bodies to initiate multiple, competing responses; instead, emotions coordinate our body systems to efficiently and effectively respond to events. This is why emotions are a highly efficient information processing system.[5]

There are, in fact, many single-culture studies that demonstrate coherence among emotion response systems (reviewed in Matsumoto, Nezlek, & Koopmann, 2007). The cross-cultural evidence, however, is just starting to emerge. We (Matsumoto et al., 2007) reanalyzed the data from the Scherer studies described earlier and examined the relationships among the self-reported expressive behaviors, emotional experiences, and physiological sensations. There were moderately sized correlations between these three systems of responses across the respondents in all 27 countries analyzed. There were also consistent correlations between verbal and nonverbal expressions, as well as between emotion intensity and physiological sensations, all of which suggest coherence in an underlying neurophysiological reality. Moreover, this coherence was true cross-culturally.

Summary. Research on biological emotions indicates that these emotions are a universal psychological phenomenon that is based in the evolution of the species. Humans are born with a core set of emotions that are biologically innate and genetically encoded. They allow us to appraise events and situations in reliable and predictable ways; thus the same types of underlying psychological elicitors are found across cultures. When emotions are elicited they trigger a host of responses, and these responses appear to be part of a universal emotion package. They are associated with unique physiological signatures in both the central and autonomic nervous systems, which are part of a coordinated response system that prepares individuals to fight, flee, or jump for joy. They are expressed universally in all humans via facial expressions regardless of race, culture, sex, ethnicity, or national origin. As such, humans can also universally recognize emotions in others, and this has important social meaning. Overall, these universal processes allow us to adapt, respond, and cope with problems that occur in our social lives and environments, aiding us to live, work, and function more effectively, regardless of the culture in which we are embedded (see Table 2.3 for a summary of the characteristics of biological emotions).

As we mentioned, one of the cornerstones of biological emotions is the fact that each of them has a universal nonverbal signal in the face. The universality of facial expressions is an important aspect of biological emotions

Table 2.3   Characteristics of Biological Emotions

Universality in . . .	Description
Emotion antecedents	The same kinds of events trigger the same emotions in all cultures, especially events found in nature or in basic social relationships.
Emotion appraisal processes	The processes people use to evaluate events that trigger emotions are universal, especially concerning their underlying psychological themes.
Physiological responding	Each emotion turns on a unique and specific physiological signature that primes the body for action.
Cognitive gating	Each emotion produces unique and specific channeling of mental activities, attention, and thought.
Subjective emotional experience	Each emotion produces a unique subjective feeling state, also known as *affect*.
Expressive behavior	Each emotion produces unique nonverbal behaviors, including facial expressions, voice, and body.
Response coherence	The responses produced by an emotion are organized and orchestrated so as to allow for organized responding to events with minimal conscious deliberation, ensuring that different body systems do not compete with each other.

and served as the impetus for much of the research that has occurred in psychology over the past four decades. But this was not always the case, and for many years psychology believed facial expressions of emotion were learned gestures. We now describe the scientific evidence underlying the conclusion that these expressions are universal.

Scientific Evidence for the Universality of Facial Expressions of Emotion

Original Debates Concerning Universality Versus Culture Specificity and the Original Universality Studies

Darwin (1872) originally suggested that emotions and their expressions had evolved across species, were evolutionarily adaptive, biologically innate, and universal across humans and even nonhuman primates.

According to Darwin, all humans, regardless of race or culture, possessed the ability to express emotions in exactly the same ways, primarily through their faces and, to a lesser extent, in the voice (see Chapter 3). Darwin (1872) claimed, in his principle of serviceable habits, that facial expressions are the residual actions of more complete behavioral responses. He wrote *The Expression of the Emotions in Man and Animals* to refute the claims of Sir Charles Bell, the leading facial anatomist of his time and a teacher of Darwin's, about how God designed humans with unique facial muscles to express uniquely human emotions.[6] Relying on advances in photography and anatomy (Duchenne de Boulogne, 1862/1990), Darwin engaged in a detailed study of the muscle actions involved in emotion and concluded that the muscle actions are universal, and their precursors can be seen in the expressive behaviors of nonhuman primates and other mammals.

Darwin's work, however, drew heavy criticism, especially from noted anthropologists such as Margaret Mead and Ray Birdwhistell. They noted vast differences in expressive behavior across cultures and concluded that the facial expressions could not be universal. Instead, they argued that emotional expressions had to be learned differently in every culture, and just as different cultures have different spoken languages, they must have different expressive languages of the face as well.

Between Darwin's original writing and the 1960s, only seven studies attempted to test the universality of facial expression. Unfortunately, these studies were inconclusive so that unequivocal data speaking to the issue of the possible universality of emotional expression did not emerge at that time (Ekman, Friesen, & Ellsworth, 1972). Thus, an influential review of the literature (Bruner & Tagiuri, 1954) concluded that facial expressions were not universal but learned.

It was not until the mid-1960s when psychologist Sylvan Tomkins resurrected interest in the study of emotions and faces with the publication of his landmark volumes (Tomkins, 1962, 1963). Tomkins then conducted the first study demonstrating that facial expressions were reliably associated with certain emotional states (Tomkins & McCarter, 1964). Later, Tomkins recruited Paul Ekman and Carroll Izard to conduct what is known today as the "universality studies."

In the first set of studies, these researchers obtained judgments of faces thought to express emotions panculturally and demonstrated that all cultures agreed on the emotions portrayed in the expressions (Ekman, 1972, 1973; Ekman & Friesen, 1971; Ekman, Sorenson, & Friesen, 1969; Izard, 1971). Collectively these findings demonstrated the existence of six universal expressions—anger, disgust, fear, happiness, sadness, and surprise—as judges from around the world agreed on what emotion was portrayed in the faces.

These early studies were open to the criticism that the results were flawed because the cultures studied were relatively industrialized, and people in those cultures may have learned how to interpret the faces shown because of shared visual input through mass media such as movies or magazines. To address this criticism Ekman and colleagues (Ekman & Friesen, 1971; Ekman et al., 1969) conducted two studies with two preliterate tribes—the Fore and the Dani—in the highlands of New Guinea. In the first study, Ekman showed that the tribespeople could reliably recognize the faces of emotion posed by Westerners; in the second study, films of the tribespeople expressing emotions were shown to Americans who had never seen New Guineans before, and the Americans were able to recognize the emotions portrayed by the New Guineans. Thus the ability to recognize facial expressions of emotion did not occur because of learning through mass media or other shared visual input.

In addition to the judgment studies just described, some of the most important findings related to universality came from Friesen's (1972) cross-cultural study of expressions that occurred spontaneously in reaction to emotion-eliciting films. In that study American and Japanese participants viewed neutral and highly stressful films while their facial behaviors were recorded. Coding of the facial behaviors that occurred when viewing the films identified the same expressions associated with the six emotions mentioned previously and corresponded to the facial expressions portrayed in the stimuli used in the previous judgment studies. Individuals from both cultures showed the same expressive patterns; thus, this study provided the first evidence that facial expressions of emotion were universally produced.

Subsequent Research Documenting the Universality of Facial Expressions of Emotion

Since the original universality studies already described, more than 30 studies examining judgments of facial expressions have replicated the finding of universal recognition of emotion in the face (Matsumoto, 2001). In addition, a meta-analysis of 168 datasets examining judgments of emotion in the face and other nonverbal stimuli indicated universal emotion recognition well above chance levels (Elfenbein & Ambady, 2002a). It would be very difficult to obtain such robust and consistent findings if expressions were not universally recognized. Even when low-intensity expressions are judged across cultures (Ekman et al., 1987; Matsumoto et al., 2002), there is strong agreement across cultures as to the emotion in the expression. Research from the past two decades has also demonstrated the universal recognition of a seventh emotion—contempt (Ekman & Friesen, 1986; Ekman & Heider, 1988; Matsumoto, 1992; Matsumoto & Ekman, 2004).

Besides studies of posed expressions, there have been over 75 studies that demonstrated that these very same facial expressions are produced by individuals all over the world when emotions are elicited spontaneously (Matsumoto, Keltner, Shiota, O'Sullivan, & Frank, 2008). These findings are impressive, given that they have been produced by different researchers around the world, in different laboratories using different methodologies, with participants from many different cultures, but all converging on the same pattern of results. Thus today there is strong evidence for the universal facial expressions of seven emotions (see Figure 2.1).

Figure 2.1   The Seven Basic Emotions and Their Universal Expressions

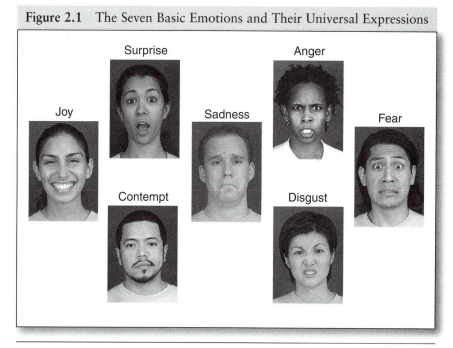

Source: © David Matsumoto

Identifying the Source of Universal Facial Expressions

Facial expressions of emotion are not only universally recognized and produced. Several lines of research indicate that they are biologically innate, and we describe these briefly here.

Studies of blind individuals. A strong source of evidence for the biological basis of emotion-expression linkages comes from studies of congenitally blind individuals. Early case and anecdotal studies (Dumas, 1932; Eibl-Eibesfeldt, 1973; Freedman, 1964; Fulcher, 1942; Goodenough, 1932; Thompson, 1941) reported many similarities between blind and sighted individuals in their spontaneous facial expressions of emotion. The findings from these studies have been bolstered more recently by studies that have actually measured the spontaneous facial behaviors of blind individuals when emotions were aroused, showing similarities with the facial behaviors of sighted individuals in both children (Cole, Jenkins, & Shott, 1989) and adults of many different cultures (Galati, Miceli, & Sini, 2001; Galati, Sini, Schmidt, & Tinti, 2003).

One of our most recent studies contributed to this literature by comparing the spontaneous facial expressions of congenitally and noncongenitally blind judo athletes at the 2004 Athens Paralympic Games with the sighted athletes from the 2004 Olympic Games (Matsumoto & Willingham, 2009). The blind athletes came from 23 cultures. If congenitally blind individuals from vastly different countries and cultures produce exactly the same facial configurations of emotion in the same emotionally evocative situations as sighted athletes, this is strong evidence for the biological basis of their source because these individuals could not have possibly learned to produce these expressions through visual observation.

This study found near-perfect concordance between the blind and sighted athletes in their expressions. For example, correlations between the blind and sighted athletes' individual facial muscle movements were $r(32) = .94$, $p < .01$; $r(32) = .98$, $p < .01$; and $r(32) = .96$, $p < .01$, for match completion, receiving medal, and on the podium, respectively. Moreover, the expressions of the blind athletes functioned in exactly the same ways as the sighted athletes. For example, winners displayed all types of smiles, especially Duchenne smiles, more frequently than the defeated athletes, who displayed more disgust, sadness, and combined negative emotions. Duchenne smiles are smiles that involve not only the smiling muscle (*zygomatic major*), which raises the lip corners, but also the muscle surrounding the eyes (*orbicularlis oculi*), which raises the cheeks, thins the eyes, and lowers the eye cover fold. Duchenne smiles have been reliably associated with true positive emotions (Ekman et al., 1990; Frank & Ekman, 1993). When receiving the medal, winners (gold and bronze) displayed all types of smiles and Duchenne smiles more frequently than did the defeated (silver medalists), who displayed more non-Duchenne smiles (see Figures 2.2, 2.3, and 2.4).

We believe that these studies provide strong evidence for a biologically based emotion-expression linkage that is universal to all people of all

Figure 2.2   Comparison of Blind and Sighted Athletes Who Just Lost a
Match for a Medal

Source: © Bob Willingham. Reprinted with permission.

Figure 2.3   Comparison of Blind and Sighted Athletes Who Just
Won a Match

Source: © Bob Willingham. Reprinted with permission.

Figure 2.4   Comparison of Blind and Sighted Athletes Who Just Won a Match and Were Overcome With Emotion

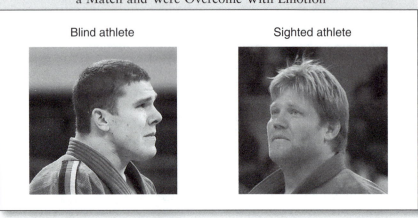

Source: © Bob Willingham. Reprinted with permission.

cultures. Some may argue that these individuals may have learned to produce those expressions tactilely, but one would have to argue that they are able to feel different expressions that occur spontaneously—i.e., rapidly, automatically, and unconsciously—on themselves or others, and then are able to spontaneously produce them, and that this occurs across all cultures studied. This proposition is hardly defensible.[7]

Evidence from twin and family studies. Another source of evidence for possible biological sources of emotion-expression linkages comes from studies of twins and family relatives. Facial behaviors of blind individuals are more concordant with their kin than with strangers (Peleg et al., 2006). And some facial expressions to emotionally provocative stimuli are more concordant among monozygotic twin pairs than dizygotic twins (Kendler et al., 2008). These studies are strongly suggestive of a hereditable, genetic component to facial expressions of emotion.

Evidence from the developmental literature. More evidence for the biological bases of facial expressions of emotion comes from the developmental literature. The same facial musculature that exists in adult humans exists in newborn infants and is fully functional at birth (Ekman & Oster, 1979). As such, infants have a rich and varied repertoire of facial expressions including those that signal not only emotional states but also interest and attention (Oster, 2005). There is widespread consensus that smiling; distaste, the infant precursor of adult disgust; and crying, the universal signal of sadness/distress, occur in neonates (Oster, 2005). There is some controversy as to when other differentiated and discrete negative emotions occur. Some authors suggest that discrete negative emotions exist from birth or shortly thereafter and emerge according to a maturational timetable (Izard, 1991; Izard & Malatesta, 1987; Tronick, 1989). Others suggest that infants, at least within the first year of life, display relatively undifferentiated or modulated negative expressions, which ultimately transform into more differentiated, discrete expressions later (Camras, Oster, Campos, & Bakeman, 2003; Oster, 2005). Discrete expressions of anger and sadness have been reported in the early part of the second year of life (Hyson & Izard, 1985; Shiller, Izard, & Hembree, 1986). Regardless, by the time of preschool, children display discrete expressions of the other emotions as well (Casey, 1993). It is difficult to conceive of how this occurs if the children did not have the biological capability to do so in the first place.

Evidence from nonhuman primates. Another line of evidence comes from studies of nonhuman primates. For years ethologists (Chevalier-Skolnikoff, 1973; Geen, 1992; Hauser, 1993; Snowdon, 2003; Van Hoof, 1972) have noted the morphological similarities between human expressions of emotion and nonhuman primate expressions displayed in similar contexts. Van Hoof (1972) described the evolution of the smile and laugh along two different evolutionary tracts across early mammals, monkeys, apes, chimpanzees, and humans. Redican (1982) suggested that among nonhuman primates, facial displays described as grimaces and open-mouth grimaces were akin to the human emotions of fear and surprise; that the tense-mouth display was similar to anger and that both combined formed the often-identified threat display; and that nonhuman primates show a play face that is similar to the happy face of humans. He also suggested that the nonhuman pout served a similar function to the human sad face. Ueno, Ueno, and Tomonaga (2004) demonstrated that both infant rhesus macaques and infant chimpanzees showed different facial expressions to sweet and bitter tastes, but that the chimps' facial expressions were more similar to human facial expressions than to that of the macaques. However, even some of the smaller apes, such as siamangs (*Symphalangus syndactylus*), noted for their limited facial expression repertoire, have distinguishable facial expressions accompanying sexuality, agonistic behavior, grooming, and play (Liebal, Pika, & Tomasello, 2004). de Waal (2002) suggested that for some states a species more closely related to humans than chimpanzees, the bononos, may have more emotions in common with humans.

The most recent research has gone beyond demonstrating equivalence in morphological descriptions of expressions to identifying the exact facial musculature used in producing the expressions being described.[8] The facial expressions considered to be universal among humans have been observed in nonhuman primates (de Waal, 2003). Chimpanzees have a fully functional facial musculature that, while not as differentiated as that of humans, includes the same muscles that are used in emotional expressions (Bard, 2003; Burrows, Waller, Parr, & Bonar, 2006). The additional facial muscles for humans are related to speech and articulation, speech illustration, conversation regulation, and the ability to eat while talking (Ekman & Friesen, 1969). Moreover, the chimpanzee facial musculature produces many of the same appearance changes in the face as does the human musculature, according to a comparison of the human and chimpanzee versions of the Facial Action Coding System (Vick, Waller, Parr, Pasqualini, & Bard, 2007).

When all of these bodies of evidence are considered together, along with the studies documenting the universality of facial expressions of emotion, it is difficult to not conclude that facial expressions of emotion are not only universal but biologically innate.

The Forms and Functions of the Universal Emotions and Their Expressions

When you read other people's emotions, knowing what triggered them and their functions are the two keys to understanding what to do about them. We discussed earlier the triggers of each of the biological emotions— that is, the underlying universal psychological themes that elicit them. Here we talk about what functions each emotion serves (see Table 2.2).

The prototypical expression[9] of anger involves the brows drawn down and together, the upper eyelids raised, the lower eyelids tensed, and the lips tightened. Recall that anger is triggered by goal obstruction. One of the central appearance features of anger is the lowering of the brows and simultaneous staring or glaring of the eyes (which occurs because the upper eyelids are raised against the lowering of the brows). Whenever people in the world are angry, they have perceived something that has obstructed an important goal of theirs. This is a universal aspect of anger elicitation. Now, what was the goal, and how was it obstructed? These are aspects of anger that are culturally and individually variable. What is universal is the underlying psychological theme—goal obstruction. The function of anger, therefore, is to remove the obstacle. The emotion of anger helps us to remove obstacles by preparing us to fight. That is why our physiology turns on the way it does and our cognitions focus in targets.

Contempt is the emotion of moral superiority and is expressed by a unilateral (one-sided) tightening of the lip corner or smile. Whenever contempt is elicited, the individual has perceived an action or person that is beneath him or her. The function of contempt is to assert one's moral superiority over something or someone else. While anger is very active, preparing people to fight, contempt is relatively passive, as the contemptuous person is making a statement about his or her relative superiority.

Disgust is the emotion of contamination. There are two versions of the disgust expression, one involving the wrinkling of the nose, the other a raising of the upper lips (which creates a horseshoe appearance at the nasolabial fold outside our nostrils). Both versions produce a scrunching motion in the middle of the face. Disgust is the emotion that is elicited when we come into contact with rotten, offensive objects. It is an interesting emotion because people are disgusted not only at objects—feces, urine, spoiled milk, insects—but they are also disgusted at other people. That is, humans can generalize emotional reactions from specific objects that directly assault our senses of sight, smell, or taste to more abstract concepts, like political philosophy or opinion. The function of disgust is to eliminate the contaminated object or idea.

Fear occurs when one perceives a threat to one's physical or psychological well-being. One of the main characteristics of the fear expression is the large amount of white shown above the eyes. Fear is expressed by a raising and drawing together of the brows, a raising of the upper eyelids, tensing of the lower eyelids, and stretching the lips horizontally. The function of fear is to help us avoid threats and reduce the impending harm. That is why our bodies set in motion actions to prepare us to escape or freeze, both of which can be very adaptive responses to potentially harmful stimuli.

Sadness is triggered by the loss of valuable objects. It is expressed by a raising of just the inner corners of the eyebrows, a raising of the cheeks, drooping of the upper eyelids, and a downturn of the lip corners. Of course the lost object can be a person, part of one's body, inanimate objects, or psychological, such as self-esteem or respect. A good synonym of sadness is distress, and you will see us refer to these emotions interchangeably throughout this book. The function of sadness is to shut down one's mind and body and to recoup one's resources. At the same time another function of sadness is to call for help. It's a distress signal.

Surprise is the emotion of sudden, novel objects. It is expressed by a raising of the brows and upper eyelids, and a dropping of the jaw; thus, the surprise expression is open and round (compared to fear, which is horizontal and tense, despite sharing some similarities with surprise). Surprise is often the briefest of emotions because one cannot stay surprised for very long about the same thing. Surprise often gives way to another emotion very quickly such as fear or joy. The function of surprise is to help individuals orient to the surprising event and thus process more information about it before possibly reacting in other ways.

Happiness or joy is triggered by goal attainment. It is expressed by a raising of the lip corners and raising of the cheeks, crow's feet wrinkles, and a narrowing of the eyes. We feel these positive emotions when our needs are met. The function of this emotion is to ensure future motivation toward goals, facilitating goal-directed behaviors.[10]

Different Types of Facial Expressions of Emotion

The Neuroanatomical Roots of Facial Expressions of Emotion

Research on the neuroanatomy of facial expressions of emotion has demonstrated that there are two distinct neural pathways that mediate facial expressions, each originating in a different area of the brain (Matsumoto & Lee, 1993; Rinn, 1984). The pyramidal tract drives voluntary facial actions and originates in the cortical motor strip, whereas the extrapyramidal tract drives involuntary emotional expressions and originates in the subcortical areas of the brain (see Figure 2.5). The subcortical areas of the brain are those areas that we share with our animal relatives. These areas are concerned with body functions related to fighting, fleeing, feeding, and reproduction. Emotional signals from this area of the brain coordinate and orchestrate a whole series of physiological, cognitive, and behavioral responses. One of these is a facial expression.

The cortical motor strip is the area of the brain that controls voluntary movement. Studies of this area have demonstrated that the part of our bodies that receives the largest degree of innervation from this area, and thus which is under the greatest degree of voluntary control, is our hands. This makes sense as we learn to use our hands for many complex and subtle movements. The next largest part of our bodies represented on the cortical motor strip is our face, and within the face, our lower face is more highly represented. This also makes sense because we learn to use the many muscles we have in our lower face not only for eating but also speech articulation, which is a learned activity also involving many complex and subtle movements.

Thus when we are emotional not only do signals emanate from the subcortical areas of the brain, telling our bodies and faces to fire; signals also emanate from the cortical motor strip telling us how we need to control our emotions and expressions as well. Our facial expressions, therefore, are under the dual neural control of both the cortical and subcortical areas of the brain.

Figure 2.5 Neuroanatomical Roots of Emotional Expressions

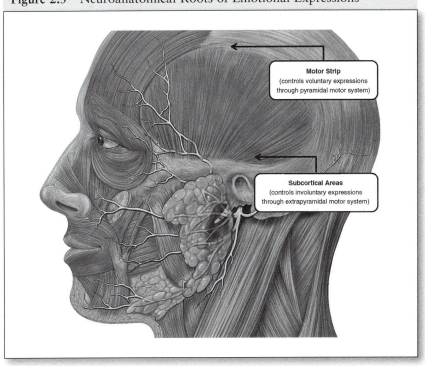

Motor Strip
(controls voluntary expressions
through pyramidal motor system)

Subcortical Areas
(controls involuntary expressions
through extrapyramidal motor system)

Source: Patrick J. Lynch, medical illustrator; C. Carl Jaffe, MD, cardiologist.

Macro, Micro, Subtle, and Partial Expressions

Because of this dual neural control, there are different ways in which the distinct facial expressions of emotion actually appear on the face. When single emotions occur and there is no reason for them to be modified or concealed, expressions typically last between 0.5 to 4 seconds (s) on the face and will often involve the entire face (Ekman, 2003). We call these *macro-expressions*, and they occur whenever we are uninhibited, alone, or with family and close friends. Because macroexpressions last for several seconds, they are relatively easy to see on the face, if one knows what to look for.

Some expressions occur much more quickly, less than 0.5 s and sometimes as fast as 67 milliseconds (ms). These are known as *microexpressions*. Micro-expressions are likely signs of emotions that one wishes to conceal.[11] They occur so fast that most people cannot see or recognize them in real time.

The idea that microexpressions exist has its roots in Darwin's (1872) inhibition hypothesis that suggested that facial actions that cannot be controlled voluntarily may be produced involuntarily even if the individual is trying to control his or her expressions.[12] Research on the neuroanatomical bases of emotional expressions already described suggests how this occurs. In the instance when an emotion is elicited, but the individual wishes to conceal this emotion, the two distinct neural pathways that mediate facial expressions fire at the same time. These conflicting signals produce a neural "tug of war" over control of the face, allowing for the quick, fleeting leakage of microexpressions.

The existence of microexpressions was verified almost a century after Darwin by Haggard and Isaacs (1966) while scanning films of psychotherapy sessions.[13] Later Ekman and Friesen (1974) demonstrated that microexpressions occurred in their frame-by-frame analysis of interviews with depressed inpatients. Most recently, Porter and ten Brinke (2008) demonstrated that microexpressions occurred when individuals attempted to mask or squelch their emotional expressions.[14]

Because microexpressions are signs of concealed emotions, the ability to detect them may be important for individuals such as health care workers, psychotherapists, law enforcement officers, or anyone whose profession requires face-to-face interactions. This could benefit the development of rapport, trust, and collegiality in making credibility assessments, evaluating truthfulness and detecting deception, and providing the basis for better cooperation, negotiation, or sales. But because they are so quick, observers may miss them when they occur; to wit, they were only detected initially when films were analyzed in frame-by-frame detail (Ekman & Friesen, 1974; Haggard & Isaacs, 1966). We have developed training tools to help people improve their ability to recognize microexpressions when they occur (see www.humintell.com). Studies have shown a significant correlation between one's ability to recognize microexpressions and his or her ability to detect emotionally arousing lies (Ekman & O'Sullivan, 1991; Frank & Ekman, 1997; Frank, Hurley, Kang, Pazian, & Ekman, 2011; Warren, Schertler, & Bull, 2009). And our latest studies in this area have shown that training with our tools produces a reliable benefit that lasts beyond the training session and carries over into the work environment (Matsumoto & Hwang, in press-b).

A third category of facial expressions of emotion is known as *subtle expressions*. Contrary to the full-face, high-intensity macroexpressions, subtle expressions are low-intensity emotional expressions that occur when a person is just starting to feel an emotion, when the emotional response is of low intensity, or when a person is trying to cover up his or her emotions but is not entirely able to do so. They can involve the same muscles as in a full-face expression, just expressed at very low intensities. Or for the expressions that involve multiple areas of the face, subtle expressions can involve just parts of the face, such as just the brows and eyes area or just the mouth area; these are known as partial expressions.

Although microexpressions have received a lot of media attention in the past few years, research has shown that the ability to read subtle expressions better predicts the ability to detect deception than the ability to read microexpressions (Warren et al., 2009). This actually makes sense because even though microexpressions are clearly signs of concealed emotions, they probably occur much less frequently than subtle expressions. Moreover, studies of microexpressions have shown that they are often partial expressions, shown in either the upper or lower half of the face (Frank et al., 2011; Porter & ten Brinke, 2008). This is true not only in deceptive situations but in most emotional situations in everyday life. Thus the ability to see and recognize subtle expressions likely has a much higher benefit for practitioners.

We have developed tools to help train people to see and recognize subtle expressions (see www.humintell.com). One of our latest studies has also demonstrated that people using our training tools can reliably improve their ability to see subtle expressions (Hwang & Matsumoto, 2010). Given that subtle expressions occur in real life more frequently than micros or macros, and given that the ability to recognize subtle expressions is associated with the ability to detect deception, the availability of tools to train the ability to see subtle expressions is a major advantage for practitioners.

What Else Does the Face Signal?

Recall that our faces not only involuntarily react when an emotion is aroused, but we can deliberately pose expressions to convey all sorts of messages. For example, we use our faces for each of the following purposes in addition to signaling emotions:

- *Speech illustration.* Just as we learn to use our hands to gesticulate and illustrate our speech, we also learn to use our faces to do so as well. For instance, people often raise their brows when being inquisitive and lower their brows when they lower their voices.
- *Conversation regulation.* Just as we use our hands and tone of voice to regulate turn taking in conversation, we provide cues to others that we are either done talking and it's their turn, or not, through our faces as well.
- *Emblematic gestures.* These are movements that symbolically give verbal meaning that can be conveyed by words. Although most of the time emblematic gestures are considered via hand movements, we also have emblematic gestures conveyed by the face, such as the doubtful look produced by raising the upper lip and pushing the lower lip up, or skepticism shown by a raised outer portion of a single eyebrow.

- *Cognition.* We use our faces to signal when we're thinking, or confused, often furrowing our brows when concentrating or perplexed. We also purse our lips when conducting mental searches.
- *Talking and eating.* We use the muscles around the mouth area for talking and eating and especially speech articulation.
- *Expressive regulation.* We also use the facial muscles to regulate our emotion signals, like "keeping a stiff upper lip" or by clamping down on our jaws and keeping our mouth shut.
- *Physical exertion.* We often use our faces as part of whole-body responses to aid in effortful physical activities engaged by the rest of the body, such as when lifting heavy weights or throwing something. (Ever watch the faces of weight lifters or baseball pitchers?)

One of the biggest mistakes that practitioners make when learning to read facial expressions of emotion is that they *overinterpret* many different types of facial behavior as emotional expressions. This problem is compounded by the fact that despite the large number of muscles we have in the face, sometimes the exact muscles used in signaling emotions are also used in signaling other, nonemotional states. Or, people can mimic joy by smiling when they are not feeling joy. They can pretend they are angry by posing an anger face. Thus for practitioners it becomes very important to be able to separate the true emotional signals from other nonemotional facial behaviors (noise) if one is trying to read emotions.

Reading Faces in Practice: Application Implications

Being able to separate signal from noise in reading facial expressions of emotion can give practitioners in a wide variety of professions an edge in their line of work. Emotions are reactions to things that matter to that person, and they occur in conversations, interactions, interviews, or interrogations. Facial expressions annotate the content of the words that are being spoken and the context in which the interaction is occurring. Reading these signals can give the practitioner an idea of what is important to the expresser and why. They can help the skilled practitioner generate important insights into the mental states, motivations, intentions, and personalities of the expressers. They are important signs of trustworthiness, cooperation, and honesty. And they can be used as signs of deception, or lack of forthrightness.

For all of these reasons the ability to read other people's facial expressions of emotion can be an important tool in one's toolkit for anyone whose job involves interacting with others. This is true for anyone involved in security, intelligence, or law enforcement (such as checkpoint security, intelligence field officers and analysts, police, fire, and first responders); health care workers (physicians, nurses, social workers, dentists, psychotherapists, psychiatrists, counselors, coaches); lawyers, judges, and other officers of the courts; salespersons, negotiators, and mediators; consumer product and marketing researchers—just about anyone. And it can help people in their everyday lives as well, from interactions at home with family, with friends, and in the community.

Because facial expressions of emotion are part of our evolutionary history and are a biologically innate ability, we all have the ability to read facial expressions of emotion. And it is an ability that gets better on the job and in our everyday lives. This is especially true for macroexpressions. But most people are not very good at recognizing micro or subtle expressions. And there are many individual differences in this skill; some people are naturally better than others. Fortunately, as mentioned, tools have been developed to help people improve their skills regardless of what level of natural ability they have. Thus, if one is in a profession where the ability to read facial expressions of emotion—especially micro and subtle expressions—may help one be more efficient or accurate, then there are resources available to do so. The second part of this book contains many reports from practitioners in many different professions who have received such training and describe how that improved skill has helped them in their work.

But let's also be clear that improved ability to read facial expressions, or any nonverbal behavior for that matter, is just the first step. What one does with the information is an important second step in the process of interaction. Being overly sensitive to nonverbal behaviors such as microexpressions and other forms of nonverbal leakage can be detrimental to interpersonal outcomes as well, as discussed in literature on eavesdropping (Blanck, Rosenthal, Snodgrass, DePaulo, & Zuckerman, 1981; Elfenbein & Ambady, 2002b; Rosenthal & DePaulo, 1979). Individuals who call out other's emotions indiscriminately can be considered intrusive, rude, or overbearing. Dealing effectively with emotion information of others is also likely to be a very crucial part of the skill set one must have to interact effectively with others. Knowing when and how to intervene, or to adapt one's behaviors and communication styles, or engage the support and help of others, are all tactical skills that must be brought into play once emotions are read.

Notes

1. We use the word "social" here in the broadest sense, which includes interactions not only with other humans, but also other living beings, such as snakes, bears, wild pigs, etc. Emotions would certainly have elicited adaptive reactions in these interactions as well.

2. But also see the work on unconscious emotions (Winkielman & Berridge, 2004).

3. Research suggests that some other emotions may also share some characteristics with biological emotions. Expressive behaviors typically associated with shame, embarrassment, or pride, for example, have been observed in nonhuman animals (de Waal, 1989), but evidence for their cross-cultural expression, universal physiological signatures, and antecedents and reactions is still lacking.

4. Whether or not we engage in that behavior, however, is dependent on a host of factors, including the context, who else is involved, the consequences of our actions, and the behaviors that we learned are acceptable and appropriate in that context (Matsumoto & Wilson, 2008).

5. Of course the most efficient response is not always the best response. Emotions were incredibly helpful throughout our evolutionary history in that they allowed humans to respond immediately to events in the environment that enabled them to adapt and survive. In today's world, however, one may argue that this archaic system may sometimes (often?) get in the way of making the best, most rational decisions about how to respond to the world, and it may be that the efficiency of our emotion systems can get us in trouble from time to time.

6. To wit, Darwin penciled in the margin of Bell's book, "He never looked at a monkey" (Darwin, 1872).

7. Interestingly, there have been a number of studies that have examined the ability of congenitally blind individuals to voluntarily pose facial expressions of emotion, all of them reporting difficulties in doing so and inconsistency between what is posed and what actually occurs on the face spontaneously (Dumas, 1932; Fulcher, 1942; Galati, Scherer, & Ricci-Bitti, 1997; Mistschenka, 1933; Ortega, Iglesias, Fernandez, & Corraliza, 1983; Rinn, 1991; Webb, 1977). This difficulty is congruent with the necessity of having to see the expressions on oneself (in a mirror) or in others in spontaneous situations in order to mimic the expression when requested.

8. The importance of specifying the exact muscles underlying facial expressions can be understood by recognizing the difference in ethologists' verbal descriptions of fear, play, and threat faces of apes. A nonfearful threat involves a tense mouth and lips with no teeth showing. When fear is involved, as is common when subordinate animals are threatening those superior to them in the social hierarchy, the lips are stretched back thereby showing teeth. This seeming smile is not a smile at all, but a fear grimace. By contrast, in the much reported "play face" of apes, the corners of the lips go up as they do in human smiles. The difference between lateral and diagonal movement is crucial.

9. For each of the emotions, we describe what is known as the full-face, prototypical expression. The prototypical expression describes the total muscle movements and appearance changes in the entire face that are involved when the emotion is elicited. These are likely the forms of the emotions we are born with. Variants of these prototypical expressions occur when components of the prototypical expressions are expressed. These are related to partial or subtle expressions described later in this chapter.

10. A note about happiness is necessary here. In English the term "happiness" can refer both to a state as well as to a trait, the former being a reaction while the

latter is a cognitive evaluation of one's overall life situation. With regard to the former, Ekman (2003) described different types of enjoyable emotions including sensory pleasures, amusement, contentment, excitement, relief, wonder, ecstasy, elevation, gratitude, fiero (pride in accomplishment), *naches* (pride in one's children), and *schadenfreude* (joy in another's misfortunes). We would add triumph. With regard to the latter, terms such as "satisfaction with life" or "subjective well-being" are synonymous with dispositional cognitive evaluations of one's life situation. It is important to distinguish the specific type of "happiness" studied because happiness as a transient state is very different from happiness as cognitive evaluations, and the relationship between culture and "happiness" is likely to differ depending on which one is studying. The meaning of happiness is different at different ages (Mogilner, Kamvar, & Aaker, in press). Thus we will use the term "joy" to better describe this transient emotional state.

11. This claim is consistent with the theoretical and empirical work on microexpressions to date. It may be that microexpressions are also signs of rapidly processed but unconcealed emotional states. Future research will need to investigate this and other possibilities.

12. This idea may actually have earlier roots in the work of Duchenne (1862/1990), who demonstrated a difference in specific facial muscles between smiles of true enjoyment and nonenjoyment smiles. Darwin's inhibition hypothesis was different in that it suggested that suppressed emotional expressions could leak out involuntarily.

13. Relatedly, Condon and Ogston (1967) published a microanalysis of interactional behavior. While not focused on facial expressions, they employed a micro-level, frame-by-frame analysis of nonverbal behavior in a psychotherapeutic interview of a mother, father, and child. They suggested that nonverbal behavior can be analyzed with such precision and that such micro-level nonverbal behaviors signal something meaningful about the mental states of the encoders.

14. To our knowledge Porter and ten Brinke's (2008) study was the first empirical study published in a peer-reviewed journal that presented the individual characteristics of microexpressions, as previous evidence for microexpressions was limited to book chapters and books. Many peer-reviewed articles on expression in deceptive situations that have mentioned the micro momentary speed of various expressions exist (e.g., Ekman, Hager, & Friesen, 1981; Frank & Ekman, 1993, 1997; Frank, Ekman, & Friesen, 1993), but they mainly focused on the form of the expressions— i.e., the presence or absence of specific facial muscles, ala Duchenne's (1862/1990) work mentioned earlier.

References

Bard, K. A. (2003). Development of emotional expressions in chimpanzees (Pan troglodytes). *Annals of the New York Academy of Sciences, 1000,* 88–90.

Barr, C. L., & Kleck, R. E. (1995). Self-other perception of the intensity of facial expressions of emotion: Do we know what we show? *Journal of Personality and Social Psychology, 68,* 608–618.

Blanck, P. D., Rosenthal, R., Snodgrass, S. E., DePaulo, B. M., & Zuckerman, M. (1981). Sex differences in eavesdropping on nonverbal cues: Developmental changes. *Journal of Personality and Social Psychology, 41*(2), 391–396.

Boucher, J. D., & Brandt, M. E. (1981). Judgment of emotion: American and Malay antecedents. *Journal of Cross-Cultural Psychology, 12*(3), 272–283.

Bower, G. H. (1981). Mood and memory. *American Psychologist, 36*(2), 129–148.

Bower, G. H., Lazarus, R., LeDoux, J. E., Panksepp, J., Davidson, R. J., & Ekman, P. (1994). What is the relation between emotion and memory? In P. Ekman (Ed.), *The nature of emotion: Fundamental questions. Series in affective science* (pp. 301–318). New York: Oxford University Press.

Brandt, M. E., & Boucher, J. D. (1985). Concepts of depression in emotion lexicons of eight cultures. *International Journal of Intercultural Relations, 10,* 321–346.

Bruner, J. S., & Tagiuri, R. (1954). The perception of people. In G. Lindzey (Ed.), *Handbook of social psychology* (Vol. 2, pp. 634–654). Cambridge, MA: Addison-Wesley.

Buck, R. W. (1999). The biological affects: A typology. *Psychological Review, 106*(2), 301–336.

Burrows, A. M., Waller, B. M., Parr, L. A., & Bonar, C. J. (2006). Muscles of facial expression in the chimpanzee (Pan troglodytes): Descriptive, comparative, and phylogenetic contexts. *Journal of Anatomy, 208,* 153–167.

Camras, L. A., Oster, H., Campos, J. J., & Bakeman, R. (2003). Emotional facial expressions in European-American, Japanese, and Chinese infants. In P. Ekman, J. J. Campos, R. J. Davidson, & F. B. M. de Waal (Eds.), *Emotions inside out: 130 years after Darwin's "The expression of the emotions in man and animals"* (Vol. 1000, pp. 135–151). New York: New York Academy of Sciences.

Casey, R. J. (1993). Children's emotional experience: Relations among expression, self-report, and understanding. *Developmental Psychology, 29*(1), 119–129.

Chevalier-Skolnikoff, S. (1973). Facial expression of emotion in nonhuman primates. In P. Ekman (Ed.), *Darwin and facial expression* (pp. 11–89). New York: Academic Press.

Clore, G. L., & Ortony, A. (1988). Semantic analyses of the affective lexicon. In V. Hamilton, G. H. Bower, & N. H. Frijda (Eds.), *Cognitive science perspectives on emotion and motivation* (pp. 367–397). Amsterdam: Martinus Nijhoff.

Clore, G. L., & Ortony, A. (1991). What more is there to emotion concepts than prototypes. *Journal of Personality and Social Psychology, 60*(1), 48–50.

Clore, G. L., Ortony, A., & Foss, M. A. (1987). The psychological foundations of the affective lexicon. *Journal of Personality and Social Psychology, 53,* 751–766.

Cole, P. M., Jenkins, P. A., & Shott, C. T. (1989). Spontaneous expressive control in blind and sighted children. *Child Development, 60*(3), 683–688.

Condon, W., S,, & Ogston, W. D. (1967). A segmentation of behavior. *Journal of Psychiatric Research, 5,* 221–235.

Cosmides, L., & Tooby, J. (2000). Evolutionary psychology and the emotions. In M. Lewis & J. M. Haviland-Jones (Eds.), *Handbook of emotions* (2nd ed., pp. 91–115). New York: Guilford Press.

Darwin, C. (1872). *The expression of emotions in man and animals.* New York: Oxford University Press.

Davidson, R. J., Scherer, K., & Goldsmith, H. H. (Eds.). (2003). *The handbook of affective sciences.* New York: Oxford University Press.

de Waal, F. B. M. (1989). *Chimpanzee politics: Power and sex among apes.* Baltimore: Johns Hopkins University Press.

de Waal, F. B. M. (2002). Apes from Venus: Bonobos and human social evolution. In F. B. M. de Waal (Ed.), *Tree of origin: What primate behavior can tell us about human social evolution* (pp. 39–68). Cambridge, MA: Harvard University Press.

de Waal, F. B. M. (2003). Darwin's legacy and the study of primate visual communication. In P. Ekman, J. Campos, R. J. Davidson, & F. B. M. de Waal (Eds.), *Emotions inside out: 130 years after Darwin's "The expression of emotions in man and animals"* (pp. 7–31). New York: New York Academy of Sciences.

Dimberg, U., & Ohman, A. (1996). Behold the wrath: Psychophysiological responses to facial stimuli. *Motivation & Emotion, 20*(2), 149–182.

Duchenne de Boulogne, G. B. (1990). *The mechanism of human facial expression.* New York: Cambridge University Press. (Original work published 1862)

Dumas, F. (1932). La mimique des aveugles [Facial expression of the blind]. *Bulletin de l'Academie de Medecine, 107,* 607–610.

Eibl-Eibesfeldt, I. (1973). The expressive behavior of the deaf-and-blind born. In M. von Cranach & I. Vine (Eds.), *Social communication and movement* (pp. 163–194). London: Academic Press.

Eibl-Eibesfeldt, I. (1989). *Human ethology.* New York: Aldine de Gruyter Press.

Eisenberg, N., Fabes, R. A., Miller, P. A., Fultz, J., Shell, R., Mathy, R. M., et al. (1989). Relation of sympathy and distress to prosocial behavior: A multimethod study. *Journal of Personality and Social Psychology, 57,* 55–66.

Ekman, P. (1972). Universal and cultural differences in facial expression of emotion. In J. R. Cole (Ed.), *Nebraska symposium on motivation, 1971* (Vol. 19, pp. 207–283). Lincoln: Nebraska University Press.

Ekman, P. (Ed.). (1973). *Darwin and facial expression; a century of research in review.* New York: Academic Press.

Ekman, P. (1992). An argument for basic emotions. *Cognition & Emotion, 6*(3–4), 169–200.

Ekman, P. (1993). Facial expression and emotion. *American Psychologist, 48*(4), 384–392.

Ekman, P. (1999). Basic emotions. In T. Dalgleish & T. Power (Eds.), *The handbook of cognition and emotion* (pp. 45–60). Sussex, UK: John Wiley & Sons.

Ekman, P. (2003). *Emotions revealed* (2nd ed.). New York: Times Books.

Ekman, P., Davidson, R. J., & Friesen, W. V. (1990). The Duchenne smile: Emotional expression and brain physiology: II. *Journal of Personality & Social Psychology, 58*(2), 342–353.

Ekman, P., & Friesen, W. V. (1969). The repertoire of nonverbal behavior: Categories, origins, usage, and coding. *Semiotica, 1,* 49–98.

Ekman, P., & Friesen, W. V. (1971). Constants across culture in the face and emotion. *Journal of Personality and Social Psychology, 17,* 124–129.

Ekman, P., & Friesen, W. V. (1974). Nonverbal behavior and psychopathology. In R. J. Friedman & M. Katz (Eds.), *The psychology of depression: Contemporary theory and research* (pp. 3–31). Washington, DC: Winston & Sons.

Ekman, P., & Friesen, W. V. (1986). A new pan-cultural facial expression of emotion. *Motivation & Emotion, 10*(2), 159–168.

Ekman, P., Friesen, W. V., & Ellsworth, P. (1972). *Emotion in the human face: Guidelines for research and an integration of findings.* New York: Pergamon Press.

Ekman, P., Friesen, W. V., O'Sullivan, M., Chan, A., Diacoyanni-Tarlatzis, I., Heider, K., et al. (1987). Universals and cultural differences in the judgments of facial expressions of emotion. *Journal of Personality & Social Psychology, 53*(4), 712–717.

Ekman, P., Hager, J., & Friesen, W. V. (1981). The symmetry of emotional and deliberate facial actions. *Psychophysiology, 18,* 101–106.

Ekman, P., & Heider, K. G. (1988). The universality of a contempt expression: A replication. *Motivation & Emotion, 12*(3), 303–308.

Ekman, P., Levenson, R. W., & Friesen, W. V. (1983). Autonomic nervous system activity distinguishes among emotions. *Science, 221*(4616), 1208–1210.

Ekman, P., & Oster, H. (1979). Facial expressions of emotion. *Annual Review of Psychology, 30,* 527–554.

Ekman, P., & O'Sullivan, M. (1991). Who can catch a liar? *American Psychologist, 46*(9), 913–920.

Ekman, P., Sorenson, E. R., & Friesen, W. V. (1969). Pancultural elements in facial displays of emotion. *Science, 164*(3875), 86–88.

Elfenbein, H. A., & Ambady, N. (2002a). On the universality and cultural specificity of emotion recognition: A meta-analysis. *Psychological Bulletin, 128*(2), 205–235.

Elfenbein, H. A., & Ambady, N. (2002b). Predicting workplace outcomes from the ability to eavesdrop on feelings. *Journal of Applied Psychology, 87*(5), 963–971.

Ellsworth, P. C., & Scherer, K. (2003). Appraisal processes in emotion. In R. J. Davidson, K. R. Scherer, & H. H. Goldsmith (Eds.), *Handbook of affective sciences* (pp. 572–595). New York: Oxford University Press.

Esteves, F., Dimberg, U., & Ohman, A. (1994). Automatically elicited fear: Conditioned skin conductance responses to masked facial expressions. *Cognition and Emotion, 8*(5), 393–413.

Frank, M. G., & Ekman, P. (1993). Not all smiles are created equal: The differences between enjoyment and nonenjoyment smiles. Special issue: Current issues in psychological humor research. *Humor: International Journal of Humor Research, 6*(1), 9–26.

Frank, M. G., & Ekman, P. (1997). The ability to detect deceit generalizes across different types of high-stake lies. *Journal of Personality and Social Psychology, 72,* 1429–1439.

Frank, M. G., Ekman, P., & Friesen, W. V. (1993). Behavioral markers and recognizability of the smile of enjoyment. *Journal of Personality & Social Psychology, 64*(1), 83–93.

Frank, M. G., Hurley, C. M., Kang, S., Pazian, M., & Ekman, P. (2011). Detecting lies in a counter terrorism scenario. *Manuscript in preparation.*

Fredrickson, B. (2001). The role of positive emotions in positive psychology: The broaden-and-build theory of positive emotions. *American Psychologist, 56*(3), 218–226.

Fredrickson, B., & Losada, M. F. (2005). Positive affect and the complex dynamics of human flourishing. *American Psychologist, 60*(7), 678–686.

Freedman, D. G. (1964). Smiling in blind infants and the issue of innate versus acquired. *Journal of Child Psychology and Psychiatry, 5,* 171–184.

Fridlund, A. (1994). *Human facial expression: An evolutionary view.* San Diego, CA: Academic Press.

Friesen, W. V. (1972). *Cultural differences in facial expressions in a social situation: An experimental test of the concept of display rules.* Unpublished doctoral dissertation, University of California, San Francisco.

Frijda, N. H., Kuipers, P., & ter Schure, E. (1989). Relations among emotion, appraisal, and emotional action readiness. *Journal of Personality and Social Psychology, 57*(2), 212–228.

Fulcher, J. S. (1942). "Voluntary" facial expression in blind and seeing children. *Archives of Psychology, 272, 5*–49.

Galati, D., Miceli, R., & Sini, B. (2001). Judging and coding facial expression of emotions in congenitally blind children. *International Journal of Behavioral Development, 25*(3), 268–278.

Galati, D., Scherer, K. R., & Ricci-Bitti, P. E. (1997). Voluntary facial expression of emotion: Comparing congenitally blind with normally sighted encoders. *Journal of Personality and Social Psychology, 73*(6), 1363–1379.

Galati, D., Sini, B., Schmidt, S., & Tinti, C. (2003). Spontaneous facial expressions in congenitally blind and sighted children aged 8–11. *Journal of Visual Impairment & Blindness, July,* 418–428.

Geen, T. (1992). Facial expressions in socially isolated nonhuman primates: Open and closed programs for expressive behavior. *Journal of Research in Personality, 26,* 273–280.

Goodenough, F. L. (1932). Expression of emotions in a blind-deaf child. *Journal of Abnormal and Social Psychology, 27,* 328–333.

Haggard, E. A., & Isaacs, K. S. (1966). Micro-momentary facial expressions as indicators of ego mechanisms in psychotherapy. In L. A. Gottschalk & A. H. Auerbach (Eds.), *Methods of Research in Psychotherapy* (pp. 154–165). New York: Appleton-Century-Crofts.

Haidt, J. (2001). The emotional dog and its rational tail: A social intuitionist approach to moral judgment. *Psychological Review, 108*(4), 814–834.

Hauser, M. (1993). Right hemisphere dominance for the production of facial expression in monkeys. *Science, 261,* 475–477.

Hertenstein, M. J., & Campos, J. J. (2004). The retention effects of an adult's emotional displays on infant behavior. *Child Development, 75*(2), 595–613.

Hwang, H. S., & Matsumoto, D. (2010). *Training improves the ability to recognize subtle facial expressions of emotion.* Paper presented at the Annual Convention of the Association for Psychological Science, Boston, MA.

Hyson, M. C., & Izard, C. E. (1985). Continuities and changes in emotion expressions during brief separation at 13 and 18 months. *Developmental Psychology, 21*(6), 1165–1170.

Izard, C. E. (1971). *The face of emotion.* East Norwalk, CT: Appleton-Century-Crofts.

Izard, C. E. (1991). *The psychology of emotions.* New York: Plenum.

Izard, C. E. (2007). Basic emotions, natural kinds, emotion schemas, and a new paradigm. *Perspectives on Psychological Science, 2*(3), 260–280.

Izard, C. E., & Malatesta, C. (1987). Perspectives on emotional development I: Differential emotions theory of early emotional development. In J. S. Osofsky (Ed.), *Handbook of infant development.* New York: Wiley.

Keltner, D. (1995). The signs of appeasement: Evidence for the distinct displays of embarrassment, amusement, and shame. *Journal of Personality and Social Psychology, 68,* 441–454.

Keltner, D., & Buswell, B. N. (1997). Embarrassment: Its distinct form and appeasement functions. *Psychological Bulletin, 122*(3), 250–270.

Keltner, D., & Kring, A. M. (1998). Emotion, social function, and psychopathology. *Review of General Psychology, 2*(3), 320–342.

Kendler, K. S., Halberstadt, L. J., Butera, F., Myers, J., Bouchard, T. J., & Ekman, P. (2008). The similarity of facial expressions in response to emotion-inducing films in reared apart twins. *Psychological Medicine, 38*(10), 1475–1483.

Klinnert, M. D., Campos, J. J., & Sorce, J. F. (1983). Emotions as behavior regulators: Social referencing in infancy. In R. Plutchik & H. Kellerman (Eds.), *Emotion: Theory, research, and experience* (pp. 57–86). New York: Academic Press.

Klinnert, M. D., Emde, R. N., Butterfield, P., & Campos, J. (1986). Social referencing: The infant's use of emotional signals from a friendly adult with a mother present. *Developmental Psychology, 22*(4), 427–432.

Lazarus, R. (1991). *Emotion and adaptation.* New York: Oxford University Press.

LeDoux, J. E., & Phelps, E. A. (2008). Emotional networks in the brain. In M. Lewis, J. M. Haviland-Jones, & L. Feldman Barrett (Eds.), *Handbook of emotions* (3rd ed., pp. 159–179). New York: Guilford Press.

Levenson, R. W. (1999). The intrapersonal functions of emotion. *Cognition and Emotion, 13*(5), 481–504.

Levenson, R. W. (2003). Blood, sweat, and fears: The autonomic architecture of emotion. In P. Ekman, J. Campos, R. J. Davidson, & F. B. M. de Waal (Eds.), *Emotions inside out: 130 years after Darwin's "The expression of the emotions in man and animals"* (Vol. 1000, pp. 348–366). New York: New York Academy of Sciences.

Levenson, R. W., & Ekman, P. (2002). Difficulty does not account for emotion-specific heart rate changes in the directed facial action task. *Psychophysiology, 39*(3), 397–405.

Levenson, R. W., Ekman, P., & Friesen, W. V. (1990). Voluntary facial action generates emotion-specific autonomic nervous system activity. *Psychophysiology,* 27(4), 363–384.

Levenson, R. W., Ekman, P., Heider, K., & Friesen, W. V. (1992). Emotion and autonomic nervous system activity in the Minangkabau of West Sumatra. *Journal of Personality & Social Psychology,* 62(6), 972–988.

Liebal, K., Pika, S., & Tomasello, M. (2004). Social communication in siamangs (Symphalangus syndactylus): Use of gestures and facial expressions. *Primates,* 45(1), 41–57.

Matsumoto, D. (1992). More evidence for the universality of a contempt expression. *Motivation & Emotion,* 16(4), 363–368.

Matsumoto, D. (2001). Culture and emotion. In D. Matsumoto (Ed.), *The handbook of culture and psychology* (pp. 171–194). New York: Oxford University Press.

Matsumoto, D. (2006). Culture and cultural worldviews: Do verbal descriptions of culture reflect anything other than verbal descriptions of culture? *Culture and Psychology,* 12(1), 33–62.

Matsumoto, D., Consolacion, T., Yamada, H., Suzuki, R., Franklin, B., Paul, S., et al. (2002). American-Japanese cultural differences in judgments of emotional expressions of different intensities. *Cognition & Emotion,* 16(6), 721–747.

Matsumoto, D., & Ekman, P. (2004). The relationship between expressions, labels, and descriptions of contempt. *Journal of Personality and Social Psychology,* 87(4), 529–540.

Matsumoto, D., & Hwang, H. S. (in press-a). Culture and emotion: The integration of biological and cultural contributions. *Journal of Cross-Cultural Psychology.*

Matsumoto, D., & Hwang, H. S. (in press-b). Evidence for training the ability to read microexpressions of emotion. *Motivation and Emotion.*

Matsumoto, D., Keltner, D., Shiota, M. N., O'Sullivan, M., & Frank, M. G. (2008). What's in a face? Facial expressions as signals of discrete emotions. In M. Lewis, J. M. Haviland, & L. Feldman Barrett (Eds.), *Handbook of emotions* (pp. 211–234). New York: Guilford Press.

Matsumoto, D., & Lee, M. (1993). Consciousness, volition, and the neuropsychology of facial expressions of emotion. *Consciousness & Cognition: An International Journal,* 2(3), 237–254.

Matsumoto, D., Nezlek, J., & Koopmann, B. (2007). Evidence for universality in phenomenological emotion response system coherence. *Emotion,* 7(1), 57–67.

Matsumoto, D., & Willingham, B. (2009). Spontaneous facial expressions of emotion of congenitally and non-congenitally blind individuals. *Journal of Personality and Social Psychology,* 96(1), 1–10.

Matsumoto, D., & Wilson, J. (2008). Culture, emotion, and motivation. In R. M. Sorrentino & S. Yamaguchi (Eds.), *Handbook of motivation and cognition across cultures* (pp. 541–563). New York: Elsevier.

Mauro, R., Sato, K., & Tucker, J. (1992). The role of appraisal in human emotions: A cross-cultural study. *Journal of Personality and Social Psychology,* 62(2), 301–317.

Mauss, I. B., Levenson, R. W., McCarter, L., Wilhelm, F. L., & Gross, J. J. (2005). The tie that binds? Coherence among emotion experience, behavior, and physiology. *Emotion, 5*(2), 175–190.

McCrae, R. R., & Costa, P. T. (1999). A five-factor theory of personality. In L. A. Pervin & O. John (Eds.), *Handbook of personality: Theory and research* (2nd ed., pp. 139–153). New York: Guilford Press.

McCullough, M. E., Bono, G., & Root, L. M. (2007). Rumination, emotion, and forgiveness: Three longitudinal studies. *Journal of Personality and Social Psychology, 92*(3), 490–505.

Mineka, S., & Cook, M. (1993). Mechanisms involved in the observational conditioning of fear. *Journal of Experimental Psychology: General, 122*(1), 23–38.

Mistschenka, M. N. (1933). Ueber die mimische Gesichtsmotorik der Blinden [Facial mimicking motor behavior in blind individuals]. *Folida Neuropathologica Estoniana, 13,* 24–43.

Mogilner, C., Kamvar, S. D., & Aaker, J. L. (in press). The shifting meaning of happiness. *Social Psychological and Personality Science.*

Ortega, J. E., Iglesias, J., Fernandez, J., M., & Corraliza, J. A. (1983). La expression facial en los ciegos congenitos [Facial expression in the congenitally blind]. *Infancia y Aprendizaje, 21,* 83–96.

Oster, H. (2005). The repertoire of infant facial expressions: An ontogenetic perspective. In J. Nadel & D. Muir (Eds.), *Emotional development* (pp. 261–292). New York: Oxford University Press.

Panksepp, J. (2007). Neurologizing the psychology of affects: How appraisal-based constructivism and basic emotion theory can coexist. *Perspectives on Psychological Science, 2*(3), 281–296.

Panksepp, J. (2008). The affective brain and core consciousness: How does neural activity generate emotional feelings? In M. Lewis, J. M. Haviland-Jones, & L. Feldman Barrett (Eds.), *Handbook of emotions* (3rd ed., pp. 47–67). New York: Guilford Press.

Peleg, G., Katzir, G., Peleg, O., Kamara, M., Brodsky, L., Hel-Or, H., et al. (2006). Heriditary family signature of facial expression. *Proceedings from the National Academy of Sciences, 103*(43), 15921–15926.

Porter, S., & ten Brinke, L. (2008). Reading between the lies: Identifying concealed and falsified emotions in universal facial expressions. *Psychological Science, 19*(5), 508–514.

Redican, W. K. (1982). An evolutionary perspective on human facial displays. In P. Ekman (Ed.), *Emotion in the human face* (pp. 212–280). New York: Cambridge University Press.

Rinn, W. E. (1984). The neuropsychology of facial expression: A review of the neurological and psychological mechanisms for producing facial expressions. *Psychological Bulletin, 95,* 52–77.

Rinn, W. E. (1991). Neuropsychology of facial expression. In R. Feldman & B. Rime (Eds.), *Fundamentals of nonverbal behavior* (pp. 3–70). New York: Cambridge University Press.

Roseman, I. J. (1984). Cognitive determinants of emotion: A structural theory. *Review of Personality & Social Psychology, 5,* 11–36.

Roseman, I. J., Dhawan, N., Rettek, S. I., & Naidu, R. K. (1995). Cultural differences and cross-cultural similarities in appraisals and emotional responses. *Journal of Cross-Cultural Psychology, 26*(1), 23–48.

Rosenthal, R., & DePaulo, B. M. (1979). Sex differences in eavesdropping on nonverbal cues. *Journal of Personality and Social Psychology, 37*(2), 273–285.

Scherer, K. R. (1986). Vocal affect expression: Review and a model for future research. *Psychological Bulletin, 99,* 143–165.

Scherer, K. R. (1997a). Profiles of emotion-antecedent appraisal: Testing theoretical predictions across cultures. *Cognition & Emotion, 11*(2), 113–150.

Scherer, K. R. (1997b). The role of culture in emotion-antecedent appraisal. *Journal of Personality & Social Psychology, 73*(4), 902–922.

Scherer, K. R., Schorr, A., & Johnstone, T. (Eds.). (2001). *Appraisal processes in emotion: Theory, methods, research.* New York: Oxford University Press.

Scherer, K. R., & Wallbott, H. (1994). Evidence for universality and cultural variation of differential emotion response-patterning. *Journal of Personality & Social Psychology, 66*(2), 310–328.

Shiller, V. M., Izard, C. E., & Hembree, E. A. (1986). Patterns of emotion expression during separation in the strange-situation procedure. *Developmental Psychology, 22*(3), 378–382.

Snowdon, C. T. (2003). Expression of emotion in nonhuman animals. In R. J. Davidson, K. Scherer, & H. H. Goldsmith (Eds.), *Handbook of affective sciences* (pp. 457–480). New York: Oxford University Press.

Susskind, J. M., Lee, D. H., Cusi, A., Feiman, R., Grabski, W., & Anderson, A. K. (2008). Expressing fear enhances sensory acquisition. *Nature Neuroscience, 11,* 843–850.

Tangney, J. (2003). Self-relevant emotions. In M. R. Leary & J. P. Tangney (Eds.), *Handbook of self and identity* (pp. 384–400). New York: Guilford Press.

Thompson, J. (1941). Development of facial expression of emotion in blind and seeing children. *Archives of Psychology, 37,* 1–47.

Tiedens, L. Z., Ellsworth, P. C., & Mesquita, B. (2000). Stereotypes about sentiments and status: Emotional expectations for high- and low-status group members. *Personality and Social Psychology Bulletin, 26*(5), 560–574.

Tomkins, S. S. (1962). *Affect, imagery, and consciousness* (Vol. 1: The positive affects). New York: Springer.

Tomkins, S. S. (1963). *Affect, imagery, and consciousness* (Vol. 2: The negative affects). New York: Springer.

Tomkins, S. S., & McCarter, R. (1964). What and where are the primary affects? Some evidence for a theory. *Perceptual and Motor Skills, 18*(1), 119–158.

Tooby, J., & Cosmides, L. (2008). The evolutionary psychology of the emotions and their relationship to internal regulatory variables. In M. Lewis, J. M. Haviland-Jones, & L. Feldman Barrett (Eds.), *Handbook of emotions* (3rd ed., pp. 114–137). New York: Guilford Press.

Tracy, J. L., & Robins, R. W. (2004). Putting the self into self-conscious emotions: A theoretical model. *Psychological Inquiry, 15*(2), 103–125.

Tronick, E. Z. (1989). Emotions and emotional communication in infants. *American Psychologist, 44*(2), 112–119.

Tsai, J. L., & Levenson, R. W. (1997). Cultural influences of emotional responding: Chinese American and European American dating couples during interpersonal conflict. *Journal of Cross-Cultural Psychology, 28,* 600–625.

Ueno, A., Ueno, Y., & Tomonaga, M. (2004). Facial responses to four basic tastes in newborn rhesus macaques (Macaca mulatta) and chimpanzees (Pan troglodytes). *Behavioural Brain Research, 154*(1), 261–271.

Van Hoof, J. A. R. A. M. (1972). A comparative approach to the phylogeny of laughing and smiling. In R. A. Hinde (Ed.), *Nonverbal communication* (pp. 209–241). Cambridge, England: Cambridge University Press.

Vick, S.-J., Waller, B. M., Parr, L. A., Pasqualini, M. S., & Bard, K. A. (2007). A cross species comparison of facial morphology and movement in humans and chimpanzees using the Facial Action Coding System (FACS). *Journal of Nonverbal Behavior, 31,* 1–20.

Warren, G., Schertler, E., & Bull, P. (2009). Detecting deception from emotional and unemotional cues. *Journal of Nonverbal Behavior, 33,* 59–69.

Webb, C. (1977). The use of myoelectric feedback in teaching facial expression to the blind. *Biofeedback and Self-Regulation, 2*(2), 147–160.

Winkielman, P., & Berridge, K. C. (2004). Unconscious emotion. *Current Directions in Psychological Science, 13*(3), 120–123.

3

The Voice

Mark G. Frank, Andreas Maroulis, and Darrin J. Griffin
University at Buffalo, State University of New York

Wе have all heard the phrase, "It's not what you say, but how you say it." This phrase exists in our parlance because we have come to recognize that the nonverbal elements that accompany the spoken word are as important as the actual words in imparting meaning to speech. In fact, when we speak we unleash three distinct types of information upon our listeners through the voice *channel*, of which one is verbal, and the other two are nonverbal. The first subchannel is the *verbal* subchannel, and it consists of the actual words we speak. The second subchannel is the speech *style* subchannel, which consists of the patterns of pausing and other irregularities of speech that accompany the words spoken. The third subchannel is the speech *tone* subchannel, which consists of the acoustic properties of speech such as loudness and pitch. We consider the verbal, style, and tone aspects of speech *subchannels* because they are each capable of sending separate and unique messages; however, unlike the 3 independent channels of face, voice, and body we referred to earlier, these subchannels are all interdependent. You can make a facial expression without uttering a sound. You can gesture at someone without uttering a sound. However, once you utter a sound, each sound will have at minimum a tone and a style. You cannot have a speech style without a tone. Likewise, once you articulate words, they will have tone and style. Most of the time these three subchannels impart roughly the same message, but at other times they can impart different, even contradictory, messages. Think of someone uttering the phrase, "This will be fun." Can you think of a way to say this exact phrase such that it will make a listener believe this *actually* will be fun? Can you think of a way to say this exact phrase such that it will make a listener believe this will *not* be fun at all, possibly even painful? Those elements of your speech that you altered with each utterance of that phrase that enabled you to change its meaning are the nonverbal subchannels of your speech. This is how sarcasm works. But these nonverbal subchannels are about more than sarcasm; they reveal information about our enduring demographic traits, such as our gender, approximate age, and even our native language. They also reveal information about our more transient states, such as our emotions, attitudes, and whether we are engaged in a lot of mental effort as we speak. All of these things can be communicated above and beyond the words we choose to speak.

The Nonverbal Elements of Speech

Given that this book focuses on nonverbal communication, we will focus more on the second and third subchannels—the style and tone—and be considerably more skimpy in discussions about the first subchannel—the words. The style and tone of speech are often lumped together under the term *prosody*. But prosody, or the "music" of speech, is a subcategory of all the various noises we can make, such as disfluencies, pauses, laughs, yawns, and grunts, which are collectively called *paralanguage* (Duncan, 1969; Trager, 1961). Paralanguage tends to be a catch-all category for any information derived from the voice that is not the actual spoken word (Knapp, 1972). However, the line between paralinguistic and verbal information is blurrier than one might think. For example, we can take a medium that, on the surface, has no room for nonverbal communication—e-mail or text messaging. After all, how can we convey tone and style patterns with just written words? WELL? HOW CAN WE? HURRY UP! YOU ARE TAKING TOO LONG!! Although the words on this page are a strictly verbal medium, you have just witnessed what happens to those words through punctuation and capitalization. These two elements of written speech reinstall some of the nonverbal elements common to spoken speech. This is now generally agreed-upon e-mail or text message etiquette—do not capitalize one's writing, as it is akin to shouting at someone in a face-to-face conversation. And of course raising one's voice is a nonverbal signal. Also, the punctuation marks—question marks, exclamation points—serve to change the tone of the written word in the mind of the reader. The question mark causes the reader to raise the pitch at which one hears that sentence in the mind's ear, whereas the exclamation point causes the reader to raise the volume of the speech in the mind's ear. Similarly, we can use periods, ellipses, or dashes . . . to . . . build . . . drama, through the strategic use of pausing. We all know that a well-timed pause can change an otherwise mildly interesting story into an uproarious joke. Someone who excels at this is known to have "comedic" timing.

These punctuation techniques all have nonverbal behavioral analogues in any real-time conversation. But the 21st century has taken us beyond mere capitalization and punctuation as techniques to put nonverbal signals back into the written conversation. The most obvious type of nonverbal injection is the emoticon, which is a collection of letters or symbols designed to portray (usually) a facial expression of emotion (see Chapter 2). The classic, and we think first, emoticon was the sideways smiley face, denoted by a colon and closing parenthesis—for example, :). These have become so popular that most word processing software will automatically convert any colon-closing parentheses to this: ☺. Many text messaging programs also now list a series of circle-faces with various expressions to drop into one's text message; for example, if your day is not going as well—☹. These emoticons serve the same function in written speech as they do in spoken speech. Thus, someone who says to you, "You are being a jerk," and then smiles, is just being ironic and playfully teasing you. However, if someone writes you a text message that says, "You are being a jerk," its actual meaning is unclear. But if someone writes you the same text message that instead says, "You are being a jerk :)," the irony is now clear due to the presence of the smile. As we've seen throughout this book, nonverbal communication adds nuance, shading, and depth of meaning to all communication, and strictly verbal media—e-mail, text messaging—deprives us of most of that. So, being primarily face-to-face creatures, we humans have figured out ways to create and inject nonverbal information back into these media. What is important to note from this discussion is that although we will review the science concerning nonverbal signals in the voice separate from the verbal, in reality it may be impossible to cleave them so neatly. But we will soldier forth.

Mechanics of Vocal Production

The human voice, like the human face (see Chapter 2), has dual influences on its actions, which is illustrated by Figures 3.1 and 3.2. Typically speech starts with various thoughts in the brain, and then signals from the outer or neo cortex—Broca's speech area—activate the cortical motor strip that then signals the jaw, tongue, lips, vocal cords, larynx, and diaphragm to initiate the movements producing the sounds that compose the words representing the thoughts (see Figure 3.1; Fry, 1979). However, if an emotion is aroused, then the inner limbic system of the brain sends signals that engage the autonomic and somatic nervous systems, which then alter blood flow, blood pressure, muscle tension, mucus secretion, respiration, and so forth (see Figure 3.2; Robinson, 1972). These physiological changes then alter the length, shape, and smoothness of the movements of the various body parts that are responsible for the sounds of speech, thus changing the tone, energy, loudness, and other measurable elements of the voice (Scherer, 1989). Both of these systems can send signals simultaneously to the throat structures, which is why it is referred to as a dual system. However, unlike the face, where there is a direct connection between the limbic system and the facial muscle movements, the voice instead features more indirect connections to the muscles and other associated elements

Figure 3.1   Approximate Brain Signal Pathways for Deliberate Speech (External View of Brain)

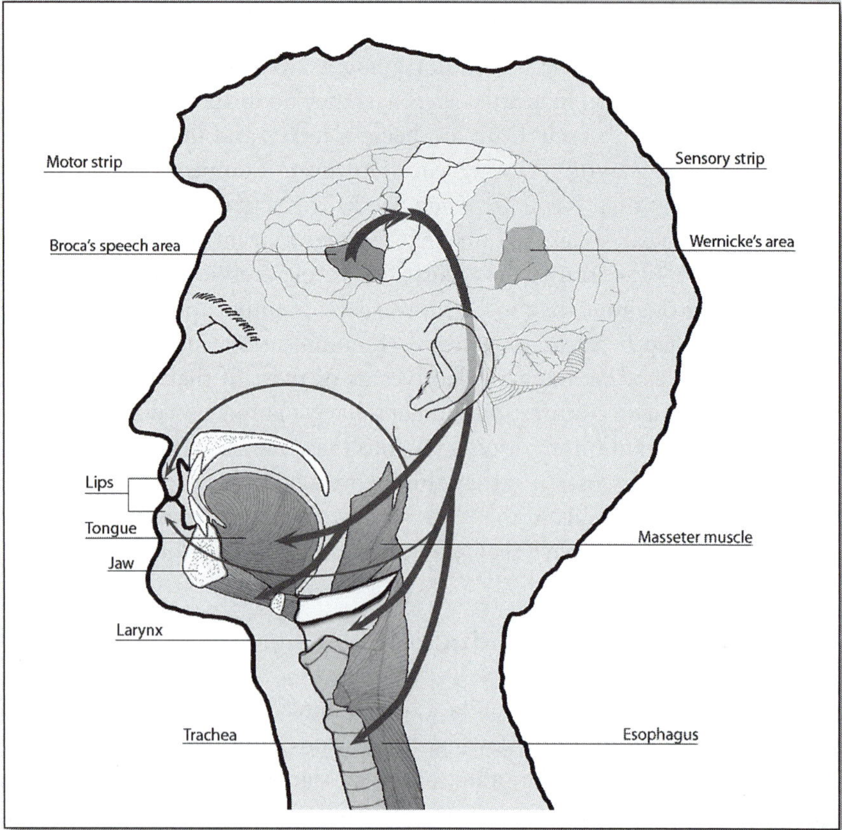

Figure 3.2   Approximate Brain Signal Pathways for Emotional
Reactivity Affecting Speech (Cut-Away View of Brain)

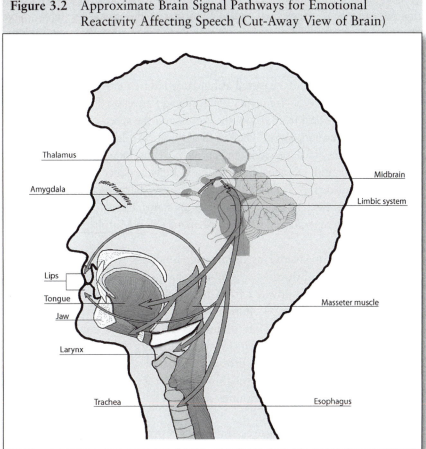

that surround the body parts responsible for speech. This does not mean we should discount their effects on the paralinguistic subchannels of speech, as small changes to any of the body elements can produce measurable acoustic changes in the voice (Scherer, 1989). But what this strongly suggests is that nonverbal measures accompanying speech may be a useful source of information about the speaker's transient states.

Measurement of Nonverbal Voice Characteristics

The sound of a human voice is composed of many distinct and measurable qualities that make each of our voices sound, for the most part, unique (Nolan, 1983). It is these nonverbal elements that tend to make our voices recognizable to others.

There are a number of quantifiable measures of nonverbal information that we can extract from the voice. The most popular measures, which have also been productive from a research point of view in that they predict various behaviors or emotional states, include the following *tonal* qualities.

Pitch. Often denoted and measured as fundamental frequency or F_0, pitch is the measurement of the vocal frequency. Pitch changes are caused by a combination of air pressure upward from below the larynx and the speed of vibration of the vocal folds (Lieberman, 1961). The length of the vocal folds also influences pitch such that shorter folds produce higher pitch. Thus individuals with shorter folds—children and women—tend to have higher-pitched voices than men (Daniloff, Schuckers, & Feth, 1980). Scientists have been interested in not only mean changes in pitch as indicators of various states, but also the variability in pitch over a statement (called *jitter*; Lieberman, 1961; Murphy, 2000).

Loudness. Often measured as *amplitude,* loudness is the measure of the intensity or energy of the voice. Loudness changes are caused by the combination of air pressure upward from below the larynx and the tension of the larynx (Zemlin, 1968). Loudness is often hard for scientists to measure accurately because unless a microphone is attached at a constant distance from the mouth, any head movements will artificially change the amplitude of the signal measured. However, gross changes in loudness—shouting versus whispering—can be captured reliably even if the microphone is not at a controlled distance from the mouth.

Timbre. Often hard to measure, timbre is a representation of the *quality* of the voice. It is considered hard to measure because there are many possible characteristics that can go into the timbre, and many scientists see it as the measure of anything that is neither loudness nor pitch (McAdams & Bregman, 1979). Timbre can then be thought of as the difference in two voices when their loudness and pitch are identical. A number of factors can produce timbre changes, including different sorts of phonation (Daniloff et al., 1980), which modifies the vibrations of the larynx. Often timbre differences are attributable to differences in the configuration of an individual's mouth, nose, throat, and so forth, along with their basic tension (Scherer, 1989).

Resonance. Often measured by the presence of *formants* in the spectrum of a voice, resonance refers to the specific pronunciation sounds of different consonants, vowels, and other sounds (Fant, 1960). These sounds are differentially generated by slight changes in the positions and movements of the tongue, lips, larynx, and so forth.

Here are some other popular and productive nonverbal measures that we can extract from the voice within the *style* subchannel.

Speech rate. This is usually measured as words per minute or words per second. A change in the speech rate can often indicate higher cognitive load or mental effort on the part of the individual (Sillars, Coletti, Parry, & Rogers, 1982). It can also reflect the effects of an emotion, with a decrease for a lower-arousal emotion like sadness or disgust, but an increase for higher-arousal emotions like anger and fear (Johnson, Emde, Scherer, & Klinnert, 1986).

Response length. This is the amount of time a person spends talking. There is some evidence that when people are lying they choose to utter shorter statements (Zuckerman, Koestner, & Driver, 1981).

Speech latency. This is the measurement of the time it takes someone to respond to another. It is the period that spans the end of one person's statement or question to the beginning of the other person's response. It is sometimes referred to as speech hesitation. Longer speech latencies—i.e., slower to respond—have been shown to be reliable measures of higher cognitive load or mental effort (DePaulo et al., 2003; Goldman-Eisler, 1968).

Pauses. This is the time between spoken words. There are two types of pauses—*filled* and *unfilled*. A filled pause is when an individual fills the pause with noise but not necessarily a word. An example of this is when someone says *um,* or *ah,* in between words, as in, "I went to the, uh, zoo." The *uh* fills that pause with sound. An unfilled pause simply does not have the sound involved. For example, "I went to the . . . zoo." Scientists count the number, rate, and duration of pauses. When people are thinking on their feet, they tend to have more pauses (Goldman-Eisler, 1968).

Speech errors. These are various dysfluencies or disturbances in speech, such as repeating words, stuttering, grammar errors, slips of the tongue, false starts, and any incoherent sounds that are uttered (Kasl & Mahl, 1965). As with many of these other measures, they are typically measured as the rate of errors or disturbances per unit of time. An increase in the rate of these disturbances often indicates a higher cognitive load, and in particular, the disturbances marked by repeated particular words and phrases seem to be compelling (DePaulo et al., 2003).

Although scientists can measure all these *style* qualities precisely, they often have trouble measuring some of the *tonal* qualities (e.g., like timbre).

In face-to-face encounters with others it is often our less precise general impressions of the tone and style that influence our perceptions of them. Thus, a person's voice may be described as dull, harsh, or breathy, from which we infer other traits about that person (Scherer, 1984). Likewise, we can detect pronunciation changes associated with accents and then use that information to infer someone's ethnicity.

Information Derived From the Nonverbal Subchannels of the Voice

Paralinguistic information provides a cavalcade of information, most of which we process without much thought. If a stranger calls us on the telephone, we usually develop a mental picture of the caller. Research shows we can be surprisingly good at this; participants were able to match audio samples from strangers to their photographs at 76.5% accuracy, significantly higher than chance (50%; Krauss, Freyberg, & Morsella, 2002). However, some aspects of appearance we are very good at detecting from voice (e.g., gender) and others not so well (e.g., shoe size). To make this analysis manageable we will separate the characteristics into *enduring*, stable traits (e.g., age, gender) of the individual, *transient* dynamic states of the individual (e.g, emotions), and *interactive tools* of the individual (e.g., turn-taking cues).

Enduring traits. These refer to relatively stable demographic or personality characteristics of people. The first thing to note is that we are good at recognizing *identity*. If we are presented with a 2.5 minute audio clip of someone with whom we are familiar speaking, then we can accurately identify them 98% of the time (Hollien, Majewski, & Doherty, 1982). Other studies have shown that audio clips of familiar individuals saying, "Hello! How are you?" are recognized nearly 100% of the time (Abberton & Fourcin, 1978). People are also accurate identifying famous people from voice, although on average not as well as with familiar people from their lives. If someone has to come up with the name of the famous person from his or her own free recall, then the person is 26.6% accurate; but when given a multiple choice listing of names to select, then accuracy rises to 69.9% (van Lancker, Kreiman, & Emmorey, 1985). These high accuracy levels are likely due to the fact that no two individuals sound exactly alike. The reason we don't sound exactly alike is that we all differ in the size and position of our voice apparatus, which will have corresponding consequences for our typical levels of pitch, timbre, and resonance.

Age is another characteristic that we recognize well. A long-ago study found that 4,000 listeners could estimate quite accurately the age of the 9 unknown speakers on a radio broadcast (Pear, 1931). When participants in other studies were given voice samples and asked to match them to photos of the speaker, they were able to identify age quite well, and age was one of the strongest driving factors (Krauss et al., 2002). It appears that as we get older, voice pitch deepens—dramatically for males in puberty—stabilizes into adulthood, but then rises slightly after age 70 (Masaki & Seiji, 2008). Also, disturbances in fundamental frequency increase, and speech rate decreases, with age (Hummert, Mazloff, & Henry, 1999). Surprisingly, perceived hoarseness in the voice was not a predictor of age (Gorham-Rowan & Laures-Gore, 2006).

Gender is detected at very high rates as well (Pear, 1931). Even when presented with just 6 vowel sounds per speaker, detectors were able to identify accurately gender 96% of the time (Lass, Hughes, Bowyer, Waters, & Bourne, 1976). This is likely due to female voices being higher pitched but also more variable and with lower resonance than male voices (Ko, Judd, & Blair, 2006).

Ethnicity is often identified based upon the accent of the speaker; that is, the speaker has an Irish, Australian, Jamaican, Italian, German, Japanese, or Korean accent that betrays his or her ethnicity. Identifying race within a culture is a bit trickier. Judges who were presented with a pair of sustained *a* sounds, taken from a black or a white American speaker, were able to accurately classify who was who 60% of the time (Walton & Orlikoff, 1994). However, social class, or at least an early 1960s version of social class, as reflected in education levels, tends to be better and more reliably recognized than race (Harms, 1961).

Personality is not as tightly tied to vocal qualities, but some types of personality seem to have certain characteristics that make them identifiable. For example, extroverts tend to talk louder, with a faster speech rate, shorter pauses, and more variable pitch than introverts (Lippa, 1998; Siegman, 1987). Dominance is also associated with lower pitch and greater loudness (Hall, Coats, & Smith Lebeau, 2005; Puts, Gaulin, & Verdolini, 2006).

Transient states. Although the word "transient" may imply that something is not significant, in fact, these characteristics have received the most attention of all in the nonverbal research literature on the voice. Transient characteristics of people include their emotions and mental processing efforts.

Due to the nature of human emotion, described in great detail in Chapter 2, research on vocal expression of *emotion* parallels many of the same issues confronted by research on facial expressions of emotion, including many of the same controversies. For example, voice scientists debate which labels best describe the emotion family represented by a particular vocal tone (Juslin & Laukka, 2003; Scherer, 1986). Scientists also debate whether vocal expressions of the emotions are best understood as categorical entities with their own properties (e.g., Laukka, 2005; Scherer, 1984), or whether they are better and more parsimoniously understood as conveying varying amounts of the dimensions of arousal and pleasure (e.g., Bachorowski, 1999). What interests scientists is the degree to which research on vocal expression further confirms or refutes the categorical, hardwired view of emotions suggested by research on facial expression.

As you recall from Chapter 2, emotions are a bio-psycho-social response designed to aid us in adapting to and coping with events that have immediate consequences for our welfare. Clearly other animals feature vocalizations that communicate threats, danger, the nature of relationships, and even their emotional states (e.g., Kitchen, Cheney, & Seyfarth, 2003). Chapter 2 showed compelling evidence that our facial expressions of emotion are universal; that is, expressed similarly and recognized across all cultures. The question is whether the voice shows the same qualities. Darwin (1872/1998) thought so and described many paralinguistic correlates of various emotional states. As you see from Figures 3.1 and 3.2, as with the muscles of facial expression, different parts of the brain can independently send signals to the speech production apparatus in the throat. The fact that discrete emotional signals are sent should produce more bounded changes in the voice structures within each discrete emotion, which in turn would produce some distinguishing sound qualities corresponding to each emotion. This means individuals should agree on which emotion term to label a vocal portrayal of an emotion made by either a layperson or actor. We would expect people from many different cultures should also agree as to which vocal portrayal represented which emotion. However, given that there are not direct inputs from the subcortical structures of the brain into the specific vocal apparatus, only in the supporting structures, we would likely expect the levels of agreement to be lower than those for the face because the interposition of layers of body between these connections may muffle the correspondence and thus render their relationship less precise than the face. This is exactly what we find in the research literature (see review by Scherer, 2003).

A comprehensive review of the literature examining the emotions of anger, fear, happiness, and sadness showed significantly greater-than-chance agreement for all 4 emotions, both within and across cultures (Juslin & Laukka, 2003). And, as suggested earlier, the agreement rates were typically less than the agreement rates reported for facial expressions. The agreement rates for facial expressions of emotion are typically anywhere from 60% to 95% for expressions of anger, contempt, disgust, fear, happiness, sadness, and surprise, with the greatest agreement on happiness. The agreement rates for the vocal expressions of emotion range from approximately 54% to 70% for judgments made within a given culture, to approximately 32% to 64% for judgments made across cultures. Note that despite being lower, they were still significantly higher than chance agreement (which for these data is 14%[1]). For both within and across cultures, the pattern was the same—the highest agreement levels were for the vocal expressions of anger and sadness, and the lowest agreement level was for happiness[2] (Juslin & Laukka, 2003). This is opposite to what we typically find in the facial expressions, where the highest agreement rate is almost always happy facial expressions. We should exercise some caution when comparing the relative importance of face and voice, as there are likely cultural factors that may push or pull for the different expressive channels. For example, when presented with facial and vocal expressions of emotion, the Japanese tend to be a bit more influenced by voice than face, compared to the Dutch (Tanaka et al., 2010); however, we should be careful about generalizing from a single study. But the upshot of the cross-cultural findings on voice is that the pattern is similar to the findings on the face—that there appear to be universals on voice production of emotion, even when the groups are relatively isolated from Western culture (e.g., Bryant & Barrett, 2008; Scherer, Banse, Wallbott, & Goldbeck, 1991).

Although anger, fear, happiness, and sadness have received the most study, smaller numbers of studies have examined agreement for emotions such as disgust, contempt, boredom, embarrassment, guilt, shame, and many shades of positive emotion, such as amusement, relief, contentment, and so forth. The results for these emotions are slightly more mixed. For example, shame (Banse & Scherer, 1996) and guilt often do not show high agreement rates (e.g., 22%, with chance being 7%), although they are occasionally misclassified as sadness (Simon-Thomas, Keltner, Sauter, Sinicropi-Yao, & Abramson, 2009). Disgust shows irregular agreement patterns, sometimes significantly high agreement (93.5%; Sauter, Eisner, Calder, & Scott, 2010; Simon-Thomas et al., 2009) and sometimes insignificantly low agreement (15%; Banse & Scherer, 1996). This may be due to the techniques used to elicit disgust in the vocalists, as scientists have noted that disgust utterances elicited by emotional films tend to feature significantly higher F_0, whereas disgust elicited by actor portrayal tends to produce disgust utterances with significantly lower F_0 (Scherer, 1989). In contrast, embarrassment has shown lower but still significant above-chance agreement (17%; Simon-Thomas et al., 2009), as has contempt (60%; Banse & Scherer, 1996; 46%; Sauter et al., 2010; 34%; Simon-Thomas et al., 2009).

Another interesting aspect of voice research is that these scientists have spent more time differentiating amongst different positive emotion states than scientists studying the face. For example, researchers have examined agreement rates for laypeople's expressions of various positive emotions and found significant agreement for amusement (81%), relief (76%), interest (66%), enthusiasm (42%), pleasure (35%), awe (30%), and triumph (29%). They did not find significant agreement on compassion, gratitude, love, contentment, desire, or pride (Simon-Thomas et al., 2009). Other researchers found the same high agreement for distinguishing amusement (76.5%), relief (64.7%), pleasure (58.8%), triumph (achievement; 70.6%), and in this case also contentment (23.5%; Sauter et al., 2010; 46%; Sauter & Scott, 2007). Interest has also had consistent high agreement levels, and so has its opposite—boredom—at similarly high rates (75% and 76%, respectively; e.g., Banse & Scherer, 1996; Scherer, 1989). Surprise, although at times confused with fear, can also be reliably detected (81.3%; Sauter et al., 2010).

There are other emotions that have also been assessed in the voice under the labels of anxiety, stress, laughter, and crying. These are likely subsumed under the general rubric of fear, joy/happiness, and distress/sadness emotion labels (see Chapter 2 for a more detailed discussion of conceptual issues with emotion). But staying with the terminology used by the researchers, they have reported that we can detect a person's anxiety better in the voice by itself as compared to the face itself (e.g., Harrigan, Wilson, & Rosenthal, 2004). Some of the qualities associated with anxiety are similar to fear, such as speech disturbances, pauses, and stutters (Harrigan, Suarez, & Hartman, 1994). Stress has usually been measured in the context of deception, with a variety of measures purported to measure vocal stress associated with telling a lie—although often to no avail (Hollien & Harnsberger, 2006). Laughter is seen in all cultures, yet the actual acoustic properties vary greatly, suggesting that laughter may serve a few different functions, ranging from extreme joy to nervousness (Grammer & Eibl-Ebesfeldt, 1990). Crying is also found in all cultures and tends to be mostly associated with sadness (Klineberg, 1940)—but can be seen at times at supposedly happy occasions (Vingerhoets & Cornelius, 2001).

There are also nonverbal features in the speech that tend to reflect an individual's higher mental effort, or *thinking*. These include longer speech latencies, slower speech, and more pauses (Greene & Ravizza, 1995). There is also some evidence to suggest that people engaged in higher mental effort also are less immediate, which includes speaking in a more monotone fashion (Kraut & Poe, 1980).

Methodological cautions when studying transient states. There are likely methodological reasons—along with the biological architecture issues (discussed earlier)—that contribute to these relatively reduced (but still statistically significant) agreement rates for various emotions conveyed by the voice. The first was mentioned earlier—that vocal portrayals of a given emotion can vary greatly depending upon the method used to elicit it—e.g., disgust portrayals featured higher pitch when elicited by a film, yet featured lower pitch when self-generated by actors (Pittam & Scherer, 1993). Recordings of spontaneous vocal expression of emotion, taken from real-life spontaneous emotion situations (e.g., airline pilots during panic situations; Kuroda, Fujiwara, Okamura, & Utsuki, 1979), suffer from this same problem—the event triggers for the emotion differ drastically. These sorts of materials also suffer from other problems inherent in using natural spontaneous material, such as often poor quality recordings, short samples, a single speaker, and uncertainty as to the true underlying emotional state of the speaker as he or she spoke (Scherer, 2003). Second, when instead exerting experimental control by employing posed vocal emotions, researchers have noted much larger individual differences in people's abilities to pose an emotion in their voices as compared to their faces (Scherer, 1989). Thus the prototype for each vocal emotion will likely be more variable. Third, this individual difference factor becomes particularly problematic in much of voice research because many studies feature only one or two stimulus speakers doing the vocal portrayals; thus, any deviant or poor portrayal will have a disproportionate effect on suppressing the agreement rates. Fourth, and consistent with the previous observation, voice researchers have not been able to document with great precision the exact parameters of each of these emotions expressed in the voice. Much of this is likely due to both technical *capabilities* and *limitations* to measure the voice. Technical advances have allowed researchers to carve up and represent vocal signals in hundreds of ways; for example, F_0 is studied for emotions by measuring its mean, its variance, its range, its contours (change patterns), high-frequency energy, shift regularity, formants, formant precision, amplitude mean, range, variability (e.g., Banse & Scherer, 1996), and other variables that are often hard to describe and still not quite settled by researchers, like *timbre* (e.g., McAdams & Bregman, 1979). Furthermore, technological advances have enabled the discovery of new complex and detailed measures (e.g., new energy measures and/or synthetic vocal recreations; e.g., Laukka, 2005). Thus the measurement tools used to study the voice are continually changing. Ironically, the fact that new measures are being uncovered actually speaks strongly to the technical *limitations* that plague the study of voice. Scientists have lamented that many unique paralinguistic characteristics of speech have yet to be quantified (Scherer, 2003). Thus the measurement canvas upon which scientists may apply their tools is also shifting. In contrast, scientists studying facial expressions only need to observe the facial muscles, of which there are only 46 possible facial muscle movements. Moreover, there are only 2 ways to measure facial expressions—visually, using a human- (e.g., FACS; Ekman & Friesen, 1978) or computer-driven system based on human coding (e.g., CERT; Bartlett et al., 2006), or physically with electromyography (e.g., Fridlund, Ekman, & Oster, 1987; see Chapter 2). The final consideration when researching the tone qualities of each emotion is that all the measurements must be within-subject measurements (i.e., compare a person's emotional tone with his or her neutral tone), as there are vast differences between individuals in voice pitch and timbre, etc. If one examines the pitch of any 5 males and 5 females, and then plots them on a graph, for the most part one will see the top 5 pitch levels to be the females and the bottom 5 the males, independent of any emotional manipulation. Likewise, this within-subject comparison helps the scientist control for many of the unknown factors that compose timbre and resonance, etc.

In summary, given the indirect innervation of the vocal tract, the lack of consensus on the exact prototype of each emotional signal, and the myriad possible vocal measurements and characterizations of those measurements of each emotion, it is reasonable to expect that emotions expressed through the voice would not show the same levels of agreement as the face. Despite that, and the other methodological considerations when studying the voice, the research seems to have converged across posed, induced, and spontaneous vocal expressions of emotion to show that there are markers for each of the basic emotions in the voice and that the pattern of results looks very similar to the pattern of results found when studying facial expressions of emotion. Table 3.1 shows a summary of the basic emotions identified in the

Table 3.1   Basic Summary of Acoustic Profile and Strength of Evidence for Universality of the Basic Emotions as Expressed Through the Voice

Emotion	F_0	Loudness	Speech Rate	Strength of Finding
Anger	+	+	+	Excellent
Contempt	–	–	0	Fair
Disgust	–	–	–	Fair/Good
Fear	+	+/–	+	Good/Excellent
Happiness	+	+	+	Excellent
Sadness	–	–	–	Excellent
Surprise	+	0	+	Fair

Note: + = an increase; – = a decrease; 0 = no significant change in the given characteristic for that particular emotion facial literature and provides a rough subjective assessment of their characteristic acoustic properties and the strength of the voice research data supporting them as a universal signal of human emotion.

Interactive tools in the voice. These characteristics refer to those paralinguistic characteristics of the voice that can be directed outward toward others and thus affect interactions in some observable way. For example, the paralinguistic information associated with speech influences *comprehension* of information, such that people are more likely to remember information that is presented by a speaker with more variable pitch and amplitude in his or her speech than one who has less (e.g., Glasgow, 1952). People are more likely to be *persuaded* by people who not only vary pitch and amplitude but also speak with fewer pauses, shorter latencies, and faster speech (Apple, Streeter, & Krauss, 1979; Leigh & Summers, 2002; Miller, Maruyama, Beaber, & Valone, 1976). Related to this topic is the phenomenon of "motherese," in which a parent speaks in exaggerated pitch and amplitude changes that seem to be more effective in grabbing the attention of a prelinguistic child (Fernald, 1992).

Paralinguistic information is essential in managing conversations (e.g., *turn taking*) as well. Have you ever wondered why you don't have to say "over" (like an astronaut) whenever you finish speaking during a conversation—and how your conversation partner seems to know when to speak and when to wait his or her turn? How do we have orderly conversations without (usually) speaking over each other? The reason is that people make subtle adjustments in their voice pitch, amplitude, and style to signal that they are finished speaking (Duncan & Fiske, 1977). Let's examine the steps.

First, a speaker needs to request a turn. To do so, he or she may accelerate his or her rate of backchannel (see Chapter 1) *ums* and *ahs* to the speaker and/or may stutter starts with an initial word or sounds ("I . . . I . . . I . . ."; Wiemann & Knapp, 1975). Second, once the new speaker has the floor, he or she will maintain his or her turn by sensing when others wish to interject and deploy various tone and style signals to keep the floor. For example, the speaker will increase his or her speech rate, loudness, and rate of filled pauses in order to prevent openings for the other to start talking (silence of course allows others a golden opportunity to cut in; Lallgee & Cook, 1969; Rochester, 1973). Third, when the speaker is finished, he or she will typically drop his or her pitch and stretch the final word or syllable (Capella, 1985). If it is a question to which one wishes an answer, then the pitch rises at the end. Regardless, this is a signal to the other that the speaker is finished and is allowing others to speak. And, if this listener wishes that speaker to continue, the listener need only smile and nod and utter backchannel *mm-hm, mm-hm* for as long as he or she wishes the speaker to speak.

Finally, there is a perspective that argues that the main purpose of paralinguistic information is to *provoke* directly the behavior of others, rather than to be a basic expression of various internal emotional or other processes (Owren, Rendall, & Bachorowski, 2003). This model still accepts the evolutionary origins of the vocal signal but instead suggests that the vocal acoustics serve the organism by driving the emotional reactions of others; for example, laughter and crying have been shown to provoke strong emotional reactions (Hatfield, Hsee, Costello, Weisman, & Denney, 1995; Neumann & Strack, 2000). This may in fact be the case, as most of our nonverbal communication will affect others in unspecified ways, dependent upon context. We recognize in our definition of emotion that there is not only a biological and a psychological aspect to emotions, but a social component to them as well (see Chapter 2). Thus, this perspective on the voice may be true, but it does not mean one must reject the perspective that these paralinguistic clues are manifestations of internal states. Both can be true.

Application Implications

As with the face, there are many potential uses of nonverbal clues in the voice. Sometimes, we may find ourselves only having access to the voice, as in a telephone call. Or maybe we hear a discussion in an adjoining room, where the voices are muffled enough to not hear the words spoken, but we find we can still determine the general emotional tenor of the conversation. Or, we can use the information gleaned from the voice in a face-to-face conversation to help identify subtle emotions or to determine when someone is engaged in extra mental effort. This information will be discussed a bit more in Chapter 6 and in some of the contributions from our Part II practitioner chapters.

Computer and other scientists have used these voice markers to try to develop software that can read emotional or emotion-like states in the voice (e.g., Hollien, 2000). These devices have been sold to various law enforcement agencies and to private industry to facilitate information gathering and deception detection, although their accuracy rates have not been impressive (e.g., Hollien & Harnsberger, 2006). Regardless, this is a field that will continue to grow.

Conclusion

Although all three subchannels of information in the voice are important, the two nonverbal subchannels—tone and style—have elements that are universally produced and recognized. The nonverbal elements associated with voice have been used in predicting outcomes that other behavioral clues have not. We can identify people by their voices. The fact that you can replicate the data from these research studies yourself speaks to the robustness of the phenomenon. You can demonstrate the ability to recognize enduring traits by asking your friend to close his or her eyes and then play TV or Internet video of someone talking. Then ask your friend to describe this speaker in as much detail as he or she can. Your friend will likely describe this person's age, gender, education, and maybe ethnicity or part of the country in which this person was raised fairly accurately. Similarly, you can demonstrate the ability to recognize transient states by asking your friend to say this exact statement word-for-word 4 times: "These pretzels are making me thirsty." Each time have your friend portray a different emotion, and likely you will accurately detect each (but you will have to look away or close your eyes, as you'll find that your friend will make the facial expression that accompanies that emotion as well when trying to replicate the emotion in the voice). Finally, you can demonstrate the interactive tools by having a conversation with your friend and then inserting various random pauses, or ending your sentences with lowered pitch, or just stop saying *mm-hm*. See how long it takes you to discombobulate your friend. It won't be long.

Thus in any applied setting, voice clues are going to be very important. Later, you will see our contributors talk about their importance in psychiatric assessment, negotiation and the law, and their controversial role in the study of interpersonal deception.

Notes

1. This paper reported Rosenthal and Rubin's (1989) *pi* statistic, which is a measure of agreement controlling for the number of response alternatives—which then enables better comparisons across studies with different response options. Chance for *pi* is .50, and perfect agreement is 1.00. The original Juslin and Laukka (2003) paper reports *pis* ranging from .93 to .74. However, in the previous chapters the data have typically been reported as percentage agreement, so we recalculated these *pis* back to percentage agreement but assumed 7 response options to make this back calculation. Thus, the percentages reported are good estimates but not exact.

2. They also studied tenderness, but that had the lowest agreement and the fewest number of studies (only 1 cross-cultural study with 3 speakers).

References

Abberton, E., & Fourcin, A. J. (1978). Intonation and speaker identification. *Language and Speech*, 21(4), 305–318. doi: 10.1177/002383097802100405

Apple, W., Streeter, L. A., & Krauss, R. M. (1979). Effects of pitch and speech rate on personal attributions. *Journal of personality and social psychology*, 37(5), 715–727. doi: 10.1037/0022-3514.37.5.715

Bachorowski, J. A. (1999). Vocal expression and perception of emotion. *Current Directions in Psychological Science, 8*(2), 53–57. doi: 10.1111/1467-8721.00013

Banse, R., & Scherer, K. R. (1996). Acoustic profiles in vocal emotion expression. *Journal of personality and social psychology, 70*(3), 614–636. doi: 10.1037/0022-3514.70.3.614

Bartlett, M. S., Littlewort, G., Frank, M. G., Lainscsek, C., Fasel, I., & Movellan, J. R. (2006). Automatic recognition of facial actions in spontaneous expressions. *Journal of Multimedia, 1*(6), 22–35.

Bryant, G. A., & Barret, H. C. (2008). Vocal emotion recognition across disparate cultures. *Journal of Cognition and Culture, 8*(1–2), 135–148. doi: 10.1163/15677 0908x289242

Cappella, J. N. (1985). Production principles for turn-taking rules in social interaction: Socially anxious vs. socially secure persons. *Journal of Language and Social Psychology, 4*(3–4), 193–212. doi: 10.1177/0261927x8543003

Daniloff, R., Schuckers, G., & Feth, L. (1980). *The physiology of speech and hearing: An introduction.* Englewood Cliffs, NJ: Prentice-Hall.

Darwin, C. (1998). *The expression of the emotions in man and animals.* New York: Oxford University Press. (Original work published 1872)

DePaulo, B. M., Lindsay, J. J., Malone, B. E., Muhlenbruck, L., Charlton, K., & Cooper, H. (2003). Cues to deception. *Psychological Bulletin, 129*(1), 74–118.

Duncan, S. (1969). Nonverbal communication. *Psychological Bulletin, 72*(2), 118–137. doi: 10.1037/h0027795

Duncan, S., & Fiske, D. W. (1977). *Face-to-face interaction: Research methods and theory.* Hillsdale, NJ: Erlbaum.

Ekman, P., & Friesen, W. V. (1978). *The facial action coding system.* Palo Alto, CA: Consulting Psychologists.

Fant, G. (1960). *Acoustic theory of speech production.* The Hague, The Netherlands: Mouton.

Fernald, A. (1992). Human maternal vocalizations to infants as biologically relevant signals: An evolutionary perspective. In J. H. Barkow, L. Cosmides, & J. Tooby (Eds.), *The adapted mind: Evolutionary psychology and the generation of culture* (Vol. xii, pp. 391–428). New York: Oxford University Press.

Fridlund, A. J., Ekman, P., & Oster, H. (1987). Facial expression of emotion. In A. Siegman & S. Feldstein (Eds.), *Nonverbal behavior and communication* (pp. 143–224). Hillsdale, NJ: Erlbaum.

Fry, D. B. (1979). *The physics of speech.* Cambridge, UK: Cambridge University Press.

Glasgow, G. M. (1952). A semantic index of vocal pitch. *Communication Monographs, 19*(1), 64–68.

Goldman-Eisler, F. (1968). *Psycholinguistics: Experiments in spontaneous speech.* London, New York: Academic Press.

Gorham-Rowan, M. M., & Laures-Gore, J. (2006). Acoustic-perceptual correlates of voice quality in elderly men and women. *Journal of Communication Disorders, 39*(3), 171–184. doi: 10.1016/j.jcomdis.2005.11.005

Grammer, K., & Eibl-Eibesfeldt, I. (1990). The ritualisation of laughter. In W. A. Koch (Ed.), *Natürlichkeit der Sprache und der Kultur* (pp. 192–214). Bochum, Germany: Brockmeyer.

Greene, J. O., & Ravizza, S. M. (1995). Complexity effects on temporal characteristics of speech. *Human Communication Research, 21*(3), 390–421. doi: 10.1111/j.1468-2958.1995.tb00352.x

Hall, J. A., Coats, E. J., & Smith LeBeau, L. (2005). Nonverbal behavior and the vertical dimension of social relations: A meta-analysis. *Psychological Bulletin, 131*(6), 898–924. doi: 10.1037/0033–2909.131.6.898

Harms, L. S. (1961). Programmed learning for the field of speech. *Communication Education, 10*(3), 215–219.

Harrigan, J. A., Suarez, I., & Hartman, J. S. (1994). Effect of speech errors on observers' judgments of anxious and defensive individuals. *Journal of Research in Personality, 28*(4), 505–529. doi: 10.1006/jrpe.1994.1036

Harrigan, J. A., Wilson, K., & Rosenthal, R. (2004). Detecting state and trait anxiety from auditory and visual cues: A meta-analysis. *Personality and Social Psychology Bulletin, 30*(1), 56–66. doi: 10.1177/0146167203258844

Hatfield, E., Hsee, C. K., Costello, J., Weisman, M. S., & Denney, C. (1995). The impact of vocal feedback on emotional experience and expression. *Journal of Social Behavior and Personality, 10*(2), 293–313.

Hollien, H. (2000). The concept of ideal voice quality. In R. D. Kent & M. J. Ball (Eds.), *Voice quality measurement* (pp. 13–24). San Diego, CA: Singular Publishing Group.

Hollien, H., & Harnsberger, J. (2006). *Voice stress analyzer instrumentation evaluation.* Final Report CIFA Contract—FA 4814-04-0011. Gainesville: University of Florida.

Hollien, H., Majewski, W., & Doherty, E. T. (1982). Perceptual identification of voices under normal, stress and disguise speaking conditions. *Journal of Phonetics, 10*(2), 139–148.

Hummert, M. L., Mazloff, D., & Henry, C. (1999). Vocal characteristics of older adults and stereotyping. *Journal of Nonverbal Behavior, 23*(2), 111–132. doi: 10.1023/a:1021483409296

Johnson, W. F., Emde, R. N., Scherer, K. R., & Klinnert, M. D. (1986). Recognition of emotion from vocal cues. *Archives of General Psychiatry, 43*(3), 280–283.

Juslin, P. N., & Laukka, P. (2003). Communication of emotions in vocal expression and music performance: Different channels, same code? *Psychological Bulletin, 129*(5), 770–814. doi: 10.1037/0033-2909.129.5.770

Kasl, S. V., & Mahl, G. F. (1965). Relationship of disturbances and hesitations in spontaneous speech to anxiety. *Journal of Personality and Social Psychology, 1*(5), 425–433. doi: 10.1037/h0021918

Kitchen, D. M., Cheney, D. L., & Seyfarth, R. M. (2003). Female baboons' responses to male loud calls. *Ethology, 109*(5), 401–412. doi: 10.1046/j.1439-0310.2003.00878.x

Klineberg, O. (1940). *Social psychology* (Vol. 5). New York: Holt.

Knapp, M. L. (1972). Toward an understanding of nonverbal communication systems. *The Journal of Communication, 22*(4), 339–352.

Ko, S. J., Judd, C. M., & Blair, I. V. (2006). What the voice reveals: Within- and between-category stereotyping on the basis of voice. *Personality and Social Psychology Bulletin, 32*(6), 806–819. doi: 10.1177/0146167206286627

Krauss, R. M., Freyberg, R., & Morsella, E. (2002). Inferring speakers' physical attributes from their voices. *Journal of Experimental Social Psychology, 38*(6), 618–625. doi: 10.1016/s0022-1031(02)00510-3

Kraut, R. E., & Poe, D. (1980). Behavioral roots of person perception: The deception fudgments of customs inspectors and laymen. *Journal of Personality & Social Psychology, 39*(5), 784–798.

Kuroda, I., Fujiwara, O., Okamura, N., & Utsuki, N. (1979). Method for determining pilot stress through analysis of voice communication. *Aviation, Space, and Environmental Medicine, 47*(5), 528–533.

Lallgee, M. G., & Cook, M. (1969). An experimental investigation of the function of filled pauses in speech. *Language and Speech, 12*(1), 24–28.

Lass, N. J., Hughes, K. R., Bowyer, M., Waters, L. T., & Bourne, V. T. (1976). Speaker sex identification from voiced, whispered, and filtered isolated vowels. *Journal of the Acoustical Society of America, 59*(3), 675–678.

Laukka, P. (2005). Categorical perception of vocal emotion expressions. *Emotion, 5*(3), 277–295. doi: 10.1037/1528-3542.5.3.277

Leigh, T. W., & Summers, J. (2002). Effects of salespersons' use of nonverbal cues. *Journal of Personal Selling and Sales Management, 22*(1), 41–53.

Lieberman, P. (1961). Perturbations in vocal pitch. *Journal of the Acoustical Society of America, 33*(5), 597–603.

Lippa, R. (1998). Gender-related individual differences and the structure of vocational interests: The importance of the people, Äìthings dimension. *Journal of Personality and Social Psychology, 74*(4), 996–1009. doi: 10.1037/0022-3514.74.4.996

Masaki, N., & Seiji, N. (2008). Changes in speaking: Fundamental frequency characteristics with aging. *Folia Phoniatrica et Logopaedica, 60*(3), 120–127.

McAdams, S., & Bregman, A. (1979). Hearing musical streams. *Computer Music Journal, 3*(4), 26–60.

Miller, N., Maruyama, G., Beaber, R. J., & Valone, K. (1976). Speed of speech and persuasion. *Journal of personality and social psychology, 34*(4), 615–624. doi: 10.1037/0022-3514.34.4.615

Murphy, P. J. (2000). Spectral characterization of jitter, shimmer, and additive noise in synthetically generated voice signals. *The Journal of the Acoustical Society of America, 107*(2), 978–988.

Neumann, R., & Strack, F. (2000). "Mood contagion": The automatic transfer of mood between persons. *Journal of personality and social psychology, 79*(2), 211–223. doi: 10.1037/0022-3514.79.2.211

Nolan, F. (1983). *The phonetic bases of speaker recognition. Cambridge studies in speech science and communication.* Cambridge, UK: Cambridge University Press.

Owren, M. J., Rendall, D., & Bachorowski, J. A. (2003). Nonlinguistic vocal communication. In D. Maestripieri (Ed.), *Primate psychology* (pp. 359–394). Cambridge, MA: Harvard University Press.

Pear, T. H. (1931). *Voice and personality.* Great Britain: Chapman & Hall.

Pittam, J., & Scherer, K. R. (1993). Vocal expression and communication of emotion. In M. L. Lewis & J. Haviland (Eds.), *Handbook of emotions* (pp. 185–197). New York, London: Guilford Press.

Puts, D. A., Gaulin, S. J. C., & Verdolini, K. (2006). Dominance and the evolution of sexual dimorphism in human voice pitch. *Evolution and Human Behavior, 27*(4), 283–296.

Robinson, W. P. (1972). *Language and social behaviour.* Harmondsworth, Middlesex: Penguin.

Rochester, S. R. (1973). The significance of pauses in spontaneous speech. *Journal of Psycholinguistic Research, 2*(1), 51–81. doi: 10.1007/bf01067111

Rosenthal, R., & Rubin, D. B. (1989). Effect size estimation for one-sample multiple-choice-type data: Design, analysis, and meta-analysis. *Psychological Bulletin, 106*(2), 332–337. doi: 10.1037/0033-2909.106.2.332

Sauter, D., & Scott, S. (2007). More than one kind of happiness: Can we recognize vocal expressions of different positive states? *Motivation and Emotion, 31*(3), 192–199. doi: 10.1007/s11031-007-9065-x

Sauter, D. A., Eisner, F., Calder, A. J., & Scott, S. K. (2010). Perceptual cues in non-verbal vocal expressions of emotion. *The Quarterly Journal of Experimental Psychology, 63*(11), 2251–2272. doi: 10.1080/17470211003721642

Scherer, K. R. (1984). On the nature and function of emotion: A component process approach. In K. R. Scherer & P. Ekman (Eds.), *Approaches to emotion* (pp. 293–317). Hillsdale, NJ: Erlbaum.

Scherer, K. R. (1986). Vocal affect expression: A review and a model for future research. *Psychological Bulletin, 99*(2), 143–165. doi: 10.1037/0033-2909.99.2.143

Scherer, K. R. (1989). Vocal correlates of emotional arousal and affective disturbance. In H. Wagner & A. Manstead (Eds.), *Handbook of social psychophysiology* (pp. 165–197). Oxford, England: John Wiley & Sons.

Scherer, K. R. (2003). Vocal communication of emotion: A review of research paradigms. *Speech Communication, 40*(1–2), 227–256. doi: 10.1016/s0167-6393 (02)00084-5

Scherer, K. R., Banse, R., Wallbott, H. G., & Goldbeck, T. (1991). Vocal cues in emotion encoding and decoding. *Motivation and Emotion, 15*(2), 123–148. doi: 10.1007/bf00995674

Siegman, A. W. (1987). The telltale voice: Nonverbal messages of verbal communication. In A. W. Siegman & S. Feldstein (Eds.), *Nonverbal behavior and communication* (2nd ed., pp. 351–433). Hillsdale, NJ, England: Erlbaum.

Sillars, A. L., Coletti, S. F., Parry, D., & Rogers, M. A. (1982). Coding verbal conflict tactics: Nonverbal and perceptual correlates of the "avoidance-distributive-integrative" distinction. *Human Communication Research, 9*(1), 83–95. doi: 10.1111/j.1468-2958.1982.tb00685.x

Simon-Thomas, E. R., Keltner, D. J., Sauter, D., Sinicropi-Yao, L., & Abramson, A. (2009). The voice conveys specific emotions: Evidence from vocal burst displays. *Emotion, 9*(6), 838–846. doi: 10.1037/a0017810

Tanaka, A., Koizumi, A., Imai, H., Hiramatsu, S., Hiramoto, E., & de Gelder, B. (2010). I feel your voice: Cultural differences in the multisensory perception of emotion. *Psychological Science, 21*(9), 1259–1262. doi: 10.1177/0956797610380698

Trager, G. L. (1961). The typology of paralanguage. *Anthropological Linguistics, 3*(1), 17–21.

van Lancker, D., Kreiman, J., & Emmorey, K. (1985). Familiar voice recognition: Patterns and parameters. Part I: Recognition of backward voices. *Journal of Phonetics, 13*(1), 19–38.

Vingerhoets, A. J. J. M., & Cornelius, R. R. (2001). *Adult crying: A biopsychosocial approach* (Vol. 3). Philadelphia: Routledge.

Walton, J. H., & Orlikoff, R. F. (1994). Speaker race identification from acoustic cues in the vocal signal. *Journal of Speech & Hearing Research, 37*(4), 738–745.

Wiemann, J. M., & Knapp, M. L. (1975). Turn taking in conversations. *Journal of Communication, 25*(2), 75–92.

Zemlin, W. R. (1968). *Speech and hearing science; anatomy and physiology.* Englewood Cliffs, NJ: Prentice-Hall.

Zuckerman, M., Koestner, R., & Driver, R. (1981). Beliefs about cues associated with deception. *Journal of Nonverbal Behavior, 6*(2), 105–114. doi: 10.1007/bf00987286

4

Body and Gestures

David Matsumoto and Hyi Sung Hwang
San Francisco State University and Humintell, LLC

I n the last two chapters we've covered facial expressions and voice, two of the most important channels of nonverbal behavior. In this chapter we cover gestures, gaze, interpersonal space, touch, body postures, and gait. Although the vast majority of research on nonverbal behavior from the past half century has focused on face and voice, there is a critical mass of evidence and information on these other channels of nonverbal behavior that provides us with a wealth of information for use in practical situations. At the same time, this area of nonverbal communication is also replete with myths about nonverbal behaviors that go far beyond the evidence. Our goal in this chapter, therefore, is twofold: first, to highlight what is known based on the scientific evidence and second, to dismiss myths that are not substantiated by that evidence.

Gestures

Gestures are primarily hand movements (although they occur in head and facial movements as well) that are used basically for two purposes—to illustrate speech and convey verbal meaning. Gestures are interesting because they are a form of *embodied cognition*; that is, they are movements that express some kind of thought or the process of thinking (Kinsbourne, 2006).

They likely coevolved with adaptations in our physical anatomy and cognitive and language capabilities (Bouissac, 2006). This allowed for more rapid and efficient communication systems that went beyond words and verbal language (Capirci & Volterra, 2008).

Gesturing lightens cognitive load when a person is thinking of what to say. For example, when people are given a memory task and simultaneously have to explain how to do a math problem, they remember more items if they gesture when explaining the math (Goldin-Meadow, Nusbaum, Kelly, & Wagner, 2001). Being allowed to point when counting items allows one to be more accurate and quicker; when people are not allowed to point, even nodding allows greater accuracy (Carlson, Avraamides, Cary, & Strasberg, 2007). Gestures help to smooth interactions (Chartrand & Bargh, 1999) and facilitate some aspects of memory (Butterworth & Beatie, 1978). For these reasons gestures can give important insights into the mental states and mental representations of speakers.

Gestures can be broadly classified into two categories—those that co-occur with speech and those that can occur independently of speech. The former are called *speech illustrators* while the latter are called *emblems*. We discuss both now.

Speech Illustrators (Illustrators)

Speech illustrators (or just "illustrators" for short) are movements that are directly tied to speech and serve to illustrate or highlight what is being said. Illustrators can be classified into 6 categories (Efron, 1941; Freedman & Hoffmann, 1967):

1. *Batons* are movements that emphasize a word or phrase, sometimes temporally, much like a chronometer (think of an orchestra conductor with a baton).

2. *Ideographs* are movements that draw a thought or sketch a path.

3. *Deictic movements,* such as pointing.

4. *Spatial movements* illustrate spatial relationships, like marking the distance between two places with one's hands or fingers.

5. *Kinetographs,* which depict bodily action.

6. *Pictographs,* which draw a picture of their referent.

Batons and ideographs typically have no meaning without the accompanying words, and they may even appear nonsensical if performed without speech. The other illustrators may have some verbal content, even without the accompanying words. But all speech illustrators are associated with verbal behavior on a moment-to-moment basis (Kita et al., 2007) and are directly tied to speech content, verbal meaning, and voice volume. They likely occur outside of or with minimal conscious awareness and intention.

The study of culture and gestures has its roots in the work of David Efron (Boas, Efron, & Foley, 1936; Efron, 1941), who examined the gestures of Sicilian and Lithuanian Jewish immigrants in New York City. Efron found that there were distinct gestures among immigrant Jews and Italians who adhered to the traditional culture but that those gestures disappeared as people were more assimilated into the larger American culture, and their children adopted the gestures typical of Americans. This work was followed initially by that of Ekman and his colleagues (Ekman, 1976; Friesen, Ekman, & Wallbott, 1979), who documented cultural differences in emblematic gestures among Japanese, Americans, and New Guineans. Morris and his colleagues (Morris, Collett, Marsh, & O'Shaughnessy, 1980) have also documented many cultural differences in gestures (more to follow).

Cultures differ in rules about the appropriateness of both the amount and type of these various illustrative gestures. Some cultures, such as Latin and Middle Eastern cultures, strongly encourage the use of large, illustrative gestures when speaking; people from these cultures are highly expressive in their gesticulation (Kendon, 1992, 1995). In Italy, for instance, one is expected to "speak with your hands." Other cultures are much more reserved in their use of gestures. The British, for example, gesticulate less than Italians when speaking (Graham & Argyle, 1975), and large gestures are considered impolite in British culture. East Asian cultures discourage the use of such gestures, especially when in public; thus, people from these cultures are even more reserved in their gesticulation. In East Asian cultures large gesticulation may be considered not only impolite but also aggressive.

Cultural differences exist in not only the overall frequency, expansiveness, and duration of illustrator usage, but also in forms. When counting, for example, Germans use the thumb for *1*, while Canadians and Americans use the index finger (Pika, Nicoladis, & Marentette, 2009). People of different cultures also use different gestures while describing motion events (Kita, 2000; Kita & Ozyurek, 2003; McNeill, 2000).

Cultural differences also exist for pointing. In the US and many Western European cultures, for instance, we learn to point to things using our index finger. In other cultures, however, such as Japan, people learn to point with their middle finger, which of course resembles an obscene gesture in many cultures. It is not uncommon to be in a meeting with a Japanese person and witness him or her pointing to an object using the middle finger, or to witness people on Japanese television doing so.

Emblematic Gestures (Emblems)

The other purpose of gestures is to convey verbal meaning without words. These are known as *symbolic gestures, emblematic gestures,* or *emblems.* Just as every culture has its own verbal language, every culture also develops its own emblem vocabulary in gestures. Emblematic gestures are culture specific (and some are gender specific within cultures). This is true not only of national cultures but also of organizational cultures (e.g., the military, sports teams). Unlike illustrators, emblems can stand on their own without speech and convey verbal meaning, such as the American A-OK sign (forming a circle with the index finger and thumb, remaining fingers extended), the peace sign (index and middle fingers up in a *V* shape, palm facing outward), or OK (thumb up, hand in fist). A not insignificant amount of most cultures' emblems are devoted to insults or obscenities. Emblems are true body language, with clear verbal meanings.

Emblems are an important part of any cultural language because they allow for communication across distances when voices cannot be readily heard or when speech is not allowed or wise. Referees of American football and umpires of baseball have their own emblem vocabularies to communicate across a field. Baseball teams also develop their own emblem vocabularies to communicate with each other across distance in ways that are unknown to opposing teams. Militaries develop their own emblem vocabularies in order to communicate in both open situations (e.g., salute) and stealthily (e.g., stop, look, stay).

Because emblems are culture specific, their meanings across cultures are often different and sometimes offensive. The American A-OK sign, for example, can mean "OK," "orifice" with sexual connotations, "money," or "zero" depending on the culture. Placing both hands at the side of one's head and pointing upward with the forefingers signals that one is angry in some cultures; in others it refers to the devil; and in others it means that one wants sex (is horny). The reversed peace sign—index and middle fingers up in a *V* shape, with the palm facing inward—is an insult in England and Australia meaning "screw you." Most Americans don't know that. In fact, former president George H. W. Bush happily made this emblem gesture to a protest crowd during a visit to Australia in January, 1992, much to the puzzlement of the Australian public. (See Figure 4.1 for examples of other emblems.)

It's interesting to consider the origins of emblematic gestures, many of which are not known. The gestures probably originated at some point in the history of a culture when they pictorially represented something meaningful to that group of people, were reinforced among the group members, and then transmitted across generations (the latter a major characteristic of

Figure 4.1   Examples of Culturally Unique Emblems

| Apology in Nepal | "Too hot to touch" in China | "Oh my eye! (You liar)" in Iran |

The first two pictures above show examples of emblems with different meanings in two cultures. In Nepal, the ears are grabbed as a realization that one has offended the ears of another person by saying something impolite or otherwise offensive. In China, the earlobe is grabbed after touching something hot as the earlobe is the coolest part of the skin, and it is believed it will relieve the pain in the burned finger. This has evolved into an emblem that means "too hot" in general. The third picture shows an example of an emblem from Iran. There, when you want to say someone is lying, you act as if you have been struck in the eye and say, "Oh my eye!" The meaning is that when someone tells you a lie it is like being struck in the eye.

Source: © David Matsumoto

the definition of culture; see Chapter 5). One popular theory about the reversed peace sign just described, for instance, suggests that it goes back centuries to when England and France were at war. The English longbowmen had devastated the French in previous engagements and thus were very feared. However, it took a lot of strength to draw the longbow with the middle and index fingers. When English longbowmen were captured, the French cut off their index and middle fingers in order to render them useless as archers should future battles occur. As a crude form of psychological warfare, the English longbowmen raised these two fingers to the French before battle in order to show that they were able to defeat them on the battlefield. It was also a way to tell the French that they still had their fingers. Even the famous middle-finger gesture of obscenity was mentioned in the literature of ancient Rome dating at least two thousand years ago (Morris et al., 1980). Its widespread use is thought to have been a consequence of the spread of the Roman Empire.

Although the movements associated with emblems are culture specific, there appears to be universality in the content themes, functions, and reasons why cultures have a rich vocabulary of emblems (Morris et al., 1980). For example, rituals concerning greetings and salutations, references to locomotion or mental states, and insults are aspects of life that occur in all cultures and for which it would be convenient to be able to signal without words. Thus it makes sense that all cultures develop some emblems for these universal aspects of life. But the specifics of the movements associated with each emblem are different, as these are influenced by national and linguistic boundaries, cultural influx across history due to wars or immigration, and the richness of the word or phrase signaled in the verbal dictionaries of the cultures (Morris et al., 1980).

Morris and colleagues (1980) argued that emblems also arose from gesturing particular symbols. For example, the crossed fingers for good luck was originally a surreptitious "sign of the cross" to signal to another that one was a Christian, then became just the sign of the cross to ward off Satan, and finally just "good luck." Morris called other emblems "relic" emblems, in that they were trace representations of specific behaviors. For example, the Greek "moutza" is an insult emblem that involves a forward hand gesture, palm outward, with fingers spread upward. It was the original "talk to the hand" that we now see with younger people. The moutza is a representation of tossing garbage or urine, or possibly wiping cinders or other effluent on the face of another. Its origins were thought to be ancient Greece where the public would toss their garbage or urine on prisoners as they were transported through the streets. This no longer occurs, but that gesture remains as a relic of that action and today is used as an insult or a curse.

There are also "hybrid" gestures. These refer to gestures that are originally associated with one language but come to be used with another language. Hybrid gestures occur among immigrants and bi- or multilingual individuals. They were first observed by Efron (1941), who reported about a US-born Eastern Jewish individual who used a classical Eastern Jewish culture gesture (fist clenched, thumb outstretched, describing a scooping motion in the air as if digging out an idea) even when speaking English. Another type of hybrid gestures was described by Morris and colleagues (1980), who detailed the combining of two different gestures (the flat hand chop threat gesture of Tunisia combined with the A-OK [ring] gesture to produce a ring-chop hybrid gesture). Other early studies documented that immigrants often use gestures from their original culture when using their second language (Scheflen, 1972). More recent studies have shown that the cross-linguistic transfer of gestures seems to occur from a high-frequency gesture culture to a low-frequency culture (Pika, Nicoladis, & Marentette, 2006).

Although emblems are culture specific, our latest research suggests that a number of them are becoming universally recognized, such as *come, go, hello, goodbye, yes,* and *no* (Hwang, Matsumoto, LeRoux, Yager, & Ruark, 2010). These results are likely being driven by the strong influence of mass media around the world, particularly television and the Internet, where people can view the behaviors of different cultures and begin to learn how to decode them. We predict that it is only a matter of time before a universal set of emblematic gestures is also panculturally produced as well. But make no mistake—emblematic gestures are learned like language and are not biologically wired like the facial and vocal expressions of emotion discussed in Chapters 2 and 3.

Face and Body Gestures

Although gestures are typically considered hand movements, it's important to remember that our facial expressions and head movements can also gesticulate. In the face, for instance, we learn to use our brows as speech illustrators, often raising them when raising our voices or lowering them when lowering our voices. Sometimes we don't even have to use our voices; musicians often raise their brows when reaching for a high note and lower their brows when playing lower and stronger notes. We can also use our eyebrows to highlight or underline elements of our speech. The mother of one of the editors of this book would interrogate him and his siblings in the morning about whether they had made their beds. If she asked the question with immobile eyebrows, then not making the bed was treated as a misdemeanor offense. If she asked the question with raised eyebrows (to emphasize its importance), then not making the bed was elevated to a felony offense, worthy of an immediate harsh lecture with orders to march straight upstairs, right now, and make that bed, and with resultant threats for removal of afterschool playtime with friends.

Many of our facial muscles, especially in the lower face, are used for speech articulation, thus requiring us to move our faces in specific ways to vocalize speech. In fact, some of our facial muscles may have direct links to the voice box, which is why you can hear when a person is smiling even on the telephone. Because different languages require different sounds, people of different cultures move their faces differently in order to pronounce their languages. People who do not normally speak a particular language will often report that their jaws feel sore at the end of a day of speaking this infrequent language because of these different movements. This is akin to the soreness one might feel in the legs if one has not jogged in quite some time.

We also gesture using our heads, the most common gestures being the emblems "yes" and "no." In the United States, as in many cultures of the world, these head gestures are nods and shakes of the head. But while most people of most cultures nod their head yes and shake their head no, these are also culturally determined, as some cultures of the world do not do so.

Even simple gestures such as nodding go a long way to influencing interactions. In one study, participants were instructed to tell a group about a problem, and one member of the group was assigned to help that person. Helpers who nodded (and smiled) were rated by third parties to be more effective than those who did not; the helpees also rated the helpers as more understanding and warm (D'Augelli, 1974). In another study, physical therapists who nodded, smiled, and frowned were associated with both short- and long-term improvements in their client's functioning (Ambady, Koo, Rosenthal, & Winograd, 2002). A meta-analysis of studies examining physician-patient communication concluded that head nods, forward lean, direct body orientation, uncrossed legs and arms, and arm symmetry were positively associated with different patient outcomes (Beck, Daughtridge, & Sloane, 2002). Finally, head nods can also help manage conversations in what is known as backchannel communication. Showing slight nods, along with occasional audible *mm-hm*s, communicates that one is attentive and following the conversation and wishes the speaker to continue. We are often unaware that we even do this. The previous chapter suggested as an experiment to try not smiling or nodding or saying *mm-hm* in your next conversation in order to see how your partner reacts.

We also gesture with our bodies. In the United States and many other cultures, the emblem for "I don't know" is a shrug. Shrugs are often displayed in our shoulders but also by our hands or even our faces. Gestures, therefore, are produced by our entire bodies, including our hands and facial expressions, and can be used to both illustrate speech and convey verbal meaning by themselves. It is no wonder that this is a complex communication system rich with meaning, and to miss these emblems would mean that one misses much of the conversation.

Gaze

Gaze is a powerful nonverbal behavior, most likely because of its evolutionary roots in animals. Research on both humans and nonhuman primates has shown that gaze is associated with dominance, power, or aggression (Fehr & Exline, 1987) as well as affiliation and nurturance (Argyle & Cook, 1976). The affiliative aspects of gazing begin in infancy (Fehr & Exline, 1987) as infants attend to adults as their source of care and protection. The power of gaze is exemplified in "the staring game," in which two individuals stare at each other until one breaks off the stare or smiles; the individual that does so is the loser. Interestingly, such staring games are also done in animal societies and establish dominance hierarchies.

These meanings and functions of gaze and visual attention are similar across cultures, and all cultures create rules concerning them because both aggression and affiliation are behavioral tendencies that are important for group stability and maintenance. But cultures differ in the amounts of gaze and visual attention considered appropriate. Arabs, for example, gaze much longer and more directly at their partners than do Americans (Hall, 1963; Watson & Graves, 1966). Watson (1970), who classified 30 countries as either a "contact" culture (those that facilitated physical touch or contact during interaction) or a "noncontact" culture, found that contact cultures engaged in more gazing and had more direct orientations when interacting with others, less interpersonal distance, and more touching. Within the United States, ethnic groups differ in gaze and visual behavior (Exline, Jones, & Maciorowski, 1977; LaFrance & Mayo, 1976).

Relatedly, gaze is often used as a nonverbal sign of respect, although different cultures produce different rules concerning gaze as a sign of respect. In the United States, individuals are taught to "look the other person in the eye" or to "look at me when you're talking." For Americans, looking directly at the individual to whom one is talking is a sign of respect. In many other cultures, however, the same behavior is a sign of disrespect, and looking away or even looking down is a sign of respect (along with bowing the head down; interestingly, we don't hear of cultures, however, where looking up with the head tilted back is respectful, probably because these behaviors are typically associated with the universal expression of contempt). Thus it is easy for intercultural conflict to occur as a result of these gestural differences, as Americans may judge people of other cultures as disrespectful or insincere when in fact these people may have been acting in deference. After learning about this cultural norm from one of your authors, a courtroom judge confessed to him in horror that she may have given convicted defendants from one cultural group slightly harsher sentences because she had thought these individuals were disrespecting the court by not looking her in the eye. At the same time, people of other cultures can easily judge Americans to be more aggressive than Americans intend.

Stereotypes about gaze also belie judgments of deception and credibility. In the United States, a commonly held belief is that a liar will not look someone straight in the eye. And most people around the world also believe this to be the number-one cue of deception (the Global Deception Research Team, 2006). Not only is that probably not true (there is little or no empirical support for this myth), but the cultural differences just mentioned compound the situation even more, allowing Americans to believe that foreigners are lying when in fact they might simply be acting deferentially. We'll also discuss this issue more in Chapter 5 on culture and Chapter 6 on deception.

Interpersonal Space

The use of space in interpersonal interactions is another important nonverbal behavior and is called *proxemics*. Hall's (1966, 1973) classic work in this area specified four different levels or zones of interpersonal space use depending on social relationship type: intimate, personal, social, and public. These zones are like concentric invisible bubbles that surround the person. He suggested that interpersonal distance helps to regulate intimacy by controlling sensory exposures because the possibility of sensory stimulation (smells, sights, touch) is enhanced at closer distances. This meaning and function of space is a universal aspect of life that exists across cultures; thus it makes good sense that cultures regulate the use of space as such regulation is necessary for social coordination; violations of space bring about aversive reactions (Sussman & Rosenfeld, 1978).

People of all cultures appear to use space according to the four major distinctions proposed by Hall (1966, 1973), but they differ in the size of the spaces they attribute to them. In the United States, Hall suggested that intimate distances are less than 18 inches (46 cm), personal distances are 18 inches to 4 feet (1.2m), social distance is 4 to 12 feet (3.66 m), and public distances are greater than 12 feet (see Figure 4.2). A study of people from

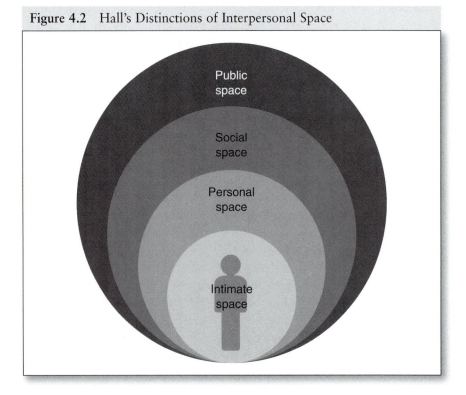

Figure 4.2   Hall's Distinctions of Interpersonal Space

five different cultures (American, Swedish, Greek, Southern Italian, and Scottish), for example, showed that the cultures were similar in the order of the distances for different types of transaction, but there were significant mean differences in the actual distances used (Little, 1968). In general, results from various studies suggest that cultures around the Mediterranean, Middle East, or of Latin origin interact at closer distances. Arab males, for example, tend to sit closer to each other than American males, with more direct, confrontational types of body orientations (Watson & Graves, 1966). They also use greater eye contact and speak in louder voices. Arabs, at least in the past, learned to interact with others at distances close enough to feel the other person's breath (Hall, 1963, 1966). Latin Americans tend to interact more closely than do students of European backgrounds (Forston & Larson, 1968), and Indonesians tend to sit closer than Australians (Noesjirwan, 1977, 1978). Italians interact more closely than either Germans or Americans, and Colombians interact at closer distances than do Costa Ricans (Shuter, 1976). When interacting with someone from their same culture, Japanese sat the farthest away, Venezuelans the closest, with Americans in the middle (Sussman & Rosenfeld, 1982); interestingly, in the same study, foreigners who spoke in English adopted the American conversational distance compared to when speaking with others from their home country in their native language. Cultural differences in the use of space even occurred when individuals set dolls to interact with each other (Little, 1968).

But it is also important to remember that it is not necessarily the culture of the interactants per se that is the main determining factor of the appropriate interpersonal spacing to take in an interaction. Rather, the major single factor determining distances appears to be the relationship of the interactants. The specific content or affective tone of the interaction is the next most important (Little, 1968).

Another thing to recognize is that much of the information we have about the use of interpersonal space involves dyadic interaction. We have much less research about the use of space among groups of people, especially strangers. Anecdotally, it appears that cultures valuing relatively more space among dyadic interactants, such as those in East Asia, don't have strong rules about maintaining such space among crowds of strangers. Anyone with experience in a crowded rush hour train in downtown Tokyo or crowded marketplaces in China can attest to this. But Americans in the United States tend to value some degree of personal space even when among crowds of strangers and are offended or insulted if people "invade" that space. We often have to create rules for contexts in which our preferences may be violated, such as in elevators. The intimacy equilibrium hypothesis (Argyle & Dean, 1965) suggests that people take steps to reinstate their space; in an elevator, one would stare at the numbers, visually removing the space offender. Similarly, a bar will have seats all facing forward, thus directing eye gaze forward, enabling a stranger to sit at the edge of our intimate zone without causing major offense. Thus the rules of space use may differ across different contexts as well as cultures.

Finally, one often-overlooked aspect of space usage is the influence of age. A meta-analysis of studies demonstrated that personal space gradually and steadily increases between ages 3 and 21 (Hayduk, 1983). This has been found to be true in both naturalistic and experimental settings. Adults as well as children are influenced by age differences; when a 5-year-old intrudes on the rear space of an adult, the adult generally turns toward and speaks to the child. When 10-year-olds do so, the adults generally move, lean away, or fidget.

Touch

Another important nonverbal behavior is touch. Touch is related to the use of interpersonal space because it requires close physical contact. Some writers consider interpersonal touch as one of humankind's earliest and most basic forms of communication (Knapp, 1972; Morris, 1971), probably owing to its importance in early mother-infant caretaking. Anecdotally, touch has long been considered a sign of positive emotion, closeness, comfort, and compassion. As such, we learn to communicate many messages via touch. In academia the study of touch is known as *haptics*.

Recent research has gone beyond examining the relationship between touch and general positive emotion by demonstrating that touch communicates distinct emotions, such as anger, fear, disgust, love, gratitude, and sympathy across cultures (Hertenstein, Holmes, McCullough, & Keltner, 2009; Hertenstein, Keltner, App, Bulleit, & Jaskolka, 2006). Among family members, the amount of touching—embraces, handholding, arms around shoulders—is positively associated with the intensity of smiling of family members, and these relationships predict positive behaviors outside of the home as well (Oveis, Gruber, Keltner, Stamper, & Boyce, 2009).

We all learn what is and is not appropriate with regard to touching others and being touched. There are interesting sex differences in reactions to touch. In surveys, men and women both agree that being touched by close friends of the opposite sex is pleasant and touch from a same-sex person is unpleasant; but being touched by an opposite-sex stranger is unpleasant for women but pleasant for men (Heslin, Nguyen, & Nguyen, 1983). When there is no justification for the touch, men seem to have more aversive reactions to being touched than women and like an intruding toucher less (Sussman & Rosenfeld, 1978).

A number of interesting studies have demonstrated a link between touch and compliance. In one of the first studies to do so (Kleinke, 1977), money was left on the shelf of a phone booth in an airport. An experimenter approached the person who next used the phone, asking if he or she found the money. There were large differences in compliance as a function of whether or not the experimenter touched or did not touch the person; 96% of the people who were touched returned the money whereas only 63% of the people who were not touched did. Touch has also been shown to increase compliance to signing petitions and completing research surveys (Patterson, Powell, & Lenihan, 1986; Willis & Hamm, 1980).

The meaning and function of touch are likely similar across cultures, and just as cultures regulate space, they also regulate touch, by creating different rules about the amounts of touching behavior deemed acceptable. As mentioned previously, Watson (1970) classified 30 countries as either a "contact" culture (those that facilitated physical touch or contact during interaction) or a "noncontact" culture. Recent research has generally confirmed this prediction (McDaniel & Andersen, 1998), but it has also called for sharpening these generalizations by taking into account context and relationship (Remland, Jones, & Brinkman, 1991). Regardless, violations of the cultural rules regarding touch are likely to be interpreted in the same way as those of space, producing aversive consequences.

While all of the examples until now in this section have involved one person touching another, another form of nonverbal behavior involves a person touching him or herself. These movements are called "adaptors" or "manipulators" because they allow the individual to adapt to internal or external stimuli (e.g., scratching an itch) or because they allow for the manipulation of a part of the body (rubbing one's arms to soothe oneself). While of course everyone engages in these types of nonverbal behaviors often, *changes* in the frequency, duration, or intensity of these may have important meaning to the mental state of the individual. Individuals under duress, for example, may show an increase in their manipulators that appear to soothe or caress the body, or in actions that appear fidgety.

Postures and Gait

Postures communicate attitudinal states and general affect, as opposed to the very specific emotions communicated by face and voice. These attitudinal and general affective states include preference (liking versus disliking), orientation (closed or open), and attention (direct or indirect). These various dimensions can be summarized as communicating general positivity as well as status relationships (Mehrabian, 1968a, 1968b, 1969). For example, body orientation—the degree to which a person's shoulders and legs are turned in the direction of rather than away from another interactant—is associated with attitude toward the interactant; the least direct orientation occurs for disliked interactants while more direct orientations occur for liked others. Open arms and legs in a seated position generally communicates a more positive attitude and openness, whereas arms akimbo (arms on hips) generally is associated with more negative attitudes.[1]

A handful of studies have examined whether body postures can be signals of more discrete emotional states, not just general positivity-negativity. For example, when actors posed emotions of pride, happiness, anger, and sadness, they walked with longer strides and exhibited more exaggerated foot pounding (heavy footedness) when posing anger than when posing the other emotions (Montepare, Goldstein, & Clausen, 1987). In another study (Coulson, 2004), observers viewed 176 computer-generated mannequin figures and judged them for the presence or absence of 6 emotions—anger, disgust, fear, happiness, sadness, and surprise. Observers could not distinguish disgust, fear, and surprise beyond chance levels. Anger, sadness, and happiness, however, were reliably attributed to a large number of postures, with some obtaining greater than 90% agreement rates. Anger was conveyed by a backward head tilt, absence of a backward chest bend, no abdominal twist, arms raised forward and upward, and weight transfers either forward or backward. Happiness was conveyed by a backward head tilt, no forward movement of the chest, and arms raised above shoulder level and straight at the elbow. Sadness was conveyed by a forward head tilt, forward chest bend, to twisting, and arms at the sides. In yet another study (Montepare, Koff, Zaitchik, & Albert, 1999), observers saw 3-second video clips of actors portraying angry, happy, sad, or neutral emotional situations.[2] The observers were able to judge which emotion was being portrayed beyond chance levels. Subsequent ratings of the body movements indicated that angry videos were rated as jerkier, stiffer, and harder than the other emotions; anger body movements were also more expanded, fast, and had more action.

One of the limitations with these sets of studies, however, is that actors were asked to portray emotion through their posture or gait, which raises the possibility that the produced behaviors were mimes of an emotion but not really what happens when emotions are elicited spontaneously and naturally. And there is surprising little systematic research on the production or interpretation of the meaning of postures across cultures. The studies that do exist suggest that people of different cultures interpret postures according to the same dimensions (i.e., positivity, openness, status) but place different weights of importance on specific aspects of these dimensions (Kudoh & Matsumoto, 1985; Matsumoto & Kudoh, 1987).

Another aspect of nonverbal behaviors related to whole-body movement is gait, which is the pattern of movement of the body when walking. Studies where individuals wear bulky sweatshirts, with reflectors on their shoulders, elbows, hips, knees, and other joints, have shown that observers can accurately judge the sex of the person by their gait alone (Kozlowski & Cutting, 1977). Recent research has uncovered fascinating new findings. For instance, gait patterns are different when people are asked to simulate different emotional states or while listening to different types of music (Janssen et al., 2008). Gait also offers some cues to a person's personality characteristics and can be used as cues to determine sexual advances or inappropriate touching (Sakaguchi & Hasegawa, 2006); slow walkers with slow length strides and personality traits implying vulnerability were identified as targets for inappropriate touching. One study examined judgments of the emotional state of individuals carrying a concealed handgun versus a concealed 1-liter bottle and found that observers' judgments correlated with arm swing and gait (Blechko, Darker, & Gale, 2009). The suggestion that the additional emotional load involved with deceptive behavior may produce gait abnormalities has a number of interesting practical applications, such as security screening (see Chapter 6 on deception).

These gait differences manifest themselves in various disorders as well. For example, depressed patients show decreased stride length, decreased coordination of arms in movement, and slower velocity (Lemke, Wendorff, Meith, Buhl, & Linneman, 2000). Parkinson's patients also show reduced stride but can be trained to expand the stride by employing various visual clues, again suggesting some volitional control over the movement (Lewis, Byblow, & Walt, 2000).

Only a handful of studies have examined cross-cultural differences in gait and perceptions of it. Montepare and Zebrowitz (1993) obtained judgments from Korean observers of 5- to 70-year-old Americans as they walked from one end of a room to the other and back, and they compared those judgments to those previously obtained from American observers (Montepare & Zebrowitz-McArhur, 1988). There was cross-cultural agreement in perceptions of age, sex, strength, and happiness, but cross-cultural differences on perceptions of dominance. The authors suggested that some reactions to gait information may be universal while others are more influenced by culture.

There has been some interesting research in the speed with which individuals across cultures typically move through their cities (Kirkcaldy, Furnham, & Levine, 2001; Levine & Bartlett, 1984; Levine, Lynch, Miyake, & Lucia, 1989; Levine & Norenzayan, 1999). These studies have demonstrated that pace is associated with punctuality, coronary heart disease, and a variety of attitudinal and personality traits. These studies, and the relative lack of studies on culture, posture, and gait, suggest that this area is ripe for study.

Nonverbal Behaviors and Rapport

We end this chapter with a brief discussion of the relationship between nonverbal behaviors and rapport. Establishing rapport is very important to so many practitioners who work in face-to-face interactions. Rapport is crucial if one is trying to obtain information, whether it be in a job interview, medical or psychiatric intake, or police interrogation. Rapport occurs when a relationship is in harmony or concordance; in layperson's terms, rapport occurs when two people are "on the same wavelength" or "on the same page." Rapport greases the wheels of social interaction and makes it much more likely that one can obtain reliable and trustworthy information.

Several techniques are commonly and popularly thought to establish and maintain rapport. One of the most popular involves mirroring the other person's behaviors in body posture, tone of voice, or speech. Another involves invoking a sense of obligation by giving gifts or doing favors without being asked. Yet another involves finding an area of commonality and building a sense of camaraderie.

A number of scientists have examined the relationship between nonverbal behaviors and rapport, and a few key nonverbal behaviors have been shown to positively influence the development of rapport. Mirroring is known as the "chameleon effect" in the scientific literature, referring to a tendency to adopt the postures, gestures, and mannerisms of interaction partners (Chartrand & Bargh, 1999), and in general it has been supported by the available evidence as producing positive regard for the other. But some studies also show null or even negative effects on rapport as a function of mirroring (LaFrance & Ickes, 1981). These data suggest that mirroring may positively influence rapport if it is done naturally and subconsciously (or at least appears to be so); if an interactant partner feels that one is deliberately trying to mirror behaviors, the partner is likely to feel manipulated, diminishing the chances for rapport building. Other nonverbal behaviors found to be associated with rapport include smiling (Rotenberg et al., 2003); direct body orientation, uncrossed legs, symmetrical arms, and moderate eye contact (Harrigan, Oxman, & Rosenthal, 1985); and congruent limbs and forward-leaning postures (Trout & Rosenfeld, 1980).

Touch may also be a way to build rapport. Finding a way to innocuously add touch to an interaction—like shaking hands with two hands or placing one hand on the partner's shoulder when shaking hands—can facilitate rapport building. But one needs to be very careful about the context in which touching occurs, as it may be inappropriate to touch at all, especially across cultures or genders.

Tickle-Degnen and Rosenthal (1990) have suggested that the development of rapport is a dynamic process involving three interrelating components, mutual attentiveness, positivity, and coordination, and that the relative weighting of these components changes across time. In early interactions, positivity and attentiveness may be more important than coordination. Later, however, coordination and attentiveness may be more important than positivity.

Application Implications

Many of the concepts discussed in this chapter seem to have straightforward implications for any interaction. For example, gestures can inform us about the cultural group of the individual. Gait can provide important information for not only security officers but also physicians. Rapport is likely essential in any sort of interview context, be it a job interview, police interrogation, or a first date. Information on gesture, posture, gait, and use of interpersonal space is often quite useful because the individual is often unaware that he or she is producing these behaviors. At the same time, observers have to be careful not to overinterpret these behaviors. With the exception of the emblematic gestures, these other signals from the body are not as clear-cut as what we have seen on the face and voice in the previous two chapters. The behaviors in this chapter often complement other signals, adding nuance to other clearer basic signals in the face and voice. But at times these behaviors will contradict other signals, and that can allow for interesting insights into others. We will see more about that in Chapter 6.

Conclusion

In previous chapters we explored the complex world of faces and voices. In this chapter we have seen how incredibly sophisticated our nonverbal behavior system is by examining gestures, gaze, space, touch, body postures, and gait. Each of these nonverbal channels communicates a wealth of information about emotional states, cognitions, intent, personality, and attitudes. Not paying attention to these various channels means that we may miss a lot of what occurs in conversation.

Although there are many resources regarding nonverbal behaviors in the general press, our intent was to bring to bear the latest scientific evidence available in each of the relevant areas so that researchers and practitioners can use knowledge based in evidence rather than experience, stereotype, or myth. Nowhere is this clearer than in this chapter's final section on rapport. Most practitioners view the establishment of rapport as a necessary if not crucial part of their professional interactions and for good reason, as rapport is so important in the creation of a platform for credible information exchange or gathering.

Another aspect of all nonverbal behaviors that is important for a complete understanding involves an appreciation of the influence of culture on nonverbal behaviors. While we have discussed culture sporadically throughout this chapter and previously, we devote the entire next chapter to this very important topic.

Notes

1. But be careful to not overinterpret arm crossing, especially in chairs with no armrests. In these situations the frequency of arm crossing may increase as a way of resting the arms.

2. To be sure, body movements in even brief video clips are different from static postures. Static postures, like the universal facial expressions of emotion, have "snapshot" qualities; that is, they convey meaning without movement.

References

Ambady, N., Koo, J., Rosenthal, R., & Winograd, C. H. (2002). Physical therapists' nonverbal communication predicts geriatric patients' health outcomes. *Psychology and Aging, 17*(3), 443–452.

Argyle, M., & Cook, M. (1976). *Gaze and mutual gaze.* New York: Cambridge University Press.

Argyle, M., & Dean, J. (1965). Eye contact, distance, and affiliation. *Sociometry, 28,* 289–304.

Beck, R. S., Daughtridge, R., & Sloane, P. D. (2002). Physician-patient communication in the primary care office: A systematic review. *Journal of the American Board of Family Practice, 15*(1), 26–38.

Blechko, A., Darker, I. T., & Gale, A. G. (2009). The role of emotion recognition from nonverbal behaviour in detection of concealed firearm carrying. *Proceedings of the Human Factors and Ergonomics Society 53rd Annual Meeting, 53*(18), 1363–1367.

Boas, F., Efron, D., & Foley, J. P. (1936). A comparative investigation of gestural behavior patterns in "racial" groups living under different as well as similar environmental conditions. *Psychological Bulletin, 33,* 760.

Bouissac, P. (2006). Gesture in evolutionary perspective. *Gesture, 6*(2), 189–204.

Butterworth, B., & Beatie, G. (1978). Gesture and silence as indicators of planning in speech. In R. Campbell & P. Smith (Eds.), *Recent advances in psychology of language: Formal and experimental approaches* (pp. 347–360). New York: Plenum.

Capirci, O., & Volterra, V. (2008). Gesture and speech: The emergence and development of a strong and changing partnership. *Gesture, 8*(1), 22–44.

Carlson, R. A., Avraamides, M. N., Cary, M., & Strasberg, S. (2007). What do the hands externalize in simple arithmetic? *Journal of Experimental Psychology: Learning, Memory, and Cognition, 33*(4), 747–756.

Chartrand, T. L., & Bargh, J. A. (1999). The chameleon effect: The perception-behavior link and social interaction. *Journal of Personality and Social Psychology, 76*(6), 893–910.

Coulson, M. (2004). Attributing emotion to static body postures: Recognition accuracy, confusions, and viewpoint dependence. *Journal of Nonverbal Behavior, 28*(2), 117–139.

D'Augelli, A. R. (1974). Nonverbal behavior of helpers in initial helping interactions. *Journal of Counseling Psychology, 21*(5), 360–363.

Efron, D. (1941). *Gesture and environment.* Oxford, England: King's Crown Press.

Ekman, P. (1976). Movements with precise meanings. *Journal of Communication, 26*(3), 14–26.

Exline, R. V., Jones, P., & Maciorowski, K. (1977). *Race, affiliative-conflict theory and mutual visual attention during conversation.* Paper presented at the American Psychological Association Annual Convention, San Francisco.

Fehr, B. J., & Exline, R. V. (1987). Social visual interactions: A conceptual and literature review. In A. W. Siegman & S. Feldstein (Eds.), *Nonverbal behavior and communication* (Vol. 2, pp. 225–326). Hillsdale, NJ: Lawrence Erlbaum.

Forston, R. F., & Larson, C. U. (1968). The dynamics of space: An experimental study in proxemic behavior among Latin Americans and North Americans. *Journal of Communication, 18*(2), 109–116.

Freedman, N., & Hoffmann, S. P. (1967). Kinetic behavior in altered clinical states: Approach to objective analysis of motor behavior during clinical interviews. *Perceptual & Motor Skills, 24,* 527–539.

Friesen, W. V., Ekman, P., & Wallbott, H. (1979). Measuring hand movements. *Journal of Nonverbal Behavior, 4*(2), 97–112.

Global Deception Research Team. (2006). A World of Lies. *Journal of Cross-Cultural Psychology, 37*(1), 60–74.

Goldin-Meadow, S., Nusbaum, H., Kelly, S. D., & Wagner, S. (2001). Explaining math: Gesturing lightens the load. *Psychological Science, 12*(6), 516–522.

Graham, J. A., & Argyle, M. (1975). A cross-cultural study of the communication of extra-verbal meaning by gestures. *International Journal of Psychology, 10,* 57–67.

Hall, E. T. (1963). A system for the notation of proxemic behaviors. *American Anthropologist, 65,* 1003–1026.

Hall, E. T. (1966). *The hidden dimension.* New York: Doubleday.

Hall, E. T. (1973). *The silent language.* New York: Anchor.

Harrigan, J. A., Oxman, T. E., & Rosenthal, R. (1985). Rapport expressed through nonverbal behavior. *Journal of Nonverbal Behavior, 9*(2), 95–110.

Hayduk, L. A. (1983). Personal space: Where we now stand. *Psychological Bulletin, 94*(2), 293–335.

Hertenstein, M. J., Holmes, R., McCullough, M., & Keltner, D. (2009). The communication of emotion via touch. *Emotion, 9*(4), 566–573.

Hertenstein, M. J., Keltner, D., App, B., Bulleit, B. A., & Jaskolka, A. R. (2006). Touch communicates distinct emotions. *Emotion, 6*(3), 528–533.

Heslin, R., Nguyen, T. D., & Nguyen, M. L. (1983). Meaning of touch: The case of touch from a stranger or same sex person. *Journal of Nonverbal Behavior, 7*(3), 147–157.

Hwang, H. S., Matsumoto, D., LeRoux, J. A., Yager, M., & Ruark, G. (2010). *Cross-cultural similarities and differences in emblematic gestures.* Paper presented at the 2010 Congress of the International Association of Cross-Cultural Psychology, Melbourne, Australia.

Janssen, D., Schollhorn, W. I., Lubienetzki, J., Folling, K., Kokenge, H., & Davids, K. (2008). Recognition of emotions in gait patterns by means of artificial neural nets. *Journal of Nonverbal Behavior, 32*, 79–92.

Kendon, A. (1992). Some recent work from Italy on quotable gestures ("emblems"). *Journal of Linguistic Anthropology, 2*(1), 72–93.

Kendon, A. (1995). Gestures as illocutionary and discourse structure markers in Southern Italian conversation. *Journal of Pragmatics, 23*, 247–279.

Kinsbourne, M. (2006). Gestures as embodied cognition: A neurodevelopmental interpretation. *Gesture, 6*(2), 205–214.

Kirkcaldy, B., Furnham, A., & Levine, R. (2001). Attitudinal and personality correlates of a nation's pace of life. *Journal of Managerial Psychology, 16*(1), 20–34.

Kita, S. (2000). How representational gestures help speaking. In D. McNeill (Ed.), *Language and gesture: Window into thought and action* (pp. 162–185). Cambridge, England: Cambridge University Press.

Kita, S., & Ozyurek, A. (2003). What does cross-linguistic variation in semantic coordination of speech and gesture reveal? Evidence for an interface representation of spatial thinking and speaking. *Journal of Memory and Language, 48*, 16–32.

Kita, S., Ozyurek, A., Allen, S., Brown, A., Furman, R., & Ishizuka, T. (2007). Relations between syntactic encoding and co-speech gestures: Implications for a model of speech and gesture production. *Language and Cognitive Processes, 22*(8), 1212–1236.

Kleinke, C. I. (1977). Compliance to requests made by gazing and touching experimenters in field settings. *Journal of Experimental Social Psychology, 13*, 218–223.

Knapp, M. L. (1972). *Nonverbal communication in human interaction.* New York: Holt, Rinehart, and Winston.

Kozlowski, L. T., & Cutting, J. E. (1977). Recognizing the sex of a walker from a dynamic point light display. *Perception and Psychophysics, 21*, 575–580.

Kudoh, T., & Matsumoto, D. (1985). Cross-cultural examination of the semantic dimensions of body postures. *Journal of Personality & Social Psychology, 48*(6), 1440–1446.

LaFrance, M., & Ickes, W. (1981). Posture mirroring and interactional involvement: Sex and sex typing effects. *Journal of Nonverbal Behavior, 5*(3), 139–154.

LaFrance, M., & Mayo, C. (1976). Racial differences in gaze behavior during conversations: Two systematic observational studies. *Journal of Personality and Social Psychology, 33*(5), 547–552.

Lemke, M. R., Wendorff, T., Meith, B., Buhl, K., & Linneman, M. (2000). Spatiotemporal gait patterns during over ground locomotion in major depression compared with healthy controls. *Psychiatric Research, 34,* 277–283.

Levine, R. V., & Bartlett, K. (1984). Pace of life, punctuality, and coronary heart disease in six countries. *Journal of Cross-Cultural Psychology, 15*(2), 233–255.

Levine, R. V., Lynch, K., Miyake, K., & Lucia, M. (1989). The Type A city: Coronary heart disease and the pace of life. *Journal of Behavioral Medicine, 12*(6), 509–524.

Levine, R. V., & Norenzayan, A. (1999). The pace of life in 31 countries. *Journal of Cross-Cultural Psychology, 30*(2), 178–205.

Lewis, G. N., Byblow, W. D., & Walt, S. E. (2000). Stride length regulation in Parkinson's disease: The use of extrinsic, visual cues. *Brain, 123,* 2077–2090.

Little, K. B. (1968). Cultural variations in social schemata. *Journal of Personality and Social Psychology, 10*(1), 1–7.

Matsumoto, D., & Kudoh, T. (1987). Cultural similarities and differences in the semantic dimensions of body postures. *Journal of Nonverbal Behavior, 11*(3), 166–179.

McDaniel, E., & Andersen, P. A. (1998). International patterns of interpersonal tactile communication: A field study. *Journal of Nonverbal Behavior, 22*(1), 59–75.

McNeill, D. (2000). Analogic/analytyic representations and cross-linguistic differences in thinking for speaking. *Cognitive Linguistics, 11*(1–2), 43–60.

Mehrabian, A. (1968a). Inference of attitudes from the posture, orientation, and distance of a communicator. *Journal of Consulting & Clinical Psychology, 32*(3), 296–308.

Mehrabian, A. (1968b). Relationship of attitude to seated posture, orientation, and distance. *Journal of Personality and Social Psychology, 10*(1), 26–30.

Mehrabian, A. (1969). Significance of posture and position in the communication of attitude and status relationships. *Psychological Bulletin, 71*(5), 359–372.

Montepare, J., Goldstein, S. B., & Clausen, A. (1987). The identification of emotions from gait information. *Journal of Nonverbal Behavior, 11*(1), 33–42.

Montepare, J. M., & Zebrowitz, L. A. (1993). A cross-cultural comparison of impressions created by age related variations in gait. *Journal of Nonverbal Behavior, 17*(1), 55–68.

Montepare, J. M., & Zebrowitz-McArhur, L. (1988). Impressions of people created by age-related qualities of their gaits. *Journal of Personality and Social Psychology, 55*(4), 547–556.

Montepare, J., Koff, E., Zaitchik, D., & Albert, M. (1999). The use of body movements and gestures as cues to emotions in younger and older adults. *Journal of Nonverbal Behavior, 23*(2), 133–152.

Morris, D. (1971). *Intimate behaviour.* New York: Random House.

Morris, D., Collett, P., Marsh, P., & O'Shaughnessy, M. (1980). *Gestures: Their origins and distribution.* New York: Scarborough.

Noesjirwan, J. (1977). Contrasting cultural patterns on interpersonal closeness in doctors: Waiting rooms in Sydney and Jakarta. *Journal of Cross-Cultural Psychology, 8*(3), 357–368.

Noesjirwan, J. (1978). A rule-based analysis of cultural differences in social behavior: Indonesia and Australia. *International Journal of Psychology, 13,* 305–316.

Oveis, C., Gruber, J., Keltner, D., Stamper, J. L., & Boyce, W. T. (2009). Smile intensity and warm touch as thin slices of child and family affective style. *Emotion, 9*(4), 544–548.

Patterson, M. L., Powell, J. L., & Lenihan, M. G. (1986). Touch, compliance, and interpersonal affect. *Journal of Nonverbal Behavior, 10*(1), 41–50.

Pika, S., Nicoladis, E., & Marentette, P. F. (2006). A cross-cultural study on the use of gestures: Evidence for cross-linguistic transfer? *Bilingualism: Language and Cognition, 9*(3), 319–327.

Pika, S., Nicoladis, E., & Marentette, P. F. (2009). How to order a beer: Cultural differences in the use of conventional gestures for numbers. *Journal of Cross-Cultural Psychology, 40*(1), 70–80.

Remland, M. S., Jones, T. S., & Brinkman, H. (1991). Proxemic and haptic behavior in three European countries. *Journal of Nonverbal Behavior, 15*(4), 215–232.

Rotenberg, K. J., Eisenberg, N., Cumming, C., Smith, A., Singh, M., & Terlicher, E. (2003). The contribution of adults' nonverbal cues and children's shyness to the development of rapport between adults and preschool children. *International Journal of Behavioral Development, 27*(1), 21–30.

Sakaguchi, K., & Hasegawa, T. (2006). Person perception through gait information and target choice for sexual advances: Comparison of likely targets in experiments and real life. *Journal of Nonverbal Behavior, 30,* 63–85.

Scheflen, A. E. (1972). *Body language and the social order: Communication as behavioral control.* Englewood Cliffs, NJ: Prentice Hall.

Shuter, R. (1976). Proxemics and tactility in Latin America. *Journal of Communication, 26*(3), 46–52.

Sussman, N. M., & Rosenfeld, H. M. (1978). Touch, justification, and sex: Influences on the aversiveness of spatial violations. *Journal of Social Psychology, 106,* 215–225.

Sussman, N. M., & Rosenfeld, H. M. (1982). Influence of culture, language, and sex on conversational distance. *Journal of Personality and Social Psychology, 42*(1), 66–74.

Tickle-Degnen, L., & Rosenthal, R. (1990). The nature of rapport and its nonverbal correlates. *Psychological Inquiry, 1*(4), 285–293.

Trout, D. L., & Rosenfeld, H. M. (1980). The effect of postural lean and body congruence on the judgment of psychotherapeutic rapport. *Journal of Nonverbal Behavior, 4*(3), 176–190.

Watson, O. M. (1970). *Proxemic behavior: A cross-cultural study.* The Hague, Netherlands: Mouton.

Watson, O. M., & Graves, T. D. (1966). Quantitative research in proxemic behavior. *American Anthropologist, 68,* 971–985.

Willis, F. N., & Hamm, H. K. (1980). The use of interpersonal touch in securing compliance. *Journal of Nonverbal Behavior, 6,* 49–55.

5

Cultural Influences on Nonverbal Behavior

David Matsumoto and Hyi Sung Hwang
San Francisco State University and Humintell, LLC

Although there are some nonverbal behaviors that have universal and probably biologically based roots, culture influences nonverbal behavior in profound ways. Just as members of every culture learn to communicate differently with verbal language, they also learn to communicate differently with nonverbal language as well. When interacting with people of different cultures, therefore, one deals not only with different verbal languages but with different nonverbal behavior, too. That is why even if people gain language fluency, they are not perceived as culturally fluent unless they adopt the mannerisms and associated nonverbal behaviors of that culture and language. These differences make *inter*cultural interactions more complex and difficult than *intra*cultural interactions and lead to greater potential miscommunication. We will come back to this point at the end of the chapter. First we review some of the main research findings from the literature examining the influence of culture on the various aspects of nonverbal behavior and discuss how these influences contribute to the intercultural communication process. We begin our presentation by explaining exactly what we mean when we say "culture."

What Is Culture?

Defining Culture

"Culture" means many things to many people. For most it is conflated with race, nationality, and ethnicity. But culture is not the same as these other social constructs, and to understand its influence on nonverbal behavior and communication we need to have a working definition of it. We define human culture as *a unique meaning and information system, shared by a group and transmitted across generations* (Matsumoto, 2007; Matsumoto & Juang, 2007). Culture gives meaning to social contexts, social roles, identities, relationships, and settings. Our cultures determine what it means to be a husband or wife, child, work colleague, acquaintance, or even stranger. Culture determines what being in private or public means. Given these various meanings, cultures create rules we call *norms* that help to determine what is appropriate or not in our behaviors with specific people in specific contexts. Culture is the meaning and information afforded to these contexts, relationships, and norms.

Cultural meanings and information enhance social coordination, allowing for greater differentiations among social groups, institutionalize cultural practices and customs, and prescribe social norms and expectations for all important aspects of social life such as mating, aggression, and cooperation. Without culture we would have social chaos. With culture we have social order (see Figure 5.1). For example, rules concerning how and where we drive are culturally determined. With these rules there is order. Can you imagine a society without rules for how we should all drive and share the road? There would be pandemonium. Sure, different societies have different rules because of their different cultures. But within each society the social order that culture brings aids the members in ensuring their survival in the environment in which they live. These rules are solutions for living; because groups communicate their solutions across generations, each generation need not create entirely new solutions, ensuring efficiency for survival.

Human cultures are evolved potentials (albeit more recent in evolutionary history than the emotion system).[1] The emergence of human cultures coincides with the evolution of a host of complex cognitive abilities including language (Premack, 2004), self-other knowledge, the ability to know that other people not only are intentional agents but can share intentions (Tomasello, 1999; Tomasello, Carpenter, Call, Behne, & Moll, 2005), and the ability to continually build upon improvements and discoveries (ratcheting; Tomasello, Kruger, & Ratner, 1993). Many of these coincide with the

Figure 5.1   The Function of Culture

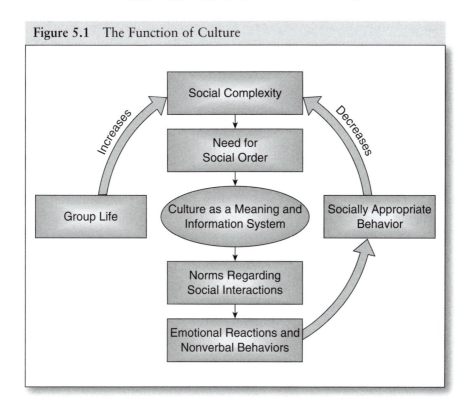

development of the higher cortical areas of the brain and the language areas (as opposed to the location of the emotion system, which is in the phylogenetically older, subcortical areas).

Culture is a response to ecological and environmental context (DeKay & Buss, 1992; Georgas, van de Vijver, & Berry, 2004). It is the complex of ways that emerges when groups address ecological challenges to meet biological needs and social motives. Culture is a set of time-tested solutions for the problem of how to survive and reproduce. It enables groups to meet basic needs of survival, procreate and produce offspring, put food on the table, provide shelter from the elements, and care for daily biological essentials. It also allows for complex social networks and relationships, enhancement of the meaning of normal, daily activities, and the pursuit of well-being. It allows us to be creative in music, art, drama, and work, to seek recreation, and to engage in sports and organize competitions, whether in the local Little League or the Olympic Games. It allows us to search the sea and space, to develop an education system, and to create mathematics. It allows us to go to the moon, to create a research laboratory on Antarctica, and send probes to Mars and Jupiter. Unfortunately, it also allows us to have wars, create and improve on weapons of mass destruction, and recruit and train terrorists.

Contrasting Culture With Other Social Constructs

So what's the difference between culture and other social constructs? Culture is often marked by verbal language, and different language groups typically have different cultures. Even if the language is the same, different dialects of a language often denote different cultures. English, for example, is the primary language of England, parts of Canada, the United States, Australia, New Zealand, and parts of the Caribbean. But there are differences in the use of English in each of these countries, and they denote interesting differences in their cultures. Even within these countries there are different dialects and regional differences in the language that denote differences in local and regional cultures. In the United States, for instance, English is vastly different among the West Coast, Hawaii, the Deep South, and Boston. These linguistic differences co-occur with interesting cultural differences.

Nationality refers to a person's country of origin, and countries typically have their own cultures. This is because countries are associated with each of the factors that influence culture. For example, countries are defined by specific boundaries that describe their ecology—geography, climate, and natural resources. Countries also have their own unique sociocultural history, language, government, and economic base, all of which affect culture. Countries have differences in mean levels of aggregate personality traits, which can affect culture. But be careful; *country* is a geopolitical demarcation while *culture* is not, and there can be people of vastly different cultures living in the same country and even speaking the same language but living, thinking, and behaving very differently. This is true in many countries of the Middle East, Eastern Europe and Russia, and China. Conversely, people can be of the same or very similar culture, but living in different countries, such as Kurdish people in Turkey, Iraq, and Iran, or Pashtun people living in Pakistan and Afghanistan.

The word *ethnicity* is derived from the Greek *ethnos*, meaning people of a nation or tribe, and is usually used to denote one's racial, national, or cultural origins. In the United States, for example, ethnic groups include African Americans, Asians and Pacific Islanders, Hispanics and Latinos, and Native Americans. Thus, ethnicity is generally used in reference to groups characterized by a common nationality, geographic origin, culture, or language (Betancourt & Lopez, 1993). Understanding the relationship between ethnicity and culture can be tricky. To the extent that ethnicity refers to national origins, it may denote aspects of culture. But just because a person's ancestry is from a particular region of the world doesn't necessarily mean that person shares the culture of his or her place of origin. This is especially true of immigrants whose families have lived in a host country for generations. While they may have a certain ethnic origin, they may be culturally indistinguishable from the host culture.

Sex refers to the biological differences between men and women. The term *sex roles* is used to describe the behaviors and patterns of activities men and women may engage in that are directly related to their biological differences and the process of reproduction (such as breast-feeding). In contrast, *gender* refers to the behaviors or patterns of activities that a culture deems appropriate for men and women. *Gender role* refers to the degree to which a person adopts the gender-specific and appropriate behaviors ascribed by his or her culture. Describing and understanding psychological gender differences requires us to go beyond the biological differences between men and women. Gender differences are thus cultural differences, and the size and nature of gender differences actually differ across cultures.

Groups that share a common meaning and information system that is transmitted across generations of group members have culture. This is true not only for the groups described earlier but also for groups with disabilities, groups with different sexual orientations, different organizations, and gangs. Different companies have their own cultures. Militaries have their own culture, and even within the military different branches of the military often have their own culture.

What is not culture? Race is not culture, although many people use the terms interchangeably. The problem with race is that there is considerable controversy surrounding what it is (Anderson & Nickerson, 2005). Many contemporary scholars suggest that there are three major races—Caucasoid, Mongoloid, and Negroid—but past studies of the origins of race have proposed as many as 37 different races (Yee, Fairchild, Weizman, & Wyatt, 1993). Although laypersons typically use skin color, hair, and other physical characteristics to define race, most physical anthropologists use population gene frequencies. Regardless of which biological or physical characteristics one uses to define race, the concept of race is much less clear-cut than previously believed (Lewontin, Rose, & Kamin, 1984). Some authors have suggested that the distinctions among races are arbitrary and dubious at best (Zuckerman, 1990). Even studies of genetic systems, including blood groups, serum proteins, and enzymes, have shown considerably more within-group than between-group variation, suggesting that racially defined groups are actually more similar than different. Race, therefore, is a social construction (Smedley & Smedley, 2005), not culture, and people of different cultures differ in their definitions of race. In some cultures, race is a continuum along a dimensional scale, not a categorical or nominal entity (Davis, 1991). Many Brazilians believe that race is not heritable and varies according to economic or geographic mobility (Eberhardt & Randall, 1997). In some countries, socioeconomic mobility is associated with changes in perceptions of physical properties such as skin color and hair texture (Eberhardt & Randall, 1997).

Culture is also not personality. Just because a person is a member of a certain culture doesn't necessarily mean that he or she harbors all of the exact same qualities of that culture. To think so is to rigidly stereotype people. *Personality* refers to the individual differences that exist among individuals within groups. Culture is a macro, social, group-level construct. It is the social psychological frame within which individuals reside, much like the structure of our houses and homes. *Personality* refers to the unique constellation of traits, attributes, qualities, and characteristics of individuals within those frames. Cultures may value or favor certain personality types. For example, the United States seems to value extroverts, and thus shy children are often given remedial pushes by their parents to socialize more to overcome their "disability" (Kagan, Snidman, Arcus, & Reznick, 1994).

Culture as we have defined it is not the same as popular culture, which generally refers to trends in music, art, and other expressions that become popular among a group of people. Certainly popular culture and culture as we have defined it share some similarities—perhaps most important, the sharing of an expression and its value by a group of people. But there are also important differences. For one, popular culture does not necessarily involve sharing a wide range of psychological attributes across various psychological domains. Culture as we defined it involves a system of rules that cuts across attitudes, values, opinions, beliefs, norms, and behaviors. Popular culture may involve sharing in the value of a certain type of behavioral expression but does not necessarily involve a way of life. A second important difference concerns cultural transmission across generations. Popular culture refers to values or expressions that come and go as fads or trends within a few years. Culture is relatively stable over time and even across generations (despite its dynamic quality and potential for change).

Culture and Facial Expressions of Emotion

Cultural Differences in Expressing Emotion

We learned in Chapter 2 about the universality of facial expressions of emotion and their probable biological, genetic basis. Thus people all around the world have the capacity to express their emotions in exactly the same ways on their faces. And in many situations people of all different cultures do so, such as when alone or with close friends and family.

But there are many cultural differences in how people manage and modify the universal facial expressions. The first evidence for cultural differences in expression was in a different condition of Friesen's (1972) study described in Chapter 2. In the first condition, the Americans and Japanese viewed highly stressful films alone and produced the same facial expressions. In a subsequent condition, they viewed the films in the presence of an older, male experimenter. In this second condition, cultural differences emerged; whereas the Americans continued to express their negative emotions, the Japanese were more likely to smile.

Ekman and Friesen (1969) coined the term *cultural display rules* to account for cultural differences in facial expressions of emotion. These are rules learned early in childhood that help individuals manage and modify their emotional expressions depending on social circumstances. This concept explained the cultural differences observed in Friesen's (1972) study. In the first condition of the experiment, there was no reason for display rules to modify expressions because the participants were alone and their display rules were inoperative. In the second condition, display rules dictated that the Japanese mask their negative emotions in the presence of the experimenter, as it was considered impolite in Japanese culture to make such expressions in the presence of a higher-status person (Ekman, 1972; Friesen, 1972).

When the concept of display rules was proposed originally as a mechanism of expression management, Ekman and Friesen (1969, 1975) noted seven ways in which expressions may be managed. Individuals can express emotions as they feel them with no modification. But individuals can also amplify (exaggerate) or deamplify (minimize) their expressions; for instance, feelings of sadness may be intensified (amplification) at funerals or minimized (deamplification) at weddings. People can mask or conceal their emotions by expressing something other than what they feel, as when nurses or physicians hide their emotions when speaking with patients with terminal illness, or when employees in service industries (e.g., flight attendants) interact with unruly customers. Individuals may also learn to neutralize their expressions, expressing nothing, such as when playing poker (poker face). People can also qualify their feelings by expressing emotions in combination, such as when feelings of sadness are mixed with a smile, with the smile commenting on the sadness, saying to others, "I'll be OK." Individuals can also simulate emotions—displaying them even though they are not felt at all. These behavioral modification responses have been found to occur when spontaneous expressive behaviors have been studied (Cole, 1986; Ekman & Rosenberg, 1998). See Table 5.1 for summary of the characteristics of display rules.

Thus, display rules explain why facial expressions of emotion can be both universal and culture specific. We are all born with the capacity to show emotions on our faces. And when we are in situations that allow us to express ourselves freely without modification, our faces show the same expressions for the same emotions all over the world. But people of different cultures learn different display rules about how to manage and modify their expressions depending on social circumstances. In one culture it may be okay to express your anger or frustration to your colleague, friend, or spouse; in another it may not be. But when displayed, the expressions have the same form across cultures; to our knowledge there is no evidence that people of different cultures express the same emotion differently, or express different emotions with the same expression; they just manage the use of the underlying, universal emotional expressions.

Table 5.1   Characteristics of Different Types of Cultural Display Rules

Label	Description	Example
Express	Express an emotion as it is felt with no modifications	Expressing an emotion "as is," as when alone or with close friends or family
Amplify	Exaggerate the expression of an emotion so that what is displayed is more than what is felt	Laughing loudly at your boss's bad joke even though it is only mildly amusing
Deamplify	Reduce the intensity of the expression so that what is displayed is less than what is felt	Scolding a child when angry, showing that you're angry but not enraged
Neutralize	Show nothing	Poker face; stone-faced
Qualify	Express the emotion but with another expression to comment on the original emotion. The second expression is often a smile.	Smiling even though one feels miserable; the smile lets people know that things are okay or will be okay even though you're in distress
Mask	Don't show what one truly feels and instead show something else altogether	Smiling even though one is entirely angry at something or someone
Simulate	Display an emotion even though one is not felt at all	Feigning that one is angry or happy or sad when one is not

Fast Sequencing of Universal and Culture-Specific Expressions

As other studies documenting cultural differences in expression began to pepper the literature (Argyle, Henderson, Bond, Iizuka, & Contarello, 1986; Edelmann et al., 1987; Gudykunst & Nishida, 1984; Gudykunst & Ting-Toomey, 1988; Matsumoto & Kupperbusch, 2001; Noesjirwan, 1978; Waxer, 1985), a consensus in the field emerged that when emotions are aroused, the displays are *either* universal *or* culture specific, depending on context. In our latest work, we showed that emotional displays can be both for the same person in the same context, if displays are examined *in sequence across time*. To demonstrate this possibility, we went back to the study of Olympic athletes (Matsumoto, Willingham, & Olide, 2009) originally discussed in Chapter 2. A previous study demonstrated that their first, immediate facial reactions upon match completion were universal—joy for the winner, sadness/distress for the loser (Matsumoto & Willingham, 2006). The subsequent expressions, however, were not analyzed in that study. Thus we examined changes in the Olympic athletes' expressions after their initial reactions were examined and classified them into one of several regulation strategies. We then examined the relationship between these expressive styles and cultural variables such Hofstede's (2001) cultural dimensions and country demographics such as population density and affluence. Although the athletes' initial reactions were universal, their subsequent expressions were culturally regulated and reliably associated with population density, affluence, and individualism[2]. Athletes from urban, individualistic cultures expressed their emotions more; athletes from less urban, more collectivistic cultures masked their emotions more. Thus, if we examine the image sequence in Figure 5.2 from left to right across time, we initially see the winner of the judo match express the universal emotion of joy. Shortly thereafter in the middle image his expression changes to something more neutral looking, as we can see him pressing his lips together, likely trying to conceal his joy in order to conform to the display rule to not "show up" his opponent. But in the third image we see that joy leaking out again, as of course this is the Olympics and the victory would make that person the best in the world. We imagine most of us would likely have difficulty fully containing our joy in that circumstance.

The speed by which some of these expression changes occurred was surprisingly fast. The average amount of time between the first, universal expression and the subsequent, culturally specific expression was 1 second. And that time estimate was likely too slow. (It was limited by the photographic

Figure 5.2   An Example From the 2004 Athens Olympic Games

| Immediately at match completion | A few seconds later . . . | A few seconds after that . . . |

Source: © Bob Willingham. Reprinted with permission.

equipment we used in that study, which date-time stamped each image to the second.) In our experience analyzing videos of people in emotionally evocative situations, we notice that people can cycle through several different emotional expressions in fractions of a second.

Thus emotional expressions can be both universal and culture specific in the same individuals in the same context, provided that expressions are examined across time. This makes perfect sense, because all humans are cultural beings. Moreover, expressive styles involving greater modification of the original initial reaction require more time for display than expressive styles involving relatively less modification, likely because the former recruit greater neurocognitive resources. Expressive modes that allow for the continued expression of the initial emotion or only slight modifications of its intensity (deamplification) require less such modification and, thus, result in shorter elapsed times from the initial response.

The fact that expressions change across time and are more culturally variable subsequent to an initial, immediate, universal emotional reaction explains why beliefs about the pervasiveness of cultural differences in expression exist. When intense emotions are aroused, attention is often drawn to the stimulus event and *not* the expressive behaviors of the individuals in that event. While attention is given to the eliciting event, immediate universal reactions occur but are missed. When attention returns to the individuals, they are already beginning to engage in culturally regulated behavior. Such a process may perpetuate beliefs about the cultural variability of expressive behavior. Because we tend to believe our experiences, it is easier to believe the existence of cultural differences in expressive behavior because that's what we often see.

A Worldwide Mapping of Cultural Display Rules

Despite the fact that even though the concept of cultural display rules was critically important in psychology, cross-cultural research on them was fairly dormant after its inception. In the early 1990s we revived the study of cultural display rules by documenting differences in display rules between Americans and Japanese (Matsumoto, 1990) and among Asian, Hispanic, African, and European Americans within the United States (Matsumoto, 1993). Subsequently, we created the Display Rule Assessment Inventory (DRAI), in which participants choose a behavioral response when they experience different emotions in different social situations (Matsumoto, Takeuchi, Andayani, Kouznetsova, & Krupp, 1998). Preliminary studies using this measure demonstrated cultural differences in display rules but also provided evidence for their internal and temporal reliability and for their content, convergent (with measures of emotion regulation), discriminant (correlations with personality controlling for emotion regulation), external, and concurrent predictive validity with personality (Matsumoto, Yoo, Hirayama, & Petrova, 2005).

More recently we (Matsumoto et al., 2008) administered the DRAI in over 30 countries, examining universal and culture-specific aspects to display rules and linking the cultural differences to culture-level individualism vs. collectivism. Despite the larger potential range of scores, most countries' means on overall selection of appropriate expression for different emotion situations (i.e., endorsement of expression) fell around the midpoint, and there was relatively small variation around this mean, suggesting a universal norm for expression regulation.[3] And individuals of all cultures endorsed expressions toward ingroups more than toward outgroups, indicating another universal effect. Collectivistic cultures endorsed less expressivity overall than individualistic cultures, suggesting that overall expressive regulation for all emotions is central to the preservation of social order in these cultures. This finding is commensurate with the behavioral findings from previous studies (Friesen, 1972; Matsumoto & Kupperbusch, 2001; Matsumoto, Willingham, et al., 2009). Individualism was also positively associated with higher expressivity norms in general and for positive emotions in particular. And it was positively associated with endorsement of expressions of all emotions toward ingroups but negatively correlated with all negative emotions and positively correlated with happiness and surprise toward outgroups. Cumulatively, these findings suggest a fairly nuanced view of the relationship between culture and expression endorsement that varies as a function of emotion, interactant, and overall expressivity endorsement levels.

Figure 5.3 is a graphical representation of the relationship between individualism and overall expressivity endorsement across cultures. The X-axis refers to individualism vs. collectivism, and as you go from left to right, the countries are more individualistic and less collectivistic. The Y-axis refers to overall expressivity endorsement, and as you go up the scale, expressivity endorsement increases. The United States, Canada, Australia, and New Zealand are all fairly individualistic and also have relatively high expressivity endorsement scores; members of these cultures tend to be the most expressive. It's interesting that they are all English-speaking countries and share a common heritage with England. South Korea, Indonesia, Malaysia, and Hong Kong are more collectivistic and tend to have the lowest expressivity scores.

Figure 5.3   Graphical Representation of the Relationship Between Individualism and Overall Expressivity Endorsement

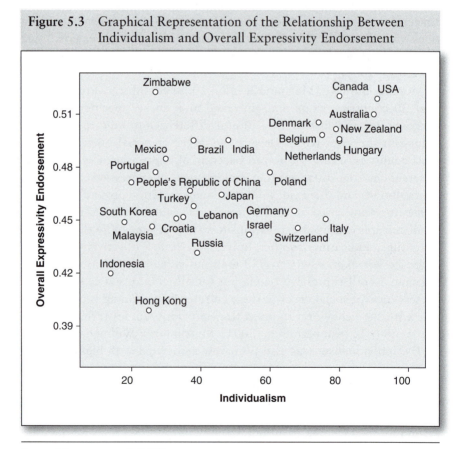

Source: Matsumoto et al. (2008).

Cultural Similarities and Differences in Judging Emotion

Because facial expressions of emotion are universal, it's not surprising that there is overwhelming evidence that demonstrates that the seven universal facial expressions are panculturally recognized (Elfenbein & Ambady, 2002b; Matsumoto, 2001).[4] And cultures are similar in other aspects of emotion judgment as well. For example, there is pancultural similarity in judgments of relative intensity among faces; that is, when comparing expressions, people of different countries agree on which is more strongly expressed (Ekman et al., 1987; Matsumoto & Ekman, 1989). There is also pancultural agreement in the association between perceived expression intensity and inferences about subjective experiences (Matsumoto, Kasri, & Kooken, 1999). People of different cultures also agree on which emotion label they would select after their initial judgments of the emotions portrayed in an expression (Biehl et al., 1997; Ekman et al., 1987; Matsumoto & Ekman, 1989), suggesting pancultural agreement in the multiple meanings derived from universal faces. So when people see angry faces, they primarily see anger but also a bit of disgust. When they see fearful faces, they primarily see fear but also a bit of surprise. This agreement may exist because of overlap in the semantics of the emotion categories, antecedents and elicitors of emotion, or in the facial configurations themselves.

There are cultural differences in emotion judgments as well; for instance, on the absolute levels of recognition agreement across cultures (Biehl et al., 1997; Elfenbein & Ambady, 2002b; Matsumoto, 1989, 1992; Matsumoto et al., 2002). Recognition rates for universal faces tend to be higher in the United States and Western Europe compared to African or Asian countries. There are also cultural differences in attributions about the intensity of expressions (Biehl et al., 1997; Ekman et al., 1987; Matsumoto, 1990, 1993; Matsumoto et al., 2002; Matsumoto et al., 1999); Americans tend to see facial expressions of emotion as more intense than people of other cultures.

*An Ingroup Advantage to Facial
Emotion Recognition?*

One type of cultural difference in emotion judgment that has received attention by researchers recently concerns the possibility of an *ingroup advantage* in emotion recognition (Elfenbein & Ambady, 2002b). This refers to the tendency for individuals to more accurately recognize emotional expressions produced by members of their own culture rather than those produced by another. Researchers arguing for the existence of this effect have suggested that it occurs because of "emotion dialects"—culturally derived, minor variants of emotional expressions (Elfenbein, Beaupré, Levesque, & Hess, 2007; Wickline, Bailey, & Nowicki, 2009). Presumably people are more accurate when judging such expressions because those expressions are differentially used in their culture. For instance, raising an eyebrow could be a sign of skepticism in one culture. If people of that culture judged expressions of encoders raising an eyebrow, they are likely to respond that the expression was one of skepticism. People from another culture, however, may not think it skepticism because the expression may not be used in that culture, or it may have a different meaning in that culture.

Unfortunately, none of the research reported to date claiming to support the ingroup hypothesis has used spontaneous expressions that would support a dialect theory. Instead, all of the research cited to support the hypothesis has involved expressions that were posed by members of different cultures, and these were not equivalent across cultural groups (Elfenbein & Ambady, 2002a, 2002b; Elfenbein et al., 2007).[5]

Recently we tested the dialect theory of the ingroup effect using spontaneous expressions produced by members of different cultures in a naturalistic field setting (Matsumoto, Olide, & Willingham, 2009). The expressions came from Matsumoto and Willingham's (2006) study of expressions produced by athletes during the judo competition of the 2004 Athens Olympic Games. Across all emotions studied, the ingroup advantage hypothesis was *not* supported, suggesting that the effect reported in previous studies may be localized to nonequivalent, posed expressions. That means that the cultural ingroup advantage hypothesis may occur only with posed mimes. Mimed expressions may not be valid analogs of naturally occurring expressions when emotions are aroused spontaneously because they may include extraneous muscle movements or not include muscle movements that spontaneously would be present. Innervated muscles may also be at different intensity levels or symmetries from spontaneous expressions. Any of these possible characteristics of posed, voluntarily expressions may be sufficient to produce the dialects proposed by Elfenbein and colleagues (2007) that in turn produced the ingroup effect in the past. Future studies need to examine if indeed the cultural dialects Elfenbein and colleagues suggest occur actually do occur in real life and if these truly produce ingroup advantages in emotion recognition. The data to date suggest they do not.

Judging Faces in Context

Despite the fact that facial expressions in real life always occur in context, most mono- or cross-cultural judgment studies, including those described earlier, present them fairly acontextually. Writers have long debated the relative contribution of face and context in contributing to emotion messages by studying congruent and incongruent face-context combinations (Bruner & Tagiuri, 1954; Ekman & O'Sullivan, 1988; Fernberger, 1928; Russell & Fehr, 1987). One type of study in this genre is that which examines the linkage between an emotion-eliciting context and a facial expression, which we have called *response linkage* (Matsumoto & Hwang, 2010). Studies involving congruent response linkages have found an additive effect (Bruner & Tagiuri, 1954; Knudsen & Muzekari, 1983), which probably occurred because of the increased signal clarity in the overall emotion message when two different signal sources provide the same message. Interestingly, studies involving incongruent response linkages have generally demonstrated a face superiority effect, indicating that the signals in the face tend to override the signals provided by the context (Ekman & O'Sullivan, 1988; Ekman, O'Sullivan, & Matsumoto, 1991; Frijda, 1969; Goldberg, 1951; Nakamura, Buck, & Kenny, 1990).

But do these effects exist across cultures? We conducted two studies involving observers from the United States, Japan, and South Korea, who judged facial expressions of anger, sadness, and happiness presented together with a congruent or incongruent emotion-eliciting context (Matsumoto, Hwang, & Yamada, in press). When faces were congruent with contexts, the agreement rates in judgments were near perfect, with no cultural differences. This suggests that our (and others') previous work documenting cultural differences in emotion recognition rates may have been the result of methodological artifacts, at least partially, due to the fact that observers were asked to make judgments of emotion solely from faces. In reality, such judgments are made from multiple cues present in both faces and contexts, and it makes sense that when multiple cues are given cultural differences are eliminated. When faces and contexts were incongruent, there were both face and context effects, and the relative contributions of each were moderated by culture. American judgments were more influenced by faces, whereas Japanese and South Korean judgments were more influenced by context. The results provided a more nuanced view of how both culture and emotion moderate judgments of faces in context—by showing how face and context effects occur simultaneously—and how cultural differences existed in the judgments.

Understanding Cultural Influences on Nonverbal Behaviors

As we learned in Chapter 4, culture has a large influence on all the other nonverbal behaviors as well. Cultures differ, for example, in the amount and type of speech-illustrative gestures. Cultures also create their own emblematic gesture vocabularies to signal words or phrases with hand, head, or body movements. Cultures create rules concerning gazing and visual attention because both aggression and affiliation are behavioral tendencies that are important for group stability and maintenance. Gaze is often used as a nonverbal sign of respect. But because different cultures produce different rules concerning gaze, respect is conveyed through increased gaze in some cultures and decreased gaze in others. Culture influences the use of our voices; expressive cultures use louder voices with high speech rates, whereas less expressive cultures use softer voices with lower speech rates. Pronunciations of some languages require the production of different sounds and rhythms to the voice that may be associated with different emotions (e.g., the guttural quality of some Germanic languages, the up and down rhythms of Mandarin). Cultures regulate the use of interpersonal space and assign different amounts of space to different types of interactions. Cultures regulate the use of touch. There appears to be cross-cultural agreement in the interpretation of body postures but cross-cultural differences in gait, especially with regard to average speed of walking.

The existing literature strongly suggests that culture influences nonverbal behavior in important and profound ways. We believe that cultural differences in nonverbal behavior can be summarized according to cultural norms associated with the overall expressivity that is encouraged or discouraged in specific cultures (see Table 5.2). In broadest terms, on one hand, *Expressive* cultures are likely to use facial expressions and gestures more frequently, with greater intensity and duration, speak in louder voices, use direct gaze, and feature relaxed and open postures at closer distances. On the other hand, *Reserved* cultures are likely to use fewer facial expressions and gestures, speak in softer voices, avoid direct gaze, and display more rigid, closed postures at relatively greater distances.[6]

When considering cultural influences on nonverbal behavior (or any psychological process) we cannot ignore the powerful role of context in moderating those influences. Although the distinction between Expressive and Reserved cultures just described can likely describe general tendencies for behaviors, there are certainly contexts in which members of *Expressive* cultures are very reserved. Similarly there are many contexts in which members

Table 5.2 Nonverbal Characteristics of Expressive and Reserved Cultures

	Type of Culture	
Channel	Expressive	Reserved
Face	Many facial expressions, animated, regularly show emotions, use of face to amplify and illustrate speech	Fewer facial expressions, less emotions, more controlling expressions
Gesture	Many illustrating gestures, large motions, higher frequency of emblem usage	Fewer illustrating gestures, smaller motions, lower frequency of emblem usage
Voice	Louder voices, deeper range, higher speech rate	Softer voices, diminished range, lower speech rates
Gaze	Direct gaze at eyes of people to whom one is speaking	Less direct gaze at eyes of people to whom one is speaking
Interpersonal space and touch	Closer distances in interaction, more likely to touch	Farther distances in interaction, less likely to touch
Posture	More relaxed, open postures	More rigid, closed postures

of *Reserved* cultures are very expressive. The difference in behavior across contexts, in fact, is larger in some cultures. In previous work we have suggested that *context differentiation* is an important and meaningful dimension of cultural variability (Matsumoto et al., 2009). High context-differentiating cultures make larger distinctions in behavior according to context, whereas low context-differentiating cultures make relatively less such distinctions. Behaving in different ways in different contexts can be viewed as a sign of maturity in some cultures but as a sign of hypocrisy in others.

It's important to appreciate why cultural differences in the use of nonverbal behaviors exist. Earlier in this chapter we suggested that one of the functions of culture is to enhance social coordination and decrease the possibility for social chaos. Doing so facilitates our survival. Therefore, cultures create rules to regulate emotional reactions, expressions, and nonverbal behaviors because these expressions and behaviors have the potential to threaten social coordination and social cohesion. Cultural rules are manifested in norms, values, attitudes, traditions, customs, and heritage and are communicated across generations. The regulation of expressions and nonverbal behaviors, in turn, helps to grease social interactions, ensuring social order, preventing chaos, and ensuring survival (see again Figure 5.1).

Application Implications

It is clear to see how and why one would need to understand culture in any applied setting. You could make huge mistakes. Recall the story from the previous chapter of the courtroom judge giving harsher sentences to defendants of a culture that expressed respect in a way opposite to US culture. You may think you have a business agreement with another person from a different culture because that person is smiling. But he or she may only be acting polite, or even expressing confusion. In some Asian cultures, it would be considered impolite to contradict or say no to another person. Therefore, there are often nonverbal clues to help understand the difference between a spoken "yes" that means yes, and a spoken "yes" that means no (often in the paralinguistic features of speech). This has implications in security/customs as well. For example, an Australian customs officer mentioned to one of the authors how he could not understand why Japanese tourists would appear stressed and lie about where they bought their goods by responding yes to both "Did you buy that in Australia?" and "Did you buy this in Japan?" It turned out that information about cultural norms solved this problem, and when he shifted to asking "Where did you buy these items?" he noted much more truthful responses and relaxed accompanying nonverbal behaviors.

Conclusion

Cultural differences in nonverbal behavior make intercultural interactions and communications more difficult than intracultural communication. Intercultural communication is likely to be marred by uncertainty and ambiguity, not only because of questions concerning the verbal messages but also because of cultural differences in the nonverbal behaviors associated with the verbal messages. These are likely to lead to aversive reactions that further increase the potential for misunderstanding, miscommunication, and misattributions about intent or character, which disrupts social coordination and increases the potential for conflict. Even without knowing or feeling it, intercultural interactions can produce greater competition and less cooperation in interaction (Matsumoto & Hwang, in press). It's easier for people from *Expressive* cultures to judge those from *Reserved* cultures as being untrustworthy, inscrutable, sly, or shifty. At the same time, it's easier for people from Reserved cultures to judge those from Expressive cultures as arrogant, loud, rude, immature, or vulgar. Many of these aversive reactions occur unconsciously and automatically because they are rooted in cultural filters for interpreting the appropriateness of behavior in general, and nonverbal behavior in particular, that are developed from early on through the process of enculturation.

Many of these interpretations and attributions, however, may be misguided or downright incorrect because the cultural filters with which one uses to interpret the nonverbal behavior of others may or may not be the cultural framework within which the person's behavior is rooted. Thus when considering nonverbal behavior in the context of intercultural interactions, it is important to realize that cultural differences in nonverbal behavior exist, that engaging with such differences may produce negative emotional reactions, and that these differences and reactions are a normal and inevitable part of the communication process. By creating these kinds of expectations, and by being mindful of our own and others' reactions as well as their face, reputation, honor, or status, we can begin to ensure that intercultural interactions are not an obstacle but instead a platform for staging the development and exchange of ideas and the sharing of goals in new and exciting ways not actualized by intracultural communication.

Notes

1. An "evolved potential" refers to a capability of humans (and other organisms) that presumably has emerged in the process of evolution and natural selection. The evolution of advanced cognitive abilities and language probably allowed for the emergence of human cultures as we know them today.

2. Individualism vs. collectivism (IC) is a well-known dimension of cultural variability (Hofstede, 2001; Triandis, 1995). Individualistic cultures foster the needs, wishes, and desires of individuals over ingroups; collectivistic cultures foster the needs of ingroups over those of individuals.

3. Thus, regulating one's emotional expressions is an essential part of being a socialized human in any culture.

4. In fact, studies documenting high levels of cross-cultural agreement in emotion recognition were an important part of the initial evidence for the universality of facial expressions of emotion and form an important part of the overall evidence as well.

5. Equivalence is an important concept in cross-cultural research methodology. The lack of equivalence in measures, methods, or stimuli introduces bias, which precludes valid cross-cultural comparisons (van de Vijver & Leung, 2011).

6. The distinction between Expressive and Reserved cultures is related to Hall's (1966, 1973) distinction of high-context and low-context cultures, as well as Watson's (1970) classification of contact and noncontact cultures. Our distinction is different, however, as we believe there is sufficient evidence to suggest that cultural differences extend beyond any single channel of nonverbal behavior and encompass the entire constellation of nonverbal behaviors involved in interaction. At the same time, we do not believe that there is a unidimensional, positive relationship among all of the various channels of nonverbal behavior; some cultures may facilitate more or less expression differentially across channels. Differences in the relationships among channels across cultures may be an interesting avenue of research in the future.

References

Anderson, N. B., & Nickerson, K. J. (2005). Genes, race, and psychology in the genome era. *American Psychologist, 60*(1), 5–8.

Argyle, M., Henderson, M., Bond, M., Iizuka, Y., & Contarello, A. (1986). Cross-cultural variations in relationship rules. *International Journal of Psychology, 21,* 287–315.

Betancourt, H., & Lopez, R. S. (1993). The study of culture, ethnicity, and race in American psychology. *American Psychologist, 48*(6), 629–637.

Biehl, M., Matsumoto, D., Ekman, P., Hearn, V., Heider, K., Kudoh, T., et al. (1997). Matsumoto and Ekman's Japanese and Caucasian facial expressions of emotion (JACFEE): Reliability data and cross-national differences. *Journal of Nonverbal Behavior, 21,* 3–21.

Bruner, J. S., & Tagiuri, R. (1954). The perception of people. In G. Lindzey (Ed.), *Handbook of social psychology* (Vol. 2, pp. 634–654). Cambridge, MA: Addison-Wesley.

Cole, P. M. (1986). Children's spontaneous control of facial expression. *Child Development, 57,* 1309–1321.

Davis, F. G. (1991). *Who is black? Our nation's definition.* University Park: Pennsylvania State University Press.

DeKay, W. T., & Buss, D. M. (1992). Human nature, individual differenecs, and the importance of context: Perspectives from evolutionary psychology. *Current Directions in Psychological Science, 1*(6), 184–189.

Eberhardt, J. L., & Randall, J. L. (1997). The essential notion of race. *Psychological Science, 8*(3), 198–203.

Edelmann, R. J., Asendorpf, J., Contarello, A., Georgas, J., Villanueva, C., & Zammuner, V. (1987). Self-reported verbal and non-verbal strategies for coping with embarrassment in five European cultures. *Social Science Information, 26,* 869–883.

Ekman, P. (1972). Universal and cultural differences in facial expression of emotion. In J. R. Cole (Ed.), *Nebraska symposium on motivation, 1971* (Vol. 19, pp. 207–283). Lincoln: Nebraska University Press.

Ekman, P., & Friesen, W. V. (1969). The repertoire of nonverbal behavior: Categories, origins, usage, and coding. *Semiotica, 1,* 49–98.

Ekman, P., & Friesen, W. V. (1975). *Unmasking the face: A guide to recognizing the emotions from facial cues.* Englewood Cliffs, NJ: Prentice Hall.

Ekman, P., Friesen, W. V., O'Sullivan, M., Chan, A., Diacoyanni-Tarlatzis, I., Heider, K., et al. (1987). Universals and cultural differences in the judgments of facial expressions of emotion. *Journal of Personality & Social Psychology, 53*(4), 712–717.

Ekman, P., & O'Sullivan, M. (1988). The role of context in interpreting facial expression: Comment on Russell and Fehr (1987). *Journal of Experimental Psychology: General, 117*(1), 86–88.

Ekman, P., O'Sullivan, M., & Matsumoto, D. (1991). Confusions about context in the judgment of facial expression: A reply to "The contempt expression and the relativity thesis." *Motivation & Emotion, 15*(2), 169–176.

Ekman, P., & Rosenberg, E. L. (Eds.). (1998). *What the face reveals: Basic and applied studies of spontaneous expression using the Facial Action Coding System (FACS).* New York: Oxford University Press.

Elfenbein, H. A., & Ambady, N. (2002a). Is there an ingroup advantage in emotion recognition? *Psychological Bulletin, 128*(2), 243–249.

Elfenbein, H. A., & Ambady, N. (2002b). On the universality and cultural specificity of emotion recognition: A meta-analysis. *Psychological Bulletin, 128*(2), 205–235.

Elfenbein, H. A., Beaupré, M. G., Levesque, M., & Hess, U. (2007). Toward a dialect theory: Cultural differences in the expression and recognition of posed facial expressions. *Emotion, 7*(1), 131–146.

Fernberger, S. W. (1928). False suggestions and the Piderit model. *American Journal of Psychology, 40,* 562–568.

Friesen, W. V. (1972). *Cultural differences in facial expressions in a social situation: An experimental test of the concept of display rules.* Doctoral dissertation, University of California, San Francisco.

Frijda, N. H. (1969). Recognition of emotion. In L. Berkowitz (Ed.), *Advances in experimental social psychology* (Vol. 4, pp. 167–224). New York: Academic Press.

Georgas, J., van de Vijver, F. J. R., & Berry, J. W. (2004). The ecocultural framework, ecosocial indices, and psychological variables in cross-cultural research. *Journal of Cross-Cultural Psychology, 35*(1), 74–86.

Goldberg, H. D. (1951). The role of "cutting" in the perception of the motion picture. *Journal of Applied Psychology, 35,* 70–71.

Gudykunst, W. B., & Nishida, T. (1984). Individual and cultural influences on uncertainty reduction. *Communication Monographs, 51*(1), 23–36.

Gudykunst, W. B., & Ting-Toomey, S. (1988). Culture and affective communication. *American Behavioral Scientist, 31*(3), 384–400.

Hall, E. T. (1966). *The hidden dimension.* New York: Doubleday.

Hall, E. T. (1973). *The silent language.* New York: Anchor.

Hofstede, G. H. (2001). *Culture's consequences: Comparing values, behaviors, institutions and organizations across nations* (2nd ed.). Thousand Oaks, CA: Sage.

Kagan, J., Snidman, N., Arcus, D., & Reznick, S. J. (1994). *Galen's prophecy: Temperament in human nature*. New York: Basic Books.

Knudsen, H. R., & Muzekari, L. H. (1983). The effects of verbal statements of context on facial expressions of emotion. *Journal of Nonverbal Behavior, 7*(4), 202–212.

Lewontin, R. C., Rose, S., & Kamin, L. J. (1984). *Not in our genes: Biology, ideology, and human nature*. New York: Pantheon Books.

Matsumoto, D. (1989). Cultural influences on the perception of emotion. *Journal of Cross-Cultural Psychology, 20*(1), 92–105.

Matsumoto, D. (1990). Cultural similarities and differences in display rules. *Motivation & Emotion, 14*(3), 195–214.

Matsumoto, D. (1992). American-Japanese cultural differences in the recognition of universal facial expressions. *Journal of Cross-Cultural Psychology, 23*(1), 72–84.

Matsumoto, D. (1993). Ethnic differences in affect intensity, emotion judgments, display rule attitudes, and self-reported emotional expression in an American sample. *Motivation & Emotion, 17*(2), 107–123.

Matsumoto, D. (2001). Culture and emotion. In D. Matsumoto (Ed.), *The handbook of culture and psychology* (pp. 171–194). New York: Oxford University Press.

Matsumoto, D. (2007). Culture, context, and behavior. *Journal of Personality, 75*(6), 1285–1319.

Matsumoto, D., Consolacion, T., Yamada, H., Suzuki, R., Franklin, B., Paul, S., et al. (2002). American-Japanese cultural differences in judgments of emotional expressions of different intensities. *Cognition & Emotion, 16*(6), 721–747.

Matsumoto, D., & Ekman, P. (1989). American-Japanese cultural differences in intensity ratings of facial expressions of emotion. *Motivation & Emotion, 13*(2), 143–157.

Matsumoto, D., & Hwang, H.-S. (2010). Judging faces in context. *Social and Personality Psychology Compass, 3*, 1–10.

Matsumoto, D., & Hwang, H.-S. (in press). Cooperation and competition in intercultural interactions. *International Journal of Intercultural Relations*.

Matsumoto, D., Hwang, H.-S., & Yamada, H. (in press). Cultural differences in the relative contributions of face and context to judgments of emotion. *Journal of Cross-Cultural Psychology*.

Matsumoto, D., & Juang, L. (2007). *Culture and psychology* (4th ed.). Belmont, CA: Wadsworth.

Matsumoto, D., Kasri, F., & Kooken, K. (1999). American-Japanese cultural differences in judgments of expression intensity and subjective experience. *Cognition & Emotion, 13*, 201–218.

Matsumoto, D., & Kupperbusch, C. (2001). Idiocentric and allocentric differences in emotional expression and experience. *Asian Journal of Social Psychology, 4*, 113–131.

Matsumoto, D., Olide, A., & Willingham, B. (2009). Is there an ingroup advantage in recognizing spontaneously expressed emotions? *Journal of Nonverbal Behavior, 33*, 181–191.

Matsumoto, D., Takeuchi, S., Andayani, S., Kouznetsova, N., & Krupp, D. (1998). The contribution of individualism-collectivism to cross-national differences in display rules. *Asian Journal of Social Psychology, 1,* 147–165.

Matsumoto, D., & Willingham, B. (2006). The thrill of victory and the agony of defeat: Spontaneous expressions of medal winners at the 2004 Athens Olympic Games. *Journal of Personality and Social Psychology, 91*(3), 568–581.

Matsumoto, D., Willingham, B., & Olide, A. (2009). Sequential dynamics of culturally-moderated facial expressions of emotion. *Psychological Science, 20*(10), 1269–1274.

Matsumoto, D., Yoo, S. H., Fontaine, J. R. J., Alexandre, J., Altarriba, J., Anguas-Wong, A. M., et al. (2009). Hypocrisy or maturity: Culture and context differentiation. *European Journal of Personality, 23,* 251–264.

Matsumoto, D., Yoo, S. H., Fontaine, J. R. J., Anguas-Wong, A. M., Arriola, M., Ataca, B., et al. (2008). Mapping expressive differences around the world: The relationship between emotional display rules and individualism v. collectivism. *Journal of Cross-Cultural Psychology, 39*(1), 55–74.

Matsumoto, D., Yoo, S. H., Hirayama, S., & Petrova, G. (2005). Validation of an individual-level measure of display rules: The display rule assessment inventory (DRAI). *Emotion, 5*(1), 23–40.

Nakamura, M., Buck, R. W., & Kenny, D. A. (1990). Relative contributions of expressive behavior and contextual information to the judgment of the emotional state of another. *Journal of Personality and Social Psychology, 59*(5), 1032–1039.

Noesjirwan, J. (1978). A rule-based analysis of cultural differences in social behavior: Indonesia and Australia. *International Journal of Psychology, 13,* 305–316.

Premack, D. (2004). Is language the key to human intelligence? *Science, 303,* 318–320.

Russell, J. A., & Fehr, B. (1987). Relativity in the perception of emotion in facial expressions. *Journal of Experimental Psychology: General, 116*(3), 223–237.

Smedley, A., & Smedley, B. D. (2005). Race as biology is fiction, racism as a social problem is real: Anthropological and historical perspectives on the social construction of race. *American Psychologist, 60*(1), 16–26.

Tomasello, M. (1999). *The cultural origins of human cognition.* Cambridge, MA: Harvard University Press.

Tomasello, M., Carpenter, M., Call, J., Behne, T., & Moll, H. (2005). Understanding and sharing intentions: The origins of cultural cognition. *Behavioral & Brain Sciences, 28,* 675–735.

Tomasello, M., Kruger, A. C., & Ratner, H. H. (1993). Cultural learning. *Behavioural and Brain Sciences, 16,* 495–552.

Triandis, H. C. (1995). *New directions in social psychology: Individualism and collectivism.* Boulder, CO: Westview Press.

van de Vijver, F. J. R., & Leung, K. (2011). Equivalence and bias: A review of concepts, models, and data analytic procedures. In D. Matsumoto & F. J. R. van de Vijver (Eds.), *Cross-cultural research methods in psychology.* New York: Cambridge University Press.

Watson, O. M. (1970). *Proxemic behavior: A cross-cultural study.* The Hague, Netherlands: Mouton.

Waxer, P. H. (1985). Video ethology: Television as a data base for cross-cultural studies in nonverbal displays. *Journal of Nonverbal Behavior, 9,* 111–120.

Wickline, V. B., Bailey, W., & Nowicki, S. J. (2009). Cultural in-group advantage: Emotion recognition in African American and European American faces and voices. *Journal of Genetic Psychology, 170*(1), 5–29.

Yee, H. A., Fairchild, H. H., Weizman, F., & Wyatt, E. G. (1993). Addressing psychology's problems with race. *American Psychologist, 48*(11), 1132–1140.

Zuckerman, M. (1990). Some dubious premises in research and theory on racial differences: Scientific, social and ethical issues. *American Psychologist, 45*(12), 1297–1303.

6

Deception

Mark G. Frank and Elena Svetieva
University at Buffalo,
State University of New York

There is no shortage of hints, tips, and suggestions in magazines, newspapers, and general-public books about secret "telltale" signs of deception. Many television programs feature characters that can detect lies rapidly and accurately based solely on nonverbal behavior. The reason for this popularity is easy to see. Most people would love to be able to read the minds of others, although likely for self-serving reasons. On the one hand, we might use our newfound powers to exploit other people, to gain advantages, and obtain things we could not otherwise obtain. On the other hand, we might also be able to avoid hurting others' feelings and smooth our social interactions. Unfortunately—or fortunately—we cannot peer into the heads of other people to view their thoughts, feelings, or intended actions. So we make our best-guess estimate about what others are thinking, feeling, or intending by listening to their words and observing their actions and, for the most part, taking them at face value (Grice, 1975). This is despite the fact that people do not always express themselves honestly. In fact, people admit to deceiving others routinely, on the average of once or twice a day (DePaulo, Kashy, Kirkendol, Wyer, & Epstein, 1996).

This means that at some point we have all deceived others—you, us, everyone. Our joke around the laboratory is that 99% of people admit to having told a lie, and the remaining 1% are liars. We do not speak the first words that jump into our minds, and we do not tell people exactly what we feel about them at any given point. Politeness dictates that the speaker refrains from telling the pure ragged truth. Politeness also dictates that the listener refrain from scouring every communication uttered by the speaker for any sign of deception. The costs are too great in terms of energy and attention. Thus an implicit deal is struck between speakers and listeners—I won't say everything exactly as I feel, and you won't scrutinize everything I say—and this deal is the key social lubricant of our society.

But there are times when this social lubricant ignites into a social grease fire. And that occurs in situations where the expectations are clear that deception is not authorized—a violation of trust in a trust-dependent relationship; a criminal act concealed from police, a terrorist act concealed from security officers, a feigning of symptoms during a medical examination, and so forth. Whereas in our day-to-day world of polite interactions there is no continual and compelling need to detect someone else's true state of affairs, in these other situations it may be life and death. We call these latter situations "high stakes" situations because a person who chooses to deceive in these situations may stand to gain some large reward by lying successfully (sex, unneeded narcotics, or even literally getting away with murder), or faces a strong punishment for getting caught in the lie (losing custody of children, being placed in jail, or even being shot by security guards).

Thus, to know what others truly think, feel, and intend in these high-stakes situations, we may resort to what Goffman (1963) terms "stealing" information—we observe the subtle behaviors a person emits involuntarily and use them to deduce what that person truly believes. These behaviors are frequently nonverbal, expressed without awareness, and for this they are a potentially fertile source of information about a person's true state of mind.

This chapter will outline many of the issues associated with nonverbal communication and deception. We will examine what we mean by deception and lying, how they might trigger various nonverbal behaviors, and how well we can detect these signs or signals when they do occur. Along the way, we hope to disabuse readers of many of the popular myths about secret nonverbal telltale deception signs.

What Do We Mean by Lying and Deception?

Often the terms *deception* and *lying* are used interchangeably, but we think there is an important difference. We believe deception is the superordinate category, of which one subcategory is telling a lie. We define *deception* as any action or phenomenon that misleads someone; *lying* is an act whereby someone *deliberately* misleads another and does so without notifying that person that he or she will be misleading them (Ekman, 1985/2001). The words *deliberate* and *prior notification* are the crucial distinguishing characteristics of a lie. Deception may or may not be a deliberate act, whereas a lie is always deliberate. Thus, a tiger may deceive its prey by having a striped coat that blends into its environment, but the tiger does not wake up that morning, look into his closet, and choose a striped coat over another design. Nonetheless, the tiger does not lie, but it deceives. A second implication of the word *deliberate* is that it means that someone who presents you with inaccurate information is not necessarily lying. What is important is whether this person believes what he or she is saying is true. If this person truly believes that the information he or she has told you is accurate, then it is *not* a lie, no matter how outlandish (Frank & Ekman, 2004a). But if the person knows the information he or she told you is inaccurate and misleading, then what that person said *is* a lie. This issue was at the crux of the political debate over whether former president George W. Bush lied about the weapons of mass destruction in Iraq. If he *knew* for sure there were no weapons, then he lied when he said Saddam Hussein had them. If he truly *believed* there were weapons of mass destruction, for whatever reason, then he did *not* lie. Most experts now agree there were no such weapons, so the president was inaccurate; but if he believed the faulty information, then he did not lie to the public.

The *prior notification* part of the definition prevents some common daily events from being called lies. For example, there are those times where we may pay money for others to mislead us, as when we buy a movie ticket to watch an actor pretend to be Abraham Lincoln, Moses, or a mad scientist. Likewise, some situations explicitly or implicitly allow for people to not be 100% truthful, for example, bluffing in poker, or price negotiations (see Chapter 13 by Andy Boughton on negotiation and his take on the pervasiveness of deception in those situations). Thus we enter these types of situations "on notice" that we may require the other or ourselves to conceal the truth. The latitude for misleading is limited by laws and rules written to articulate those limits—for example, one cannot lie about a known structural flaw in the object for sale, or play poker with marked cards, and so forth.

These definitional distinctions are not just an academic exercise; they have implications for the nonverbal behaviors that can betray a lie. If people believe they are telling the truth, then for all intents and purposes they will look and behave like a truth teller, independent of the accuracy of the information they present. For this chapter we will be addressing the research associated with lying, not deception in general, and all the behaviors we will discuss are dependent upon the individual *knowing* he or she is misleading someone.

The Research on Nonverbal Clues to Lying

The first thing to note about behavioral clues to lying is that there is no single behavior or combination of behaviors that occurs only when we tell a lie (Zuckerman, DePaulo, & Rosenthal, 1981). This does not mean that there are no signs or signals associated with lying—there are. It is just that scientists have discovered that none of them are exclusive to lying; that is, these behaviors can occur for reasons other than lying. Thus the fictional Pinocchio's nose grew only when he told a lie; his nose did not grow when he was nervous about turning into a real boy. Likewise, there is no sign or signal whose absence indicates the truth (Ekman, 1985/2001).

The basic finding on behavioral clues to lying, based on the most recent comprehensive meta-analysis of all published research studies, concluded that liars tend to behave in ways that make them appear more tense and less forthcoming than truth tellers (DePaulo et al., 2003). Theoretically, tension and reticence make sense given that all human expressive behavior is generated either by emotional reactions or cognitive activity (corresponding to tension and appearing less forthcoming, respectively). Emotional reactivity as involved in lying refers to the behaviors associated with feelings caused by the act of lying itself or attempts to falsify or conceal feelings (DePaulo et al., 2003; DePaulo, Stone, & Lassiter, 1985; Ekman, 1985/2001; Ekman & Frank, 1993; Vrij, 2008; Zuckerman et al., 1981). Cognitive activity as involved in lying refers to the behaviors associated with the extra mental effort and dexterity it takes to fabricate a story and to maintain it, as well as the behaviors associated with memory recollection that suggest a person actually experienced an event and is not fabricating an account (Yuille, 1989). Virtually all scientists agree that emotions and cognition are the main underpinnings for all behavioral clues to deceit (e.g., Ekman & Friesen, 1969; Knapp & Comadena, 1979; Mehrabian, 1971; Zuckerman et al., 1981). We note that some scientists have made a distinction between emotions and cognition as somehow being competing approaches to lie detection;

that is, there is an "emotional" approach and a "cognitive" approach (e.g., Vrij, 2004, 2008; cf. Zuckerman et al., 1981). We believe this is an error, as no scientist that we know in this field actually thinks that the behavioral clues are *either* emotional *or* cognitive. This straw man argument confounds and conceals, rather than clarifies, the nature of human lying by creating a false dichotomy. It is like saying there are two competing models of human survival—the food approach or the water approach. Although they carry different implications for short-term survival, in the long term both are essential to survival.

We are also going to add to the cognitive- and emotional-based clues two other offshoot categories of clues to lying that have not received as much scientific attention—signs of strategic behavioral control and changes in instrumental movements. Strategic behavioral control refers to the techniques liars employ to deliberately conceal or camouflage their behavioral signs of thinking and feeling; for example, by consciously limiting their hand, finger, head, and facial movements (Ekman & Friesen, 1972; Vrij, Akehurst, & Morris, 1997; Zuckerman et al., 1981). Changes in instrumental movements refer to the leakage of movements that betray an intended movement or motor action, or the deformation of a normal movement pattern associated with locomotion or other instrumental action, like reaching for objects, etc. These change clues can be generated by emotional or cognitive activity, but they can also be generated as a function of the size and weight of an external object (such as a handgun or suicide bomber vest) along with the direction or intensity of movement toward a target (Diedrich & Warren, 1998; Lee, Roan, & Smith, 2009a; Lee, Roan, Smith, & Lockhart, 2009b; see also Chapter 7 by Carl Maccario).

Expressive Channels

Regardless of the origin of any behavioral clue, there are only five families of behavioral clues found within 3 main behavioral channels, all of which have been discussed in Chapters 2, 3, and 4 on the face, voice, and body, respectively. We have the facial channel, which includes facial expressions and eye movements. We have the body channel, which includes manipulators, illustrators, emblems, posture, and other movements. We also have the voice channel, which contains three subchannels, two of which are nonverbal—the vocal style and vocal tone. The remaining channel is strictly verbal—the actual words spoken. However, given the nonverbal focus of this book, we will not discuss verbal clues to lying. Suffice to say, we do believe they are a very important, useful, and promising avenue for identifying clues to deceit, particularly as that body of research has gone on to identify not only reliable memory-based markers of lying in the word choices of people, but has also derived tactical strategies to exploit the nature of human memory to further separate the behavioral patterns of liars and truth tellers (Frank, Yarbrough, & Ekman, 2006; Hazlett, 2006; Vrij et al., 2008).

Finally, although there is no "Pinocchio" response, individuals seem to have their preferred mode of expression when lying such that their patterns of face, body, and voice channel behavior is similar when they are lying to conceal a theft or when they are lying about a strongly held opinion (Frank & Ekman, 2004b; Hirsch & Wolf, 2001). So, as poker players acknowledge, most people seem to have a distinct behavioral movement pattern or "tell" when lying (Hayano, 1980). But not everyone does, and some people are flawless liars ("natural performers," Ekman, 1985/2001), so we should exercise some caution here.

Cognitive-Based Nonverbal Clues to Lying

A liar has to conceal, fabricate, or distort information in order to lie. When questioned, the liar must come up with an alibi, adjust it to any new pieces of evidence presented, and try to speak his or her story in a way that looks natural and does not arouse suspicion. Balancing all these tasks requires much more mental effort that telling the unadorned truth. Moreover, the act of keeping the truth concealed, covering actions, remembering the false alibis, creating and describing events that have not happened, or portraying events in a way to allow multiple interpretations to confuse the lie catcher (and confusion can be as effective as misleading for the liar) adds significantly more to the cognitive processing load of a liar compared to a truth teller. We note that additional mental effort is not solely the domain of the outright liar; however, a person who must tell an uncomfortable truth to another or answer a complicated question will also engage in additional mental effort to develop the proper and polite phrasing. These put-upon truth tellers may appear behaviorally similar to liars. The only way to distinguish between these is to assess the context in which the mental effort is generated and to make a judgment as to why this extra effort might be needed. If it does not make sense—e.g., you ask a very simple question like "What is your name?" and you see these signs—then it may be more likely to be a lie, or at least a sign that the person has thought about lying to you. However, this will never be foolproof, as even in this example the responder may be thinking through all the motives and implications for why this questioner wants to know his or her name.

This higher cognitive load and extra mental effort tends to manifest itself in the *vocal style* channel, through a paralinguistic array of behaviors such as longer speech latencies, increased speech disturbances, less verbal and vocal involvement, less talking time, and so forth (DePaulo et al., 2003). However, we need to remind ourselves, as we saw in Chapter 3 on the voice, that these behavioral patterns are assessed as changes from someone's normal, truthful style of behavior (what we call a person's baseline behavior). And we must remind ourselves that these behaviors are signs of thinking on one's feet and not guaranteed proof that a person is lying.

These cognitive clues can appear in the *face channel* as well. When a person is thinking hard, his or her blink rate may change (Vrij et al., 2009). Although it is (erroneously) believed that liars may shift their eyes around more, the overall trend is that they do not, nor are their patterns of eye contact or gaze aversion different from truth tellers (DePaulo et al., 2003). There is some evidence that liars press their lips more, but it is uncertain as to whether this is to control an emotional reaction or whether it is an action like lip pursing that occurs when people think harder.

Finally, we can see these clues in the *body channel* as well. Research consistently shows that liars tend to have a reduced rate of illustrators (hand or head movements that accompany speech; see Chapter 4) due to the higher cognitive load of lying. This causes them to focus so much on their stories that their other behavioral modalities shut down (relatively speaking; Ekman & Friesen, 1972). Others have argued that the reduction is caused by deliberate control of these body actions (e.g., Vrij, 1995), and we'll address that later when we discuss strategic behavioral management.

Application implications. In applied settings, the relationship between cognitive clues and lying is considerably more complicated than what we see in the laboratory setting. For example, that liars have longer response latencies (hesitations) than truth tellers is a fairly robust research finding (Zuckerman et al., 1981). In the laboratory, this is usually measured fairly cleanly—one just counts the videotape frames of silence between the end of the interviewer's question and the beginning of the research participant's answer. But herein lies the limitation. In the lab, the interviewer and participant engage in a fairly clean question-response, question-response type of back and forth pattern. Participants do their best to be cooperative and simply answer the question put to them. What we've noted instead, after many years viewing real-life law enforcement type interviews, is that people in actual high-stakes situations—like criminal suspects—often use more complicated responses than typical research participants' good-faith efforts to answer the questions posed to them. The suspect's response may be about something not related to the topic, it may involve repeating back the question, it may involve other techniques that we believe—at their essence—are about postponing telling information that can be proven to be a lie. These tricks increase the response latency because although the liar is speaking, he or she is not answering the question until much later in the response. For example, in the lab the interviewer asks, "Is everything you've told me the truth?" The research participant may hesitate, may say "um," but will more than likely say yes. In actual law enforcement interviews, suspects' responses to that same question might be, "That's a great question. I'm glad you asked me that. Why do you think I would I lie to you? Of course I'm telling the truth." Or, they might say, "Why would you question my credibility? I told you before, I don't lie." Now be a scientist—how would you measure response latency in these criminal examples? If you apply standard rules for measuring response latency, you would measure the period of time after the last word of the question—" . . . the truth?"—and the beginning of the answer—"That's a great question . . ." But note—that preamble about "That's a great question . . ." is not addressing the question at all. Practically speaking, the response latency period measurement should end at " . . . Of course I'm telling the truth," which happens much later in the response. So which is the correct response latency period measurement? This has now become a bit more of a subjective judgment to determine when the answer to the question was actually spoken. Thus applying the established research coding rules about the beginning of *any* response, regardless of whether it addresses the question, may produce misleading results that hide a potential diagnostic clue. But obfuscating-type responses and their corresponding paralinguistic markers may be the nature of lie telling in the real world. Interestingly, this more complicated real-world understanding of clues such as this does fit nicely with what was written by four of our Part II contributors, who together have well over 100 combined years experience dealing with criminal-type lies.

Emotional-Based Nonverbal Clues to Lying

Lies can generate emotional reactions, ranging from the excitement and pleasure of "pulling the wool over someone's eyes" to fear of getting caught, to feelings of guilt, or to feelings of distress, disgust, or contempt (Ekman, 1985/2001; Frank & Ekman, 1997). These emotions are generated by our cultural beliefs that lying is one of the worst things one can do. We can also lie about what we feel; for example, we might pretend we like our friend's favorite politician when in fact we are disgusted by that politician. As we know from the Chapters 2 and 3 on facial expressions and voice, Darwin

(1872/1998) first suggested that emotions tend to manifest themselves through reliable, measureable changes in the facial expression and voice tone. Conversely, research has also shown that the presence of these facial expressions and changes in voice tone can be reliable indicators that an emotion has been aroused (see review by Matsumoto, Keltner, Shiota, O'Sullivan, & Frank, 2008).

The involuntary nature of the emotions, along with their resultant facial expression and vocal tone, means they will often "leak" out in the nonverbal behavior despite the liar's intention to conceal them. As such, these emotional signals are involuntary products of the actual emotion, where behavioral intentions are expressed in the face and voice (Ekman, 2003), and behavioral action tendencies (Frijda, 1986) are expressed in the body. Therefore, to the extent a liar feels fear of getting caught or other emotions, he or she is more likely to "leak" signs of these emotions in the face, voice, and body—these include traces of the facial expression of fear, raised voice tone, increased manipulators, sweat, and body orientation more conducive to escape or avoidance. A "leakage hierarchy" was proposed to account for the relative importance of the different behavioral channels in leaking these emotional signs (Ekman & Friesen, 1969). Given the strength and clarity of each signaling system, these signs are most likely to appear in the face, as shown by facial expressions of emotion (micro or macro; Frank & Ekman, 1997), followed by the vocal tone (higher pitch in fear; Streeter, Krauss, Geller, Olson, & Apple, 1977), and then in the body (increased manipulators, nervous leg movements, etc.; Ekman, 1985/2001; Ekman, O'Sullivan, Friesen, & Scherer, 1991). Note that if a deception situation does not generate strong emotions, these emotion-based signals will not exist (Frank & Ekman, 1997). Also note that if the deception situation elicits strong levels of fear independent of lying—for example, if the subject is being tortured—then again we would not expect signs of fear to predict lying (as they would be demonstrated equally by truth tellers). But if there is a scenario in which the stakes are high for getting caught, but the interview and other potential sources of fear are reduced—e.g., the interrogator builds rapport and is kind to the subject—then signs of fear could be a significant predictor of lying (e.g., Frank & Ekman, 1997; Frank, Hurley, Kang, Pazian, & Ekman, 2011; Frank, Yarbrough, & Ekman, 2006; Matsumoto, Hwang, Skinner, & Frank, 2011).

Our own work has found that liars are more likely to demonstrate fear, distress, disgust, and contempt compared to truth tellers (Frank & Ekman, 1997; Frank, Hurley, et al., 2011; Matsumoto et al., 2011). When someone is not motivated to conceal his or her emotions, that person's expression tends to last between ½ and 4 seconds in length (Ekman, 1989). However, in deception situations, where the liar is motivated to conceal his or her emotions, often these facial expressions of emotion are micro momentary, that is, they last for less than ½ of a second, or what has been called a "micro expression" (Ekman & Friesen, 1969; Frank, Hurley, et al., 2011; Haggard & Isaacs, 1966). The reason for micro expressions is found in our basic neuroanatomy. To briefly review from Chapter 2 on the face, the two parts of the brain that send impulses to the face in essence send contradictory messages and thus fight for control of the face. The involuntary emotion part sends a signal to express the emotion, whereas the voluntary motor control part sends a signal to suppress or mask the emotion (Frank, Matsumoto, Ekman, Kang, & Kurylo, 2011). In a recent paper we classified 71 liars and 61 truth tellers at 72% accuracy based on the presence or absence of a negative facial expression of emotion (Frank, Hurley, et al., 2011). Untrained observers could only detect these lies at chance (50%). Of those negative expressions, 51% were ½ a second or faster, and 30% were ¼ of a second or faster. Those participants who stipulated that they tried to control their facial expressions showed them at the same rate as those who did not try to control their expressions. This is consistent with other work that showed subjects were able to reduce, but not eliminate, elements of their facial expressions when they were instructed to conceal them in a lying situation (Hurley & Frank, 2011).

Meta-analytic studies suggest that liars do appear more nervous than truth tellers, with less facial pleasantness, higher vocal tension, higher vocal pitch, greater pupil dilation, and increased fidgeting (DePaulo et al., 2003). If the lie itself is about emotions—e.g., telling someone that one feels calm, when in fact one is nervous—the research shows that signs of the truly felt emotion appear in the face and voice despite attempts to conceal, although these signs are often subtle and brief (Ekman & Friesen, 1969; Ekman, Friesen, & O'Sullivan, 1988; Frank & Ekman, 1997, 2004b; Frank, Matsumoto, et al., 2011; Porter & ten Brinke, 2008). Chapter 2 on the face articulates these specific muscle movements.

Emotions during lying can also manifest through the voice and body. There is a literature looking at "stress" in the voice that occurs with lying. This stress is likely the emotion of fear, but it may also include a dose of vocal control that may produce micro momentary tremors in the voice (Lippold, 1971). Regardless, technological approaches to measuring these vocal signs of lying have not been impressive, with the highest accuracies for distinguishing truth from lies being around 62% (with guessing being 50%; Hollien & Harnsberger, 2006; Hopkins, Benincasa, Ratley, & Grieco, 2005). It also seems that higher accuracy levels are obtained with longer speech samples; studies that had liars and truth tellers utter only yes or no responses tend to show detectability not much better than chance (e.g., Horvath, 1978).

Emotions have been implicated in producing various body clues to deceit, such as the presence of adaptors (manipulators, which seem to increase with discomfort; see Chapter 4) or foot and head movements or postural shifts (Zuckerman et al., 1981). In fact, manipulators such as putting a hand over one's mouth, or touching one's nose or face, have in the past been referred to as "red flag" indicators of deception (Inbau, Reid, & Buckley, 1986). One study even suggested that a nose touch was a telltale lie indicator for former president Clinton (Hirsch & Wolf, 2001). However, current research has suggested that manipulators are not very good indicators of lying (DePaulo et al., 2003). Likewise, foot, leg, or head movements, although they might express some nervousness or other emotion, have not been shown to be strong, reliable clues to lying (DePaulo et al., 2003).

Application implications. The strong role for emotions in betraying deception means that to the extent that a lie features higher stakes for getting caught, we would expect to see more of these signs of emotion in liars compared to truth tellers. But as we've seen, if the liar has nothing to lose and nothing to gain by having the lie discovered, or if that lie is not central or important to his or her sense of self, we would not expect the liar or truth teller to feel much emotion (Ekman, 1985/2001; Frank & Ekman, 1997). Yet the majority of the current research literature on deception has examined low-stakes trivial lies with no consequences for getting caught. In contrast, applied contexts tend to involve high stakes that mean strong punishments for the liar who gets caught and potentially large rewards for the liar who is able to fool others. Thus the majority of the research literature may not be fully relevant to the real-world applications in security, law enforcement, or the courts (Frank, 2005). This means that one must exercise caution even when examining otherwise excellent meta-analyses of the research literature on deception, as these often lump together high- and low-stake studies, of which the vast majority are of the low-stakes variety. The most recent and comprehensive meta-analysis (DePaulo et al., 2003) did separate high and low motivation, which, although akin to high and low stakes, is not quite the same thing (e.g., one can be motivated without feeling fear of getting caught). These authors reported that different clue patterns emerged in the high versus low motivation studies, with more emotion-based clues such as appearing tense being prominent in the high-motivation studies:

> Social actors were more tense overall when lying compared with when telling the truth, and this effect was significant only when they were motivated to succeed . . . For studies in which there was no special incentive for succeeding, cues to deception were generally weak. (DePaulo et al., 2003, p. 97)

Finally, we must be cautious about overinterpreting emotional clues. They are simply clues that the person is feeling an emotion. The observer still has to figure out why this person is feeling that emotion. Is the subtle sign of fear in the face and voice the fear of a liar who is afraid of getting caught, or is it the fear of a truth teller who is afraid that he or she is not being believed? (called the "Othello error" by Ekman, 1985/2001).

Strategic Nonverbal Behavioral Management Clues

In an applied setting, such as a security checkpoint, liars and truth tellers both try to appear truthful and take concrete steps to conceal signs that might suggest a lie. Some researchers have argued that this results in a series of strategic moves and countermoves in lie telling (Buller & Burgoon, 1996); that is, individuals strategically manage their behaviors in response to suspicion or other actions on the part of the interrogator. However, that work has been criticized because it fails to make clear, a priori testable predictions (DePaulo, Ansfield, & Bell, 1996). Moreover, it is uncertain as to how this theory differentiates lying from normal communication, since truthful individuals also adjust their behaviors in response to queries (e.g., Vasilyeva & Frank, 2006). However, our bet is that we could make some better a priori estimates as to which clues liars are likely to strategically alter based upon their particular culture's beliefs about the clues that betray lying. Those cultural beliefs, valid or not, would have to be the basis from which a liar would choose his or her behavioral appearance strategy. For example, a survey of 75 countries showed that the most prevalent belief about liars' behavior is that they do not make eye contact (Global Research Team, 2006). Thus, we would predict that liars would be more likely to manage their eye contact, to the point that they may overcompensate and exaggerate the amount of their eye contact compared to truth tellers. Although a meta-analysis of behavioral clues to deceit suggested that eye contact is a very poor clue to predicting deception (average effect size $d = .01$; DePaulo et al., 2003), our frame-by-frame analysis of a high-stakes lie situation showed that liars make significantly *more* eye contact than truth tellers, but only when thinking about their reply to the particular question that forced them to tell a lie. Liars were not different from truth tellers when listening to the question put to them or whilst speaking (Frank, Kim, Kang, & Aragona, 2011). And this study showed that most liars reported afterward that they did deploy a strategy to make sure they would look the interviewer in the eye to appear truthful. Similarly, there is another strong cross-cultural belief that liars are fidgety (despite an insignificant effect size in the research literature), and thus it is not a surprise that illustrators—hand or head movements that accompany speech and are considered to be a part of speech (see Chapter 4 on the body)—are stifled when individuals tell a lie compared to when they tell the truth, thus making them appear less fidgety (Ekman & Friesen, 1972; Vrij, 1995). What this suggests is that liars—and to a lesser extent truth tellers—don't simply suppress all behaviors but strategically choose those they believe are associated with lying (Frank, Kim, et al., 2011). However, the success of various behavioral control efforts can really only be assessed by measuring changes in the frequencies or durations of various behaviors, rather than the specific presence of the behavior.

This behavioral control manifests itself in the *facial channel* through the presence of micro expressions of emotion, which are micro because of efforts to suppress them (Frank, Matsumoto, et al., 2011). Moreover, research suggests there might be a behavior whose presence does indicate specific efforts to control—more lip pressing for liars compared to truth tellers (see Chapter 2; DePaulo et al., 2003). However, we also note that even when specifically requested to control various facial behavior when lying, liars could reduce, but not eliminate, their facial behavior (Hurley & Frank, 2011). Within the *body channel,* the decreased movements are likely evidence of behavioral control (DePaulo et al., 2003; Ekman & Friesen, 1972; Vrij, 1995). Within the voice channel, shorter responses are likely a control measure (DePaulo et al., 2003).

Instrumental Behavioral Deformations

It is possible that some behavioral clues to lying may be gleaned by changes, or deformations, in the flow of body movement patterns of individuals. Some of these theorized movements—hesitation when reaching for something or disfluencies in gait—can be driven by the cognitive or emotional systems described earlier, as well as in Chapter 4 on the body. For example, the feeling of pride is expressed with the arms extended upward (Tracy & Matsumoto, 2008). Or, when actors posed emotions of pride, happiness, anger, and sadness, they walked with longer strides, and they exhibited more exaggerated foot pounding (heavy footedness) when posing anger than when posing the other emotions (Montepare, Goldstein, & Clausen, 1987). However, we should be cautious about these findings based upon 4 actors who pose emotions (see Chapter 2 for hazards with facial posing). A more controlled study examined judgments of the emotional state of individuals carrying a concealed handgun versus a concealed 1-liter bottle and found that observers judged those carrying and concealing the handgun as having more negative emotion in their gait that those concealing the bottle and that this emotion judgment correlated with arm swing and gait style (Blechko, Darker, & Gale, 2009). A similar principle may apply to contraband concealment—we could expect changes in body posture, the speed of movement, and stance adjustments in persons engaged in contraband concealment (see also Chapter 7 by Carl Maccario). Specifically, movements may be driven by impingements caused by the presence of weapons or explosives—that is, the different weight loads can cause changes in body posture and movement that may betray the fact that a person is concealing a weapon of some kind. Research has shown that differential weight loads affect normal gait kinematics or movements. When loads approaching 20% of a person's body mass are added (e.g., 40 lbs for a 200-lb person) compensatory mechanisms appear in the gait that can be readily detected (Bonnard & Pailhous, 1991).

Other studies have demonstrated that even weights equal to 10% of a person's body mass result in significant changes in stride variability—particularly when walking at 2.5, 3, and 3.5 km/hr (equivalent to normal and brisk walking speeds; Falola, Delpech, & Brisswater, 2000). A load of 10% approximates the changes that might occur in a 150-lb person carrying 15 lbs of explosives strapped to the body (which is within the range of IED loads observed from both failed and successful person-borne IEDs). Even if the load were shifted to both ankles, a 2.27 kg load creates a slower but lengthened stride (Diedrich & Warren, 1998). This suggests that explosives or a handgun (a typical .38 caliber revolver weighs 2.25 lbs, or approximately 1 kg) strapped to an ankle might also create these aberrant gait features. In addition to the emotional load often involved with deceptive behavior, these added concealed loads might elicit even stronger, and more evident, gait abnormalities. This is a hypothesis that is worth examining.

Finally, there is another way in which these instrumental behaviors can betray lying. We embody our cognitions through our action tendencies. Embodied cognition suggests that even from early infancy thinking about a movement activates centers in the nervous system responsible for movement (Kinsbourne, 2006) and that the activity of the mind is always linked to both sensory processing and centers for motor control (Wilson, 2002). Simply put, thoughts activate movement. As you read in Chapter 4 on gestures, the initial links between thinking and moving mean that bodily movement and the form of gestures are inextricably linked to the thought they accompany such that the ability to gesture facilitates lexical retrieval (Frick-Horbury & Guttentag, 1998; Krauss, 1998), and their disassociation requires inhibition on the part of the individual (Kinsbourne, 2006). This predicts that both liars and truth tellers are likely to show behavioral movements that reinforce the words they speak, that is, nodding the head when agreeing and shaking the head when disagreeing. These head movements are of course symbolic gestures or emblems (see Chapter 4). When someone's beliefs match his or her words, then these emblems should be consistent with those words (nod when saying yes, shake head when saying no). However, in the case of the liar, the beliefs in one's head are incongruent with the words one speaks— because, by definition, the liar must know the truth in order to tell a lie. Thus, the liar will be more likely to leak an emblem that is congruent with the thought (which is the truth) in his or her head but incongruent with the liar's statement. If asked, "Did you steal that money?" the truth teller is likely to speak the word "no" and shake his or her head no, whereas the liar is likely to speak the same word "no" but will be more likely to nod his or her head yes, as the liar knows "Yes, I took the money." Our current research shows exactly this. Of the 71 liars and 61 truth tellers, we found 21 cases of a subject showing a contradictory head nod or shake; 18 of the 21 (86%) occurred in the liars (Svetieva, 2010).

Summary

It is clear that not all laboratory research studies on lying and malfeasant behavior are directly relevant to understanding real-world settings due to their lack of ecological validity. We could further argue that none of the current laboratory research studies are perfectly applicable, as the stakes generated in a laboratory are not and ethically cannot be the same as those in the real world. However, the high-stakes studies are the best we have, and they can at least engage the same human systems that we have seen in our experience with the real world (cognitions, emotions, movements, strategies) and therefore provide a more complete insight into the behavioral signals that may betray lying. This will become even more evident after reading some of the accounts of our practitioners in Part II of this book.

Detecting Lies From Nonverbal Clues

The general research literature suggests that most people detect lies from behavior at levels not much better than guessing (Bond & DePaulo, 2006). The average person is around 54% accurate and tends to be more accurate spotting truths (61%) than lies (47%). This result applies to laypeople and, surprisingly, to professionals whom we entrust to catch liars (police, customs, judges, etc.). However, as with the research on nonverbal clues associated with lying, the vast majority of the research on detecting lies from behavioral clues has examined detecting lies told by research subjects in low-stake, unemotional situations. When we instead isolate and examine just those studies in which professional lie catchers judged high-stakes lies, we find that professionals are significantly better at detecting lying than the literature had suggested (67% accurate judging high stakes vs. 54% judging low stakes; O'Sullivan, Frank, Hurley, & Tiwana, 2009). The high stakes involved are able to generate emotional clues in the behavior of the liars, clues that are detectable and whose presence more closely matches the lie behaviors these professionals report seeing in the real world (Ekman & O'Sullivan, 1991; Ekman, O'Sullivan, & Frank, 1999; Frank & Ekman, 1997; Frank & Hurley, 2011; Warren, Schertler, & Bull, 2009).

We have suggested in previous work (O'Sullivan et al., 2009) that the Realistic Accuracy Model (RAM) for personality judgments (Funder, 1999) captures the key elements for accuracy in lie detection judgments. The RAM posits that four conditions need to be met before one can truly assess accuracy in a judgment (be it personality or lie detection). The first condition posits that the individual being judged must display behaviors *relevant* to a trait or, in the case of lying, relevant to a person's truthfulness. The high stakes associated with the lies found in law enforcement situations stimulate the production of emotion and its associated behaviors that are apparently relevant (e.g., Frank & Ekman, 1997). The second condition posits that these sorts of behaviors must be *available* to the judge. If the observer is too far away to see facial expressions of emotion, or to hear inconsistent statements or inappropriate breaths or sighs, the *relevant* information is not *available* to observers, thereby limiting the ability to make an accurate assessment (e.g., Frank, 2005). We have noted, for example, that much of the "real world" police interview video is shot from such a far distance that one cannot see subtle facial movements even if exhibited by the suspect; thus, a relevant clue like a micro expression of fear or contempt would not be available. It would then be an error to conclude that facial expressions are not a useful clue in these sorts of videos if they are not *available* (c.f., Mann, Vrij, & Bull, 2004). The third condition posits that the judge must actually *detect* these diagnostic behaviors. If he or she is not looking in the right place—e.g., staring at leg movements when the facial expression of fear is diagnostic, or vice versa—the judge will likely not detect the clue (e.g., Ekman & O'Sullivan, 1991; Hurley & Frank, 2011). The fourth condition posits that these behaviors must not merely be detected; they must be adequately used and *interpreted* by the judge (e.g., O'Sullivan & Ekman, 2004). For high lie detection accuracy, minimum criteria for all four conditions of this model must be met. First, a lie scenario must have stakes high enough to generate emotional clues on the part of the liars, which would produce behavioral clues more *relevant* to lies told in real-world criminal scenarios. Second, the videos being judged must be clear enough that the size of the facial image, quality of the voice recording, or the presence of body behavior replicates that seen in the type of face-to-face communication found in actual interactions, or at least allows the behavioral signals to be visible (Frank, 2005). Third, the judges must *detect* these clues, and fourth, they must properly *interpret* them. An appropriate test bed lie scenario meets the first condition, appropriate video and audio recording captures the second, and particular skills of the judges captures the third and fourth.

In fact, research has examined the skills of some judges, and there do appear to be individual differences in detection ability (Frank & Ekman, 1997). One group, called the "wizards," seems to be reliably better than 80% accurate at detecting lies (O'Sullivan & Ekman, 2004). It is not exactly clear why these individuals are better than others, but it seems early upbringing in emotional situations, along with occupations that pushed for this skill, appear to be important. We have also found that individuals with left-hemisphere brain damage, such that they could not process speech (and thus were limited to nonverbal communication), were better at detecting individuals lying about their feelings than were matched right-hemisphere damaged or non–brain damaged patient controls (Etcoff, Ekman, Magee, & Frank, 2000). Similarly, children who were physically abused but raised in institutions rather than foster care were better able to detect lies about feelings (Bugental, Shennum, Frank, & Ekman, 2001). Groups of lie catchers working together do slightly better than individuals alone. Six-person juries were slightly better at discriminating truths and lies than 6 individuals working alone; the juries' increased accuracy stemmed from them outperforming the individual judges on detecting the lies but not the truths (Frank, Feeley, Paolantonio, & Servoss, 2004).

It is likely that the ability to judge lying is not a single skill, but a skill composed of many subskills, such as the ability to recognize emotion, the ability to identify logical flaws, the ability to hear subtle changes in voice pitch, and so forth (Frank & Ekman, 1997). To that end, studies have shown that accuracy for judging high-stakes lies is correlated significantly with the ability to accurately detect micro expressions of emotion (Ekman & O'Sullivan, 1991; Frank & Ekman, 1997; Frank & Hurley, 2011; Warren et al., 2009).

Finally, the research also suggests that it is possible to train people to be better lie catchers and that even with poor training techniques, there is a small but significant training effect (Frank & Feeley, 2003). As research has progressed, and more sophisticated and targeted training has been deployed, training effects reported in the literature have become even stronger (O'Sullivan, Frank, & Hurley, 2010). And, as one can imagine, if you train on invalid clues to lying, lying detection accuracy will decrease significantly (Kassin & Fong, 1999).

Application implications. Most people would be best served to not put a lot of stock in their abilities to detect lies from behavior. Research has shown that one's confidence in his or her abilities to detect lies is uncorrelated with one's actual abilities (DePaulo et al., 1985). Given that most people are not very good lie catchers and that in real life, most lies are detected by some unimpeachable corroborating evidence (Park, Levine, McCornack, Morrison, & Ferrara, 2002), maybe we should not bother learning how to detect lying from behavior. We feel that taking such a position would be a major error. In fact, we believe that the research literature vastly underestimates how well real-world law enforcement and other professionals detect lying. Laboratory studies that test lie detection abilities will usually present a short video clip to a judge who makes a dichotomous truth-or-lie judgment. That's it; there is no other evidence or information presented to judges. Compare this to a real-world investigative interview. The law enforcement officer or court-room judge does *not* ask just a single question, observe the suspect's response for one minute, and then walk out and make a judgment. Instead, these authority figures gather multiple sources of data prior to setting foot in that interview. They have witness statements, surveillance camera footage, adjudication history of the suspect, or other potential sources of information that they can use and exploit to better evaluate truths and lies of the suspect. Moreover, they can ask questions, follow up on topics depending upon the response, go back and ask the same questions a second time, and so forth (e.g., Frank et al., 2006).

What this suggests to us is that nonverbal communication in this context may be better used as a means to obtaining other information, rather than as a means for simply making a judgment about whether a person is lying. A suspect shows a micro expression of fear when he or she denies knowing a particular drug dealer. Does it mean the suspect is lying? Or does it mean that he or she is in fear of that drug dealer? Or afraid of being disbelieved? Based on what we know from Chapter 2, we can conclude that the suspect is likely feeling an involuntary emotional blast of fear. But the law enforcement officer can then use that signal, what we would call a "hot spot" (Ekman, 1985/2001; Frank et al., 2006), to not abandon that line of inquiry but instead do the opposite by digging deeper into the suspect's knowledge of this person. Digging deeper forces the suspect to commit to specific details about his or her movements, possessions, knowledge, and so forth. These details can be compared to all the other information the law enforcement officer knows to examine them for discrepancies. And it is the presence or absence of this corroborating evidence that lets the officer know for sure whether the suspect is lying. Thus, to the law enforcement officer, the nonverbal clues are often indispensable and important, but not the only bit of information they have. We do know that when the stakes are higher, police in general are no longer at the same 54% accuracy as laypeople but instead closer to 67% (O'Sullivan et al., 2009). Now add on the ability to ask questions, follow up on answers, catch suspects in contradictions, compare suspect statements with those of disinterested witnesses or security camera data, and what you have is a system that will likely do a much better job at ferreting out a lie than the research literature suggests.

Conclusion

It seems clear that nonverbal communication and lying are more complicated by the fact there are no clear-cut guaranteed clues to deceit. Nonverbal clues can have a hugely important role in betraying a lie. But there are no clues specific to lying itself, and all the clues discussed in the chapter can arise for reasons other than lying. And, as we'll mention in the final chapter of this book, the context surrounding these behavioral clues is essential to understanding and interpreting them. For example, a fear expression can betray a lie, but it is not a sign of lying per se. A person who shows you a sign of fear when he or she tells a story about almost being killed on the drive into work is showing an emotion that fits the story. The person who shows you a sign of fear when mentioning that he or she had lunch with a brother-in-law is showing an emotion that does not fit the story (unless you find out another reason why). You will note how later chapter authors—the practitioners—have a more nuanced and complicated understanding of these behaviors than you would presume based on a simple reading of the research literature, and they will note this significance.

References

Blechko, A., Darker, I. T., & Gale, A. G. (2009). The role of emotion recognition from non-verbal behaviour in detection of concealed firearm carrying. *Human Factors and Ergonomics Society Annual Meeting Proceedings,* 1363–1367.

Bond, C. F., Jr., & DePaulo, B. M. (2006). Accuracy of deception judgments. *Personality and Social Psychology Review, 10,* 214–234.

Bonnard, M., & Pailhous, J. (1991). Intentional compensation for selective loading affecting human gait phases. *Journal of Motor Behavior, 23,* 4–12.

Bugental, D. B., Shennum, W., Frank, M. G., & Ekman, P. (2001). "True lies": Children's abuse history and power attributions as influences on deception detection. In V. Manusov & J. H. Harvey (Eds.), *Attribution, communication behavior, and close relationships* (pp. 248–265). Cambridge, UK: Cambridge University Press.

Buller, D. B., & Burgoon, J. K. (1996). Interpersonal deception theory. *Communication Theory, 6,* 203–242.

Darwin, C. (1998). *The expression of the emotions in man and animals.* New York: Oxford University Press. (Original work published 1872)

DePaulo, B. M., Ansfield, M. E., & Bell, K. L. (1996). Theories about deception and paradigms of studying it: A critical appraisal of Buller and Burgoon's interpersonal deception theory and research. *Communication Theory, 6,* 297–310.

DePaulo, B. M., Kashy, D. A., Kirkendol, S. E., Wyer, M. M., & Epstein, J. A. (1996). Lying in everyday life. *Journal of Personality and Social Psychology, 70,* 979–995.

DePaulo, B. M., Lindsay, J. J., Malone, B. E., Muhlenbruck, L., Charlton, K., & Cooper, H. (2003). Cues to deception. *Psychological Bulletin, 129,* 74–118.

DePaulo, B. M., Stone, J. I., & Lassiter, D. (1985). Deceiving and detecting deceit. In B. R. Schlenker (Ed.), *The self and social life* (pp. 323–370). New York: McGraw-Hill.

Diedrich, F. J., & Warren, W. H. (1998). The dynamics of gait transitions: Effects of grade and load. *Journal of Motor Behavior, 30,* 60–78.

Ekman, P. (1989). The argument and evidence about universals in facial expressions of emotion. In H. Wagner & A. Manstead (Eds.), *Handbook of psychophysiology: The biological psychology of emotions and social processes* (pp. 143–164). London: John Wiley.

Ekman, P. (2001). *Telling lies: Clues to deceit in the marketplace, politics and marriage.* New York: W. W. Norton & Company. (Originally published 1985)

Ekman, P. (2003). *Emotions revealed: Understanding faces and feelings.* London: Phoenix.

Ekman, P., & Frank, M. G. (1993). Lies that fail. In M. Lewis & C. Saarni (Eds.), *Lying and deception in everyday life* (pp. 184–201). New York: Guildford Press.

Ekman, P., & Friesen, W. V. (1969). Nonverbal leakage and cues to deception. *Psychiatry, 32,* 88–106.

Ekman, P., & Friesen, W. V. (1972). Hand movements. *Journal of Communication, 22,* 353–374.

Ekman, P., Friesen, W. V., & O'Sullivan, M. (1988). Smiles when lying. *Journal of Personality and Social Psychology, 54,* 414–420.

Ekman, P., & O'Sullivan, M. (1991). Who can catch a liar? *American Psychologist, 46,* 913–920.

Ekman, P., O'Sullivan, M., & Frank, M. G. (1999). A few can catch a liar. *Psychological Science, 10,* 263–266.

Ekman, P., O'Sullivan, M., Friesen, W. V., & Scherer, K. (1991). Invited article: Face, voice, and body in detecting deceit. *Journal of Nonverbal Behavior, 15,* 125–135.

Etcoff, N. L., Ekman, P., Magee, J. J., & Frank, M. G. (2000, May 11). Superior lie detection associated with language loss. *Nature, 405,* 139.

Falola, J. M., Delpech, N., & Brisswater, J. (2000). Optimization characteristics of walking with and without a load on the trunk of the body. *Perceptual and Motor Skills, 91,* 261–272.

Frank, M. G. (2005). Research methods in detecting deception research. In J. Harrigan, R. Rosenthal, & K. Scherer (Eds.), *The new handbook of methods in nonverbal behavior research.* New York: Oxford University Press.

Frank, M. G., & Ekman, P. (1997). The ability to detect deceit generalizes across different types of high stake lies. *Journal of Personality and Social Psychology, 72,* 1429–1439.

Frank, M. G., & Ekman, P. (2004a). Nonverbal detection of deception in forensic contexts. In W. O'Donohue & E. Levensky (Eds.), *Handbook of forensic psychology* (pp. 635–653). New York: Elsevier.

Frank, M. G., & Ekman, P. (2004b). Appearing truthful generalizes across different deception situations. *Journal of Personality and Social Psychology, 86,* 486–495.

Frank, M. G., Feeley, T. H., Paolantonio, N., & Servoss, T. N. (2004). Detecting deception by jury, I: Judgmental accuracy. *Journal of Group Decision and Negotiation, 13,* 45–59.

Frank, M. G., & Feeley, T. H. (2003). To catch a liar: Challenges for research in lie detection training. *Journal of Applied Communication Research, 31,* 58–75.

Frank, M. G., & Hurley, C. M. (2011). *The detection of deception and emotion by police officers.* Manuscript under review.

Frank, M. G., Hurley, C. M., Kang, S., Pazian, M., & Ekman, P. (2011). *Detecting deception in high stakes situation: I. The face.* Manuscript under review.

Frank, M. G., Kim, D. J., Kang, S., & Aragona, D. (2011). *Detecting deception in a high stakes situation: II. The eyes.* Manuscript under review.

Frank, M. G., Matsumoto, D. M., Ekman, P., Kang, S., & Kurylo, A. (2011). *Improving the ability to recognize micro expressions of emotion.* Manuscript submitted for publication.

Frank, M. G., Yarbrough, J. D., & Ekman, P. (2006). Improving interpersonal evaluations: Combining science and practical experience. In T. Williamson (Ed.), *Investigative interviewing: Rights, research, regulation* (pp. 229–255). Portland, OR: Willan.

Frick-Horbury, D., & Gutentag, R. E. (1998). The effects of restricting hand gesture production on lexical retrieval and free recall. *American Journal of Psychology, 111,* 43–62.

Frijda, N. H. (1986). *The emotions.* New York: Cambridge University Press.

Funder, D. C. (1999). *Personality judgment: A realistic approach to person perception.* San Diego, CA: Academic Press.

Global Research Team. (2006). A world of lies. *Journal of Cross-Cultural Psychology, 37,* 60–74.

Goffman, E. (1963). *Stigma: Notes on the management of spoiled identity.* Englewood Cliffs, NJ: Prentice-Hall.

Grice, H. P. (1975). Logic and conversation. In P. Cole & J. L. Morgan (Eds.), *Syntax and semantics* (Vol. 3, pp. 41–58). New York: Academic Press.

Haggard, E. A., & Isaacs, K. S. (1966). Micro-momentary facial expressions as indicators of ego-mechanisms in psychotherapy. In L. A. Gottschalk & A. H. Auerbach (Eds.), *Methods of research in psychotherapy* (pp. 154–165). New York: Appleton-Century-Crofts.

Hayano, D. M. (1980). Communicative competency among poker players. *Journal of Communication, 30,* 113–120.

Hazlett, G. (2006). Research on detection of deception: What we know vs. what we think we know. In R. Swenson (Ed.), *Educing information: Interrogation—science and art* (pp. 45–62). Washington, DC: NDIC Press.

Hirsch, A. R., & Wolf, C. J. (2001). Practical methods for detecting mendacity: A case study. *Journal of the American Academy of Psychiatry and Law, 29,* 438–444.

Hollien, H., & Harnsberger, J. D. (2006). *Voice stress analyzer instrumentation evaluation.* CIFA Contract FA 4814-04-0011 Final Report.

Hopkins, C. S., Benincasa, D. S., Ratley, R. J., & Grieco, J. J. (2005). Evaluation of voice stress analysis technology. *Proceedings of the 38th Hawaii International Conference on System Science, Waikoloa, HI.*

Horvath, F. (1978). An experimental comparison of the psychological stress evaluator and the galvanic skin response in detection of deception. *Journal of Applied Psychology, 63,* 338–344.

Hurley, C. M., & Frank, M. G. (2011). Executing facial control during deception situations. *Journal of Nonverbal Behavior, 35,* 119–131.

Inbau, F. E., Reid, J. E., & Buckley, J. P. (1986). *Criminal interrogations and confessions* (3rd ed.). Baltimore: Williams & Wilkins.

Kassin, S. M., & Fong, C. T. (2009). "I'm innocent!" Effects of training on judgments of truth and deception in the interrogation room. *Law and Human Behavior, 23,* 499–516.

Kinsbourne, M. (2006). Gestures as embodied cognition. *Gesture, 6,* 205–214.

Knapp, M. L., & Comadena, M. E. (1979). Telling it like it isn't: A review of theory and research on deceptive communications. *Human Communication Research, 5,* 270–285.

Krauss, R. M. (1998). Why do we gesture when we speak? *Current Directions in Psychological Science, 7,* 54–60.

Lee, M., Roan, M., & Smith, B. (2009a). An application of principal component analysis for lower body kinematics between loaded and unloaded walking. *Journal of Biomechanics, 42,* 2226–2230.

Lee, M., Roan, M., Smith, B., & Lockhart, T. E. (2009b). Gait analysis to classify external load conditions using linear discriminant analysis. *Human Movement Science, 28,* 226–235.

Lippold, O. (1971). Physiological tremor. *Scientific American, 224,* 65–73.

Mann, S., Vrij, A., & Bull, R. (2004). Detecting true lies: Police officers' ability to detect suspects' lies. *Journal of Applied Psychology, 89,* 137–149.

Matsumoto, D., Keltner, D., Shiota, M. N., O'Sullivan, M., & Frank, M. (2008). Facial expressions of emotion. In M. Lewis, J. M. Haviland-Jones, & L. Feldman Barrett (Eds.), *Handbook of emotions* (3rd ed., pp. 211–234). New York: Guilford Press.

Matsumoto, D., Hwang, H. S., Skinner, L., & Frank, M. G. (2011). Evaluating truthfulness and detecting deception: New tools to aid investigators. *FBI Law Enforcement Bulletin, 80*, 1–8.

Mehrabian, A. (1971). *Silent messages*. Belmont, CA: Wadsworth.

Montepare, J. M., Goldstein S. B., & Clausen, A. (1987). The identification of emotions from gait information. *Journal of Nonverbal Behavior, 11*, 33–42.

O'Sullivan, M., & Ekman, P. (2004). The wizards of deception detection. In P. A. Granhag & L. Stromwell (Eds.), *The detection of deception in forensic contexts.* (pp. 269–286). Cambridge, UK: Cambridge University Press.

O'Sullivan, M., Frank, M. G., Hurley, C., & Tiwana, J. (2009). Police lie detection accuracy: The effect of lie scenario. *Law and Human Behavior, 33*, 530–538.

O'Sullivan, M., Frank, M. G., & Hurley, C. M. (2010). Training for individual differences in lie detection accuracy. In J. G. Voeller (Ed.), *Handbook of science and technology for homeland security*. New York: Wiley.

Park, H. S., Levine, T. R., McCornack, S. A., Morrison, K. & Ferrara, M. (2002). How people really detect lies. *Communication Monographs, 69*, 144–157.

Porter, S., & ten Brinke, L. (2008). Reading between the lies: Identifying concealed and falsified emotions in universal facial expressions. *Psychological Science, 19*, 508–514.

Streeter, L., Krauss, R., M., Geller, V., Olson, C., & Apple, W. (1977). Pitch changes during attempted deception. *Journal of Personality and Social Psychology, 35*, 345–350.

Svetieva, E. (2010). *Deception and the body: Replicating, improving and extending analyses of bodily movement in deception.* Proquest/UMI. Unpublished master's thesis, University at Buffalo, State University of New York.

Tracy, J. L., & Matsumoto, D. (2008). The spontaneous expression of pride and shame: Evidence for biologically innate nonverbal displays. *Proceedings of the National Academies of Sciences, 105*, 11655–11660. doi_10.1073_pnas .0802686105

Vasilyeva, A., & Frank, M. G. (2006). *Testing interpersonal deception theory: Strategic and nonstrategic behaviors of deceivers and truth tellers, communication skills, and dynamic character of deception.* Paper presented at the annual International Communication Association Conference, Dresden, Germany.

Vrij, A. (1995). Behavioral correlates of deception in a simulated police interview. *Journal of Psychology, 129*, 15–28.

Vrij, A. (2004). Why professionals fail to catch liars and how they can improve. *Legal and Criminological Psychology, 9*, 159–181.

Vrij, A. (2008). *Detecting lies and deceit: Pitfalls and opportunities.* Chichester, England: Wiley.

Vrij, A., Akehurst, L., & Morris, P. (1997). Individual differences in hand movements during deception. *Journal of Nonverbal Behavior, 21*, 87–102.

Vrij, A., Leal, S., Granhag, P. A., Mann, S., Fisher, R. P., Hillman, J., & Sperry, K. (2009). Outsmarting the liars: The benefit of asking unanticipated questions. *Law and Human Behavior, 33,* 159–166.

Vrij, A., Mann, S., Fisher, R., Leal, S., Milne, B., & Bull, R. (2008). Increasing cognitive load to facilitate lie detection: The benefit of recalling an event in reverse order. *Law and Human Behavior, 32,* 253–265.

Warren, G., Schertler, E., & Bull, P. (2009). Detecting deception from emotion and unemotional cues. *Journal of Nonverbal Behavior, 33,* 59–69.

Wilson, M. (2002). Six views of embodied cognition. *Psychonomic Bulletin & Review, 9,* 625–636.

Yuille, J. C. (Ed.). (1989). *Credibility assessment.* Dordrecht, Netherlands: Kluwer.

Zuckerman, M., DePaulo, B. M., & Rosenthal, R. (1981). Verbal and nonverbal communication of deception. In L. Berkowitz (Ed.), *Advances in experimental social psychology* (pp. 1–59). San Diego, CA: Academic Press.

PART II

Applying the Science of Nonverbal Behavior

7

Aviation Security and Nonverbal Behavior

Carl Joseph Maccario
Transportation Security Administration

It is important to look at a little background history of aviation security before we discuss the value of what some call "behavior detection." The traditional approach in aviation has always been to detect the threat item, i.e., the gun, knife, or bomb. This mind-set came out of the late 1960s and 1970s when there was a proliferation of hijackings in aviation by various groups for the purpose of political asylum, release of political prisoners, or other political demands. Therefore, the method of threat detection primarily included metal detectors, x-ray machines, and explosives detection machines.

However, over the last three decades—culminating with the attacks of 9/11—we have seen terrorist activity shift toward using the aircraft itself as a bomb or a method of destruction. To accomplish this, terrorists adjusted their methods of defeating the traditional security by using items that cannot be so easily detected by the traditional technology. Richard Reid, known as the "shoe bomber," successfully passed through security and tried to ignite his explosive-laden shoe in an attempt to blow up a plane shortly after 9/11. Yet the fact that he had poor hygiene, no baggage, showed subtle signs of nervousness on his face, and had exceptional concern for security procedures was inconsistent with the normal baseline of passenger behavior. This caused so much concern among Israeli security that they denied him boarding on one of his flights on El Al. He later flew without incident to Paris but still received extra scrutiny, including an extended interview. His shoes, however, were never checked for explosives.

Since that time, US airports require passengers' shoes to pass through the x-ray machines. Then on December, 25, 2010, we witnessed a young Nigerian, Umar Farouk Abdul Mutallab, successfully smuggle an explosive device, not in his shoes but in his underwear, in an attempt to blow up an aircraft. The device malfunctioned.

These two events highlight the fact that the threat to aviation is constantly evolving and that terrorists in particular are constantly adapting methods and weapons to defeat current available technology and procedures. In response, aviation security professionals called for a better balance between detecting the behavior of individuals with nefarious intentions and detecting the dangerous weapons or explosives through technological means. The underwear bomber clearly underscored the need for security to pay attention to individuals' behavior as they transit security as much as we pay attention to the items they are carrying. Video and eyewitness accounts of the underwear bomber's behavior and demeanor before he passed through security clearly showed that he was acting extremely nervous, showing an unusual amount of stress (such as sweating), closely watching the security procedures, and had almost a "tunnel vision" as to what was being checked and not checked; yet no one engaged him or questioned him. It is the belief among many of us who work in the field of behavior detection that Abdul Multullab would have "folded" under questioning or if subjected to more individual scrutiny based on his nervous demeanor and other behavioral indicators of fear. Some of the many cases of drug smugglers caught at Transportation Security Administration (TSA, the agency charged with airport and other transportation security in the United States) checkpoints by TSA behavior detection officers often involve passengers who have a keen interest in security procedures, scanning the checkpoint before entering, rigid posture, minimal body movements, and a tense facial expression, almost one of fear and apprehension (see Chapter 2), unlike the other passengers who do not show those signs and go about their business of clearing security. These are often tip-offs that something is wrong. As behavior detection officers, we become concerned when we see behavioral signals that deviate from a known environment, behaviors that demonstrate extreme concern about security procedures, excessive touching of the face and head, and constantly looking around as if to see who is watching. These nonverbal indicators cause the security official to give that person more scrutiny because that person's body is giving off behavior alarms—and I call this scrutiny *human alarm resolution.*

There are many people in the field of aviation security who feel that the problem with US aviation security is that we are too focused on the item and not the person. We keep retreating back to technology to solve every threat issue, although through the failure of the shoe and underwear explosive devices, luckily we have not experienced another successful attack since 9/11.

The idea of a behavior-based security system is not a new concept to the world of aviation. However, watching people to detect suspicious behavior—behavior such as that we saw from Richard Reid and Abdul Mutallab, sweating, closely watching security, fidgeting, constantly looking around, avoiding eye contact with security officials, all before they entered security—was never a staple of airport security screening for most of the world's airports. When I worked as a behavior detection officer for a private aviation security company, we identified a money smuggler because he kept protecting the briefcase he was carrying by placing it between his feet, nervously shifting it side to side and then back and forth every time a security person walked by. He would also continually rub his head the closer he got to the security interview station. At the interview station, he could not maintain general eye contact with me as I went through the security questions; all the while continually shifting his feet and the bag. His shoulders elevated every time he answered a question almost like he was struggling for air. In the briefcase was $100,000 that he was trying to take out of the country without declaring it to US Customs, as required by law when one is carrying more than $10,000 out of the country.

The idea for behavior detection to be used in security screening situations originated with the Israeli airport security community, which implemented a number of techniques that focused on passengers' demeanor and subsequent answers to simple questions about their trip. The logic of this approach is that the passenger's nonverbal behavior and verbal responses may reveal deception and maybe even hostile intentions. This is now commonly referred to in the security world as *behavior recognition* or, as the Israelis call it, *pattern recognition.* Behavior recognition is not new to the US or international law enforcement/security community. US Customs and Border Protection and the Drug Enforcement Administration have been using nonverbal behavior indicators to decide who to search or subject to additional inquiry for several decades. The behaviors they have used were based on decades of anecdotal law enforcement experience.

There are a lot of erroneous beliefs about behavior recognition in the public and popular press. First, many civil libertarians have argued that behavior recognition is the same as racial profiling. The reality is that racial profiling is absolutely useless and ineffective as a security tool because terrorism has no stereotypical face, gender, or ethnicity. In the past 30 years there have been documented instances of Arabian terrorists, African terrorists, British terrorists, Irish terrorists, American terrorists, Japanese terrorists, Chechen terrorists, Sri Lankan terrorists, and so forth. In the United States alone, we've seen terrorist acts attempted or committed by Richard Reid, a biracial man; Farouk Abdul Mutallab, a Nigerian; and Caucasians John Walker Lindh, an American fighting with the Taliban in Afghanistan, Ted Kaczynski, the Unibomber, and Timothy McVeigh, who used a truck bomb against a US federal building in Oklahoma City. When we speak of behavior recognition as a security tool, ethnicity, race, and religion are not components of these techniques. If police officers or security officials look only for one "stereotypical terrorist" type, the real terror threat is going to walk right past them. As we've seen earlier, terrorists are always adapting their techniques to defeat the latest security innovations—and nothing would be easier to defeat than racial profiling.

Second, some people have complained about the fact that behavior detection involves people getting arrested because they happened to show signs of nervousness or some other behavioral clue that catches the eye of the security officer. This too is not true. Behavior recognition does not trigger arrest—it triggers additional observation and possibly a brief conversation with a security officer. It is the outcome of that conversation that dictates what happens next. Much of the time nothing happens next, but sometimes the individual is passed on to secondary screening. If the security officer notices something clearly illegal—illicit drugs, false travel documents, and so forth—only then is a law enforcement officer called.

Behavior recognition or suspicious behavior detection is about how a person is acting or behaving within his or her environment. The theory behind behavior recognition is that when someone is in the process of carrying out a criminal or terrorist act, that person will exhibit behavior that is out of the norm. This behavior may be a manifestation of the act or operation that the person is planning, or it could be an attempt to conceal these behaviors.

The reader will note that many times throughout this material I stress the importance of recognizing behavior indicators that may indicate possible terrorist or criminal activity. I say *may* because sometimes what you identify is indeed criminal activity, which certainly encompasses terrorist activity as well, but sometimes these behaviors may indicate simply a hypernervous person, a confused person, or some other issue that is not at all related to criminal or terrorist activities.

Much of previous practice in identifying individuals as threats was based upon informal training, that is, relying upon gut instincts or unscientifically tested ideas. Formally training personnel in behavior recognition, with an eye to the solid science, is our new approach to security. Although there is no better tool in detecting suspicious behavior than another human being, if that human being is untrained, he or she may be familiar with some indicators of potential malfeasance but will likely not be "tuned" in to recognizing them when they are anomalous. In this instance, it is important to distinguish "looking" from "seeing" and "listening" from "hearing." Therefore, formal training is essential, and luckily there are many successful models for training.

The most successful model is that of the Israelis. The Israelis are renowned for their security procedures when it comes to safeguarding their aviation industry as well as their critical infrastructure and citizens. Many countries have sought out the methods employed by the Israelis, especially after the most recent underwear bomber incident that defeated current technological screening. The Israelis have been using these methods in aviation security for 4 decades with perfect success: that is, they have had no hijackings or airport-based attacks. However, Israeli airport personnel are typically responsible for roughly 30 flights—or around 900 passengers—a day out of Ben Gurion airport, and thus they can engage every passenger with an interview and even a detailed hand search of the passenger's luggage. In contrast, the US aviation system features over 2 million passengers traveling on any given day. This type of volume restricts us from using all of the Israeli type methods, and so we needed to adapt elements of that system to our laws and logistics.

The TSA did exactly that and has been running airport checkpoints now for over 10 years. In 2006, TSA began a program called Screening Passengers by Observation Technique (SPOT), deploying formally trained behavior detection officers in a system based on the Israeli model but informed by current science (like that found in Chapter 6 of this book) along with the realities of TSA's 10 years of experience working checkpoints since 9/11. In the larger picture, the TSA behavior detection program is designed to complement the current technology-based screening for prohibited items. Behavior detection officers are trained to observe all passengers and to primarily look for behavior that is anomalous to passengers transiting through that particular checkpoint. Observing at a distance requires that these officers be skilled in the science of nonverbal behavior. According to former TSA head Kip Hawley, this TSA behavior detection program has been extremely successful in detecting both criminal activity—resulting in thousands of arrests for illegal items and fraudulent documents—and also identifying individuals who have been forwarded for further investigation due to possible terrorists ties. For example, in April 2007, CNN reported that TSA behavior detection officers identified an individual trying to carry bomb-making materials onto an aircraft at Orlando International Airport. In that particular case, the individual's behavior and appearance were contrary to the normal demeanor of the usual passenger flow. This person stood out from the rest, showing very tense body posture, minimal gross body movements, etc. He also had what you would consider an almost "pained smile" on his face, his lower mouth looked like it was smiling, but the rest of his face was tense, with the muscles around his eyes not moving at all. This arrest was one of many such successes of the program.

As mentioned previously, the logic behind the behavior recognition model is that someone trying to carry out a criminal or terrorist act will exhibit behavior that is out of the norm or inconsistent with the environment. The main way in which these inconsistent behaviors are shown is through the passenger's nonverbal behavior; that is, nonverbal behavior that deviates from normal nonverbal behavior. The norm is developed over countless hours of observation in a particular space. As an example, no one knows your workplace better than you because you are there virtually every day. No one knows your neighborhood better than you because you live there; you know what is routine and what the norm is. A passenger's behavior may be suspicious if he or she deviates from normal routines or the routines of the day-to-day activities of that environment. This deviation is driven by what I call the fear of discovery. This fear of discovery occurs even if someone feels that his or her terrorist act is proper, good, or is justified to further the individual's beliefs. In each instance, the terrorist still must defeat the security system and not be discovered. The fear of discovery manifests itself in many ways, both verbal and nonverbal, and many are discussed in Chapter 6. Many of these nonverbal indicators are behaviors people may be aware of but may not have realized that they could potentially indicate possible hostile intent or terrorism. There is nothing mystical about these behavior indicators. Security officers and police have told us time and time again that they have encountered them but could never put a face or name to that "gut" feeling or explain why "the hair on the back of their neck stood up." We do know from personal discussions with former airline employees who now work for the TSA that the demeanor of the 9/11 hijackers who transited through Newark airport was so anomalous and worrisome that these airline employees did not discard the terrorists' boarding passes as usual.

The reason humans have these reactions when they fear discovery is that this fear triggers many behavioral processes that can be detected through many nonverbal channels and outlets (see Chapters 2 and 3 in this volume for more detail on the science of this reaction). In summary, body movements involving the head, arms, legs, face, and hands all send messages that can express emotions, including anxiety, fear, nervousness, contempt, discomfort, and deceit. The body can also send messages that express our inner, unspoken feelings or thoughts, such as when we are thinking hard, searching our memories, or thinking on our feet. These behaviors, when interpreted properly and in context, can indicate potential suspicious activity or hostile intent. Of course, I won't go into all the behaviors or how they are specifically applied in security settings, but various behaviors triggered by fear include throat clearing; facial flushing; sweating; voice and body trembling; changes in voice pitch, volume, and rate of speech; choice of words, or even drying of the mouth, all basic human reactions to stress and fear. Other body behaviors include rigid body posture, minimal body movements, increased breathing rate, panting, exaggerated or repetitive grooming gestures, and exaggerated or inappropriate emotions. Other behaviors related to defeating security involve the terrorist scanning an area for the presence of police or security and showing an unusual interest in security procedures. The potential terrorist will also try to evade detection by attempting to hide his or her face by turning away when someone approaches; trying to stay out of sight, behind obstructions, or in "the shadows" in order to avoid being seen; wearing disguises or anomalous clothing; avoiding eye contact; or leaving an area when the terrorist believes he or she has been detected. Dr. David Givens, at the Center for Nonverbal Studies, Spokane, Washington, talks of how close observation of individuals and their body movements can often determine whether or not they are holding something back or hiding something they don't want you to know.

These indicators may seem somewhat obvious to some of you reading this. However, many people look but do not see. They listen but do not hear. They do not possess the knowledge on the potential value that these indicators may hold. There have been many studies done that have shown that human beings are poor observers when it comes to being aware of their surroundings and what's happening in them. It is very disheartening when you hear stories of a tragic attack or incident where the eyewitnesses are on the news describing the perpetrators' behavior and activities that "looked weird" or "definitely not normal." What were all the others looking at? I have flown through Logan Airport, where I am based for the TSA, in a suit and have been recognized by many non-TSA airport employees. Yet when I am in street clothes, it is amazing how I have walked right by those same people without being recognized! Dismissing activity as "probably nothing" or "looking" but not "seeing" is going to allow possible criminal, including terrorist, activity to go on undetected.

This new behavioral approach better balances the use of technology to meet the goal of the TSA and law enforcement to ensure a safe aviation experience. Many security officials and agencies are increasingly realizing the value of the human interaction when engaging potentially suspect activity because the only thing all terrorist attacks have in common is the presence of a human being. Not just any human being, but one who has gathered weaponry or explosives and planned and is now attempting to carry out the attack to deliver maximum casualties—all while avoiding discovery. The key is training those officials in decoding and deciphering these nonverbal indicators, with the appropriate caveats so that a credible assessment can occur. But the costs of this assessment are minor—a brief conversation. This small time cost to the traveler is balanced by the potential costs in lives and dollars caused by a successful terrorist attack. The damage to the US economy after 9/11 was measured in thousands of lives and in billions of dollars. In order to protect our way of life from terrorism, we as citizens, security, and police must seek out and engage suspicious behavior before it is too late. We cannot, post 9/11, afford to dismiss any suspicious behavior or activity when it could very well be the beginnings of terrorist preattack planning or operation. We need to find out who these people are and why they are exhibiting suspicious behavior and activity within the environment that the security officer knows intimately. Many times these situations will be resolved as being caused by some innocent reason. But sometimes they are not. It is for these cases that we must be forever vigilant.

8

A Cop's Nonverbal Journey

From Gut to Mind

Joseph Ennett
US Treasury (retired)

I am a retired law enforcement officer of 34 years. I spent 2 years as an investigator in the US Army, 8 years as a local police officer in Virginia and Missouri, and 24 years as a Special Agent in the US Treasury Department.

I realize today that the way we see people, places, and things is directly related to where we came from, where we are now, our journey along the way, and, most importantly, what we did with it all. I found that the critical process for understanding truth and lies in my career was a self-examination of the instincts, perceptions, and skills that I picked up over the years, but to fully understand this, I had to look back.

The Early Years

As most of us did, I learned the consequences of a truth and a lie as a kid growing up at home. My mother had an uncanny ability to detect a lie and frequently advised me not to try to "pull the wool over her eyes." Of course I learned how. In looking back, I realize that my instincts on truths and lies

155

began to develop there. The examination of my own instincts continued through my life experiences, professionally and personally. Acknowledging the value of my own interactions and experiences was directly related to how much growth I allowed to take place within myself, which also aided me in my understanding of human emotions in others.

So, how did I end up in law enforcement? In college I took a police science course, got my first "A" ever, went on a local police ride-along at 100 mph, and I was hooked. Law enforcement would be my career. In a "mock" interview/interrogation class while doing a practical exercise (PE), I found out what can happen to our emotions when interrogated by a professional. In a US Army CID criminal investigation school I was exposed to a polygraph or "lie detector" demonstration and saw another example of what happens when emotions are aroused. I recall that it was at this time I began to appreciate that just because a person's emotions become aroused or heightened, it is not always a sign of guilt. The PE volunteer was asked several yes or no questions but was not required to answer—yet the chart readings revealed the answers. Later in the exercise, the volunteer was asked an open-ended question: "While you were assigned in Paris did you . . ." His emotional response was off the polygraph chart (very big). Certainly any number of possibilities existed on what he could have done while in Paris. The message here was that we did not know what he had done, but his emotions were heightened with the thoughts of the possibilities. From an interrogation standpoint, if this were a real scenario, he would have become vulnerable on this topic; we would then need to follow up on this question to determine what might have caused this response, much of which may not have been deceptive at all. Regardless, this information was useful. Shortly after the CID school, my first real interrogation of a suspect took place, and I got a confession from him after an hour and a half of questioning. Later in my career, I found that the time I needed to interview would shorten.

Policing and Gut Instinct

As a local patrol officer, I worked in various parts of the city. In the high-crime neighborhoods, I began to fully hone my lie detection; that is, my "gut" feeling started to be more revealing and then trusted. I was getting to know myself better. Up until that point I had no advanced training in interviewing, but I was exposed to more and more interviews. And, as I got to know the people I encountered in my area better, I learned their patterns and behaviors. But it was still the "gut" that guided me. I learned that the intuition into emotion that began during my encounters in the military became a necessity for survival as an officer on the street. In particular, I learned that recognizing the anger that occurs at the brink of physical combat became a tool I could use to diffuse the fight before it happened. I remember as a young rookie standing, alone, looking eye to eye at an individual named "Wayne." Wayne had been fighting with his brother and stabbed him rather severely with a bottle prior to my arrival. I was there now and his anger had not left. I saw in Wayne's eyes the stare of anger, his pursed lips and combative stance. I sensed the impending violence and was able to talk with him and diffuse the anger before he picked up the broken bottle he had used moments before I had arrived. Strange as it seems, we developed respect for each other that night and as a result avoided a likely confrontation a year or so later. Taking time to "know" my adversary and myself proved to be a good thing that I carried forward.

Getting Exposed to Science and Structure

As my career broadened to the federal government, more specialized interview training from several government and private sources followed, which resulted in more structure to my interviews. This additional structure, plus the basic training on nonverbal communication, along with my gut, allowed me to become pretty successful at interviewing, and I was recognized for this. At times the interviews were quite lengthy though, as the "gut" was still often the guidance. My knowledge of people was growing. I did not perceive the journey that was ahead.

If you believe in revelations, mine was about to happen. I received formalized training on emotions and nonverbal communication taught by retired agent James Newberry and retired deputy Robert Harms. These two were trained by research psychologists Dr. Paul Ekman and Dr. Mark Frank on how to recognize signs of emotion. The training gave me the "key." I was taught about human emotions and what they looked like when someone was experiencing one. I could now make sense of and understand the "gut" feelings I had followed for many years. I now looked at communication differently, and I looked at "me" differently. One hazard I have noted is that we all tend to have a "me theory" of personality. The me theory is, in short, a description of how we tend to view the world based on our own experiences, preconceptions, prejudices, and expectations. My view changed because I could now see so much more about other people, and I also realized how much they could see in me. My interviews and interrogations became more focused, channeled, and shorter as I now had more effective tools in my toolbox. I felt that all of the training I had taken over the years on interviewing and behavioral observation, and all of the personal experiences I had with people in interpersonal interactions, came together in allowing more efficient and effective interviewing. For those of us who may golf, paint, or enjoy some other skill, using the right interview tool at the right time was just like picking the right club for the shot or the right brush for the expression. The end result is better, and knowing that our abilities are growing is very rewarding. I will admit that at first, all these different skills were a bit of information overload, where there was always something else to monitor, but I was hooked and dedicated to interviewing and toughed it out. I found that the more comfortable I became with reading facial expressions—particularly those very fleeting "microexpressions" and reading emotions through other nonverbal behavior—the shorter and more successful were my interviews. I've found that the ability to observe nonverbal behaviors results in effectively validating truth, and it allows a quicker focus on the areas of interest or "hot spots" with less distraction from extraneous information. Knowing a person's culture, family, criminal background, and even religion can be helpful in knowing how a person will display emotions. Research indicates and I concur that people's backgrounds often dictate to what extent they openly show emotions. If they "wear their emotions on their sleeve" for instance, it may be easier to determine the truth.

More Than Just Deception

This is probably a good time to emphasize that the skill of detecting emotions through nonverbal communication is not just a skill used for interrogations. Frequently, folks may think that when a law enforcement officer uses the word "interview," he or she really means interrogation. Although the interrogation of a suspect is a significant part of closing a criminal case, it is only another type of interview. The purpose of an interview or encounter with another is to determine the entire story, all of the facts. It could be talking to a clerk at a store about the best tool, the best fix for the home project, or the interview of a career criminal. Determining the truth, however, is the challenge. What do I "believe" to be the truth, and what does the person I am interviewing "believe" to be the truth? There have been a number of times that I doubted what a witness stated, but I believed the witness to honestly believe that he or she was telling the truth. A good example of this is when cooperative witnesses to a car accident tell you they saw the color of the traffic light and state honestly who they believed was at fault, only for us to find during questioning that they were not facing the accident but had turned around after hearing the crash to look at it and had only then looked at the traffic light. In cases like these, because they truly believe what they said, witnesses are inaccurate but not lying. However, I would expect that their nonverbal and verbal behaviors should be consistent when truthful, even when wrong. The challenge, I believe, is to observe those times when the verbal and nonverbal behaviors are conflicted. Do the words match the behavior? This seems to be to be the true challenge of determining whether the person told me a truth or a lie.

Case Studies in the Field

As a federal officer, I frequently worked with state, local, and other federal agencies on cases. I recall an interview where a local police officer and I teamed up on a criminal case involving a street gang member we had arrested en route to assault a rival gang member. Like most interviews, the gang member sized up me and my partner, and we sized him up. This process also involves nonverbal communication—looking at someone top to bottom, staring, changing voice pitch to gauge the reactions of others, and so forth. This gang member had an extensive criminal record (which we had obtained before the interview) involving robbery, drugs, and assault. During the preliminary interview, I made a deal with him that we could speak on level ground as long as he did not lie to me. About 15 minutes into the interview he told what I believed to be an obvious lie that I was able to detect from a small body shift back and a microexpression of happiness, displayed with a slight smile on his face (enjoying the lie). I made the decision to call him on it by saying, "Why did you just do that?" He said, "What?" And I stated, "You lied to me." The look of surprise on his face that he had been found out was priceless. I convinced him at that point that a lie would land him in jail and would separate him from his family for a long time. He then supplied the truthful information and agreed to cooperate. Normally, I would not feel it wise to place all my bets on one answer being a lie. However, in this situation I took an educated chance because the science let me know what I had seen; moreover, I was not sure I would have another opportunity with him as he was very street savvy. This is where the interviewer's discretion has to prevail. A short time after he made his statement and the interview concluded, my interview partner—who had no emotions and nonverbal behavior training—looked at me with amazement and asked, "What just happened?" By no fault of his own, he had not been able to observe the same subtle nonverbal cues that I had.

By no means are all of the interviews as easy as the previous example. My experience is that nothing replaces a good set of interview questions and ears to listen carefully to the account provided by the person being interviewed. This, accompanied by good legwork (gathering as many facts from as many sources as possible) and complete homework on the individual and situation prior to the interview, places the advantage with the interviewer. I had another joint case that involved several conspirators, all of whom were not very good criminals but were very good liars. They had all conveniently abetted each other by claiming that they were together away from the crime scene the entire day and night of the crime. The task force investigating the incidents split up into pairs of respective interagency partners to conduct our follow-ups. My partner and I agreed it was time to interview one of the possible suspects. We did our homework and set up the interview, which we agreed would be essential to the case. The interview took over an hour to complete during which I observed emotions of sadness, contempt, anger, and remorse accompanied by tears. When all was said and done, I detected an expression of guilt in his face and body. At the conclusion of the interview my partner and I disagreed on the implication of the individual's expression of guilt. I was quite sure we had been lied to because I had picked up on some conflicting body language and emotions as to parts of the alibi given to us. At the end of the day, our task force met and compared notes. Unfortunately, I was the only investigator that thought we had the right group of suspects. This was a difficult position to be in for me professionally as there were several very talented law enforcement officers on the task force. One other suspect, not connected with the group, had shown some perceived deception on a voice analysis test and was favored by some of the officers as the true guilty party as a result of this test. Well, I explained to the task force Emotions and Nonverbal Communication 101 and why I doubted the suspect I had interviewed. I told them how I saw a microexpression of happiness when he was lying about where he had been during one period of the day. Sadness was displayed at another point in the interview, which I felt to be remorse. Now I did not have to rely on my gut and could expound upon the science. The other teams agreed to reinterview their people and specifically hone in on the area of conflict that I had observed. The results of the follow-up interviews essentially destroyed the coconspirators' alibis, and their involvement in the incident became evident. The next week, following additional excellent police work, one of the suspects confessed and the others fell. Upon conviction, all received double-digit sentences in prison. Any successful interview, like most success, has an element of good luck mixed in, and this was one of those cases that had a bit of luck but also bore out the good hard work of many. I also give credit to my supervisor, who understood my explanations of the science in which I had been trained. If he did not have confidence in me, the outcome could have been much different. It is cases like this that allow you to walk away knowing you did exactly what you were supposed to do as best you could.

When we are in search of the truth or, should I say, what is believed to be the truth, there are a number of things that must be considered. People lie and withhold information for different reasons. They can be motivated by any number of things, which includes those who lie because they can and actually enjoy it. Some may lie as part of a psychological disorder, while others may lie out of perceived necessity, self-preservation, or protection of someone close to them. Although understanding that some of the motivations are best left to the mental health professionals, from the perspective of a law enforcement officer determined to find the truth, it is significant to know the motivation of the person being interviewed. It could be embarrassment, fear of being caught, fear of retaliation, or the disappointment of a respected loved one. The importance of making this judgment as an interviewer is no different from setting your goals for a professional career or the goals or expectations of a personal relationship. Knowing why—understanding the motivations— allows us to know why we are headed in a particular direction and suggests the best way to get there. As I mentioned earlier, my experience supports the research that emotions are cross-cultural and universal (see Chapter 2 on the face), but if someone is lying he or she will display differently depending on the person's background and motivations. The emotion displays may look different or be more subtle if the person holds very strong convictions in his or her beliefs (or is a frequent and accomplished liar). The indicators are there; however, it may take more in-depth interviewing to reveal them to the point I could draw a conclusion from what I observed. My approach varied depending on who I was interviewing and for what purpose. One time I interviewed a bank employee who had been served a subpoena. The employee, while cordial and pleasant in general, showed me distinct fear in his face when I asked procedural questions about a client suspected of money laundering for outside interests. I indirectly addressed his fear, and the employee admitted that he was apprehensive and feared that I thought he was involved in illegal activity. I assured him that he was not the target of my investigation. Subsequently he relaxed, in both tone and facial expressions, and he was very forthcoming and proved to be an excellent source of information on the actual individual of interest. Had I not perceived the subtle fear in his face, the interview would not have been nearly as productive. And note that this fear had nothing to do with deception.

Conclusion

It is quite clear to me that the ability to observe emotions through verbal and nonverbal communication, which complement the listening process and interaction with others, is the key to any successful interview. Whether it is a conversation with a friend, business associate, family member, or total stranger, the benefits to better communication are obvious.

When I provide training, whether to law enforcement or other groups, one of the things I always address is the caution of applying the skills we learn in our professional lives into our personal lives. I recall a two-day class we were teaching where one of the students had come in the second day and told us about his social experience the night before at a local bar. He explained to the group how he had carefully applied everything he had learned in class to assist in his interaction with other patrons, much to his glee. He declined to be specific on the results of his "interviews," but one can only imagine. On a serious note, being able to read others' emotions does present us with decisions on how we use the skill. How much do we want to know, and how much do we not? Regarding our family and friends, that can be an important decision. Using the skill to facilitate conversation to make it more rewarding can be great. Being a walking lie detector may be quite intrusive and possibly amusing to some, but it likely is not as rewarding at the end of the day. Studies have shown that it is our human nature to want to believe in each other, to trust the spoken word almost to a detriment. On the other hand, questioning the validity of everything said can be quite consuming.

This chapter has covered a lot of topics, ranging from science, training, a look at ourselves, practical application, and of course some war stories that I hope have helped illustrate some of the principles. If I could just reiterate a few key things, I would have to start with desire—the desire to seek the truth—and not just a peek at the portion you or others might want to see but the whole picture. I believe we can accomplish this by overcoming our preconceptions and our own self-imposed limitations on what we encounter. In the old days, our instructors told us not to have "tunnel vision." Today, I feel as though the basic science on nonverbal communication has taken me to a new level of appreciation for my gut instinct. It is still amazing to me how much there is to be seen in other people if I "listen" to what I see as well as hear.

Once I understood the science of human emotion, I had a new base of knowledge to draw from. The new challenge was how to apply the knowledge in my work, in everyday life, and at home. People look so different today from when I started . . . or maybe it's that I see them differently? But one thing I have learned is that once you have the knowledge, once you are able to see people completely, you are unable to ignore it; you cannot go back.

9

Anomalies and Nonverbal Behavior

Paul M. Moskal
Supervisory Special Agent, FBI (retired)

I have always believed, even as a young child old enough to have such thoughts, that I have had a special gift—to read people very well. Unlike the majority of my peers and colleagues, I felt I could detect people's levels of comfort, interest, and whether they were being deceptive. As it turns out, I think most people function under this self-delusion (which of course really works to the advantage of those who are truly gifted).

To genuinely have the ability to discern truth from people's representations would move us from mere mortals to something at least slightly more; I do believe, however, that people can improve their skill sets to read others better. I want my skill sets to be moved into the realm of radio and comic book character Lamont "the Shadow" Cranston, whose fictional psychic powers elevated him to virtual divinity in the law enforcement sphere. So when the question posed in the introduction to "the Shadow" radio program asks, "Who knows what evil lurks in the hearts of men?"—the answer is this: I do! Well, not really, but this is the part where I expose my innermost self to you for the betterment of those of you who think you have the calling.

A lifetime of experience with 32 years of lawyering, law enforcement, and counterintelligence work tells me that some people are, in fact, much better than others in discerning truths from something else. Why? Who are they? Most importantly, how do they do it?

I want to learn their secrets.

I believe that what has led me down my delusional path as a spouse, parent, neighbor, and even as a law enforcement and counterintelligence officer is to look for and identify anomalies in behavior and response—commission and omission—in both verbal and nonverbal behavior.

I believe this identification of anomalies is what we cops call "gut feelings" or intuition that can sometimes lead us down one path over another. An anomaly is some behavior or action that does not fit with the other actions or behaviors that accompany it. I think that some individuals are better than others at picking up these "anomaly cues"—either due to training, experience, sensitivity, or innate ability to process what is seen by all of us but not necessarily processed in traditional cognitive ways.

We all want to be "insiders" and have information no one else does to assist us in making insightful decisions and ferret out anomalous behavior in perceptive ways. Even in our personal lives, for example, we want to know what our friends, children, and significant others are thinking (and if their thoughts match their words and actions) so we can make decisions not only in ways that benefit us directly, but in a manner that is noticed and highlights our interpersonal skills and separates us from our peers and competitors. We see this desire reflected in our culture in movies like *What Women Want*, where the main male character can hear the inner thoughts of women he meets. We are so driven to know the truth in our relationships that we even fantasize about what our pets and animals are thinking; Dr. Doolittle, for instance, "talks to the animals" and interprets their responses unlike anyone else.

In the world of television and sports, we are driven to view programming by catchy names (*Inside the Huddle, Under the Hat, In Between the Lines*) that draw us to this desire to be able to read outward signs, nonverbal behavior, language, and the decision-making process in a way that gives us special insight, for a host of reasons—including financial gain and the ability to let our peers know we are part of the insiders club who know the truth and the benefits that come with it.

Today's booming social networking sites feed us information, globally and instantaneously, that draw us in partly because of our insatiable desire to know what others are not only really doing (Facebook/LinkedIn) but what they are really thinking at that very moment (Twitter). *As a society and as a culture we want to be able to read other people beyond what they say or manifest!*

This desire for the perfect truth has infiltrated all aspects of our lives, as reflected in our pop culture. I would argue that the law enforcement and intelligence communities have always desired the perfect truth as their end result but that the ramifications for their failure in that regard in today's world are growing geometrically. This drives those two communities to seek every advantage they can in discerning what that truth is and the ways to obtain it.

Factual evidence always supersedes behavior (verbal and nonverbal), but that luxury of having factual evidence or having the ability to obtain it does not always exist. The law enforcement and intelligence communities are driven, out of necessity, to extrapolate the truth from what is known or presented to them.

If discerning the truth were a perfect science, we would all be infallible interviewers; the reality, of course, is that interviews are not a perfect science but neither are they purely an art. There are skill sets that good interviewers avail themselves of—wittingly or unwittingly. The goal here is to cognitively identify those skill sets and develop a methodology or practice that enhances our abilities to employ them.

The adage about the necessity of being a good listener to further a conversation, and the issues presented, is self-evident. We must also absorb what is said in the complete context of the transmission of that verbal and nonverbal message—who, what, where, when, why, how, as well as what is not said or otherwise transmitted.

Even though listening is a very basic skill, we have all witnessed people who do not have that skill set or fail to employ it. Incredibly, I have witnessed many good law enforcement and intelligence officers fail to use it even though it is the touchstone from which all good interviews come. As an attorney, I have also seen counsel make similar errors during times of examination by asking questions from a predetermined list that they seem incapable of deviating from despite what answer may be given.

Interviewers may become inflexible in thinking they know the answer even before they ask the question because they have a positional, intellectual, or educational superiority—or even a level of experience that drives them to the erroneous belief that they are infallible and don't need to treat every interview with the same caution.

The Bank Robber

The following personal experience highlights my poor judgment in this regard.

I was the primary investigator for a bank robbery in the Buffalo, New York, area and had the good fortune of apprehending a bank robber a day or two after the robbery. The arrest was made primarily because of eyewitnesses who observed a "getaway vehicle" and the technology of the day, which included bank surveillance photographs of the robber and the robber's fingerprints that were recovered and matched to the person depicted in the bank surveillance photograph.

Hard evidence is a wonderful thing when it exists and is recovered. I would note, however, that inherently the most unreliable form of evidence is eyewitness identification. At its best, it is subject to the weaknesses we all have as human beings—limitations of hearing, vision, memory—and is possibly further tainted by personal biases as well as situational stress or fear and other psychological factors inherent in the situation presented or already existing in the witness. Bank surveillance photographs are notoriously poor in their memorializations for a host of reasons that go beyond this topic.

As a relatively new Special Agent with all of 3 months experience, I was confident that in this matter, the hard evidence presented irrefutable proof as to who was responsible for this bank robbery. It added to my self-infatuation with the invincibility of law enforcement in dealing with criminals and with my own strong sense of my personal skills.

After the subject's arrest, I took the opportunity to work with the bank robber for the next several months to develop a professional relationship in the hopes of solving other bank robberies and other unsolved property crimes in the area. I subsequently learned that the bank robber—and his ubiquitous friend—were house burglars who ultimately graduated to being bank robbers.

As a young but obviously skilled investigator (in my own mind), I prided myself on eliciting information that identified local burglars and with sharing that information directly with the local police. The feedback I received from local authorities was all positive in terms of the information's relevance and accuracy. I was growing in confidence that my skill set in developing a rapport with the bank robber and his friend over a several-month time frame was really resulting in sound law enforcement intelligence and producing tangible results.

As part of my almost daily meetings with these two individuals, I would routinely show them photographs of other criminals and criminal activity and would solicit their information and help. I would always have another law enforcement officer or agent with me.

During this time frame, a series of approximately half-a-dozen local bank robberies occurred. The description for the party or parties responsible for robbing the banks varied from a light-skinned black male, to a Hispanic male, to a white female. The descriptive data of the robber(s) in terms of height, weight, and build were similar. The discrepancy in the description of the gender and race, however, seemed to be the more reliable and overriding factor in the assumption that different parties were responsible for the different bank robberies. In other words, it seemed more logical that the eyewitness accounts of the height and weight of the bank robber(s) were inaccurate rather than them being mistaken about both race and gender. For this series of bank robberies, I enjoyed the benefit of hard evidence—bank surveillance photographs that, I believed, accurately reflected the eyewitness accounts, including those of the victim bank tellers, with regard to race and gender. With bank surveillance photographs in hand for at least a half-dozen robberies, I showed a series of these photographs for each robbery to both the bank robber and his always-present friend that I had developed as sources of information for criminal activity.

Because I had now been "working" with them for a number of months, I did not hesitate to show the photographs or solicit their input. I had in the interim grown confident in our relationship, which was seemingly very fruitful. In each of the instances, they would offer potential subjects or tangential information. I thought my interview technique was good—I asked questions and listened to their answers to my satisfaction. The bank surveillance photographs clearly did not depict my original bank robber turned informant who was always cooperative. His friend, who was also shown every bank surveillance photograph, was not always as cooperative, but he did not have to be because he was not charged with the original bank robbery and really had no incentive to be cooperative. I viewed him as relatively unimportant in terms of developing information; it was the individual who had been arrested for bank robbery that was the focus of my efforts and attention.

After showing the last series of bank surveillance photographs to the initial bank robber, he asked me when I was going to arrest him. I asked him what he was talking about since he had already been arrested for the bank robbery he committed several months earlier. My partner and I looked at him, trying to figure out what he was talking about. He volunteered that we knew he robbed the first bank and that his friend was in fact the getaway driver! Of course, we did not know or even suspect that there was a getaway driver, since no one saw that—including the several witnesses that did identify the getaway car that turned out to be registered to the bank robber. All of the witnesses said there was only one person in the car.

The bank robber went on to explain that his friend was the driver in the original bank robbery and that he had actually hopped in the trunk of the car to effectuate the getaway. The bank robber was convinced we knew this. He then went on to explain that the person depicted in each series of photographs from the last half-a-dozen bank robberies we had shown him and his partner was in fact his partner! He went on to articulate that we really couldn't be such idiots and that we must have known for a whole series of reasons—including that we now had shown approximately 100 pictures of the very man sitting across from us directly to him—that he was obviously the man in each and every one of the photographs.

Well, that is what my 5-year-old would call a clue. My partner and I were really and truly dumbfounded. The series of photographs really was not very helpful. They were of very poor quality, and in all candor, you could not tell if the person depicted was a man or woman, black, Hispanic, or white. As I said before, bank surveillance cameras are not always helpful—yet I relied on them to my detriment.

It was painful that both my partner(s) and I interviewed the original bank robber and his friend several times and asked them directly about the original bank robbery. Because I already had a strong evidentiary case against the obvious suspect that aligned with the known facts, I failed to ask good questions about accomplices. I also failed to ask good questions of his friend who I did not view as having any active role in the original bank robbery.

I also failed to follow up on the friend's anomalous behavior to the questions I did ask because I thought I did not need his responses. I was too self-assured, and I thought too well positioned, to carefully listen to his answers. In retrospect, I did not challenge his responses when a good investigator should have; it was appropriate that I should have conducted better interviews given the relationship the bank robber enjoyed with his friend. Hindsight being 20/20, the friend's responses were always cavalier and presented in a manner such that his body language did not comport with his spoken word—it was anomalous behavior.

The friend was always smirking when he provided a response, despite the gravity of the situation. He never remained stationary—always walking in and out of conversations—literally and figuratively speaking. His responses were almost always noncommittal and were non sequiturs. His nonverbal behavior was telling me that he was being dismissive—moving away from the detailed questions about the bank robbery.

In retrospect, good technique dictated that I should have separated the two friends and always interviewed them individually, as would normally be the case. I should have sat the friend down, made him stay in place, and answer my questions to my satisfaction rather than his. I should have controlled the interview and not allowed him to do so. Usually, honest people are not continually dismissive. I was aware that his nonverbal behavior was anomalous to his verbal responses; I mistakenly did not address it. His attitude, manifested in verbal and nonverbal behavior, demanded further scrutiny; I should have known better—I obviously didn't.

My egregious error was compounded by my cognitive decision to completely disregard the friend as being involved in the following series of bank robberies because the photographic evidence did not immediately support it. I was stuck in a time warp with the first bank robbery. The wheel man had become the robber, and the robber had become the wheel man. That did not fit my existing frame of reference for how they worked in tandem. It let me disregard asking good questions and disregard listening for good answers—without anomalies. In retrospect, the responses that the friend provided, combined with his nonverbal behavior (inappropriate smiling; walking away from the questioning under the guise of disinterest; never physically or emotionally engaging the interviewer) were cavalier and supercilious given the scenario. Despite noticing this level of communication, I failed to consider it because I had disregarded his spoken response before I had even asked the question. Ultimately, both were arrested, charged, and convicted for the series of bank robberies. Upon arrest, I told them both that I knew what was going on from the onset—as they had suspected—but that I was just building a case against them. It was not true, but my pride did not allow for honesty.

As basic as this sounds, this experience taught me the necessity of asking intelligent questions and listening for intelligent answers (not always an easy thing for many reasons) and to identify the perceived anomalies between verbal and nonverbal behavior and to incorporate them into a due diligence investigation.

If I failed to act on the detected anomalies between verbal and nonverbal behavior occurring in interviews early in my law enforcement career, I did improve with several epiphanies like my early bank robbery case. Life's experiences compiled with those indigenous to law enforcement allowed me to improve as witnessed by the following investigation.

The White-Collar Fraud

I was asked to investigate a complicated white-collar fraud case involving a variation of a Ponzi scheme that resulted in a seven-figure loss to a large company by several smaller companies and individuals over a two-year period. The primary party responsible was identified as a smaller family-owned business; neither victim nor subject companies wanted any adverse publicity. Forensic accounting determined an almost exact figure that the victim company had been defrauded of by the smaller companies. The issue, however, was complicated by the suicide of the most culpable figure from the smaller company. His demise left only close family members to work with who may, or may not, have been directly aware of the criminal conduct at the time it occurred.

Initial contacts with the remaining principal and family head were not going well in that he denied culpability and refused to denigrate the reputation of his family members as part of the resulting investigation.

During my initial in-person meeting with him, he portrayed himself to be a very religious man (I do not doubt his representation in this regard), a man who was in total control of his family as the patriarch, a man who built the family business from scratch, a man who founded many local charities, and a man who was consumed with grief over his family member's suicide.

As I left the initial meeting, he articulated surprise that I was not there to bring him a check from the larger victim company he said owed him hundreds of thousands of dollars. Several subsequent meetings took on the same tone with the patriarch crying over the personal loss resulting from the suicide, demonstrating an expressed willingness to be exposed in the small community that would result in his family's shame and humiliation once the matter became public through criminal and civil litigation, and expressing indignation that we would seek restitution, claiming it was all God's will, and if he would have to go to jail—so be it.

My last in-person meeting with the patriarch took place approximately one month after the first. It provided me an opportunity to reflect on the patriarch's allegations, statements, and nonverbal behavior. As a consequence, it afforded me a plan of action. His statements and actions provided anomalies that I wanted to clarify before I made my judgment as to his personal culpability, the culpability of the business, and which direction the investigation should take.

During the interviews, the patriarch would discuss his deceased family member reverently but would only cry when we discussed restitution—never when we discussed his personal or family loss. The anomaly was obvious— he cried as you would expect during the interviews—but the discussion of money was always the triggering factor—although I do not question his true grief—just the triggering circumstances he used to express it. As a human being, much less a law enforcement officer, this circumstance was odd.

As I mentioned, at the conclusion of our first meeting, he expressed great surprise that I was not there to give him a check for hundreds of thousands of dollars. The timing of his statement, again, was odd. I think the common experience would dictate that if someone sincerely believed he was to be given a check for hundreds of thousands of dollars, it would be one of the first topics discussed, not raised as an afterthought at the conclusion of the meeting. He didn't raise any objections to the nonpayment either.

The patriarch kept insisting he was a religious man and that God would take care of the situation. He refused to have either an accountant or attorney present despite my suggestion. He used that religious mantra repeatedly when he was confronted with documentation—literally boxes of physical evidence showing the fraud—but still refused professional guidance. In fact, I used his documentation to show him it was fabricated and part of the Ponzi scheme. It is my experience that innocent people when given the opportunity—especially in white-collar crimes—seek professional assistance. He was financially able to seek guidance, but he refused. Again, this is anomalous behavior for the innocent.

The patriarch also expressed an adamant willingness to lose the family business, for him, his spouse, and grandchildren. Here again, the trigger for this self-serving attempt for sympathy was the talk of restitution. The willingness to lose his business was never offered as an independent expression of his legal or moral innocence. The timing of his statements combined with his overdramatic hand-wringing, tears, and apparent despondency (lowered head, muffled responses, sighing) was the anomaly—not that he made them as a representation of his true feelings. The timing betrayed his verbal expression. Additionally, he turned his "despondency" on and off at will when it seemingly served him. His emotions never naturally built over the course of the interview. They would artificially appear and disappear.

I concluded that the patriarch probably did not know the day-to-day workings of his company when it acted fraudulently—but he turned a negligent blind eye to it. He was genuinely grief stricken and trying to save the family reputation. These factors complicated his articulated statements.

In our last meeting, I told him my thoughts regarding the position he found himself in and pointed out the anomalies I identified in his statements and in his actions. I noted that it wasn't only one statement or action on his part that made me question his lack of knowledge and responsibility but the confluence of anomalies. The next day he had his attorney call to make an almost-million-dollar restitution to the victims—including the larger company.

The fact pattern in this matter was muddied by a very tight familial business and personal grief. It was truly a sad situation for the patriarch. It did not, however, relieve him of his company's obligations—even as he himself ultimately decided when confronted with his own anomalous behavior.

Lessons Learned

These two stories illustrate examples of typical law enforcement interviews. Most interviews encompass situations where verbal behavior doesn't always match anticipated nonverbal behaviors.

In the first scenario, I recognized the anomalies between what was said and the nonverbal behavior that accompanied it. Of course this recognition is critical, *but* without appropriate consideration of what they may mean and responsive action, mere recognition of these types of anomalies is meaningless.

In the second scenario, I identified the anomalies between what was articulated and the nonverbal behavior that accompanied it. Importantly, however, after consideration, I took the next step and modified my interview technique to drill down to a different level.

Verbal and nonverbal behaviors do not always align. Just because they do align does not mean that what is offered is the truth. When they do not align, it is problematic and necessitates closer review to ascertain why they do not align—it does not mean someone is necessarily being deceptive.

In summary, be sensitive to identifying anomalies between what is said and the nonverbal behavior accompanying the verbal behavior. The complete context of what is seen and heard provides the interviewer a larger framework from which to make insightful decisions.

A denial with a smile may be truthful, but their anomaly calls for clarification. A denial with tears may be appropriate, but in context, if it does not ring true to the shared human experience (crying to exhibit emotional pain versus crying at inappropriate times to invoke sympathy), good interviewing technique demands closer review and follow-up to explain the anomaly.

10

Understanding Body Language and the Polygraph

Daniel H. Baxter
Polygraph Technical Director

W hen one of the authors asked me if I was interested in writing a chapter about my use of observing body language during interviews, I was somewhat taken aback and initially hesitant. It occurred to me that for at least the first 24 years of my 35-plus years of interviewing, I did not particularly concentrate on a person's body language but was more concerned about what I was asking and what the other person was saying. This self-absorption first appeared when I was a police officer interviewing people suspected of committing a crime, and it continued when I started working for the Department of Defense conducting polygraph examinations on individuals being processed for a security clearance. The polygraph is the formal name of the device commonly known (but not quite accurately) as the lie detector machine.

I suspect my initial introduction to law enforcement created the mind-set that observing a person's microexpressions or subtle movements was not that important during an interview. I recall a time as a police cadet when I watched some detectives interview a suspect. I was intrigued by the way they spoke to him and obtained a confession even though he initially denied being involved. When I asked them what they did to get the confession, the detectives told me that they lied to the guy and told him that they had a witness. I was amazed that someone could be so gullible to admit to something that he knew would possibly get him jail time.

Then in January 1975, I attended a six-month police academy, and during the course of instruction I learned how to fire a weapon, employ self-defense tactics, and write a report. I cannot recall the instructors spending one minute teaching us how to interview. I had to assume that interviewing was something everyone knew how to do before becoming an officer, thus it was unnecessary to teach.

As a street officer, I used some observational techniques, but these were more for safety than for obtaining information. We were taught to watch a person's hands for any weapons or movements to avoid being struck, but it wasn't until around 1978 that I even heard of anyone teaching nonverbal behavior. Two of our detectives went to a class (I recall that it was a one-day seminar), and they came back and provided the information to the uniformed officers. The information was very elementary. For example, the detectives told us that when people fold their arms or they raise their foot so the investigator can see the sole of their shoe, then they are using blocking mechanisms. Also, if someone touches his or her nose while the officer is talking, then the person believes that the investigator's story or statement "stinks." This was my only introduction to observing body language until the late 1990s.

I was thus armed with this information, in addition to what I learned as a police cadet, when I received my transfer to the detective division. I now felt that I was prepared to interrogate and get a confession from anyone as needed. Reality then intervened. One of my first investigations involved a 19-year-old male who had sold some stolen jewelry. Unfortunately for him, at the time, all of the pawn shops were required to keep a record of all of their transactions, and I was able to obtain the individual's name and address. Upon arresting him for the possession of stolen property, I read him his Miranda rights, and he agreed to talk to me. He claimed that he "found" the items and just decided to sell them. Using all of the interview techniques that I had learned from my co-workers, I handed him a telephone and told him to call his mother and arrange for her to bring him his toothbrush and some clean underwear. When he asked me why, I told him I didn't believe him, and he was going to jail.

To my shock, he did not make the phone call but immediately asked if he could make a deal with me. He eventually admitted to burglarizing over a dozen houses and stated that he still had some stolen property at his house. After this, I felt that I could do no wrong, and all I needed to do was to threaten to put the person in jail and he or she would confess to the crime. It sounds simple, and it did not take much work or imagination on my part. Sadly, it did not work that often. One individual who happened to have an extensive criminal record and had been in prison a good portion of his life challenged me on my threat, and when I couldn't produce evidence, he walked out of the interview smiling. It was then that I knew I had to learn to interview better, but in the early 1980s there were not many schools or even seminars teaching interviewing skills, with one exception—and that school did not place much emphasis on nonverbal behavior.

My real introduction to understanding body language actually came in 1984 when I attended the National Academy for Polygraph Sciences, taught by Richard O. Arthur. The school taught police officers how to not only conduct a polygraph examination, but also how to interview and to make judgments based on observations. Mr. Arthur was a firm believer that individuals will give off signals of distress or deception throughout the pretest interview. He stressed that it was extremely important to watch the examinee's behavior from the time he or she enters the office through the pretest interview. He told us to observe how the individual acts (look for gross body shifts, eye movements, face twitching, and self-touching) when asked nonthreatening questions and use that as a baseline of "normal" or "truthful" behavior. Then as the examiner reviews the case facts, he or she needs to look for inconsistency between the previously observed baseline responses and compare them to how the individual verbally and bodily responded to the more threatening questions. The polygraph examination then is used as a tool to confirm what the examiner initially observed and heard. Unfortunately, Mr. Arthur never really provided any in-depth ideas of what to look for. He just wanted his students to understand that when a person behaves in an unusual way the interviewer needs to investigate it.

Using my newfound interviewing tool, I started conducting polygraph examinations with various crimes. Although I still relied on the results of the polygraph to interrogate suspects when the charts indicated "deception" (it is now believed that the polygraph does not detect deception but rather records emotional responses to significant issues), I was now more in-tune with what the person was expressing via nonverbal communication. One such case I still vividly recall involved a father who was suspected of poisoning his 15-year-old daughter. The investigator learned that the father was the only other person at home when the daughter started to convulse, clutching her throat, and had to be transported to the hospital. The doctors advised the investigator that the girl's larynx was burned so severely that she probably would not be able to speak again. The father denied having any knowledge of how his daughter was injured and agreed to take a polygraph examination.

At the outset of the interview, I learned that the father worked the night shift at the local automotive plant and that his marriage was not stable. I asked him about the day in question, and he claimed to have been drinking most of the day and could not remember anything other than falling asleep on the couch and waking to his daughter's screams. When he was telling his story, I did something that I usually did not do. I watched his face and his hands. To my amazement, I felt that I was seeing something in his expressions that told me there was more to the story than what he was telling me. To this date, I cannot tell you exactly what I saw, but in recalling that interview, I remembered the look in his eyes. I like to believe that it was guilt, shame, regret, sadness, or whatever you want to call it, but it was there.

I did not interrupt or question anything he had to say at that time. Once he stopped talking, all I said was, "There is something about what happened you haven't told me, but I know you want to." With just a little lean in, dropping my head so as to not make much eye contact, and lowering my voice, I told him that I knew he was in pain and wanted to talk about the incident. Without any further pushing, he then told me that he and his wife had been having marital problems, and he wanted to get back at her in some way. That morning she made a large pot of soup and left it on the stove for their daughter to eat when she came home from school. According to the father, he had been drinking and decided that he wanted to spoil the soup and poured a can of liquid drain cleaner into it. He then fell asleep and did not awake until hearing his daughter's screams. After calling for the ambulance, he realized what he had done and disposed of the can, which the investigators never found. Without conducting a polygraph examination or using the tactics that I learned earlier in my police career (lying about non-existent evidence or threatening jail time), I was able to resolve the crime within a matter of two hours. To this date, I attribute getting the confession not to my interviewing skills, but to observing and understanding that something was causing his unusual nonverbal behavior when discussing the events of the day. I also felt that he read my body language and sensed that I understood what he was going through, thus making him more open to talking about the incident.

There were other occasions as a police detective when I began to use the observational method to try to elicit information, but I never felt comfortable in making a judgment on someone's guilt or innocence based solely on my seeing something that I could not label. In 1987 I decided to leave the police force to work for the Department of Defense as a polygraph examiner. Like everyone before me, I was required to attend an 8-week "Special

Agent" course where we learned about the mission of the agency and the different offices within the Office of Security. Part of the training involved how to interview sources and applicants (one or two days' worth of mock interviews with other students). As with my police academy training, no instructor taught the class anything about nonverbal behavior, but the main emphasis was on using an interrogation technique that emphasized obtaining confessions by employing various steps, although this model of interrogation focused more on the verbal exchanges than the nonverbal behaviors.

Because of my police experience, I quickly became known for my interrogations and obtaining information from reluctant examinees. I soon forgot about using any of my observational powers and fell into the trap of relying on the way the person verbally responded to my questions and the "physiological reactions" recorded on the polygraph. To say I was an aggressive interviewer would be putting it mildly. I did not have any problem confronting someone on any issue in order to obtain the undisclosed information. I did this by repositioning myself and going face to face and knee to knee, which is still a practice with most interrogators. I used every interrogation tool in the book with the exception of observing nonverbal behavior, which, in hindsight, may have led me to the wrong conclusion in some interviews.

I continued to rely on what I felt were my proven interviewing methods until the late 1990s. My aggressive style worked to my advantage particularly in one investigation where numerous employees were implicated in stealing tens of thousands of dollars worth of property from the US Government. I was able to obtain theft confessions from 12 of the 13 individuals using the "in your face," "you are going to jail" system that I grew up with professionally. But two of the interviews stick with me to this day. The first involved the main suspect who stole the most property. I was able to get him to talk about his involvement using my direct questioning technique and downplaying the consequences. He told me about all of the items he stole and identified the others who were involved. At one point he started to cry, and he talked about how remorseful he was in becoming involved in the thefts and stated that he only did it so others on his shift would like him. Here is one time when I felt sympathy for a suspect and bought his story. I eventually told my management that he had confessed to everything that he had stolen. Regretfully, he lied, and the next day he came in and told another investigator about additional items that he had stolen. This revelation caused me great anguish, and I vowed not to let my personal feelings influence me in any future interviews I conducted.

The other memorable interview involved the only female suspect in this investigation who never did confess. I was able to get 12 people to discuss their involvement, but why not this 13th person? Surely she was involved because she was implicated by the others, but no matter what I said or did, she refused to talk. I was later told that she mentioned to a friend that she did not like the way I spoke to her and felt my demeanor was intimidating.

No matter, I felt justified in using my tactics because we were able to retrieve the majority of stolen property and have the thieves arrested or fired. As a result of my "success," I was asked to prepare a one-day course on interviewing for the new Special Agent's class. I initially started to prepare for the class by concentrating on how to ask the "right" questions and getting the interviewee to talk. I chose to start here because I was still reluctant to buy into the utility of nonverbal assessment, mainly because I really did not understand what I was seeing, nor was I able to put into context the responses I knew I was observing. I had recognized that a change in the person's baseline nonverbal behavior was important but still did not recognize the specific meaning behind it.

During this same time I was asked to conduct a polygraph examination on a male job applicant. Initially the interview seemed very benign, with no real concerns being raised. He appeared to be attentive and very cooperative. His nonverbal behavior (sitting straight up, leaning forward as I spoke, great eye contact, spontaneous responses to my questions, and what appeared to be a sincere smile) were excellent, and I felt very comfortable talking with him. These were all positive baseline behaviors that I look for when interviewing someone, and I believed that this interview was going to go well. As I went through the examination issues with the applicant, I pretested a question regarding his involvement in any serious crime. As I described that this question included sexual misconduct, the man immediately hesitated, looked away, and appeared to grab the chair arms more tightly. These are things that I had not seen him do before. It was a change in his baseline behavior, and somehow I knew that this was significant since it appeared that he was under some type of stress when answering this particular issue. Even to this day, I am not sure if he was experiencing sadness, fear, surprise, or a little bit of each in regard to being questioned about his sexual activity, but it was obvious he did not like the topic. I immediately asked him what he was thinking, and after some delay he said that his teenaged stepdaughter "may" have seen him undressing. I questioned him about how that could have happened, and he provided an explanation that his bedroom door was open one time while he was undressing, and he noticed that she was standing near the opening. I asked him if he left the door open on purpose, which he denied. He claimed that this was the only time it occurred, and he only thought about it when I asked about any illegal sexual activity. During this pretest interview, I continued to suspect that he was withholding more information about the incident or incidents, but I did not want to bias the examination so I did not directly press him on the issue.

In the polygraph examination, the applicant exhibited significant physiological reactions to the question about having involvement in serious criminal activity. Again he denied any involvement, but, as before, his demeanor—drooping head, lowered voice, and the lack of any gestures— told me that something was there driving that unusual behavior pattern. Unlike my past interviewing behavior, I stayed behind the desk and starting talking to him about how sometimes good people get caught up in bad situations. I provided him some reassurances that everything could be resolved, but he had to come to grips with the fact that some activity had occurred. I now was giving him the opportunity to clarify it for me as well as for the staff who would recommend for or against his application.

At this point I believe he still hadn't decided whether to discuss the issue because he would not make any eye contact and only occasionally nodded to my questions. Everything about his demeanor told me that he wanted to talk about what happened; he neither interrupted me nor showed any sudden body movements that suggested he wanted to leave. Yet he did not talk about any other incidents of sexual abuse. I'm not sure what I said or did, but suddenly he mentioned that he intentionally left his bedroom door open while undressing so his stepdaughter would see him naked. I simply followed this up by asking, "What else?" After a few moments of silence on both of our parts, I heard him say that he had actually "peeked" into her bedroom and watched her undress. During these disclosures his nonverbal behaviors had suddenly changed. He was looking at me directly, again started to use gestures, which were there during our initial conversation but absent when I first brought up the sexual crime issue, and his speech, although still low in pitch, was clear with no hesitation.

At this point I realized that he was ready to talk more about his sexual proclivity toward his stepdaughter. Without me intensifying my approach— in fact, I leaned back and acted like this behavior was nothing of major consequence—he then admitted that he had been videotaping his stepdaughter while she was in the bathroom. He claimed that he never sexually touched her, but he just liked looking at her naked. Again I asked the question, "What else?" and again his prior behavior pattern of no eye contact and head dropping returned. It took a stretch of silence on both of our parts, but he finally admitted to sexually assaulting his 1-year-old adopted daughter. This had been occurring right up to the time of the polygraph examination.

After he acknowledged sexually abusing his daughter, I observed what appeared to be relief on his part. He sat up straight, looked directly at me, and in a clear voice stated that he knew what he had been doing was wrong and he needed help. I believe my success in obtaining the information was a direct result of me observing the nonverbal change in his behavior when I questioned him about having any involvement in serious criminal activity. If I had not been looking at him or had not recognized that change in his baseline, I am sure that I would not have persisted in probing him on that topic, which in turn revealed this horribly damning information. What this means is that his own body revealed his (up until then) secret motivations through his reactions to questions pertinent to those motivations; I was able to capture the subtle physiological changes through my own eyes.

I realized that observing both nonverbal and verbal behavior is a powerful tool. I decided that I needed to understand what I was seeing during my interviews as well as understand what I might be missing to help me identify emotions or other reactions that could help me and others obtain the truth. I started reading books by researchers and practitioners who have been investigating body language. Many of these individuals are well known in the communication community, such as Paul Ekman, Robert Cialdini, and Desmond Morris. Practitioners including Joe Navarro and Wendall Rudicille provided real-life experiences related to what I needed to know. Finally, talking to and working alongside university researchers, such as Mark Frank, Jennifer Vendemia, Tim Levine, Pete Blair, Judee Burgoon, and a host of others has given me a new perspective on the art of observing nonverbal behavior and the role it has in interviews. As Mark Frank once told me, there is no Pinocchio effect when it comes to detecting deception. The polygraph is a good tool that can help someone detect deception, but it is only a tool. Even as an examiner of 27 years, I am under no illusion that the polygraph is 100% accurate in detecting deception. So there needs to be alternatives to assist investigators in the pursuit of facts.

I feel that by not using my powers of observation during the first 25 years of my investigative career, I may have missed out on chances to resolve some criminal acts (or at least made my interviews easier). I believe that anyone involved in the art of interviewing (both law enforcement and individuals who are in a position to hire someone) needs to be aware of how people respond nonverbally to questions. Although changes in behavior may not be a sign of deception, they are usually a sign that some internal body process has triggered some reaction—and the cause of that trigger needs to be identified through follow-up questions. Research says that when people talk, they typically make eye contact with the receiver between 25% and 65% of the time. Thus, if interviewers are looking away 35% to 75% of the time while they talk, they will miss the nonverbal changes that could signal an opportunity to gather more accurate information. With these statistics in mind, investigators or interviewers should learn to increase their eye contact and try to identify key nonverbal cues in the person they interview and ascertain why that individual showed those nonverbal cues.

This can only happen through education, training, and practice. With that as a goal, I have been able to modify the training program for my agency, and it now places a greater emphasis on observing nonverbal behavior. In my experience, observing the individual's body posture at the beginning of the interview is a key to understanding if the person is feeling somewhat relaxed or stressed. Does the individual sit up straight and lean in or slouch and lean away? I then look at the eyes and determine if there is a pattern to their gaze time. Does it change when he or she is talking, listening, or thinking? If this happens, is it because the person is nervous, afraid, or experiencing some sadness due to some life issue that may not be related to the area under investigation? This is an area where I have to be careful and rely on observing baseline behavior before addressing the topic under investigation. Many of the individuals I have interviewed have tried to stare me down when questioned about a sensitive topic, but on other occasions some individuals have diverted their eye contact. Unfortunately, these types of eye behavior occur with both the truthful and deceptive individuals so I have been hesitant to totally rely on eye contact as a determinate of honesty.

Most of us still may not be able to identify all possible useful behavioral reactions ranging from the seven universally recognized emotions (anger, contempt, disgust, fear, happiness, sadness, and surprise) to a change in the amount of time a person takes to respond to a question, but if an investigator noticed these changes at a certain time during questioning, then the interviewer should seek to uncover why the change occurred. It might be something innocent like an embarrassing incident in a high school gym locker room, or it may be something much more serious, like the applicant described earlier who was molesting his stepdaughter. But one will only know by observing and then asking follow-up questions.

11

Nonverbal Behavior in the Courtroom

Scott Brownell
12th Judicial Circuit, State of Florida

In court we trial judges see dozens, if not hundreds, of different faces each week. Consciously or not, we read cues from their facial expressions, like a salesperson does with customers, like co-workers do with one another, like friends do when they gossip. Unfortunately, we judges are as accurate at reading the emotions on the face of another as we are at predicting a coin toss. We need to improve our accuracy for two reasons: first, although we make some of our decisions based on hard evidence like tire marks and blood tests, and also consider decisions in past cases and written memoranda, for the most part we rely on testimony and oral argument presented from the faces we see. Thus, accuracy in our determination of whose words are more reliable and honest is very valuable. Second, it seems that these days fewer people come to court with a lawyer (referred to as a *pro se* litigant). People in court without counsel frequently misinterpret the court's rulings and procedures. This appears to be true whether they win or lose. In addition, people appearing without counsel feel uncomfortable saying to the court what they are actually feeling. Nevertheless, they harbor those feelings, good or bad, for years. With no lawyer to interpret the court's actions, the person's perception of fairness or unfairness, accurate or not, comes from his or her own expectancies of what should have happened. Without a clear understanding of how the court's actions relate to those expectancies, the public's trust in the court system can be injured. Learning when and how to clarify rulings, decisions, and procedures is a valuable skill for a trial judge.

The Deceitful Witness

"Calvin," the defendant in a juvenile delinquency case, was on the witness stand, testifying in defense of three burglary charges. After direct examination from his own lawyer and a few preliminary cross-examination questions, the prosecutor asked him, "Why were you riding your bike through that neighborhood? You don't live anywhere near there, do you?"

The 15-year-old defendant confidently answered, "I was just on my way to my friend Bobby's house. I live straight down that way (points south on the map in evidence), and Bobby's house is right up this way (points north), and I just rode up this here street to get there. So I was on my bike riding to Bobby's and saw them two police cars pull up behind me on the street, and I saw the cop lights on so I stopped right up here at the end of the street. You know . . . to see what they was doing. And after a few minutes they come up to me, and then they arrest me."

Calvin was arrested for the burglary of three houses on this block of nearly identical homes. At the rear of each house was a concrete slab leading to a sliding glass door.

Because an alarm sounded in a fourth house, the police were called. They arrived at the scene about 4 minutes later and shut off the alarm. In their investigation they found three pillowcases neatly tied off, containing stolen electronics and jewelry and resting on the concrete slabs behind three other houses on that side of the street.

The arresting officer testified that it was very unusual for a burglar to steal from a home and leave the stolen items at the scene of the crime. It later made sense when he also testified that anyone could run or ride a bike through the backyards of these houses, pick up the bags, and leave the neighborhood without being seen from the street. Apparently all four homes, three with the pillowcases of stolen goods and one with the alarm, were broken into by cutting some screens and prying open the sliding glass doors. The officer testified that it took him about 3 minutes to walk from one end of this street to the other, and it would have taken less than a minute to ride a bike that distance. Calvin was arrested at the end of the same street a few houses past the home where the alarm had sounded. The officer testified that the burglaries seemed well planned and were apparently interrupted by the alarm.

Why is this important? During this testimony from the witness stand, I was watching Calvin's face. Because the juvenile delinquency trial in Florida has no jury, I am also the finder of fact. From my experience of several hundred such trials, I expected this teenager's face to show some expressions of anxiousness, anger, nervousness, or at least discomfort while testifying. But for the most part, he showed no emotion. It was as if he were reporting someone else's story. That got my attention. And then, during cross-examination by the prosecutor, when Calvin said, "And they come up to me and then they arrest me," his face changed. He had just the slightest bit of a look that reminded me of a smile. Immediately, I remembered "duper's delight."

"Duper's delight," a term coined by Professor Paul Ekman, had been explained and demonstrated in a Florida judicial education program presented by Professor Maureen O'Sullivan, not long before Calvin's trial. So duper's delight was still fresh in my mind, as was her explanation of "leakage." Before she retired, Professor O'Sullivan taught at the University of San Francisco and did research with her colleagues, professors Paul Ekman, David Matsumoto, and Mark Frank. In detecting deception, O'Sullivan advised that one must watch the face carefully and note when a facial expression, which represents a feeling, doesn't match the words spoken. This mismatch of words and expressions is a clue to possible deception. She used video recordings to demonstrate some persons who were in the act of lying. In their lies, some had an emotional expression quickly pass over their face. This was called a microexpression, and because it was not intended to be seen, it was also referred to as leakage. Finally, I recalled that one single event of leakage does not establish deception with certainty, but it does suggest that more questions should be asked. And if one sees more leakage, more microexpressions of emotions that don't fit the words, deception becomes easier to spot. And what is more useful to a trial judge than detecting deceit in the courtroom?

Professor O'Sullivan was careful to remind us that detecting leakage takes concentration and that identifying micro or fragmentary emotions on someone's face takes study and practice. She reminded us that without concentration, study, and practice, judges are no better at detecting lies than predicting the coin flip, just like almost everyone else.

Those were the basics. From this information, and after doing her recommended reading and practicing a little with my children and my wife, I became comfortable identifying two of the seven universal facial expressions of emotions. One was easy; the genuine, as opposed to the fake, smile. The eyes and muscles around the eyes tell us which is which. The microexpression of the leaked smile has the same curl of the corners of the mouth upward and the same eye action, but less so, and much quicker. The other emotional expression I was consistently identifying was the look of worry or concern, otherwise known as sadness or distress (see Chapter 2).

In Calvin's testimony, his emotion, a beginning of a smile, a happy, though quickly suppressed expression, did not match his words: "They just arrested me." I immediately asked myself, "Who, in the middle of a trial, accused of crimes he did not commit and who faces punishment he does not deserve, would show no emotion while he denied the crimes and tried to hide a smile as he said, ' . . . they come up to me and then they arrest me?'" One reasonable answer—a teenager who is enjoying pulling one over on people of authority; a person who is confident of his own success. Calvin now had my undivided attention.

The prosecutor, either skillfully or luckily, then asked, "You were arrested at the end of that street . . . so, where had you *just* come from?" And there it was. Clear as day. In an instant, Calvin's eyebrows moved up, and the inside corners of the eyebrows came almost together in what is described in Chapter 2 on facial expressions as *fear, worry, and apprehension* (see Figure 2.1). Professor O'Sullivan described it as the "look of concern and worry."

In his few minutes of testimony, while he was answering questions about this very serious problem he was facing, he had shown no worry, no concern, no anger or frustration, and no emotions. But it seemed that the last question surprised him. Unlike the other questions, he apparently had not planned his response to "Where had you *just* come from?" He had to make up his answer on the fly. If he had "just come from" his home, he would have said so and not leaked a look of worry or concern. However, if he had just come from the house with the alarm, he definitely would not want me to know. And as it turned out, there were several more surprise questions, followed by the leakage of that same look of worry and concern. He was surprised by questions so frequently that his look of worry and apprehension finally changed to a genuine expression of a sad resignation. An excellent photo of the sad resignation face is found in Figure 2.1 of Chapter 2. This last facial expression was not leaked but, rather, was quite obvious to see. The additional questions for which he was not prepared included, "Did you ever ride your bike behind those houses?" *Leakage.* "Were you riding your bike on the street when the alarm first went off?" "Yeah." "So you rode to the end of the street and waited for 3 or 4 minutes waiting for the police to arrive, didn't you?" *Leakage.* "You heard that alarm when you were behind that house, didn't you?" *Leakage.* "Why didn't you stop when you heard the alarm?" *Sad resignation.* "But the alarm had been going off for more than 3 minutes before the police came. Why didn't you keep riding to your friend's house?" *Resignation.* "Did any of the other houses have alarms?" "No. Well, I guess not." *Resignation.* After his testimony and the other evidence, which included a screwdriver found in his pocket, all of which was circumstantial, this clever, well-organized burglar was convicted.

I do not describe this trial experience to convince you that people who lie in court are easy to spot. I use it to demonstrate the possibility and genuine judicial value of improving this nonjudicial skill. Accurately reading emotions in the face of this juvenile and knowing what to do with that information improved the quality of my work, at least in this particular pursuit of justice. Without Calvin's conviction, the occupants of these homes would not have the comfort of knowing who broke into their homes, knowing that this child will pay for the necessary repairs, will apologize to them, and will be supervised closely until he is 19 or until he convinces the court that probation is no longer necessary. A couple of weeks later we held the disposition hearing. After I spent a minute or two explaining to Calvin why I didn't believe his testimony, he smiled. It was not a leaked microsmile. It was real. He said, "You are good, Judge—I never thought I'd lose." Nice kid. Lousy liar.

This suggests to the trial judge an interesting idea: rearrange your courtroom a bit. If you make some minor modifications to the hearing procedure and perhaps to the structure of the courtroom, you will be able to see the entire face of a witness. Our witness boxes are set 3 feet (1 meter) to our left, slightly below and a bit ahead of our spot at the bench. This arrangement provides a nice witness profile, but no amount of chair swiveling will give one the face-to-face view one needs for a full view of the face of the witness. Without such a view, facial expressions are very difficult to identify. For our delinquency courtroom, which has no jury box, our maintenance folks built a moveable witness stand that corrects this shortcoming. For those nonjury hearings held in the courtrooms with a jury box, I simply require that the witness be seated in the front corner of the jury box closest to the bench. Besides the witnesses, occasionally even lawyers and jurors speak words that do not match the emotions they reveal on their faces. Even they lie sometimes—not big lies, not outright lies, but still not complete honesty. With witnesses seated in the corner of the jury box, or with lawyers and jurors, the simple swivel of the chair gives one a face-to-face view.

The Party Without a Lawyer

Serving in the family division, I announced my ruling. "I am granting the restraining order. This is what that means: I am ordering that Mr. 'Johnson,' you have no contact with Ms. 'Johnson.' No contact of any kind, do you understand? And you have no contact with the children except as arranged per this order. The children's visitation transfer must occur at the downtown sheriff's office. Mr. Johnson, you must arrange for the visits by calling Ms. Johnson's mother who will contact Ms. Johnson to arrange for the pickup and drop-off of the children at the sheriff's office, and your mother-in-law will inform you of the details. There will be no other visits of any kind without a court order and no overnight visits. Do you have any questions?"

As he fiercely scowled at his wife at the other courtroom table, Mr. Johnson said, "No."

"Ms. Johnson, does this make sense? The evidence today has established that the remedies you requested in your petition should be granted. Do you understand the order?" "Yes." But Ms. Johnson looked at him, then looked down at the floor, and looked up at me and deeply exhaled. There, on her face, was that look of sad resignation, similar to Calvin's look at the end of his testimony.

As every trial judge knows, I had at least two choices here. The first was to accept their answers, call the next case, and enjoy that subtle but warm feeling of accomplishment for a job done promptly and done well. Another option was to invest a few more minutes and ask more questions. Based on some personal data collection, of no scientific value at all, I believe many trial judges place a high value on the "done" in the phrase "a job well done." Trial judges have lots of work to do. Almost all of it is done in the courtroom. For that and many other reasons, closure is a very important work ethic. In addition, although many of our decisions do not make people particularly happy, almost all of our rulings are logical, legal, and fairly reached, and nearly all of our explanations are clear. At least that is what we assume. Ask any judge. Perhaps one out of one hundred might admit to more than a rare moment when these assumptions were not true. And asking more questions does take "done" off the table for a while longer. So, why advocate asking more questions? The answer is that in some circumstances justice can be better served by doing exactly that.

Competing with the work ethic of "done" is the efficiency work ethic described as "never do the same hearing twice, when once will do." The risk for multiple hearings to occur is higher when a person without a lawyer has to draft pleadings and make the arguments. This person doesn't always ask for what he or she really wants, doesn't always understand why he or she won or lost, and doesn't always know what his or her options were. For those and many other reasons, these individuals may come back more than once to resolve their issue.

Based on that possibility, I looked at each face in the Johnson family to see if emotional expressions matched the circumstances. Although his expression seemed to match his words, hers did not. Her expressions had at least two possible meanings: "I am sad, but at least it's over" and the one that struck me as more likely, "I didn't know this is what you would do, but maybe I can get some money and come back another time with a lawyer to help me." She looked down, and she looked resigned and unhappy. She just "won" her hearing but showed no expression of relief, accomplishment, or even of some comfort. My experience is that those are the more commonly expressed feelings of litigants in her position. I expected to see evidence of those feelings here. To avoid more hearings I decided to ask more questions.

One quick way to get to the meaning of her facial expressions was to ask these two questions: "Do you feel like I heard what you were saying?" and "Do you feel that I understood what you wanted the court to do?" The first question brought her response, "Yes." But the second brought this answer, "I guess I am not going to get any money from him for the rent. He has to help with money or the kids and me could get evicted. And I just want him to get help, not to cut him off from my children. They really love him and will miss him. I am not asking for a divorce. I just think we can work this out if he will just get some help." Her short answers revealed that the court's solution of the safety problem created three more issues: a financial crisis, an overly strict visitation decision, and her desire for reconciliation if he can overcome his behavioral problems. It took only a few more minutes to rewrite the order, make the appropriate referrals, adjust the visitation, and still keep the safety issue front and center.

Spending these few extra minutes of court time made clear her need for financial support and therapy treatment that she could not articulate in her petition. It also clarified the children's needs for more contact with the father. It parenthetically addressed my need to accomplish in one hearing what might have taken two or three. In the off chance that you are wondering if those are the only reasons to carefully watch the litigants' faces in court, I suggest one more.

The judicial branch does not enforce its orders. People comply with them voluntarily, albeit unhappily, or they are forced to do so by the executive branch. As long as the public holds the judges and the system in high esteem, enforcement is not the issue it has become in countries where the public has little respect for the judicial system.

A multiyear study of the public's perception of California's trial court system (Rottman, 2005) provides a large body of information on the public's perceptions of the state's trial courts. One of its major findings is relevant to this notion of paying attention to the faces of the *pro se* litigants.

The report findings established that

> procedural fairness, the sense that decisions have been made through processes that are fair, is the strongest predictor by far of whether members of the public approve of or have confidence in the California courts. Policies that promote a sense of procedural fairness are the vehicle with the greatest potential to change how the public views the state's courts and how litigants respond to court decisions. (Part I, p. 24)

Until there is research to the contrary, I am prepared to assume this is true of Florida courts as well. Add to that the research from Professor Mac O'Barr from Duke University, who was also a presenter to Florida judges (e.g., Conley & O'Barr, 1988). His research strongly suggests that the public's perception of the court system is less driven by winning or losing than by the feeling that they were heard, understood, and permitted to say what they needed to say, i.e., procedural fairness.

As time-consuming as that sounds to the busy trial judge, in the cases where the message radiating from the face of the litigant does not fit the words said or the situation, it is a small investment with potentially enormous benefits to ask the questions, "Do you feel that I heard what you wanted to say?" and "Do you feel I understood what you wanted the court to do?" Without changing the ruling, the responses may establish a genuine need for the judge to clarify, explain, or address the litigant's misunderstandings or wrong assumptions. This is a small change of procedure in a busy courtroom day that can improve the public's perception of judicial fairness, at least for that person, on that day, in that small corner of the third branch of government, and there are also those added benefits for the trial judge.

References

Conley, J. M., & O'Barr, W. M. (1988). Fundamentals of jurisprudence: An ethnography of judicial decision making in informal courts. *The North Carolina Law Review, 66*, 467.

Rottman, D. B. (2005). *Trust and confidence in the California courts.* Available at http://www.courts.ca.gov/5275.htm.

12

Persuasion, Negotiation, and the Law

Clark Freshman
University of California,
Hastings College of Law

Lawyers succeed largely by how well they negotiate and persuade. Therefore, *much* of what works for lawyers, including how they detect lies and persuade, will work for others, be they called investigators, salespeople, lobbyists, or journalists. Though I am a professor of law to aspiring lawyers, those who attend my seminars on lie detection include executives, investigators, personal coaches, and documentary filmmakers. This chapter illustrates several ways lawyers and negotiators may succeed in both formal processes, like court, and less formal contexts, such as everyday employment negotiations, mediations, and arbitrations. In all contexts, the successful lawyer or negotiator may use nonverbal awareness to improve results in several ways: identifying emotions more likely to lead to successful results, selecting specific decision makers (be they jurors or particular managers), gauging how well certain tactics (such as active listening) work with particular people, and assessing how well alternative arguments work. Finally, of course, they may use nonverbal information to get more correct information by identifying outright lies, incomplete information, and misunderstanding.

Basic Concepts

We begin with some basic concepts and then examine a range of illustrations. Based on my experience teaching thousands of lawyers, judges, and negotiators, the most important idea to learn is a correct focus on two concepts: *sweet spots* and *soft spots*. Sweet spots indicate signs of some combination of positive emotion, rapport, and trust. This can be as simple as the presence of a true enjoyment smile, the kind involving not merely the lower part of the face but the muscles surrounding the eyes as well (Duchenne, 1862/1990; see Chapter 2 on the face). It can also involve tracking or mirroring of the body movements, voice, and speech patterns of someone else (Bernieri & Gillis, 1995; see also Chapter 4). As we will see in detail, sweet spots typically suggest that we have set a context more likely to lead to success.

The flip side to sweet spots, *soft* spots include signs of emotions usually unhelpful in negotiations, such as anger and contempt or heightened thinking. Soft spots and "hot spots" (see Chapter 6 on deception) deserve our attention as sources of valuable information, but they do not necessarily indicate that someone is lying. As others indicate, the presence of soft spots or hot spots makes deception a more likely possibility, and lawyers may often treat them with suspicion. As we will see, because these soft spots may not be lies, lawyers might sometimes better respond with compassion and empathy. (Outside the specific context of nonverbal communication and deception, therapeutic jurisprudence uses soft spots to refer to signs of emotion that may be opportunities for a lawyer to better align with a client through understanding and compassion [Winick, 1998].)

Sweet and Soft Spots in Action

Whatever the label we use, facial expression can be one primary source of soft spots and sweet spots. Raising the inner eyebrows alone may reliably reveal distress. Emotional soft spots can also include changes in voice volume, or cracking of the voice, or changes in posture, such as the fear that leaning back sometimes indicates (see Chapters 3 and 4 on the voice and gestures). Soft spots also consist of signs of heightened cognitive load—that is, the person is having to think or process information too hard for the circumstances (see Chapter 6 on deception). Some soft spots may include various ways of breaking a person's normal style of eye contact, increased speech errors, and so on (see Chapters 3 and 6 on the voice and deception).

Turning from these core concepts to illustrations, let us see first how soft spots may be ambiguous. Imagine that a lawyer represents a woman suing for employment discrimination, and the lawyer wants to find out if other employees have sued the firm. A lawyer would question various managers under oath at a deposition. Suppose the lawyer asks, "How many similar complaints have you had?" If the person looks up and pauses, there are many possibilities. Perhaps the person is just anxious from the deposition; perhaps the person is genuinely not sure if "complaints" means the many times people have told him they were sexually harassed but never filed a formal "complaint" in court; perhaps the person knows of complaints by women for lower pay but not harassment; perhaps the person knows of complaints by African American men. The lawyer would be interested in all of this information (Freshman, 2000), but the witness might sincerely and innocently not know what was intended—or the witness might know what the lawyer wants but be looking for an excuse not to share the information. If the lawyer listens only to the words, the lawyer might rush on to another question. If the lawyer catches the soft spots, however, the lawyer might ask follow-up questions and get the information. Or a lawyer might get this information from asking more targeted questions to other witnesses or requesting different documents.

So, too, soft spots in a negotiation may also be ambiguous. For example, many lawyers try to write in "most favored nation" provisions that say that a client gets treated at least as well as others. A highly desirable job candidate might insist that he or she have such a clause so no one ever gets higher pay or more vacation than this person, and if others get such better treatment, then he or she automatically gets the same. A lawyer may find himself or herself discussing a "typical" clause labeled "most favored nation" and see changes in eye contact. This could mean that the person really intends to breach this clause by giving someone else better terms, but it could also just mean that the person doesn't understand the legal jargon. In either case, the lawyer *might* want to ask additional questions or revise the contract language so it is more likely the person would honor the clause or, at least, more clearly have to pay if caught.

In part because of their ambiguous nature, soft spots not only may identify times to be more suspicious or vigilant but also times to be more compassionate. One day, on a break from teaching my law school class, I saw a microexpression of distress cross a familiar student's face. I crouched down and asked, "How's it going?" She burst into tears and gave me her cell phone. Her boyfriend had just broken up with her—by text. We sat quietly for a few moments, and I offered to excuse her from class. So, too, the lawyer may use awareness of soft spots to show compassion for a client, be it the stereotypical upset person in a marital divorce or one in the often equally emotional separation of previous business collaborators (Freshman, 2010; Winick, 1998).

So, too, judges and other officials may find compassion often the most appropriate response. When I taught the national meeting of federal administrative law judges, the organizer and I agreed on the title: "Spotting Lies—With Compassion." In that group, judges often evaluated the claims of those seeking disability from severe injuries. After a long discussion with the group's president, I realized the judges understood that the hearings might prove distressful for people, but the people might not say they were in distress. Once the judges learned about microexpressions of emotion, however, they could recognize these times. So, too, the judges might understand why slower answers might reflect the cognitive load from intense emotion rather than intentional lying.

Further Applications of Nonverbal Communication

With the understanding that nonverbal information may often have ambiguity, we can see how it may be valuable in a number of distinct ways. In negotiation settings, the mere emotion itself, regardless of whatever other information it reveals, may sometimes be quite helpful. Although interpreting deeper meanings from emotional clues may be valuable, systematic research across a range of methods shows that negotiators get better results when there is more positive and less negative emotion (Freshman, Hayes, & Feldman, 2001). When there is negative emotion, negotiators are more likely to threaten, lie, and break agreements (Forgas, 1998). Researchers have induced positive emotions with generally pleasant interventions (chocolate, music, scent) and negative ones with generally negative interventions (such as negative feedback; see Freshman et al., 2001).

All these studies show that emotion is important and give some clues about what induces different emotions in general (which music, which videos, which scents), but nonverbal awareness lets the negotiator customize behaviors to optimize emotion with particular people. In my seminars, I ask questions and let people who volunteer choose a gift: particular chocolate, different hard candy, specific nuts, gift certificates from certain stores, and so on. The point is to let people recognize that the same chocolate that puts some people in a good mood will give others a migraine. When one lawyer enters a negotiation, he or she can do his or her best to find ways to maintain and increase positive emotion and decrease negative emotion for particular people.

Apart from using nonverbal awareness to optimize emotion, all lawyers and negotiators can also use it to identify both tactics and specific arguments that are more likely to persuade particular people, be they clients, judges, or other lawyers. We often want a given result, whether winning a motion or securing a new client, and may have no preference for which tactic or argument works. Nonverbal information may reveal which tactics and substantive arguments may be most likely to succeed, even when other parties do not wish to share this information—or may not fully know their unconscious reactions.

Monitoring effectiveness of tactics. Consider tactics first. Recent negotiation folklore, popularized in such texts as the bestselling *Getting to Yes,* suggests two techniques that sometimes work with some people but alienate others. One technique called active listening involves repeating back what others say (Fisher & Ury, 1991). This supposedly makes the recipient *feel* empathy and, when the recipient disagrees with the active listening, gives the sender more accurate information to modify his or her message. It is a rich theory, but it has mixed support. Marriage researcher John Gottman, famous for predicting which marriages will end within the next 2 years by observing 15 minutes of conversation, finds active listening often does not prevent the couple from divorcing—and may make matters worse (Gottman, 1999). On the other hand, anecdotal reports suggest that some people like active listening. Nonverbal awareness, particularly of the universal emotions in the face (see Chapters 2 and 5 on the face and culture), gives the speaker the opportunity to learn how specific people react to active listening. As the speaker begins saying, "What I hear you saying," he or she might note a subtle facial expression of some universal emotion like contempt or disgust. This gives the speaker the opportunity to try active listening in a different way or simply try another approach.

Option generation. Nonverbal awareness also helps assess option generation. Again, negotiation folklore popularized by *Getting to Yes* suggests that better outcomes occur when one generates many possible options for consideration. According to the coauthor of a book on emotion and negotiation, this kind of option generation *should* generate positive emotion by respecting the universal value of autonomy (Fisher & Shapiro, 2007).

Again, brainstorming and option generation are great theories that may apply to some people, but they run against significant countervailing research on individual differences. In particular, research on choice overload suggests that those who like to do the very best ("maximizers" rather than "satisficers") feel worse when they are given more choices (Iyengar, 2010). That includes a large share of the population. In an academic context, for example, the dean might come up with six different combinations of teaching, different salary options, and so on for each faculty job candidate. With some options, he or she might notice a felt smile; with others, the dean might notice the telltale reliable signs of distress, such as a raising of the inner eyebrows (see Chapter 2 on facial expressions) or signs of heightened cognitive load. This might tell him or her which particular options resonate better with which candidates. For some though, as the dean lists various options, he or she might notice that an individual displays multiple or longer signs of negative emotion. This may mean that all the latter options are ill-suited, or it may mean that the choices overwhelmed the candidate. With other candidates, however, the dean might notice instead enjoyment smiles as the "brainstorming" continues.

Monitoring reactions to specific statements. Nonverbal information also gives important feedback on the tactic of discussion of potential litigation outcomes—also known as "threats." In one extreme example reported in 2011, one company sued another for a statement that one executive at one company said to another. According to the lawsuit, one executive suggested that failure to settle a dispute might endanger the company's government contracts and the scheduled knighting of a company executive by the queen. In marked contrast, many lawyers routinely bargain by discussing what might happen if a disagreement went to court. To many others, such as the company just discussed, such talk may seem like a threat or blackmail. Indeed, some may be so shocked at discussion of what might happen in court that they do not interrupt the discussion until they have become quite engulfed in some combination of anger, disgust, or contempt. The lawyer with nonverbal awareness may notice early subtle emotional expressions that signal the beginning of such feelings before they explode. With such awareness, a lawyer may stop the discussion and move on to another point. In some instances, the lawyer might distance herself or himself from the threat even more conspicuously, such as blaming a difficult or upset client. In other instances, a lawyer might notice that threats elicit fear or even distress in the faces of others. Depending on the nature of the goals of the client and lawyer, this fear might prompt the lawyer to persist in painting a picture of the dangers of court in order to prompt the worried adversary to capitulate or agree to more favorable terms.

Prioritizing arguments. Just as nonverbal information helps with selecting tactics such as active listening, option generation, and threats, it also helps us prioritize substantive arguments and norms. Whether face to face with a potential employee, arguing a motion to a judge, or making a closing argument to a jury, a lawyer often has several different ways to win or otherwise meet his or her interests. The importance of such arguments and their framing is common to both cooperative and problem-solving negotiators, who might call these "objective criteria" (Fisher & Ury, 1991), and competitive negotiators, who might call these "authoritative norms" (Shell, 2000).

Our research at Harvard Business School illustrates how nonverbal awareness can let negotiators recognize which particular arguments, "criteria," and "norms" may persuade particular decision makers (Freshman & Wheeler, 2011). In the study, participants role-played sellers of commercial real estate who negotiated against an actor playing an aggressive negotiator seeking to buy the property. The actor argued that the current tenants might want to buy the property themselves and, if he bought the property, might very well leave—thereby lowering the value of the property. Some participants showed fear or sadness in response to this argument—emotional soft spots. Others showed contempt. Many showed cognitive-load soft spots (Freshman & Wheeler, 2011). In real-life versions of such negotiations, then, buyers might press for even lower prices from those who showed fear, explain their reasoning better to those who showed heightened cognitive load, and, with those who showed anger, move on to another argument—such as prices of comparable properties.

Negotiation and persuasion. Although much of this chapter so far on setting emotional tone and assessing how well tactics and arguments work depends on noticing universal emotions and signs of cognitive load, it is worth noting that more specific cultural nonverbals also inform negotiation and persuasion. In the real estate negotiation study, one buyer showed several facial signs of the universal emotion of contempt and a finger movement that might well look like the emblem gesture of "giving someone the finger" as he put his hand across his face (see Chapter 4 on the body). Emblems are culturally specific body movements with clear symbolic meanings, and some believe that such emblems sometimes represent leakage of concealed or unconscious thoughts (see Chapter 4 on the body and Chapter 6 on deception). We initially interpreted the movement of the finger circling the ear as the emblem for "you're crazy"—consistent with the signs of contempt seen in the face and the finger emblem. If that were the correct interpretation, then one would want to drop this argument. An audience member at a presentation at Columbia Business School, however, noted that this movement was a widely recognized gesture for "I'm thinking about it" in response to offers on the Chicago Mercantile Exchange—something we later verified. If the negotiator really was merely thinking about the argument, then one might very well continue with the argument or repeat it later.

Monitoring others' reactions. Many of the techniques of setting the emotional tone and assessing tactics and arguments work as well in court and other more formal procedures. Indeed, nonverbal communication becomes more important because rules explicitly forbid jurors from providing feedback, and judges vary in how much they reveal before they render a decision. How much mediators and arbitrators speak, and how honestly and completely, varies widely. In any of these settings, often lawyers may win by any one of a number of arguments. For example, a lawyer for a tobacco company might argue that tobacco really does not cause cancer generally, that a particular person suing his client got cancer from some other source, that the cancer did not cause as many damages, or that the claim was brought too late. Judges and juries may reveal sympathy for some arguments, through such subtle nonverbal signs as slight nodding. When lawyers use other arguments, however, judges and juries may also have contempt or disgust revealed through microexpressions of such emotion on their faces.

Identifying deception. Finally, whether in court, at the bargaining table, or elsewhere, a lawyer may use soft spots and sweet spots to get better information—including detecting deliberate lies. As discussed earlier, the presence of what I'm calling soft spots does not prove deception. Although Chapter 6 describes all these issues, let us examine how soft spots may suggest that deception is a more likely possibility in legal contexts. Some soft spots prove more closely related to lying than others, including especially fast expressions of emotions such as fear, distress, or disgust on the face.

Consider two examples of deception in our study of bargaining at Harvard Business School. In one negotiation, one seller indicated that the tenants were very happy with the property and were likely to stay. If this were true, it would make the property more valuable. While he said this, however, he changed his level of eye contact and indeed had several full eye closures. This change in nonverbal behavior suggested some concealment. If it were a real negotiation setting, that reaction should prompt the lawyer to seek more information through further questions to the seller or to contact the tenants directly to confirm their intentions.

Another example illustrated potential deception—perhaps self-deception— about confidence. One negotiator said, "I have a very strong bargaining position." The words seemed confident, but her face revealed reliable signs of distress for just less than one second. As with deception in general, we must also entertain other hypotheses about the cause of the soft spot—in this case, the individual may simply be confused or uncomfortable but still confident and likely to hold out for a very good offer.

Conclusion

This chapter has touched on several applications of nonverbal awareness for lawyers in some detail, but space does not permit a detailed discussion of all of them. Other topics I often teach to law students, lawyers, and negotiators include video analyses that address such questions as these: How may attention to nonverbal awareness be of special benefit to minorities or "outgroups" in identifying stealth bigots or biases? How may attorneys use nonverbal awareness to gain new clients and new business from existing clients? How may attorneys use nonverbal awareness to get better information from clients—and therefore sometimes avoid sanctions for failing to provide relevant information to the court or regulators? How may attorneys identify "problem clients" who may defame them or even sue them?

Although these other questions remain for another time and place, this chapter illustrates many ways that proper attention to nonverbal information may help lawyers and negotiators alike better persuade others and get better information. So, too, the lawyer and negotiator may learn when empathy and compassion may be more appropriate. Lawyers and negotiators may still miss signs of emotion and strained thinking, misinterpret them, or pick strategies that fail. Nonverbal awareness, however, gives them another lens to complement all too frequently taught analytic skills with a rich and growing science of nonverbal awareness rather than mere guesses, habit, or stereotypes. So, too, society and others may benefit as this nonverbal awareness reduces burdens on the court system, makes efficient agreements more likely, and, with luck, helps lawyers to be agents of compassion, at least at times.

References

Bernieri, F., & Gillis, J. S. (1995). Coordinated movement in human interaction. In R. Feldman & R. Rime (Eds.), *Fundamentals of nonverbal behavior* (pp. 401–431). New York: Cambridge University Press.

Duchenne de Boulogne, G. B. (1990). *The mechanism of human facial expression.* New York: Cambridge University Press. (Original work published 1862)

Fisher, R., & Shapiro, D. (2007). *Building agreement: Using emotions as you negotiate.* London: Random House Business.

Fisher, R., & Ury, W. (with Patton, B., Ed.). (1991). *Getting to yes: Negotiating agreement without giving in.* Boston: Houghton Mifflin.

Forgas, J. P. (1998). On feeling good and getting your way: Mood effects on negotiator cognition and bargaining strategies. *Journal of Personality and Social Psychology, 74,* 565–577.

Freshman, C. (2000). Whatever happened to anti-Semitism: How social science theories identify discrimination and promote coalitions between "different" minorities. *Cornell Law Review, 85,* 313–442.

Freshman, C. (2010). Yes, and: Core concerns, internal mindfulness, and external mindfulness for emotional balance, lie detection, and successful negotiation. *Nevada Law Journal, 10,* 365–392.

Freshman, C., Hayes, A., & Feldman, R. (2001). The lawyer-negotiator as mood scientist: What we know and don't know about how mood relates to successful negotiation. *Journal of Dispute Resolution, 2002,* 1–79.

Freshman, C., & Wheeler, M. (2011). *Lies and emotional truthfulness in negotiation: A preliminary empirical report.* Unpublished notes.

Gottman, J. M. (1999). *The marriage clinic: A scientifically-based marital therapy.* New York: W. W. Norton.

Iyengar, S. (2010). *Choice: The decisions we make every day—What they say about us and how we can improve them.* London: Little, Brown.

Shell, G. R. (2000). *Bargaining for advantage: Negotiation strategies for reasonable people.* London: Penguin.

Winick, B. J. (1998). Client denial and resistance in the advance directive context: Reflections on how attorneys can identify and deal with a psycholegal soft spot. *Psychology, Public Policy, and Law, 4,* 901–919.

13

Negotiation and Nonverbal Communication

Andrew Boughton
The Edge Negotiation Group

In negotiation there is a golden rule—or if you're a *Lord of the Rings* fan, one rule to rule them all—*information is power!* The more you understand about the other party, the more power you have. Ideally, if you possessed the ability to read the other party's thoughts, you'd have clarity on some of the critical elements of his or her power. You would know the other person's level of interest (or desperation), along with his or her break points, deadlines, view of the issues, true constraints, artificial constraints, view of the market information, view of the competition, internal business objectives, and personal objectives.

You'd be in the ultimate position of power. You'd have complete clarity regarding the balance of power and how to extract maximum value depending on the circumstance. If you are involved in a decidedly distributive negotiation—where two parties are primarily concerned about price without connection to any future transactions—you can use this information as leverage to drive the price and crush the other party. If you're involved in a complex, multiparty, collaborative initiative over many years, you can identify areas of flexibility and genuine interest. You can manage the climate and strengthen the relationship by reading frustration and anger so you can address any issues to drive clarity and build consensus. The good news is that recent research has shown that people can be trained to read people and their subtle emotion expressions better (see Chapter 2).

Why Negotiation

How many times have you heard the phrase, "It's nothing personal, it's just business"? Chances are you've just been taken by someone in a deal, and the perpetrator is trying to quell your instinctual anger response. According to Dale Carnegie (1936/1981), when dealing with people, we must remember that we are not dealing with creatures of logic but creatures of emotion. Negotiation is personal; we are dealing with humans. We don't negotiate with companies; we negotiate directly with people face to face, over the phone, e-mail, Twitter, Facebook, cocktails, golf, etc. Negotiation purists strive to *maximize the value of every transaction.* However, that phrase needs to be qualified and should read, *maximize the value of every transaction given the circumstances you face.* No two negotiations were created equally. Every deal has the potential to be different, primarily because the people involved are different. If we incorporate only our own view of the situation, we see at best 50% of the picture. If instead we understand as much as possible about the other parties involved in the discussion, we can increase greatly the percentage of the picture we see.

Negotiation is steeped in conflict. Two or more parties with differing views attempt to reach an amicable arrangement. In this chapter I'm going to concentrate primarily on commercial negotiation, as political and other negotiation add other complexities. Most people involved in commercial negotiation understand the golden rule and often attempt to protect commercially sensitive information that could undermine their negotiating position. When it comes to negotiating, I want to know when the other side is exaggerating, concealing, omitting, altering, and distorting information that can materially impact the outcome of the deal. Combining verbal clues with nonverbal reactions can provide deeper insights into exactly the information one needs. For example, when I've just made a proposal, I need to understand whether it was acceptable, regardless of what the other side is telling me. I expect them to say no. What I want to know is how to interpret that no, as there are two kinds of no: the hard one that means, "I can't agree under any circumstance" and the soft one that means, "I don't want to agree, but I could agree because it's within my range."

Negotiation is perfectly suited for the application of nonverbal communication skills to decipher these different no's. Research has shown that three forms of stress tend to be responsible for triggering the subconscious leakage of information (Ekman, 1985/2001), and these are often present when negotiating. *Detection apprehension* is the fear of getting caught, and it requires that the liar face some material consequences for getting caught. In negotiation, the outcome of the deal is the consequence, and the bigger the value or importance of the deal, the more pronounced the fear can become for the liar. *Deception guilt* is the stress generated by violation of some aspect of a relationship. The level and importance of relationship in each deal is directly related to the frequency and duration of the contact. For example, distributive transactions (buying a building, asset disposal, buying a company, capital expenditure, etc.) generally require a lower-level relationship; therefore, individuals are less likely to experience any deception guilt from their statements. However, favored suppliers and important customers may require a higher-level relationship, involving a higher level of trust, and therefore the deception guilt can be very high for the liar. *Duping delight* refers to the pleasure of pulling the wool over the eyes of another and tends to be more of a factor during distributive negotiations when trust and relationship are less important.

The negotiation context offers one big advantage that law enforcement or other contexts don't—the clarity of the other person's motive. Imagine yourself seated on a park bench with people watching. It's easy to identify the emotions of the surrounding people, but it's almost impossible to infer the context of their conversation simply from watching their interactions. In law enforcement, it's often the inferred context or motive that drives the line of questioning and information gathering, but that too is uncertain. However, in negotiation we know the other party's context or motive: to get the best deal possible given the circumstance. So to circle back to my metaphor, I believe that in commercial negotiation, people watching alone provides the additional information we will need to unlock key insights into the other party's position and flexibility. In other words, we are watching for *what* people say and do because we can assume the *why* is to get a better deal. Now imagine a police officer interrogating a suspect; the *why* could be any number of possibilities (the suspect is protecting a friend, concealing a different crime, has a borderline personality, doesn't trust authority, is afraid, etc.).

Here's How to Apply Nonverbal Communication in Negotiation

Previous chapters in this book address the scientific aspects of nonverbal communication in deception (see Chapter 6). I'll focus on the application as it relates specifically to negotiation. The first step in applying deception detection techniques, as in any scenario, is establishing a baseline. People are different, just like snowflakes. In order to effectively filter out the other party's nervous energy from his or her stress signals related to the negotiation, we have to develop a baseline for him or her during the interaction. Remember, it's the verbal clues combined with nonverbal reactions that provide deeper insights. We want to develop a series of questions and assumptions based on information we already know or have little reason to suspect the individual would lie about. We can use icebreaker-type dialogue to help establish this baseline. Focus on questions where even if the person lied, there would be little consequence. For example, "Do you like to fish?" is a nice little icebreaker or, "Did you happen to catch (insert a movie, TV show, sports event, circus, etc.)?" We aren't concentrating on the person's answers; instead, we're watching his or her baseline behavior patterns. Does the person click a pen every time he or she answers, tap a foot, fidget in the seat, etc.? It's important to note that we want to identify signs that aren't present when the person is honest as well as signs that are present all the time as a result of his or her nervous tension—particularly as it relates to physical manipulations called manipulators (scratching, fidgeting, tapping feet, hands, etc.; see Chapter 4 on the body). We must also listen very carefully to the words people choose when answering. Do they use a number of unnecessary adjectives and adverbs? Are they qualifying their answers? It is the change against this baseline that will provide us the insights into their true position later on in the negotiation when we begin to question them about their issues and objectives.

Since negotiation revolves around "no" (once they've said yes you've little reason to negotiate further), we want to ask specific questions that establish a true representation of no. Pay particular attention to what people say, how they say it, and what their body says. We must make sure we have several examples. I'll often ask somewhat obvious and sometimes absurd questions. For instance, "Are you a fan of (insert something you suspect they won't be a fan of)?" I find it best to use closed-ended questions when establishing the baseline. My primary goal when I'm establishing a baseline is to understand what a hard no looks and sounds like. Everything else will indicate a soft no; that is, a level of flexibility or a desire rather than a true no.

To really develop this skill we need to increase our level of concentration while involved in the discussion. It isn't possible to "observe" everything without the aid of video equipment. Most commercial negotiators I know would never allow their sessions to be recorded. So instead of trying to identify everything, we want to focus our attention on what I refer to as the *crunch points*. A crunch point is a point in the negotiation when there is critical exchange of information between the parties. Crunch points are when the following occurs:

1. We've just asked a question of the other side.

2. We've delivered a proposal to the other side (I prefer to do it verbally).

3. The other side is posing a proposal or question to you.

In the first two crunch points, we should focus on a person's immediate reaction and subsequent statements. In the third crunch point, we should focus on the words chosen and compare them to the corresponding body language for conflicting signals. The best way to observe all of the signals during the crunch points is to actually bring a colleague with you to act as an observer to focus on the behavior of the other side. The best way to become an excellent observer is to offer to be the observer for your colleagues. There is no pause button, rewind button, or flashing lights to help you learn these skills. We have to learn what to look for, when to look for it, and then actually do it to gain the experience and confidence to be effective. Anybody can buy a gun; however, if we're untrained we're more likely to shoot ourselves in the foot.

A quick recap on how to use nonverbal communication while negotiating:

1. Establish the baseline behaviors

2. Establish what a hard no sounds and looks like

3. Focus on the crunch points to identify behavioral or verbal contradictions

Specifics to Look for in the Body

Manipulators. I've already alluded to manipulators, and a more detailed discussion of these is found earlier in this book in Chapter 4. Recall that manipulators are those little unconscious fidgets we do to relieve stress and comfort ourselves. Applying what I discussed earlier, once we've established a baseline, look for an increase in the number of manipulators in the other individuals at the table. Although everyone is different, I find identifying manipulators to be the easiest behavioral clue for colleagues to pick up and use initially. We must remember that these are only one piece to the puzzle, and ultimately you want to collect as many pieces as you can to increase your level of accuracy. Researchers have studied common manipulators (again, see Chapter 4), including some minor cultural differences in manipulators (see Chapter 5). However, anecdotally, I've filmed a couple thousand people over the last 6 years and have identified manipulators taking various forms that I've affectionately nicknamed *the rash, the clicker, the tap dance, the needle,* and *the bum shuffle.*

The rash occurs at a crunch point when the other party seems to have simultaneously contracted a tiny rash on either the nose, back of the head, arm, or chest. It's usually, but not always, on the upper body.

The clicker occurs when the other party clicks a pen at crunch points but doesn't tend to do it at other points throughout the discussion. It is based on the observation that some people click the top of their pens out of nervous habit. Just recently I filmed a participant in one of my workshops trying to click his pen (although it wasn't that type of pen) as he assured the other party that their price was too high even though it was well beneath his break point.

The tap dance occurs when the other party suddenly gets "happy feet" during the crunch points. Keep in mind that just because someone taps his or her feet incessantly doesn't mean the person is trying to deceive you. But if the individual doesn't have happy feet all the time, but only during the crunch points, this represents a change from the baseline. That may be another sign of internal discomfort with his or her answer. Note that the tap dance isn't always that easy to spot since often your view is obstructed by a table. You have to listen for the tap, look for the reverberating movement through the person's torso (the foot tap sort of rebounds through the body), or feel it on the table.

The needle is a simple variation on the tap dance; it is the result of crossing the legs. The foot, hanging in midair, bobs up and down like a needle on a polygraph machine. The needle is much easier to identify even when your view is obstructed by a table.

The bum shuffle occurs when the other party shows a slight shift in his or her seat, usually right before the individual delivers a proposal or counterproposal. It is almost as if the person is preparing themselves or cocking their bodies into position. The idea of literally squirming in your chair when being questioned has been recognized by professionals for many years (e.g., Inbau, Reid, & Buckley, 1986), although the research data is not as clear (see Chapter 6).

Although these are a few of my favorites, there are many different types of manipulators. The key is to try to look for an increase in "fidgetyness" from the other party compared to his or her baseline levels. That is going to give us an insight into the person's internal discomfort with whatever response or proposal is on the table. The higher the discomfort, the more likely the party's proposal isn't a genuine reflection of their position. Their position or response is in fact flexible.

Emblematic slips. Recall from the earlier chapter on body signals (Chapter 4) that emblems are nonverbal gestures with specific symbolic meaning within given cultures, such as a head nod for "yes" in most Western cultures. Also recall in the chapter on deception (Chapter 6) that emblems can often betray true feelings or thoughts when they contradict the spoken word. These incongruent emblems are a little more difficult to identify while negotiating because of their subtle nature. They are easier to identify when we can focus on looking for a couple of specific incongruities. The key Western culture emblems I look for leaking out at crunch points include the following:

1. The head shake while saying yes

2. The raised eyebrows prior to saying no

3. The shoulder shrug, meaning, "I don't know"

4. The open palm gesture, also meaning, "I don't know"

5. The drooping shoulders, or exhale, meaning relief

6. The hand or head pong, when the head is moving from side to side or the hand is rotating in a semicircle from side to side, meaning conflict or self-debate

Here is how emblematic slips are applied. As we deliver our proposal, we watch the other party's statement of rejection to make sure it is consistent with his or her actions. If the other party is saying no and his or her head is shaking "yes," that is a contradiction, and it's likely that our proposal is within the other party's range. A subtle variation on the head shaking "yes" is the raised eyebrow in response to our proposal. For example, we've proposed a price of $250,000, and we immediately see the other party's eyebrows raise followed by a verbal rejection. The inner dialogue in the other party's head might sound something like this: "Ahh, now we're getting somewhere, wait . . . we can get more, quick—say no." The raised eyebrows indicate a level of interest, and typically negotiators aren't interested if their rejection is a hard no. We should be cautious, however, as when establishing the baseline, we must observe if the other party tends to respond with an "uh-huh" or "yes" as a way of acknowledging that he or she heard and understands you. If so, you have to be careful that you don't mistake this pattern for a slip.

The shoulder shrug and open-palm gesture (hand shrug) have similar significance and meaning. I'm looking for these emblematic slips when the other party is answering questions and quoting pertinent facts from their perspective. Their presence typically indicates that the other party isn't 100% convinced of the information they're telling me. In other words, their statements are soft or the facts are fuzzy, and thus they have more flexibility than they'd like me to believe. Remember, the shoulder or hand shrug should be contradictory to their statement. For instance, the statement, "There's nothing I can do, my hands are tied" should typically be accompanied by the head shaking no. If instead it's accompanied with a single-shoulder partial shrug, suggesting leakage (see Chapter 6 on deception), the meaning changes to, "I'm not sure I can do that," or perhaps there is something they can do, and I may have to dig a little deeper to find it.

"Hand pong," my personal favorite, is when someone holds his or her hand out parallel to the ground generally with fingers spread apart, palm facing down, and rotates the wrist about 20 degrees back and forth, as if there is a ping pong match going on between the thumb and the pinky. This can also occur in the head and eyes as if the ping pong match is in the person's head. Quite literally, the person is thinking about two different scenarios, numbers, positions, etc. His or her internal soundtrack might sound something like this, "My break point is $325,000 so I'll offer to buy at $250,000." The hand or head pong gesture indicates that the person's proposal consists of a range, and all ranges are flexible (it is akin to the verbal slips—*about, in the region of, around*, etc.).

Negotiation is steeped in conflict and stress. Knowing when this conflict and stress is relieved is crucial for a negotiator. If the other party seems to be relieved by our proposal, that's a pretty strong indication that we've crossed their break point and entered into the bargaining range. Here's a typical situation. We've proposed a price of $250,000 to some group. The spokesperson summarily rejects the offer, while the group leader exhales and leans back in his chair as his shoulders droop ever so slightly. That is a pretty strong indication that our offer is acceptable. Here's what's going on inside the leader's head. Our previous offers were beyond his established break point, but our latest offer happened to cross over that very real demarcation point. The leader may have felt added stress as he worried the deal wouldn't close; however, our latest offer is now acceptable, albeit not optimal. Thus he now relaxes knowing the offer is within his range of acceptance. As a side note, being able to identify when your proposals are within the "acceptable" range has nothing to do with getting the other side to actually accept the proposal. Gaining acceptance is dependent on your ability to provide satisfaction to the other party, not necessarily your ability to spot their break point; however, providing satisfaction is a topic for a different book.

Specifics to Look for in the Face

Microexpressions. Microexpressions, as you read earlier in the book in the chapters on the face (Chapter 2) and deception (Chapter 6), are by far the most difficult to use effectively when negotiating. Because there is already so much to watch and listen for, it's very easy to miss key microexpressions or, even worse, misinterpret them. I recommend that negotiators plan out in advance which microexpressions they may be looking for and what their presence would indicate. Also keep in mind that their significance may change depending upon the situation.

During information exchanges I often say things to get a reaction that gives me a better read on the other party. The main reason is that I find many people have prepared and rehearsed responses to a lot of the more difficult questions to which they do not wish to respond. This is especially true in distributive deals where price is the dominant driver and the focus is short-term gain. So an assumption that is stated as if it was a fact can unlock that information. For instance, if I'm trying to calculate the other party's profit margin on a sale, it's unlikely they are going to answer that question truthfully. If I simply state my assumption—"It is common knowledge that your margin is 18%"—I can watch their reaction and gauge my accuracy. If I see a look of surprise, I'm probably close to the mark. As a side note, in certain circumstances I want my assumption to be a little more *unrealistic* in order to allow the other party to correct me. I may use a 35% margin instead of 18%; now I'm watching for a flash of anger or contempt in the face followed by a statement like, "It's nowhere near that; it's definitely single digits. Where are you getting your information?"

Depending on the situation, sometimes fear can be a crucial signal. For instance, I was involved in a negotiation where we suspected the other side was under a great deal of financial pressure from their bank and might be highly motivated by a cash payment if this was the case. By simply stating, "We heard you're unable to fulfill your loan covenants this month," we were able to observe the immediate fearful glances of three of the four individuals as their eyes darted to the leader for guidance. He very calmly responded, "I'm not sure where you heard that rumor, but it is completely untrue." However, the microexpressions of fear on the faces of his colleagues told us otherwise. As a result, the entire power dynamic shifted in our favor.

One obvious use of microexpressions is in looking for a subtle sign of joy when you are making your proposal, indicating it is within their range of acceptance. One not so obvious use of microexpressions is in managing the climate during a negotiation. Collaboration is the hallmark of truly skilled negotiators. Collaboration requires a high level of empathy in order to create trust and effectively share information to leverage each party's advantages while growing the value for all parties. Collaboration goes against many of our bodily responses to conflict and stress. Sharing information with an opposing party during the negotiation process is difficult. It is imperative that a negotiator foster the right tone and climate of the meeting to encourage trust and sharing. Watching very closely for signs of anger and frustration can help us identify and manage sensitive issues before they mushroom into roadblocks. By addressing hidden issues early we build trust and limit the miscommunication. If we're making them angry, they won't trust us or collaborate with us! When we see flashes of anger, we need to probe to uncover the issue before we can explore possible solutions.

Summary of Approach

1. Establish a baseline

2. Identify a genuine "no" response

3. Focus primarily on crunch points

4. Look for changes from the baseline

5. Look for contradictions between actions and words

6. Plan out what possible reactions you expect from the other party

That being said, remember that we are collecting clues, and it is always more accurate if there are several signs present. We can't simply focus on one area or technique. It is always recommended that if possible a negotiator use an observer to help identify and read the signs. An observer can focus 100% of his or her efforts on watching and listening while we manage the rest of the negotiation process.

I should also note that although this discussion focused on the nonverbal clues, verbal clues are highly important as well, for example, when the other party uses phrases like, "I was hoping to get . . . ," "I'd like . . . ," and "I'll start with . . . ," thus revealing the softness of their position. However, that is outside the scope of this book.

What Do You Do With This Information?

The one question I'm asked, repeatedly, by my students is, "What should I do if I catch the other side trying to deceive, conceal, omit, or change pertinent facts?" Whatever one does, I recommend we *avoid* confronting them with the information. When we accuse someone of lying we escalate the situation by evoking an emotional response that may conceal more meaningful emotional responses. They are also likely to become defensive and more irrational as a result. Instead, I suggest we take note of the information, use it to understand that the other party is telling us that their position is movable, and thus use the information to guide our next proposal.

Although there are many styles of negotiation, there's a basic split between distributive and collaborative (also called integrative) negotiation.

I use the Wheel of Negotiation (Figure 13.1) to distinguish between five distinct commercial negotiation styles:

1. Auction and bartering

2. Hard bargaining

3. Concession trading

4. Win-win

5. High dependency

The right hemisphere represents distributive negotiations, and the left hemisphere represents collaborative negotiations. Ultimately, what we do with the additional information we're able to identify depends largely on the style of negotiation we're involved in. Distributive negotiations, which are

Figure 13.1   The Wheel of Negotiation

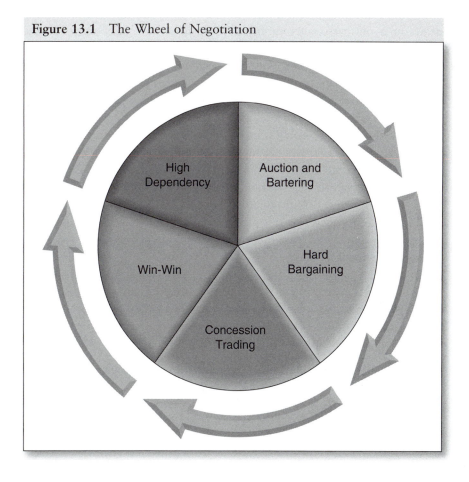

typically one-off transactions with very low levels of trust, are dominated by price negotiations. The information we're trying to uncover is used like leverage to get a better price. We're trying to identify where their break point is and then provide them enough satisfaction to get them to agree to it (no easy task, again a subject for another book). Deception detection techniques are extremely effective when used to identify the flexibility of the other party's position. We are looking for signs and signals that they are misleading about the price they will accept or are willing to pay.

When collaborating, our focus and behavior has to shift to managing the relationship and building the necessary trust. We want to use our newfound powers to identify their primary issues and interests. We need to be able to sift through the puffery and positioning, especially when they try to tell us "every issue is important." Our focus becomes managing their emotions in order to move discussions forward. Negotiation is personal! Remember, we are dealing with people. When dealing with people, we need to deal with their emotions. The ability to recognize hidden emotions can prevent unnecessary delays or avoid personality conflicts. We have to be careful and resist the temptation to leverage the information we read in this situation, otherwise we're likely to cause the negotiation to become more distributive. The concept of managing your own behaviors and emotions is an important part of the process, although it's beyond the scope of this chapter. Just remember that the ability to emote is innate, and most people interpret our reactions at least on a subconscious level. You'll want to minimize your own information leakage. The secret to all of these techniques is to practice and plan in advance.

Remember the golden rule—information is power. As we develop our powers of observation, keep in mind the following quote from Spiderman's Uncle Ben who said, "With great power comes great responsibility." We must take care not to abuse our powers of deception detection. Remember, everybody lies (including you and me), but nobody likes to be called a liar, particularly in a negotiation.

References

Carnegie, D. (1981). *How to win friends and influence people*. New York: Simon & Schuster. (Original work published 1936)

Ekman, P. (2001). *Telling lies: Clues to deceit in the marketplace, politics and marriage*. New York: W. W. Norton. (Original work published 1985)

Inbau, F. E., Reid, J. E., & Buckley, J. P. (1986). *Criminal interrogations and confessions* (3rd ed.). Baltimore: Williams & Wilkins.

14

Interpersonal Skills and Nonverbal Communication

Steve Longford
New Intelligence

It is not the strongest of the species that survive, nor the most intelligent, but the one most responsive to change.

—Undocumented quote attributed to Charles Darwin

Throughout the course of the past 8 years as a professional researcher, trainer, and facilitator, I, along with my colleagues, have encountered the term *interpersonal skills* on a regular basis. During this time it has become apparent that the term is not one that can be clearly or easily defined; however, in general, it can be described as the various capabilities and techniques used by an individual to interact with another. For a long time interpersonal skills have been packaged and grouped according to the various contexts in which they were applied, often in order to provide support or validation for their importance. The last decade has seen the emergence of interpersonal skills as a valid area that is attracting money, interest, and resources for research, training, and education. In fact, interpersonal skills aggregated and contextualized into groupings such as leadership, management, emotional intelligence, conflict resolution, and persuasion are now considered critical by many private- and public-sector organizations. This has not always been the case.

Why Were Interpersonal Skills Neglected?

In the early 1980s, the debate about whether leaders were born or made spawned a realization that regardless of the case, interpersonal skills were in need of development and enhancement. Even though leaving people to their own inherent capability was rejected as a flawed concept, it did not drive any significant increase in interpersonal skills training, for one very good reason.

At about the same time, computers were emerging as a mainstream technology that would supplant interpersonal interaction and influencing techniques or other "soft skills" training for over 20 years, especially in the workplace. In the late eighties and throughout the nineties, computer-related training became the largest single area of formal training in the Western world. In 2004, the US Bureau of Labor found that job skills training accounted for 67% of the total training hours and 48% of total training participants. Computer training took up 20% of the total training hours, the largest share of any training type. Computer training was easy to deliver, had tangible outcomes, and was considered an essential skill. Interpersonal skills, on the other hand, were more difficult to deliver well, had nebulous outcomes, and were considered a desirable, but not essential, skill. Soft skills and their associated training were relegated to the less urgent "personal development" bucket. Today, basic computer skills are assumed for most professional occupations, and while there is still a large part of the adult education sector devoted to them, it is in decline, due mostly to better user interfaces, easily accessible online packages, and the high computer literacy of school graduates entering the workforce.

This evolution has once again seen learning and development time and budgets devoted to training in areas other than computers. In a contemporary training environment where we have had both private- and public-sector clients acknowledge that personal interaction is becoming more and more critical, it is being packaged up in various ways to be relevant to the workplace. Programs such as leadership, management, performance, and team building are becoming increasingly in demand. The simple reason for this increasing awareness and reliance on interpersonal skills is because attempts at dehumanizing business and life have not been successful. In their work on the employee-customer relationship, Fleming and Apslund (2007, p. 17) define the problem as this:

> Even the most perfectly designed and built process or system is only as good as the human being who uses it. And, for many executives, because controlling quality in processes and systems is infinitely easier than similar activities with people, it seems reasonable to try and factor people out of the equation all together.

Unfortunately, factoring people out of the equation has for so many become costly, painful, destructive, and unacceptable socially, politically, economically, culturally, and even religiously. From medical malpractice lawsuits through false-termination complaints to the radicalization of displaced people, examples of the negative consequences of dealing with others poorly are commonplace. Therefore, in an attempt to reduce or eliminate the costs of dealing poorly with people, two fundamental assumptions arose in the business world that are now being challenged: 1) interpersonal skills are not as important as technical skills; and 2) interpersonal skills are innate and thus cannot be taught effectively. This challenge has also resulted in more analysis of not only what constitutes an interpersonal skill but also how specifically each skill may be of value. Finally, this challenge has also pushed us away from somewhat euphemistical expressions such as "soft skills" or "touchy feely" toward more scientifically based descriptions such as emotional intelligence and human skills.

The combination of these challenged assumptions and increased interest and awareness of interpersonal skills all points to one end goal—*to be more influential*. Interpersonal skills make people influential, and therefore those with better interpersonal skills are more influential—particularly when that influence is exercised in an ethical and sustainable manner. Experience and research confirms this notion that from birth, the ultimate goal of a human is to influence other humans.

What Is the Behavioral Intelligence Model?

Although there are many different interpersonal skills that can benefit people, the one type that I'll focus on in this chapter is the ability to read and assess nonverbal behavior. This ability is an important element of what we term "reading people" in general, which, for the purposes of our training, is defined as the process of detecting and interpreting nonverbal, verbal, and paralinguistic cues and indicators exhibited by people for the purpose of identifying and understanding their attributes and motivations. This includes reading emotions, which our training identifies as one of the most reliable clues for understanding motivations. These definitions clearly imply that detecting and deriving meaning from nonverbal behaviors is key to gaining an understanding about others; they are taught as the base skills of our Behavioral Intelligence Model. This model, simply stated, dictates that in order to influence people ethically and sustainably we require five human skills that when applied correctly, build on each other and result in greater influence:

1. Reading people

2. Reading emotions

3. Building and testing rapport

4. Understanding how people make decisions

5. Influencing others

For the purposes of our training, nonverbal behaviors include but are not limited to movements of the face or body. Our training includes where and how these actions are executed, including proximity (personal space), duration, and persistence. It also includes cues that are voluntary (conscious), habitual (fringe of consciousness), and involuntary (subconscious).

As seen earlier in this book, nonverbal behaviors are important indicators of peoples' thoughts, emotions, and intentions (see Chapters 2, 3, 4, and 6). And these indicators are extremely useful in any interpersonal domain. In the business world, for example, highly effective sales personnel are constantly looking for congruence between verbal and nonverbal cues that show their target is giving them permission to proceed. Probably more importantly, they are also on the lookout for incongruence—verbal statements of commitment combined with contradictory body or facial behavior, such as a slight shaking of the head "no" to provide insight into the level of their target's commitment. In Australia, five of our current clients in law enforcement and national security place a very high premium on training in detecting microexpressions of emotion in the face—which indicate attempts to conceal particular emotions—for targeting individuals who may be involved in illegal activities. More recently, senior managers from the finance and energy sectors have been trained to increase their capture rates of nonverbal cues such as eye contact and blink rates in order to better gauge changes in people's baseline, or normal modes of behavior, in facilitating interactions with staff. And even in basic life satisfaction, we find that knowledge of these skills can provide personal insights into one's own behavior; that is, determining if someone is casting off facial expressions or body postures that may be seen by others as hostile—for example, having a knitted eyebrow, which constitutes part of the facial expression of anger (see Chapter 2), when in fact the individual has no such intentions of sending such messages.

The training we deliver ideally capitalizes on our own natural abilities. Although the first interpersonal skill shown at birth is the ability to communicate one's needs—feed me, help me—it is not too much later that a second skill develops—the ability to read others' communication. Specifically, at its earliest onset, the purpose of reading others may be to determine opportunities and threats and to respond to them. By 12 to 18 weeks, children are very responsive to their mother's emotional expressions. When she displays joy, they do so too and look at her more and engage in more play (Termine & Izard, 1988). From as early as 5 months, babies recognize and respond appropriately to different facial expressions; for example, babies are less mobile when the adult shows anger, and they play less with their toys when he or she looks sad (Harris, 1989).

Anyone who has had children knows of the power their child has to influence right from birth and all without the power of language. It can be argued that many of the intuitive or innate skills of humans have been learned or derived during their childhood, become enhanced or modified during puberty, and are then consolidated in adulthood. Influence underpins many of our behaviors and intentions, be they to induce a smile, to engender fierce protection, to sell a car, to convince someone to look after his or her health, to seduce, to repel, to entertain, to teach, to deceive, or to empower. I am convinced that we are born influencers but that the range of our influence is limited to what we need as children to survive. As we grow older, our range of influence must grow and so too does our skill set to support this.

Who Is Interested?

My experience is that the more progressive and aware people are, whether in business, government, families, or friendships, the more they understand that effective and efficient interpersonal skills allow them to more quickly get to the real issues that cause problems and to reduce the impact these problems have on their day-to-day lives. The depth and breadth of settings in which people seek to be more effective in their interpersonal interactions is also growing.

Anecdotally, consultation with both training participants and their managers and executives reveals that although once considered predominantly vocationally based and squarely in the domain of management and leadership, interpersonal skills are now becoming not only desirable but, in some cases, mandatory in a wide variety of business and personal arenas. This has resulted in a huge boom in demand for interpersonal skills training and a corresponding boom in the development of programs that attempt to fill it. One way to understand how much importance is being placed on interpersonal skills is to look at the type of organizations and industries that I know firsthand are seeking this type of training. In Australia alone in the last 5 years, very specific and tailored nonverbal skills training has been delivered by our company to individuals from agencies and organizations involved in the following areas:

1. Law enforcement	12. Corrections	21. Rehabilitation
2. Border protection	13. Information technology	22. Marketing
3. Health and medical		23. Lobbying
4. Compliance	14. Research	24. Building and construction
5. Energy	15. University education	
6. Banking and finance	16. Infrastructure	25. Consulting
7. Insurance	17. Legal	26. Personal and families
8. Personal coaching	18. Event planning and management	27. Pharmacy
9. Counseling		28. Welfare
10. Psychology	19. School education	29. Defense
11. Immigration	20. Media	30. Automotive

The specific areas of application included the following:

Leadership	Conflict resolution
Management	Persuasion
Team building	Case management
Sales	Managing difficult behaviors
Interviewing	Treatment
Negotiation	Relationship building

While some of these applications in certain sectors may be obvious, even exaggerated, and popularized through the media, others are not. For example, television shows depict law enforcement officers as often possessing levels of interpersonal skills that result in the inducement of a confession from a criminal. Although interpersonal skills are clearly correlated with the ability to gain information in interview situations, the advances that have benefited law enforcement and, similarly, national security agencies the most have been made in the field of human source management. In particular, the increased focus on terrorism and serious organized crime has dictated a need to identify, cultivate, and maintain human sources of information (also known as "assets" or "informants") that are increasingly at risk by virtue of their association with lethal activities. Rarely motivated by money, many human sources are "handled" by personnel who require exceptional levels of interpersonal skills to keep these people happy and willing to assist. The ability to read people, in particular their nonverbal cues, is a key skill required of competent and effective human source handlers in order for them to determine important aspects of the source's motivation and personality. Thus, how do sources react to certain incentives? Do we see true enjoyment smiles (see Chapter 2)? Do we see suppressed anger? Do their bodies show the same enthusiasm as their words? All of these are potentially useful markers for the status of the relationship and motivations of individuals. One can then adjust his or her approach or incentives to keep the relationship flowing smoothly or to obtain compliance with a request.

On the other hand, television depictions of medical personnel such as doctors are in many cases not so far from the truth. Studies indicate that the root cause for many malpractice suits derives from poor communication between the doctor and the patient and that effective communication builds a rapport that tends to reduce the propensity for patients to make malpractice claims (Huntington & Kuhn, 2003; see also Chapter 16 by Sheeler). More recently there has been an argument made for the need for doctors to increase their training in detecting and interpreting nonverbal behaviors of patients, in particular expressions of overt and concealed emotion, not only to increase the effectiveness of their communication, but also to assist with other issues such as malingering, doctor shopping, drug seeking, and even clinical assessment (Archinard, 2000; Gaughwin & Longford, 2011; Mast, 2007).

Who Benefits Most From Training?

An examination of how people train and practice their skills provides a useful insight into how nonverbal behaviors are acquired. The acquisition of interpersonal skills, especially those that revolve around reading people through their verbal and nonverbal behavior, is a lifelong pursuit. On the other hand, we see a strong emerging trend of people who want to improve their ability to detect and interpret nonverbal behaviors in a much shorter time frame, and so they undertake various training programs to do this. The popularity of television shows, such as *Lie to Me* and *The Mentalist,* that feature characters who can seemingly read the minds of others based upon their observations of others' behavior has created intense interest in the detection and interpretation of nonverbal cues across a wide section of society. The ability to read and interpret nonverbal cues has become highly desirable and even fashionable because it seems to impart to the possessor of such skills supernatural powers (like the characters on TV).

Unfortunately, from my trainer experience in Australia over the past 7 years, these TV shows have also created unrealistic expectations that these skills are quick and easy to acquire and provide absolute answers to what people are thinking or hiding. I, along with a number of my contemporaries, have noticed that many participants in interpersonal skills training programs come with high anticipation of going away from training with a complete, almost omniscient capability. I regularly find it is precisely these types of participants who go away from training programs disappointed, and more importantly from an uptake point of view, they are the ones least likely to practice their techniques. This generally results in very low improvement results and ultimately a participant who is inclined to disparage techniques used for learning and applying nonverbal behaviors.

On the other hand, we have observed a number of group participants who appear to be far more likely to increase their interpersonal capability as a result of training in nonverbal behaviors. The type that shows the greatest improvement tends to be those who are receptive to scientific explanations, rather than being impressed by "magic" tricks. Postcourse assessment of training delivered by my company shows that these individuals are much more likely to continue training exercises after receiving classroom instruction. This is accentuated when these individuals have a significant realization or "a-ha" moment about their own behavior. When the belief in science and personal insight is combined, they form by far the two most important factors producing strong interpersonal skill improvement over time.

A second group of participants who show good improvement are those who can see a significant, direct, and tangible application of nonverbal skills to what is important to them. This too leads to them having a high propensity to practice their skills. Whether it be family relationships, work situations, or their own personal interactions, if the participant can consistently identify specific issues to which he or she can apply the techniques, there appears to be a greater improvement in that participant's skills over time.

Finally, there are two further groups who also appear to be more amenable to nonverbal training, but analysis of postcourse feedback has shown that their improvement levels are lower than the first two groups. Natural readers or "intuitives" often have a reasonably high degree of competence in detecting and interpreting nonverbal cues; however, they tend to lack reliability and validity in their techniques. Often training provides them with an operational language, a framework or explanation for what and how they do what they do. Improvement tends to be slower but more sustainable. Similarly, strongly process-driven individuals who can apply models and frameworks easily tend to be slower in their application of the techniques, often lacking the intuitional inputs that delineate natural readers. The upside is that they rarely make unsupportable leaps, and so interpretation often has lower utility but higher validity.

Based on feedback from course participants and the results of training impact assessments conducted with clients, we have noticed that there is a very strong correlation between the propensity to practice the techniques in real-life situations and the level of improvement in a participant's interpersonal skills. Similarly, those who are persistent with their practice and not easily disheartened by slow progress also tend to have more sustainable improvements in interpersonal skills. For example, consider the human skill of reading emotion that requires the detection and interpretation of nonverbal cues, in this case facial expressions, in order to correctly label one of seven basic emotions (see Chapter 2). We teach course participants the value of reading both concealed and expressed emotions as a means for identifying and understanding overt and underlying motivation. The challenge for training people in this area of nonverbal behavior detection and interpretation lies in creating tools that encourage practice and allow tangible measurement of improvement that is scientifically based. In this regard, software tools such as the microexpression recognition training tools, which flash quick facial expressions and ask the viewer to identify the emotion shown in the face, are vital. Examples of these tools include *MiX* (Matsumoto & Ekman, 2007) and *SubX* (Matsumoto & Hwang, 2010), programs developed and provided by American company Humintell (www.humintell.com). These tools replicate nonverbal behaviors, in this case various aspects of facial expression, and also allow users to check their answers for correctness, view the expression in slow motion, and practice recognition before testing themselves again, all the while keeping track of improvements in terms of percentages. Formal scientific studies have shown that these behaviors can be effectively and efficiently trained (Matsumoto & Hwang, 2011).

Case Examples

The acquisition of improved interpersonal skills as a result of training and practice, especially skills that revolve around nonverbal behaviors, often results in epiphany-like experiences for the practitioners. In some cases there is not actually a result as such but better detection of nonverbal cues and a clearer understanding of what has transpired in a single interaction. For example, within weeks of completing one of our training programs on detecting nonverbal behaviors a customs officer provided the following feedback to our company:

> I had my first "cluster" today and it was very interesting. The first was a classic avoidance in the funnel where the POI [person of interest] refused to walk down the line. He eventually walked the line, and then when the dog was about to search, he veered abruptly again. . . . Whilst at the carousel, he was extremely watchful of the Customs staff while they went about their work. By the time he got to the benches he was quite agitated and resented being searched. We took the first atomizer [sensing molecules of forbidden substances] and he tested positive. He then became extremely cooperative. We took another, and again [tested] positive. His body language now had become defensive, and he faced away from both myself and another dog handler. . . . Intel later revealed that he had a criminal history including possession and had also been searched with positive ion scan readings at airports prior to today.

On the other hand, a course participant who is an intuitive reader gets clear results and continues to do so. In this case she shows understanding of how she was achieving results previously as well as the improvements she is making. She provided this feedback.

> In my role, I lead a diverse team, and I often have to influence or persuade people and teams to be involved in the work that we are leading.
> The courses that I have completed . . . have helped me put some structure and a name to practices that I previously did instinctively, or did not do at all. I have significantly increased the number of times that I have been able to identify the emotion of the other party allowing me to change direction, address their concerns, and come to a conclusion that benefits all involved. It is has also supported me to increase the number of times I hear the word "yes" without hesitation.

It is also not uncommon to find that when practitioners applied newly acquired skills, regardless of their understanding of the science, it stills seemed "magical." In this case a practitioner with significant training in interpersonal skills and months of practice provided feedback on acquiring a very large home for which there had been many competing potential buyers, and his ability to read the seller allowed him to rapidly create a level of rapport that resulted in the exclusion of all other buyers.

> Yesterday morning at exchange, the [seller] and I ended up in tears . . . kind of like it had all opened a floodgate of disclosure. He used all sorts of affirmative language to describe the process and how it was handled.

> Anyway, it is an interesting story, since everything factually available pointed against the outcome [sale to me] . . . my solicitor cautioned that she had only seen this sort of story be true twice in a 40-year career. It [the non-verbal behaviors of the seller] seemed to make sense with the people and communications in front of me—being able to test things and tie people into reciprocity and commonality rapport. It was pretty intense, and my logical mind is still questioning it [the nonverbal signals I saw that contradicted logic but were accurate indicators of what eventually happened]. . . .

While each of these examples reflects a more business- and work-oriented application of the increased capability with nonverbal behaviors, there is significant feedback showing that more often it is within personal situations and relationships that there is the greatest impact. The vast majority of training course attendees are initially oriented to work situations when they commence the courses, but there is a natural overflow into their personal lives. The following was received from a participant of a 5-day human skills program approximately 2 months after course completion.

> I am currently being treated for depression (and have been for the past four years) in a combination of drugs and counseling. . . . I didn't want to do the course. . . . I felt that I was in too fragile a mental state. . . . For the first two days I didn't socialize, preferring to be quiet by myself and absorb what I was learning. Afterwards I finished . . . I was feeling much, much better—better than any counseling session had ever helped me to feel—and [later] I had a long consultation with the doctor who . . . said several key things to me: that it was interesting to him that what I had gotten out of the two days was an increased level of self-awareness, which is one of the hardest things to deal with in his usual line of work . . . and that this was crucial to my recovery. So, I started trying to use all that I was learning from the moment I left the 2-day session (for myself) and for others, and have been using it as much as possible. I've used the techniques successfully in several difficult situations at work, particularly when dealing with people that we ultimately need to have a relationship with.

Thus, this individual was able to recognize her own emotions, including what they looked like, began to notice when they occurred, and was able to take steps to funnel these into productive channels.

Conclusion

The potential outcomes of being able to leverage the nonverbal behaviors of others have far-reaching implications across a wide range of public, private, and personal situations. There is clearly a significant advantage for anyone who either possesses or acquires high levels of interpersonal skills, particularly those associated with the detection and interpretation of nonverbal behaviors. There is, however, a pressing need to document the validity of training programs through the scientific research in order to manage expectations created by the media and increase the potential for uptake of these skills through additional practice by training course attendees. The results of any increased nonverbal recognition capabilities speak for themselves, and there is no shortage of case studies and testimonials that speak directly to this fact. Ultimately, I believe there will be a snowball effect, whereby as more people realize the significant benefits that accompany increased interpersonal skills, the demand for learning about the nonverbal behaviors that underlie these skills will increase, and the subsequent practice of them will also increase, leading to happier people who make themselves and others better.

References

Archinard, M. (2000). Doctors' and patients' facial expressions and suicide reattempt risk assessment. *Journal of Psychiatric Research, 34,* 261–262.

Fleming, J. H., & Apslund, J. (2007). *Human sigma: Managing the employee-customer encounter.* New York: Gallup Press.

Gaughwin, P. M., & Longford, S. (2011). Evaluating emotion and concealed motivation in the clinical interview. *Medical Student Journal of Australia, Summer 2011.*

Harris, P. (1989). *Children and emotion: The development of psychological understanding.* Oxford, UK: Blackwell.

Huntington, B., & Kuhn, N. (2003). Communication gaffes: A root cause of malpractice claims. *Baylor University Medical Centre Proceedings, 16*(2), 157–161.

Mast, M. (2007). On the importance of nonverbal communication in the physician-patient interaction. *Patient Education and Counselling, 67,* 315–318.

Matsumoto, D., & Ekman, P. (2007). *The microexpression training tool (MiX).* Available at www.humintell.com.

Matsumoto, D., & Hwang, H. S. (2010). *The subtle expression training tool (SuBX).* Available at www.humintell.com.

Matsumoto, D., & Hwang, H. S. (2011). Evidence for training the ability to read microexpressions of emotion. *Motivation and Emotion, 35*(2), 181–191.

Termine, N., & Izard, C. (1988). Infants' reaction to their mothers' expressions of joy and sadness. *Developmental Psychology, 24,* 223–229.

US Bureau of Labor Statistics. (2004). *NLSY79 User Guide.* US Department of Labor, Bureau of Labor Statistics.

15

Nonverbal Communication in Consumer Research

Nick R. Harrington[1]
The Procter & Gamble Company

Procter & Gamble (P&G) is the world's largest consumer packaged-goods company, driven in no small part by its expertise in understanding consumer behavior. Unlike some other contributors in this book, our researchers are not trying to spot Machiavellian deception or malicious intent but instead focus on new ways to improve consumers' lives through better solutions to everyday tasks. Everyday tasks are, however, typically repetitive, often of low emotional engagement, frequently associated with removing negatives, and usually have a predictable outcome. Consequently, they are most often unconsciously enacted. Our researchers must therefore understand how consumers think and feel about tasks that they themselves have little conscious awareness of and limited ability to articulate. Historically, this has been achieved through explicit self-report measures (e.g., surveys and interviews), but these measures are susceptible to self-presentation biases and limited by restricted access to one's unconscious information. The science of human emotion, and the ability for facial expressions to express discrete emotional states nonverbally, is universally accepted. Facial expressions magnify and objectively classify consumer emotional responses and transcend language, culture, and socioeconomic differences. I will describe the qualitative application of facial expressions to aid in the interpretation of consumer responses, find inconsistency in thought and action, provide emotional weighting to verbatim responses, and identify emotional hot spots. Through these approaches we are discovering and solving unmet and unarticulated consumer needs and designing products and brands to bring more positive emotions to even everyday tasks.

Background

One of the easiest and most intuitive means of collecting market research information is to simply ask consumers—either in an interview or by choosing a number on a standard numerical scale (e.g., a 1-to-5 Likert scale). These self-reports are the most frequently used method of determining attitudes about products and for predicting future purchase behavior. These measures are easy to administer, analyze, and interpret, but they are influenced by social construction, primacy, and/or recency effects, demand characteristics, presentational styles, socially desirable responding, and acquiescence—thereby limiting their utility. Additionally, they are insensitive to the emotional drivers of behavior (e.g., Damasio, 1994; Morin, 2011; Shiv & Fedorikhin, 1999) and as a result provide an incomplete picture of what really motivates consumers.

The Difficulty of Describing Thoughts and Feelings

Why do we (consumers) find describing our thoughts and feelings so difficult? Conscious decision making is difficult and induces negative affect (e.g., Loewenstein & Learner, 2003; Schwartz, 2005); therefore, where at all possible, we (consumers) avoid it. Instead, we automatically (unconsciously) react to familiar and predictable (nonharmful) stimuli. This ensures that we maintain a low cognitive load that enables us to optimally respond to nonpredictable or previously experienced and important stimuli when they occur. As a result, much of cognition occurs unconsciously, which reduces our ability to explain or predict our everyday behavior. Neuroscience (e.g., Janoff-Bulman, 1992) provides compelling data to support the need for this unconscious filtering: "We take in 11,000,000 pieces of information a second (from our five senses), but can only process 40 of them consciously" (Wilson, 2003, p. 24).

These innate neurological, and resulting psychological, restrictions become apparent in market research contexts. Consumers who are unable to retrieve the true cause of their attitudes or behavior are faced with two options: to either admit they don't know and can't answer (the socially undesirable outcome) or to, consciously or unconsciously, fabricate a believable and socially acceptable answer. A wealth of social desirability bias research indicates that the latter option is more often selected. Wilson et al. (1993) illustrated this effect; when students were required to pick one of a number of posters and to consciously justify their preference to their professor, they were more likely to choose a poster with more obvious and less sophisticated content (e.g., a humorous cartoon cat vs. a fine art print); 3 weeks later, the same group reported significantly lower satisfaction with their posters versus students who were not required to justify their preference (the control group). The authors concluded that justifying preference (conscious cognitive effort) for the posters was difficult and that it was easier to articulate positive attributes of the cartoon than the art posters (where the appeal is more abstract), despite feelings to the contrary. Over the following weeks, the effects of social desirability bias faded, leaving only a feeling of dissatisfaction. In the social psychology literature the idea that emotionally (or affectively) charged information can unconsciously color or influence attitudes or judgments is described as the "affect as information principle" (e.g., Forgas, 1995; Schwarz & Clore, 1983; Storbeck & Clore, 2008). For example, Dutton and Aron (1974) showed that emotion (or affect) induced by being in a potentially dangerous situation (on a narrow bridge suspended high above a gorge) was transferred to a social interaction; specifically, increasing their ratings of the sexual attractiveness of a researcher pretending to be member of the national park service canvassing feedback from visitors. In a more relevant study for market researchers, Schwarz and Clore (1983) demonstrated a negative effect of rainy versus sunny weather on an explicit self-assessment of life satisfaction; moreover, the misattribution of the effect of weather (or specifically, the negative affect result from rainy weather) was abolished by drawing conscious attention to the weather before asking about life satisfaction, indicating that underlying unconscious mood was able to influence perception of specific assessment of overall satisfaction with life. Interestingly, and of concern for market research, is that the impact of affect on information increases as a task becomes more habitual and/or as less cognitive resources are available for processing. These are the conditions that occur frequently when using everyday objects or partaking in everyday tasks.

These effects are magnified further by the fact that many market research questions are related to ideas or behaviors that, although important, are of (relatively) low salience and/or engagement (e.g., use of laundry detergent) and are rehearsed to the point of becoming habitual. Habitual events are those that occur repeatedly in a stable context to the point where the context alone can cue the behavior. It has been suggested that up to 45% of everyday behavior (particularly activities with low risk) occurs habitually, and this reflects a mechanism to free cognitive resources to attend to and process more novel information (e.g., Martin, 2008; Wood & Neal, 2009). Therefore, answering questions about these behaviors requires consumers to ask themselves "why" they behaved in a certain way. This requires them to consider automatic, background, or unconscious processes to which we have little conscious access. As a result, consumers frequently respond that the ideas are "good," "OK," and "fine" and that they "would probably buy them"; in reality, these responses do not reflect what the consumer is unconsciously thinking or feeling and do not translate into behavior.

The Difficulty of Assessing Without Introspection

How do we ask consumers questions without requiring them to consciously introspect? There are techniques for capturing consumer "data" without asking questions. These tools include peripheral and central measurements of nervous system activity like galvanic skin response, pupil dilation, electroencephalography, electromyography, voice analysis, eye tracking, and psychometrics. All of these approaches are at least somewhat invasive and make the consumer interaction less natural and relaxed; moreover, many of these techniques simply measure changes in arousal versus a specific emotional state. In contrast, there is decades of research that has demonstrated that the discrete emotions of anger, contempt, disgust, fear, happiness, sadness, and surprise are manifested via expressions on the face (Matsumoto, Keltner, Shiota, Frank, & O'Sullivan, 2008; see Chapter 2) and that all humans have an innate ability to use facial expressions to express evaluations. Facial expressions of emotion have been shown to be universally expressed and recognized (e.g., Matsumoto et al., 2008; Matsumoto & Willingham, 2006) regardless of culture, race, ethnicity, gender, age, or religion (Matsumoto et al., 2008; see Chapter 5). Muscle groups responsible for facial expressions of emotion have direct linkage to subcortical areas of the brain (responsible for involuntary basic human actions like physiological changes in heart rate, blood pressure, pupil dilation, etc.) and have measurable qualities that enable confident classification even when the individual cannot articulate his or her feelings (e.g., Ekman, 2003; Ekman, Davidson, & Friesen, 1990; Ekman, Levenson, & Friesen, 1983). Importantly, the ability to recognize and decode the meaning of facial expressions precedes human ability to use formal number systems (e.g., market research rating scales) and provides the fundamental means for humans to communicate information such as emotions, motives, and behavioral intentions (Darwin, 1872/1998; Parkinson, 2005). Moreover, it has been demonstrated that within certain interpersonal scenarios, up to 93% of emotional communication occurs through facial expressions, gestures, or vocal inflections, whereas the semantic content of speech (the meaning of the respondents' words) contributed less than 10% (e.g., Mehrabian, 1971; Picard, 1998). More recently, it has been shown that while facial expressions can communicate and predict affective response to stimuli to others, this information is not always available to the individual experiencing the event and making the expression. McConnell, Dunn, Austin, and Rawn (2011) demonstrated that subjects' facial expressions regarding food preferences and food choices better predicted future choice behavior than explicit self-reports (see also North, Todorov, & Osherson, 2010; Parkinson, 2005; Picard, 2010). The fact that these facial expressions were observable to others but beyond the conscious introspection of the individual supports both the unconscious etiology of facial expressions and the ability for affective states to implicitly influence behavior.

Importance to Market Researchers

At Procter & Gamble, we know the value our consumers gain from the reduction of negative events, distress, and pain, and therefore we invest heavily in ensuring that our products serve to deliver these benefits reliably. For example, these products range from the removal of tangible "pain"—e.g., removal of cough and cold symptoms (e.g., Vicks), gastrointestinal discomfort (Metamucil, Pepto-Bismol), and tooth sensitivity (e.g., Crest, Scope)—to the removal of stains, smells, and dirt (e.g., Tide, Swiffer, Mr. Clean, Crest, Pantene), to the containment, removal, and disposal of bodily waste (e.g., Pampers, Tampax, Head & Shoulders, Bounty, Charmin, Gillette), to the enhancement, proactive maintenance, or reversal of physical or psychological negatives (e.g., PUR, Pantene, Clairol, Crest, Olay, Cover Girl, Iams).

Importance of the Face

Why do we believe facial expression analysis is beneficial in market research? Facial expressions of emotion can be captured remotely and noninvasively and therefore do not impact the behavior being studied. Facial expressions of emotion also add granularity to emotion classification, identifying distinct information that is absent in a dimensional assessment (i.e., positive or negative). Anger, fear, and sadness, for example, are all "negative" emotions, but each has its own unique source, physiological and behavioral response, and social meaning. Facial expressions can also distinguish between different types of smiles, most notably smiles of true enjoyment versus social or polite smiles (e.g., Duchenne, 1862/1990; Ekman & Friesen, 1982b; see Chapter 2). While we can generate smiles even in the absence of a positive experience, there is compelling evidence that true enjoyment smiles (also called Duchenne smiles) are difficult to voluntarily elicit. Accordingly, experiences described as having positive affect (e.g., sex, eating fat- and sugar-rich foods, social success, nurturing relationships) are driven by neurotransmitters such as dopamine and oxytocin and are commonly associated with true enjoyment smiles. Knowing this distinction can be very important in determining if consumers truly feel positive about a product or are just being polite.

Benefits of Nonverbal Analysis

How does nonverbal analysis benefit consumer research? We (Matsumoto, Hwang, Harrington, Olsen, & King, 2011) started by collecting and analyzing video from a number of different types of qualitative consumer research across a number of different P&G business categories to compare facial expression analysis with consumer verbatims. Data were analyzed from 8 studies across 4 categories in over 100 consumers assessing product usage and packaging communication. Interview data were subjected to objective coding using the *Facial Action Coding System* (FACS; Ekman & Friesen, 1978). FACS is widely acknowledged as the most comprehensive system available, identifying over 40 functionally independent muscle movements in the face (action units or AUs) that can occur at any one time. FACS coding can identify the muscles involved in any facial behavior, and certain, specific facial configurations have been reliably identified with emotion signaling (e.g., anger, contempt, disgust, fear, happiness, sadness, surprise; see Chapter 2). The analysis identified 2,986 events and 8,102 FACS AUs. The behaviors were classified by emotion type, frequency, intensity, duration, display on the face (full or partial), and consistency with verbal response.

Results. What did we learn? Facial expressions of emotion were elicited frequently during consumer research, and this was independent of the type of research being conducted. Consumers displayed a broad range of emotional expressions, expressing all of the seven universal emotional expressions and nonenjoyment smiles. As expected, based on our beliefs regarding the everyday unconscious nature of consumer packaged-goods perception, facial expressions of emotion were often of low intensity, short duration, and only partially presented. Unexpectedly, there were more negative than positive emotions and a high level of inconsistency between what the consumer said and his or her nonverbal behaviors. Full methods and results can be found in Matsumoto et al. (2011); however, a summary follows:

- Most (92%) expressions were of moderate or low intensity, with 97% presenting a partial profile. This means that the expressions are harder to code since they were more difficult to detect and are less unique.
- Disgust was the most frequently occurring emotion, followed by nonenjoyment smiles, anger, and contempt. Disgust, contempt, and anger combined accounted for 52% of all emotions classified. Smiles occurred frequently, but nonenjoyment smiles occurred much more frequently than enjoyment smiles (27% v. 4%, respectively). Enjoyment, or Duchenne, smiles were the least prevalent emotional expression coded.
- Mean expression duration was short, averaging 1.48 s, (longer durations were associated with nonenjoyment smiles, technically not signs of emotion).
- In those cases where facial expressions were associated with a verbal or survey-based assessment, consistency comparisons were made. Of 2,986 possible occurrences 1,483 were not suitable for assessment; of the remaining, 39% were inconsistent; that is to say, what the consumer said did not match his or her facial expressions.

Facial expressions to P&G stimuli were often of low intensity, short duration, and partial presentation; these findings fitted with our expectation that consumer packaged goods would produce a less intense emotional footprint than a joyous or traumatic life event. In addition, in approximately 40% of interactions with P&G researchers, consumers were verbally inconsistent about how they really "felt"; again, this fits with our beliefs about our consumers' ability to reliably access thoughts and feelings about everyday activities that exist beyond conscious introspection. Taken together, these data highlight the value of adding nonverbal behavior analyses to our standard consumer research methodologies in order to increase our ability to understand and predict consumer emotional engagement.

Further interpretation of results. The high number of negative emotions was unexpected but can be explained via at least two different mechanisms. First, it is possible that these negative emotions may have reflected the idea being tested, that is to say that the idea may not have been appealing, or the idea may have been a solution to an unpleasant problem (recall that the majority of P&G products work by effectively and reliably removing negatives). Second, respondents may have been reacting to the consumer research procedure itself; the research process requires consumers to express and justify attitudes about products or experiences that they have limited conscious access to. This can be expected to create cognitive effort and social stress, both of which are associated with negative affect. Recognizing that research may induce negative affect that is independent of the research question will be critical in experimental design and analysis in order to avoid mistakenly promoting or killing new product ideas.

The high frequency of social smiles and low frequency of true enjoyment smiles was also unexpected but, again, on reexamination was consistent with strongly held beliefs. Social smiles are exactly that, a demeanor adopted when one is in a social context, and are frequently used to soften the communication of negative information or to cover deception or express uncertainty (e.g., Ekman, 1992; Ekman & Friesen, 1982a; Ekman, Friesen, & O'Sullivan, 1988). It is thus to be expected that consumers might often try to mitigate negative responses regarding new consumer goods ideas with an insincere smile; again, recognizing this and accounting for it will enable more accurate research interpretation.

On first viewing it might seem that we should be alarmed by these findings; however, in reality the reverse is true. These data provide credence to the idea that positive affect can be delivered, not only by making happy people happier but by making dissatisfied and underserved people happier. These data and this approach empower us to use the absence of negative emotions as a predictor of success that may prove better than a myopic view focusing only on the presence of positive emotions. Moreover, awareness of the frequency of enjoyment smiles—as distinct from nonenjoyment or social smiles—ensures that researchers are trained to discriminate and avoid costly false positive emotions.

Applications

Successful proof-of-principle research has supported our concerns about the limitations of standard qualitative approaches and resulted in a program of work applying facial expressions that has provided the following:

- **A consistency check.** Expanding on the proof-of-principle work, we have used facial expressions to provide confidence that consumer verbatims and emotions are congruent. This approach has proved very successful in uncoupling the effects of research-induced self-presentation biases from emotion induced by the product idea or experience. In one study we wanted to understand the in-use barriers to acceptance of a habitually used beauty care product that was performing poorly in market; however, consumers reported that the product was "fine" and that they would "probably buy it" in the future. Facial expressions of the consumer during product usage allowed the team to isolate the moments during usage where the product failed to meet expectations. The ability to see an unconscious expectation violation provided researchers with a tangible consumer experience to initiate a conscious conversation about specific suboptimal product features and areas for improvement. Specifically, facial expressions identified an experience where consumers had developed a coping strategy to overcome negative product features that enabled habitual product use, but, it is hypothesized, these strategies would not diminish negative affect that would inhibit future purchasing behavior (despite conscious introspection to the contrary).

- **Objective measure of subjectivity.** Reliably and effectively removing negatives such as pain and discomfort is desirable and valuable to consumers. Distress, however, is a subjective measure that varies between individuals and contexts; for example, fear during a horror movie may be desirable but the same experience during a shave is not. In research with a personal grooming team we catalogued the presentation of facial expressions representing negative emotions in order to objectively profile areas of greatest sensitivity during a shave. This knowledge provided objective measures for future product design and benchmarking versus other products.
- **Illuminating unintentional communications.** The proof-of-principle research identified that we are sometimes consciously insensitive to subtle facial expressions that can have dramatic unconscious impact on affective processing. Similarly, we can unintentionally project insincerity through artwork, advertising, and branding. Work with our brand teams has helped to identify and repair the source of unexpected, and ill-defined, consumer negative feedback to product communication.
- **Identifying unarticulated emotional hot spots.** Increasingly, we are learning that the greatest insights are identified through watching consumer behavior versus waiting for consumers to identify an unmet need or product improvement; this is particularly relevant for well-rehearsed behaviors where product failure is expected and unconsciously compensated. Facial expressions provide a novel lens for behavioral observation; for example, during sensory testing for the optimal viscosity of a beauty care product, the fleeting response to suboptimal formulation thickness during dispensing, cap closure, and resulting residual mess is obvious via a micro facial expression but often missed when viewing the bigger picture and rarely recounted by the consumer. Similarly, in research evaluating perfume preference, a behavioral outcome (product choice), when everything else was equal, was better predicted via the absence of negative facial expressions than by positive self-report, further supporting the role of unconscious affect in behavioral activation.
- **Emotional weighting.** When talking to consumers about culturally or personally sensitive information or discussing hard-to-articulate topics (e.g., product aesthetics or novel technologies), consumers can hold but not verbalize strong opinions. Conversely, consumers can strongly express weakly held beliefs. Facial expression analysis has allowed us to more objectively weight and rate responses to products and experiences versus other life experiences and better understand true emotional engagement. This proved particularly useful in the assessment of a novel feminine care product where we were able to identify which elements of the product offering (packaging or in-use experience) were driving consumer satisfaction when consumers were reluctant to discuss details and verbally described all elements as "fine." Facial expression analysis allowed the team to proceed with elements associated with positive emotional responses while optimizing others.

Conclusion

Much of everyday information, including our feelings, is processed unconsciously and automatically, and we have limited access to it. The majority of P&G products and product categories fit this description. Standard market research techniques that simply ask consumers to self-report orally (e.g., in an interview) or via standardized self-report surveys are insensitive to consumer thoughts and feelings and result in incomplete or inaccurate information. Conversely, facial expressions of emotion have been conclusively demonstrated to be universally presented and recognized and are correlated with underlying neural and physiological processes (e.g., Davidson, Saron, Senulis, Ekman, & Friesen, 1990; Ekman et al., 1983; Ekman et al., 1990; Matsumoto et al., 2008; see Chapter 2).

Research described here demonstrated that even though consumer research stimuli are often familiar, are of a (relatively) low level of arousal, and involve everyday products and well-rehearsed activities (habits), we are still able to record, code, and interpret facial expressions across the emotional spectrum. The proof of concept meta-analysis revealed that consumers demonstrated more negative responses and social smiles than true enjoyment; a finding that is helping to reframe our value proposition to include effective, reliable reduction of negatives as a mechanism to create positive appeal. High levels of inconsistency between the affective content of consumer verbatims and their facial expressions of emotion highlighted the importance of identifying and minimizing conscious introspection, research-induced negative affect, and self-presentation biases. Subsequent research has extended the application of the approach and, in tandem with traditional qualitative practices, has demonstrated the ability to add objectivity to subject response, provide a measure of emotional commitment to consumer verbatims, and identify novel areas for product development that the consumer cannot consciously report.

Facial expression analysis provides an approach that heightens the ability to measure emotional responses and titrate conscious (verbal) and unconscious feedback. It also provides a mechanism to more accurately pinpoint the source of emotional hot spots. Feedback from in-house practitioners has been overwhelmingly positive, reporting the facilitation of better rapport with consumers and increasing confidence, via a validated classification process, to spot, identify, and determine the congruence of affective responses, thereby confirming this approach as a highly valuable adjunct to standard qualitative research.

Note

1. Acknowledgment to Dr. David Matsumoto and Dr. Hyi Sung Hwang for their work that contributed significantly to the content of this chapter.

References

Damasio, R. (1994). *Descartes error: Emotion, reason and the human brain*. New York: Putnam.

Darwin, C. (1998). *The expression of the emotions in man and animals* (3rd ed., P. Ekman, Ed.). New York: Oxford University Press. (Original work published 1872)

Davidson, R. J., Saron, C. D., Senulis, J. A., Ekman, P., & Friesen, W. V. (1990). Approach-withdrawal and cerebral asymmetry: Emotional expression and brain physiology I. *Journal of Personality and Social Psychology, 58,* 330–341.

Duchenne, G. B. (1990). *The mechanism of human facial expression* (R. A. Cuthbertson, Trans.). New York: Cambridge University Press. (Original work published in French, 1862)

Dutton, D. G., & Aron, A. P. (1974). Some evidence for heightened sexual attraction under conditions of high anxiety. *Journal of Personality and Social Psychology, 30,* 510–517.

Ekman, P. (1992). Are there basic emotions? *Psychological Review, 99*(3), 550–553.

Ekman, P. (2003). *Emotions revealed*. New York: Times Books.

Ekman, P., Davidson, R. J., & Friesen, W. V. (1990). The Duchenne smile: Emotional expression and brain physiology: II. *Journal of Personality and Social Psychology, 58,* 342–353.

Ekman, P., & Friesen, W. V. (1978). *Facial action coding system: Investigator's guide*. Palo Alto, CA: Consulting Psychologists Press.

Ekman, P., & Friesen, W. V. (1982a). Felt, false, and miserable smiles. *Journal of Nonverbal Behavior, 6,* 238–252.

Ekman, P., & Friesen, W. V. (1982b). *EMFACS*. Unpublished manuscript.

Ekman, P., Friesen, W. V., & O'Sullivan, M. (1988). Smiles when lying. *Journal of Personality and Social Psychology, 54,* 414–420.

Ekman, P., Levenson, R. W., & Friesen, W. V. (1983). Autonomic nervous system activity distinguishes among emotions. *Science, 221*(4616), 1208–1210.

Forgas, J. P. (1995). Mood and judgment: The affect infusion model (AIM). *Psychological Bulletin, 117*(1), 39–66. doi:10.1037/0033-2909.117.1.39. PMID 7870863.

Janoff-Bulman, R. (1992). *Shattered assumptions*. New York: Free Press.

Loewenstein, G., & Learner, J. S. (2003). The role of affect in decision making. In R. J. Davidson, K. R. Scherer, & H. H. Goldsmith (Eds.), *Handbook of affective sciences* (pp. 619–642). Oxford, UK: Oxford University Press.

Martin, N. (2008). *Habit: The 95% of behavior marketers ignore*. Upper Saddle River, NJ: Pearson.

Matsumoto, D., Hwang, H. S., Harrington, N., Olsen, R., & King, M. (2011). *Facial behaviors and emotional reactions in consumer research. Acta De Investigacion Psicologica, 1*(3), 441–453.

Matsumoto, D., Keltner, D., Shiota, M. N., Frank, M. G., & O'Sullivan, M. (2008). What's in a face? Facial expressions as signals of discrete emotions. In M. Lewis, J. M. Haviland, & L. Feldman Barrett (Eds.), *Handbook of emotions* (pp. 211–234). New York: Guilford Press.

Matsumoto, D., & Willingham, B. (2006). The thrill of victory and the agony of defeat: Spontaneous expressions of medal winners at the 2004 Athens Olympic Games. *Journal of Personality and Social Psychology, 91,* 568–581.

McConnell, A. R., Dunn, E. W., Austin, S. N., & Rawn, C. D. (2011). Blind spots in the search for happiness: Implicit attitudes and nonverbal leakage predict affective forecasting errors. *Journal of Experimental Social Psychology, 47,* 628–634.

Mehrabian, A. (1971). Nonverbal betrayal of feeling. *Journal of Experimental Research in Personality, 5,* 64–73.

Morin, C. (2011). *Neuromarketing: The new science of consumer behavior.* Symposium presentation: Consumer Culture in Global Perspective. Available at http://www.springerlink.com/content/l008038078x70166/fulltext.html.

North, M. S., Todorov, A., & Osherson, D. N. (2010). Inferring the preferences of others from spontaneous, low-emotional facial expressions. *Journal of Experimental Social Psychology, 46*(6), 1109–1113.

Parkinson, B. (2005). Do facial movements express emotions or communicate motives? *Personality and Social Psychology Review, 9,* 278–311.

Picard, R. (1998). Computing for HCI. International Conference on Human-Computer Interaction. Research methodology. *Ergonomics, 46,* 1273–1292.

Picard, R. (2010, January). Research cited in *Wall Street Journal* blogs. *Technology News & Insights.* Available at http://blogs.wsj.com/digits/2010/01/19/mit-researchers-read-consumers-faces-to-make-a-better-taste-test/.

Schwartz, B. (2005). *The paradox of choice: Why more is less.* New York: Harper.

Schwarz, N., & Clore, G. L. (1983). Mood, misattribution, and judgments of well-being: Informative and directive functions of affective states. *Journal of Personality and Social Psychology, 45,* 513–523.

Shiv, B., & Fedorikhin, A. (1999). Heart and mind in conflict: The interplay of affect and cognition in consumer decision making. *The Journal of Consumer Research, 26,* 278–292.

Storbeck, J., & Clore, G. L. (2008). The affective regulation of cognitive priming. *Emotion, 8,* 208–215.

Wilson, T. D. (2003). *Strangers to ourselves: Discovering the adaptive unconscious.* Cambridge, MA: Harvard University Press.

Wilson, T. D., Lisle, D. J., Schooler, J. W., Hodges, S. D., Klaaren, K. J., LaFleur, S. J. (1993). Introspecting about reasons can reduce post-choice satisfaction. *Journal of Personality and Social Psychology, 60,* 181–192.

Wood, W., & Neal, D. T. (2009). The habitual consumer. *Journal of Consumer Psychology, 19,* 579–592.

16

Nonverbal Communication in Medical Practice

Robert Sheeler
Mayo Clinic

The ability to interpret nonverbal communication in general and microexpressions in particular is a key development in advancing the sophistication of medical therapy. Physicians, nurses, and therapists all rely on their ability to sense when there is more to a situation than a patient is disclosing. These situations occur for a wide variety of reasons. At times, patients are intentionally disingenuous while in other instances, patients have deep feelings, and the truth may not be accessible to their conscious mind. Formal training in nonverbal communication in medical curricula is very limited, and training in interpreting microexpressions—those very fast and fleeting facial expressions of emotion—is virtually nonexistent for doctors and nurses. The most skilled diagnosticians and care providers know that the ability to take and interpret a patient's history is often the single most important skill in diagnosis and formulating successful treatment plans. There are many charged areas of patient history wherein direct and forthright communication do not reliably occur enough of the time to ensure the safety of the patient and to keep the legal risks to the health care provider from becoming excessive.

Particularly sensitive personal areas for many patients involve discussing any history of psychiatric illness or symptoms of depression or psychosis. The ability to determine reliably whether a patient might be pregnant, important regarding medication choices or potential exposure to ionizing radiation with x-ray and related procedures, is another. Sexual behavior and orientation; alcohol and recreational drug use; and domestic, physical, sexual, or emotional abuse issues are all also potentially highly charged and have high potential for less than full disclosure.

Issues related to a patient's willingness to comply or history of compliance with various therapies—be they drug treatments or lifestyle modifications—are also rife with potential concealment of the whole truth. Further, the presence of others in the room during critical communications can further confound the ability to have honest conversations, as there may be competing agendas wherein disclosing certain information may be damaging to or risky within the context of the patient's relationship with the others present. A frequent example of such a complex situation is where a clinician has to ask, due to either the risk of a test involving x-rays or a medication that could cause harm to the fetus, a young woman who is accompanied by a parent whether she might be pregnant. The ideal in such a circumstance is to have the parent leave the room. In practice, this often is not possible as the parent assumes a protective and controlling role in the exam room and getting him or her out can be awkward or frankly confrontational. In this setting, one delicately asks the question—and I have found the best thing to do is to focus intently on the young woman's face for nonverbal clues. An expression of fear often indicates the need to pursue further and engage in the confrontation if needed to get the parent out of the room to ask the question in private. Either an amused or disgusted expression from the young woman is much more reassuring that she is unlikely to be pregnant. Presumably the former response, amusement, indicates that she cannot see herself in this way at this time in her life, while the latter response, disgust, indicates that she does not find even the idea of the intimacy required to cause pregnancy something she would consider.

The Merits of Nonverbal Communication Skills to Practitioners

The ability to detect and interpret nonverbal behavior—including macro- and microexpressions—can be of substantial value in two main ways. First, these nonverbal behaviors can serve as red flags that alert the practitioner and thus allow him or her to detect areas where there is a mismatch or incongruity between the reported history and the patient's reaction. This can be a sign to stop and probe more deeply or look for answers in other ways if the question is critical to the diagnosis at hand. Second, nonverbal behaviors and microexpressions can be openings to explore meta-level issues with patients who say that their issue is one thing but where the real underlying issue that needs to be addressed is something more structural. Sensing a patient's emotional response is often a time when a skilled clinician can find out what is really going on by asking questions about underlying factors, fears, and concerns that may not have been articulated by the patient on initial direct questioning. Similarly, I have frequently encountered confrontations that appeared to be about one thing but were actually about another. For example, I have recommended to some patients that care at a specific hospice might be the best in their circumstance but then saw their accompanying spouse show a spectrum of negative nonverbal facial expressions from anger to contempt and disgust (see Chapter 2). This meant there was some other underlying issue causing the spouse to be upset. This had to be addressed directly as spouses are often intimately involved as codecision makers with the patient about major choices in care. These negative emotions are signs to explore further the spouse's feelings. I have often found that such negative emotions relate more to the spouse's feelings of failure in an inability to provide this care at home, rather than the spouse's feelings of disdain for the facility that has been suggested to provide a team approach to end-of-life care. Bringing this to the surface can be healing for both partners, and taking the discussion to this level can deepen the therapeutic relationship with the provider.

The Practitioner as Sender and Receiver

As a family medicine physician with a busy clinical practice, and as a teacher in our medical school, I have come to believe that high-level skills both in the sending and the receiving of nonverbal communication are critical to achieving the best outcomes in medicine. The ability to consciously interpret nonverbal communication and to be in touch with the signals both we and our patients send makes the practice of medicine a more intentional— and often more successful—endeavor. When both of these elements are present, it allows a resonance to develop in the clinical interaction that can form or intensify the therapeutic presence.

The three largest parts of my work involve direct patient care, teaching clinical medicine, and leading teams of people. Although one-to-one patient care is the core of medicine, the other two facets of my work offer the ability to leverage the knowledge and skills I have to improve the lives of larger numbers of people if I can do them effectively. Being able to communicate and motivate both patients and learners is summed up in the phrase I constantly use when teaching medical students: *they have to know that you care before they care what you know.*

Empathy. My observations suggest that without the ability to communicate that caring, which is done in large part through deep reflective listening and nonverbal communication, treatment outcomes are not as good. Patients seem less likely to be compliant with medication, to put up with minor side effects, and to follow through with treatment. That phrase on caring was brought home to me in one of my early practices in a small town when a patient asked me to consult with a physician in the community who was in his 80s and was winding down his practice. This physician was known to have issues with heavy alcohol use. The patient said to me that he knew that this physician had alcohol trouble but that he really cared about him and his family. He said, "I'd rather have Doc B operate on me drunk than anyone else sober." That made me step back and reassess how much loyalty truly caring about someone over time could generate in a primary care medical practice.

In the evolution of medicine toward a more patient-centered enterprise, patients need to be able to receive counsel about options and then select the ones that are best suited to their own belief systems and needs. We as their caregivers provide a human face to the world of medical technology. It is paramount that this face is not only friendly but that it serves to accurately identify their understanding and true feelings about the life-changing choices available at critical junctures in their care.

Influence. In the emergency room, these choices often come with large amounts of blood or pain. But the health choices that patients make at quieter times in their care—in terms of treating their chronic illnesses and modifying their health behaviors—may actually be more important overall. Though they are less dramatic in appearance, they can result in larger numbers of lives and dollars saved and more suffering alleviated though avoidance or prevention of problems than through rescue at the point of disaster. Hence, the role of medical caregiver as one who provides counsel and access to resources is the gem at the heart of the relationship between patients and their providers. Communication is the lens that allows that key element to come into focus.

Reading. At times there is a striking difference between what people say and what they do, the latter often having much greater impact on their health care outcomes. Nonverbal communication is a form of behavior that is half-way between saying and doing. It provides a closer link to the core emotions and beliefs of the patient. Sometimes the elements that can be discerned from this behavior are more accurate and helpful than what is available consciously to the patients themselves.

I distinctly remember the first time I actually understood the vital importance of nonverbal communication in the practice and teaching of medicine. In teaching our students in their later years of training we often will observe them taking a history or doing an exam on an established patient we have known and had an ongoing care relationship with over an extended period of time. I have learned through experience that talking to patients about their smoking habits is a delicate endeavor in the best of circumstances. Although patients always have some underlying understanding of the desirability of not smoking from a health vantage, they also have layers of behavior, emotional investment, and feelings about the times they have tried to quit and the times they have been told to quit. The image of a field of land mines comes to mind as I write this.

I observed an enthusiastic and zealous medical student who was working with me begin to take a history from one of my patients who was a long-term smoker. The patient's presenting problem was cough and shortness of breath. In the first minute of the visit the student asked the patient if he was a smoker. Upon hearing a reply in the affirmative, the student launched into an assertive and escalating series of recommendations that the patient quit smoking. Upon initiation of the discussion, the patient stiffened and straightened his body in the chair. He first crossed his arms and leaned back. Then his jaw set, his brow furrowed, and he crossed his legs. After that he leaned forward into what is usually the neutral space between examiner and patient. Then after a bit, his nostrils flared, and after another minute into the encounter, his hands became fists pressed into the arms of the chair and his eyes narrowed. Both of their voices became louder. At that point I stepped in and took over the visit before things could come to blows.

What amazed me as much as the student's arrogance was the fact that he was totally clueless about the sequence of intensifying nonverbal clues indicating that things were going badly. He did not have the slightest idea that the patient was not receptive to his recommendations nor was he even receptive to hearing about them. The student had no inkling that his intensifying efforts were causing a breakdown in the doctor-patient relationship to the point that his chances of being of service to this man's care or modifying his lifestyle choices were asymptotically approaching zero. Even at the end, when things were 40 decibels louder, he didn't seem to perceive that his chances of being punched in the nose were going up exponentially with each further attempt to recommend smoking cessation. Once I stepped in, the visit ended amicably. I was never sure—even after explaining why he was ejected from the room—that the student learned much from the experience concerning how his inability to display and read nonverbal communication cost him his ability to influence. But for me it was a life-changing moment.

Learning to Be a Better Nonverbal Communicator

How could this student—and soon-to-be doctor—miss a series of escalating clues that began with a red flag, were followed by flares in the roadway, and concluded with his running a red light? How could he not know that there was more going on? How could he not know that the skills to be a successful clinician required more than his simple and methodical attempts to modify behavior by relentless recommendations and recitations of fact devoid of any investment in understanding the dynamic interplay between doctor and patient?

I started reading everything I could find on nonverbal communication from lay literature to textbooks. The most fascinating thing I found was a description of how salespeople are trained to recognize nonverbal clues and to take specific actions when they observe them. For instance, when a client crosses his or her arms or legs and moves back, this is a time *not* to try to close a sale. A technique taught in sales is to hand that person something—a drink, a brochure, or anything that makes the client break that posture *before* you move to the phase of the sale where you try to close the deal. It hit me that most medical professionals don't even have the level of formal training or expertise that a good salesperson gets before trying to convince you to buy a used car.

I realized a number of things after this encounter about being a doctor, and also a teacher of future physicians, and I came away with even more questions. I suddenly could see the following:

1. There is a wide spectrum of communication skill levels among students and practicing nurses and physicians.

2. Many people are not very cognizant of the loud and clear messages sent through nonverbal channels.

3. Communication teaching in the field of medicine is rudimentary at best and lags behind other professions such as sales by a substantial degree.

4. What we do in medicine is mostly sales—even though we are horrified to understand this and admit it out loud. Our ability to tell patients the benefits of therapy and to motivate them to make healthy lifestyle commitments is critical to their health outcomes. Those clinicians who get the best results are not simply better at picking the right pill or doing more meticulous dissections in the operating room—they are individuals who communicate well and treat the whole person.

I started to wonder whether this type of nonverbal communication skill was something that was innate or whether it could be learned. If it was entirely innate and critically important, then the only solution would be to find a way to test for it before training an individual to work in a field such as medicine where it was of great import to succeed. If, on the other hand, it was teachable to a motivated learner, then the relevant questions became exactly what to teach, how best to teach it, and how to sufficiently impress upon the trainees the import of such learning.

People Issues in Training

In looking at the group of learners and subsequently the group of practicing physicians, nurses, and other clinicians in regard to nonverbal skills, there are three main groups:

1. Those who intuitively and/or through study have a high degree of nonverbal skill (some of whom understand they possess this skill and some who don't fully know that about themselves).

2. Those who don't have much nonverbal skill but who do possess the insight to know that they don't.

3. Those who don't have much nonverbal skill and also don't know that they don't have much skill in this area.

The first group is easy and fun to teach. Surprisingly, they are often the ones who identify these skills as being of great value and are eager to learn as much additional material as they can. The second group can be taught, but their success depends on whether they can be motivated to think that nonverbal skills are important and whether the tools and curricular time are available to enable them to succeed. The third group is the most problematic. It is not uncommon for those who have done well enough to get into a competitive training program to think highly of themselves. This last group tends to overestimate their skill in a number of areas. Unless they can be shown clear evidence both that the skill is important and that they lack such skill, then the chances of helping them to attain substantial proficiency is low. Individuals in this group frequently think the information is too basic for their skill level when it is presented, yet when observed a few years later in residency training or in practice, they will often lack even a rudimentary understanding of nonverbal communication.

My observations as well as published research suggest that women, whether it is innate skill or learned in the context of cultural teaching, are often better at interpreting nonverbal signals than men (Hall, 1978; see Chapter 5). There are also data that suggest that patients perceive women as more compassionate caregivers. They may be more nurturing, but we don't know exactly how that affects treatment. We presented at a 2010 national conference on headaches data demonstrating that across 1,225 patients, cared for by 32 physicians, male physicians prescribe differently for male migraine patients than women migraine patients, whereas women physicians prescribe similarly for both genders. At the end of the day though, women may be more tired from the higher expressive intensity of their interactions. I have seen workshop presentations from others that claim that women often use their facial muscles considerably more than men in the course of interacting with patients. If this is true, then it too can take a toll and lead to higher fatigue at the end of the day.

Topic Issues in Training

The most vital things to teach everyone who will be a clinician or a leader, based on my experience, include the following:

1. The straightforward culturally specific macro body language skills

2. The facial expressions for the basic emotions and how to recognize these when they appear as microexpressions

3. The ability to recognize the nonverbal cues that they themselves give off and, subsequently, to understand the underlying emotional states, beliefs, and drivers behind their own internal dynamic

Gaining confidence in understanding and reading nonverbal communications can increase a person's confidence and leadership abilities in both direct and indirect ways. Directly, it makes the person feel surer of himself or herself because one can specifically trust what he or she is seeing and know that one's interpretations are correct. Even if someone is good at interpreting nonverbal communication on an intuitive basis, there is always that nagging question of whether one is correct in his or her intuition and subjective interpretations. Once someone learns specific solid skills based on expert teaching, then one not only feels a sense that something adds up to a specific message, but one actually knows based on objective data that he or she is highly likely to be correct in that assessment. Indirectly, this can enhance one's overall sense of well-being, confidence, and sureness in one's self, which may lead to calmness that projects leadership. It can also give one the basis to act and transform his or her work unit into a more benevolent place.

Conclusion: How to Deploy Nonverbal Knowledge

Whether in your role as a physician, or in any clinical or interpersonal encounter, once you notice something nonverbally, you have three options:

1. Notice the signal, ponder the meaning, and recalibrate your approach without in any way directly engaging the sender of the signal.

2. Use this as a red-flag moment that will allow you to probe more deeply with gentle, noninvasive approaches such as "You seem uncomfortable" or "Is there more to that than you have shared with me so far?"

3. Directly and openly confront the person—in effect, calling the game. This is the intense option and can escalate the situation. But it can also be transformative, especially of negative behaviors that can poison the workplace. To execute this strategy requires the highest degree of certainty that you are right about the nonverbal communication—which is yet another reason to study this realm as fully and as formally as possible. If you root out behaviors that center around contempt, anger, and disgust, you can make your workplace a safer and more uplifting place to work. This will also make it a more healing environment for patients. The reason that such behaviors often persist is twofold: there is often an underlying issue or unresolved emotion *and* the person has gotten away with it over time, usually through plausible deniability since most lack the skill to say with certainty that the behavior of the other was negative in character.

Mentoring, reading, and formal courses of study are all ways that can help a person become more proficient in nonverbal communication. In the practice of medicine and in leadership roles, nuanced high-level communication skills are of critical import to success. Finding others with similar interest and using your combined commitment can help to bring these elements into your corporate culture and into the larger world to the benefit of all. The invisible becomes visible, and once it is present it can be transformative *and* healing.

Reference

Hall, J. A. (1978). Gender effects in decoding nonverbal cues. *Psychological Bulletin, 85*, 845–857.

17

Nonverbal Behavior and Psychiatric Observation

Michael R. Privitera
University of Rochester Medical Center

I t is the evaluation of both verbal and nonverbal behaviors that allows for the optimal psychiatric assessment of patients and for one to determine the patient's potential imminent risk to self and others. I say this as a psychiatrist with 31 years of experience in the field of assessments and treatment of mental disorders. This experience has ranged from inpatient and outpatient care of psychiatric patients to the assessment and treatment of "psychiatric" manifestations in medically or surgically ill patients. Some of the treatment modalities used include individual, couples, family, and group psychotherapy. I apply a variety of psychotherapy theoretical constructs within these modes; the specific approach chosen depends upon the situation and setting. I prescribe psychotropic medications—such as antidepressants, antipsychotics, antianxiety medication, and mood-stabilizing medications—and also apply somatic treatments such as light therapy, electroconvulsive therapy, and many other emerging biological treatments.

Training to become a psychiatrist includes a group of core premedical courses while in college, then 4 years of medical school, followed by 4 years of psychiatry residency training. Residency training is done by means of lectures and supervision by more experienced and trained physicians and the latter years particularly by the psychiatrists and psychologists.

This supervision occurs directly or indirectly during the trainee's provision of care to patients. The trainee is taught to take painstaking care in being aware of and recording descriptions of the patient's behaviors and words and to bring these observations to their supervisor. Some of the modalities used in recording and conveying these words and behaviors, to be brought into supervision meetings, include a verbal recounting of the sessions, process notes (written or typed notes that summarize words and behaviors of the patient during the session), audiotapes—often augmented by the trainee's recollection of events—or videotapes made of sessions. It is by these various methods that trainees learn the value of verbal plus nonverbal behaviors in the assessment and treatment of patients.

Verbal behavior, such as the words selected by the patient, is very important in the communication and understanding of subjective feelings. The so-called "Freudian slip" is an example of words spoken that may give a window into unconscious processes of the person. Assessing why a patient may choose certain words can help understand interpersonal dynamic issues—e.g., why a patient who doesn't know me personally or professionally calls me by my first name instead of "Doctor" often can be illuminating.

Dependence on words alone fails us in many situations. One significant example is when a patient has alexithymia, which is the inability to put feelings into words. Such patients under periods of stress may manifest a host of medical (psychosomatic) symptoms and will be unable to make the conscious connection between these symptoms and their anxiety, relevant life stressors, or depressed feelings—all of which get expressed somatically (communicated) through physical symptoms. Patients may, however, appear depressed or anxious to the observer, and this assessment includes interpretation of nonverbal behaviors. There are many other instances where nonverbal clues can facilitate accurate assessments as well. Communication by both verbal and nonverbal means needs to be better understood to more fully help our patients. This chapter will be devoted to describing how a variety of nonverbal behaviors (NVBs) can be used in psychiatric and psychological settings.

Mental Status Examination

The most useful way to understand the utility of nonverbal behavior in a psychiatric setting is to examine it in the context of the mental status examination (MSE). The MSE is the central method used in the initial and ongoing evaluation of patients and uses verbal and nonverbal behaviors to do so.

The following categories, behaviors, and potential interpretations are included, but I emphasize that *the situational context must be considered*. The interpretations are best considered hypotheses that need further information to confirm or refute by all collateral data sources available. The data sources may include friends, family, care providers, and relevant past or current medical information. These interpretations of nonverbal behavior are presented to illustrate to the reader the enormous amount of potentially informative nonverbal behavior available to an observant psychiatrist.

Initial Observation of the Environment

There are a number of potentially useful nonverbal clues in the initial scan of the environment. First, assuming the patient is present—where did he or she choose to sit? A new patient coming in for evaluation, clearly taking what was the therapist's chair from among the chair choices, might have difficulty with authority or have self-esteem issues in having to lower the perceived power of the therapist. This is often seen in personality disorder patients. In contrast, a patient who shows hyper-respect for the therapist's seat may be overly concerned about compliance; in fact, this can be a window into the patient's thought processes of order, respect, and authority issues. Other seating clues arise as well—those who choose the chair with the back to the wall may suggest paranoia, self-protection, over even possibly Post-Traumatic Stress Disorder. Those who choose the chair closest to the door may also suggest paranoia, as well as the need for an escape route, or simply ambivalence about being there. A more malignant intention might be to prevent a person from leaving, blocking the exit (see Chapter 4 for more on body and proxemic issues).

Initial Observation of the Patient

Clothing. There are a number of static or appearance clues that also may be useful to the psychiatrist. The first is the *style* of dress. A patient who is formally dressed—"over the top" for the occasion—has anticipation of an interpersonal interaction, likely believes in the importance of first impressions, cares what others think, has status issues, and may be compensating for low self-esteem. A patient who is casually dressed—still within the bounds of appropriateness for the situation—may be more laid back, less worried about first impressions, and even may be making a "rebellious, antiestablishment" statement if very "dressed down" for the occasion. In contrast, a patient who is disheveled or malodorous may be indicative of someone having difficulty functioning due to some medical or mental illness or substance abuse. A patient who wears revealing clothing—sexually suggestive, in other words—may be either unconsciously attempting to keep others at bay by distracting people from his or her own psychological vulnerability or may be using this style of dress to control the session or interview. Thus, it also could be a conscious attempt to manipulate others, as often seen in Borderline or Antisocial Personality Disorders. As my previous supervisor once said about a female patient who dressed provocatively and spoke suggestively, "This isn't love . . . this is war." This revealing dress also might suggest some past history of boundary violations, such as physical or sexual abuse.

Second, the *appropriateness* of the dress for the weather can also be informative. A patient who is wearing a sweater in 90-degree (32°C) weather might inform about some health issue like cold intolerance associated with hypothyroidism. It might also be due to homelessness (wearing all the clothes the person owns), some state of intoxication, or another disorder impairing cognitive functions of consciousness, attention, orientation, and recall.

Grooming. The way in which the patient keeps his or her hair—neat, messy, overly controlled, plastered down, etc.—can give a sense of the orderliness of the individual. Likewise, the presence or absence of facial hair (e.g., presence or absence of heavy beard, large mustache, etc.) may suggest either someone who is aloof or available for interaction. Within grooming we can also classify a little-mentioned nonverbal clue—*odors*. A bad-smelling person suggests unkempt, poor hygiene—often associated with schizophrenia and psychotic processes so severe that they interfere with activities of daily living (ADLs) like hygiene—or motivation and drive impairments that occur in severe depression and also interfere with ADLs. Grooming can also indicate severe substance abuse disorders—where the whole day revolves around maintaining intoxication, leaving little desire or ability to spend time on hygiene. Bad smells may be clues to some untreated oral infection, or leg infection with diabetes, and so forth. Sweet-smelling breath may also suggest diabetes. There are other clues as well—the smell of gasoline or gunpowder, alcohol, and so forth provide some clues as to recent activities.

Dynamic behaviors. The behaviors shown *prior to approach (and later during approach)* can signal anger, distress, anxiety, depression, and so forth. A patient with clenched teeth suggests tension, anxiety, and possible anger. A patient with clenched fists suggests anger or internal distress.

A patient who is pacing suggests agitation, anxiety, and worry. A patient engaged in hand-wringing suggests psychic pain; this is often seen in severe depression.

Initial Observation of the Approach

There are useful clues in the body language, touch, and eye contact of the patient. First, as one approaches it will be easier to detect whether the patient is *sweating* or not and whether that is appropriate to the weather or time. Excess sweating may suggest nervousness or some endocrine disorder. Sweat or dryness can also indicate a patient's level of anxiety—typically, sweating hands or armpits might suggest strong anxiety, but dry hands would indicate calm. Second, we can also assess the *handshake,* or absence of a handshake. Absence (in a Western culture) may suggest being alert for paranoia, even contamination fears, as in Obsessive-Compulsive Disorder. A strong handshake, or even a two-handed handshake, suggests strong involvement and someone who is psychologically present. Third, the *distance* at which the patient stands from the therapist or evaluator may be informative as well; if there is less respect for personal space, this may suggest possible boundary violations in this patient's life (e.g., sexual abuse). If the psychiatrist's personal space is violated, and the individual is agitated, makes strong eye contact ("locking eyes" with the psychiatrist), and has clenched fists, this may warn about imminent violence.

The pattern of *eye contact* is also informative. A patient who does not make eye contact may be from a culture where respect is shown through the lack of eye contact (see Chapter 5 on culture). The patient may also suffer from Asperger's Disorder, where one of the criteria for its diagnosis is poor eye contact, or some form of autism. In contrast, a patient who makes too much eye contact may signal other states. In some psychotic individuals, staring can be an aggressive maneuver of visually "consuming" another person. A glare can indicate some paranoia, hostility, or both (see earlier warning about potential assault). A patient whose eyes dart around the room may be scanning for data and paranoid, or the patient may be in a self-protective mode as part of hypervigilance.

The patient with *dilated pupils* suggests possible excessive adrenaline flow and internal distress. The patient's pupils should be able to constrict with light; if they don't constrict with light, then we need to consider toxicity from medication or illegal drug use with anticholinergic side effects, such as dry mouth, constipation, urinary retention, etc., as well.

Observation of Patient Interaction

As the interaction continues, *vocal* clues can become useful (see Chapter 3). A patient who speaks in a hypophonic (soft, low) voice may have some laryngeal or neurologic problem, or it may mean the patient is delusional as these patients often whisper because they feel that they are being overheard by spirits. In contrast, a patient with overly loud speech may have bad hearing, may have some disinhibition caused by a frontal lobe injury or tumor, or intoxication may be causing this disinhibition. A loud patient may also be in a manic episode if the general motor activity levels are high as well, the speed of speech is rapid, and there is increased libido, energy, spending, etc. A monotone patient may be overly self-absorbed, preoccupied, excessively detail oriented, or even depressed. Typically, the speech pause times lengthen for the depressed patient and revert to normal when the patient's depressive episode is treated (a psychomotor phenomenon).

The *target* of the eye contact during the interaction is also informative—does the patient continually look at a particular family member while talking or describing incidents? Is he or she "checking" for a family member's reaction? This suggests some coaching by or fearful relationship with the target of the eye contact. A patient who rolls his or her eyes displays sarcasm, suggesting strong distrust or mocking of the interviewer.

Within the realm of *gross body movement,* we can detect signs of anxiety or impatience in leg bouncing, foot tapping, or finger drumming (see Chapter 4). A patient who is twirling a pen or other instruments suggests that he or she may not really be listening to what the interviewer is saying or may be impatient and wants the process to speed up. Quickened movements, along with rapid, hard-to-interrupt speech, followed by increasingly wide social interactions with numerous other people and an increased walking pace, may suggest a possible manic episode.

Within the finer movements of the patient's *facial expressions* we can detect specific emotions, as described earlier in this book (see Chapter 2). In the context of a psychiatric setting, this information takes on further significance. For example, a patient who shows facial expressions that are incongruent with his or her environment may be responding to some internal stimulation or dialogue. The patient may appear overly happy or overly distressed depending upon the content of the thoughts going through his or her mind. Sometimes the patient may specifically deny having hallucinations but may appear as if he or she is responding to them internally, talking to himself or herself, or making movements or grimaces consistent with internal dialogue but inconsistent to the external environmental situation. In such circumstances, the auditory hallucinations may be instructing the patient to not reveal that they are occurring—for a host of delusional, mostly paranoid reasons, e.g., believing that his or her internal delusional world is the world to be trusted as "real" and the outside world (real world) cannot be trusted.

There are even a few very specific signs in the facial expression associated with depression. One is the omega sign (as in the Greek letter omega, ω; see expression of sadness in Figure 2.1 in Chapter 2). This omega shape is found at the root of the nose from the contraction of the *corrugator* muscle of the forehead. Another sign involves the nasolabial fold of face (the line running obliquely from the side of the nose to the corners of the mouth). This fold relaxes in depression and becomes flattened, but when the patient begins to recover, this fold will tighten and be demarcated again. This noticeable facial change will occur before the patient can consciously report improvement in mood. This change along with other early psychomotor improvements can be examples of how the patient is "the last to know" he or she is getting better. Upon seeing such clues, the psychiatrist can expect the patient's subjective improvement soon.

In general, the *level of expressivity* in the face and body is also a clue to the psychiatric state. Patients can have flat or restricted affect—i.e., a narrow range of responses. This may be associated with the internal state of the lack of ability to respond to humor or joy, known as anhedonia. In contrast, appropriate affect for the event under discussion reflects responsiveness to the environment and the content of discussion, suggesting a patient who is engaged and may have the ability to positively respond to his or her environment. If the psychiatrist observes a rapid switching of affect, this might suggest an ultrarapid cycling of mood or be due to a neurologic condition such as a nonmotor (no visible movement) seizure disorder. At the extreme is emotional incontinence, or a dysregulation of emotion, uncontrollable outbursts of exaggerated, involuntary facial expressions, and pathological crying or laughter—all of which may be signs of serotonergic system damage. Certain strokes and multiple sclerosis can cause this condition.

Case Examples

In my career, there have been a number of instances where awareness of nonverbal behavior helped me make accurate diagnoses—of both the psychiatric disorder and contemporaneous safety and treatment issues. The following case examples demonstrate how the assessments of NVBs turned out to be life changing or lifesaving for the patients or the clinicians involved.

The Man Who Needed to Get Out of the Cold

A man presented himself to the emergency room reportedly because he had "no place to stay," and "it was freezing outside." He presented disheveled, inadequately dressed for the weather, and malodorous, having been living on the streets for a couple of months. He told the emergency room (ER) nurse evaluator that he was not hearing voices and denied suicidal or homicidal ideation. When the patient didn't think he was being observed, I noted that he was mumbling to himself and appeared to be responding to internal stimuli, getting agitated with what appeared to be an argument with the persona of the voice. I overheard him making statements threatening to kill the voice persona. He appeared frightened, his pupils were dilated, his fists were clenched, and he was pacing and sweating. He refused antipsychotic medication in the emergency room. Although he denied hallucinations when asked, he was committed involuntarily to the hospital as we deemed him a risk to self—due to inadequate self-care due to psychosis (NVB clues such as being disheveled, inadequately dressed for the weather, and malodorous)—and to others (NVB clues such as dealing with the internal stimuli voice persona in a life-threatening manner that could easily be displaced to persons nearby by paranoid distortions of reality, as manifested by clenched fists, dilated pupils, anger expressions, sweating, agitation, etc.). Thus, NVBs of his physical and mental decompensation helped diagnose his psychotic state as well as assess his risk of being an imminent danger to himself and others, even though direct verbal behaviors from the patient did not do so.

The Heartbroken Woman

A 24-year-old female patient thought to be suicidal by her family was brought to the ER by her family. She denied having suicidal ideation to the medical student in the ER, yet family reported that she stayed to herself, no longer exercised at the gym, turned down her friends' requests to go out, wasn't eating, and was noted to be tearful after the breakup with her boyfriend 3 weeks ago. I noticed that she looked sad, and she admitted that she was not enjoying things and had a restricted range of affect on her face. The muscular tone of the nasolabial folds of her face was diminished bilaterally, and she was clearly not reactive to attempts of her father to be positive and cheer her up. She was psychomotorically retarded, staying in one position for a long period of time. She appeared to be giving lip service to the idea of getting psychiatric help as an outpatient "eventually," and she had many excuses why she couldn't commit to making an appointment now from the emergency room. The patient had attempted to hang herself 2 weeks ago, interrupted by a friend's random visit, but she didn't seek help and minimized this behavior by saying she is past the previous suicidal ideation and is "just fine" now. Her mother noticed that she had been giving away personal items to friends, and recently she was witnessed buying three large bottles of extra-strength Tylenol, allegedly "to keep these in my pantry so I don't have to go out as often this winter." She was involuntarily hospitalized—on the assessment of acute suicidality, based upon her clearly depressed presentation, in the setting of a recent failed suicide attempt, and substantial indirect evidence such as lack of cooperation with treatment in the past and buying large amounts of Tylenol that she could use to poison herself. But the key factors to identifying the depth of her depression, hence the justification for committing her against her will, were these NVBs: her nonreactivity to attempts to cheer her, the strong facial clues, and the lack of body and posture movements that were incongruent with her verbal communication. Weeks later, when she was clinically better, she admitted that her plan was to kill herself when she was discharged from the emergency room visit that was referred to earlier, and she was grateful to us that we kept her against her will.

The Paranoid Man

A 22-year-old man arrived in the Psychiatric Emergency Department, accompanied by his mother after using cocaine for several weeks, staying away from home, and not eating or drinking. He was angry at the government for spying on him, guarded, suspicious, and his eyes were darting around the room. He kept staring at the TV monitor (that was off) for long periods of time but denied he was hearing voices, had paranoid ideation, or was getting messages from the TV. He had been telling his mother that the CIA was after him because he checked an Independent Party website before Election Day last year. He denied that he had any weapons on him when we asked but then clutched the front of his trousers over a pocket. He would not talk to the examiner further. The decision was made to search him with security guards present based upon the NVBs of clutching his pocket in the setting of agitation and paranoid delusions. A large steak knife was found in the particular pants pocket that he was guarding. He later admitted that he didn't trust us when we asked about the weapon, and he thought we'd take the knife away so that the CIA could come in to get him once he was rendered defenseless.

The Rude Boy

In a videotaped family therapy session, a teenage boy was being rude to his mother in the session, while the father, though silent, was noticed (by my supervisor during residency) to be smiling, and my supervisor sensed this to be nonverbal encouragement of the boy to act this way toward his mother. My supervisor also suspected, on the basis of this NVB observation, that interpersonal problems between the mother and father were significant. He hypothesized that the father's smile was a mechanism by which the father would indirectly punish the mother for their interpersonal difficulties via the rude behavior of their son. Using this information, I held the next session with just the parents to discern and work on the issues of their relationship in order to correct the pathological dynamic before having further sessions that would include the teenage son. In future family sessions, the father took an active role in supporting his wife and clearly would tell his son that his rude behavior was unacceptable. Thus, we were able to align the verbal and nonverbal behaviors, which enabled us to correct a core family difficulty.

The Vietnam Vet

A 58-year-old Vietnam veteran was brought in by the police after menacing customers at a local restaurant if they wouldn't continue to listen to what he was saying for long periods of time about social injustice issues, especially about how veterans were forgotten and poor. He had been off his medications from the VA Medical Center for 3 months, as he had been previously diagnosed with Bipolar I Disorder and Narcissistic Personality Disorder. He had recently become homeless due to being evicted from his apartment by threatening and then attempting to assault his landlord. During the interview in the ER, I shook his hand and introduced myself. The patient initially started out calm and seemed somewhat rational. However, his affect quickly became tense, his eyes widened and his lips narrowed in an angry expression, his pupils were dilated, and his voice became louder. He began waving his hands in the air and pounding his fist on the arm of the chair. He positioned his chair closer than mine to the door by getting up to take a tissue and then moving his chair more toward the door each time he got up. I sensed the potential for violence toward me as the patient was slowly cornering me. It was clear that his behavioral dyscontrol of his manic irritability and anger, all in the setting of his Narcissistic Personality Disorder, could easily escalate to violence if he perceived any slight to his sense of self while in this psychotic state. I told the patient how important what he was saying was (an important intervention in working with an agitated narcissistic individual) and how he probably represents the feelings of many other veterans too. After briefly summarizing what the patient said so he knew he was heard, I then excused myself under the pretext of having to get to the bathroom so that I could give him my full attention. Outside the interview room, I talked with security and the ER nurse with the plan that if he escalated further he may need restraints and to prepare the restraint bed. Security officers came in with me to finish the interview, but in a more concise, contained way, and I offered the patient medication at the end, which he took. Thus an assault to me was avoided by picking up on the NVB signs of potential physical violence, such as cutting off my access to the door, tension, dilated pupils, psychomotor agitation, loud voice, increased psychomotor activity of waving hands, and pounding fists. Hence, I was able to keep safe while also serving the needs of the patient. Moreover, the respect for the patient in my demeanor, and handshake, may have later helped this patient trust me enough to take medication to help his mania.

These examples illustrate that in clinical settings, nonverbal communication is important to establish and maintain the provider-patient relationship and can strongly influence the client's adherence to treatment—hence greatly affecting outcome and patient satisfaction with care. NVBs coming from the clinician are key to the patient's perception of the level of clinician compassion and concern in his or her care. As shown, NVBs are essential to the accurate diagnosis of psychiatric conditions and assessment of intention in the analysis of risk to self or other determinations.

Conclusion

Although the variety of nonverbal behaviors described here are not fully comprehensive, nor are they specifically definitive (pathognomonic) of any of the psychiatric states described, they do point out the wide amount of potentially useful information found across all sorts of nonverbal communication domains. As mentioned earlier, one would still need to cross-check those signals with information from medical charts, other verbal and nonverbal behaviors, family statements, and so on. However, NVBs are presented as a rich resource of information, highly useful and at times indispensable in the evaluation of patients. Mental illness and violence risk assessment instruments tend to emphasize verbal communication in combination with other static risk factors. The behavioral clues referred to in this chapter occur in the initial observation of the environment, the patient, the initial approach, and the subsequent interaction with the patient. As can be seen from the earlier descriptions, it is the combination of verbal and nonverbal behaviors that allows for the optimal psychiatric assessment of the disorder and, additionally, to assess the patient's risk to himself or herself and others. Note that these behaviors are bidirectional, and hence those VBs and NVBs coming from the clinician are just as important in establishing patient rapport and trust.

NVBs are important as a gauge to the evaluator's interaction with the patient, as well as the patient's interaction with others in session, thus giving enormous insights into how to best manage significant interpersonal dynamics. NVB is not really taught as a stand-alone subject in medical school. However, NVBs should be routinely taught and used to harvest enormously useful information for the good of the patient, the clinician, and society.

18

Synthesis and Conclusion

*Mark G. Frank, Hyi Sung
Hwang, and David Matsumoto*

W ell, that was quite a journey through the applied world of nonverbal communication. All the Part II contributors illuminated so many interesting observations and ideas. In this final chapter we will put their contributions into some context, identify the themes that emerged from those chapters, and discuss how that information may further inform science and practice so that our understanding of nonverbal communication can expand beyond the current state of knowledge.

We did not insist that our contributors follow a strict format for what they wrote; we provided them with a general set of guideposts to consider. We suggested that they tell us who they are and how nonverbal communication has or has not been helpful in their work, provide some examples of nonverbal communication that they encountered—including specific behaviors they might have noticed—and mention the sorts of things they learned about nonverbal behavior. We did not share drafts of their chapters with each other; thus, they were all written independently, although the three of us did comment on earlier drafts of each chapter. These comments were mainly structural. The only consistent content comment was a request to provide specific behavioral examples. So a contributor might say something like, "I noticed he was upset . . . ," and our comment would be, "Please detail the specific behavioral clues that caused you to notice or believe he was upset." This approach allowed us to better draw out the lessons learned from these applied settings, and it enabled us to correlate the various behaviors they noted with those reported in the scientific literature.

What follows is commentary on each chapter in the order they appeared. We will discuss any given observations when they first arise and thus won't need to discuss them at length if they reappear in a later contributor's chapter. This will mean slightly longer commentary on the earlier chapters. Then we'll conclude by distilling some common themes derived from these applied settings that can be directed back toward the scientific study of nonverbal communication.

Chapter Commentary

Chapter 7—Aviation Security and Nonverbal Behavior

Maccario's work is fascinating at so many levels and timely during our "age of terrorism." Maccario highlights a number of interesting points about trying to detect potential individuals with malintent in a semichaotic environment like an airport. The most compelling amongst his many insights involve the derivation of what he uses, a novel leveraging of the environment, as well as a clarification of the purpose of his techniques.

First, Maccario mentions that his work was rooted in that of the Israelis. The Israelis derived their work from hard experience and observation, tied with science, according to our Israeli colleagues. In essence, the Israeli approach is the same one that we believe makes this book unique—an acceptance of the role of real-world observation in deriving principles of behavior. Often in the scientific world, real-world observations are instantly dismissed because they usually do not conform to the tenets of good experimental science because one cannot run a clean, clear controlled experiment in the real world. But that throws out potentially useful information that should in fact inform science. And the success rate to date that the Israelis have had regarding aircraft hijacking or assault has been perfect (i.e., no successful hijackings) since they employed their tactics in the 1970s. It only makes sense to pursue this approach. However, scientists have attacked this approach, claiming it has not been validated. Yet, if you look at the behaviors Maccario describes, many of them are the same behaviors validated by scientists as what we've mentioned in Chapter 6 on deception and Chapters 2, 3, and 4 on the face, voice, and body. But there are a few that have not. For example,

Maccario discussed how manipulators can be a reliable clue to malfeasance (see Chapters 4 and 6), even though the published research data suggest that they are not a very strong or useful clue. We note later that Boughton's chapter on negotiation, along with work of some other contributors, also make a point to highlight manipulators and other body actions. What we know about manipulators is that they increase with discomfort; this suggests either that our contributors are being misled, believing this to be a reliable clue when it is in fact an illusion, or that maybe our laboratory studies just do not generate nearly the stress levels that real-world counterterrorism officers or negotiators face. Thus, it may be that the laboratory science *underestimates* the utility of manipulators as a reliable nonverbal signal because laboratory science cannot generate the discomfort levels found in real life. Moreover, it is likely we could not ethically generate such levels in the laboratory, but instead we would have to do some selected analysis of real-world cases to assess the utility of manipulators.

Second, Maccario also adds a novel observation concerning baseline behaviors. Normally when a scientist discusses baseline behaviors, he or she is referring to the individual's normal or typical style of behavior in situations when he or she is not engaged in deception or a hostile act. We scientists then make an *intra*individual comparison, as we contrast the individual's baseline behavior to behavior when he or she might be deceptive or about to engage in hostilities. That is, in a laboratory we can ask a subject to tell the truth once, and then tell a lie once, and compare his or her behaviors when lying and telling the truth—what is known as a within-subject comparison (intraindividual comparison). Maccario instead proposes to make *inter*individual comparisons, by comparing a given individual's behavior to that of the normal or typical behaviors shown by travelers within the airport environment. He advocates for his officers' knowledge of the environmental baseline on the basis of the fact that he and his security officers are present in the airport 8 hours a day, 5 or so days a week, and thus they know intimately the flow and patterns of this particular environment above and beyond that of any given traveler. We three editors travel by airplane a lot more than the average person, yet we might be in airports two to four times a month, for no more than 2 hours per visit, which is nowhere near the amount of time his officers spend observing people. He believes that this environmental baseline knowledge can compensate for many of the inherent problems posed by using an intraindividual baseline in the airport environment because we don't know what this specific potential terrorist looks like when he or she is not planning on disrupting aviation. Maccario's idea is that the environmental baseline, derived from countless hours of being in an airport environment, can help fill that knowledge gap to identify the behaviorally anomalous individual. Thus the baseline is not necessarily someone's own behaviors, but the general behavior of the crowd. This shift to an interindividual baseline makes sense under these circumstances.

This observation also provokes our scientific minds to reconsider the published research on lie detection abilities. Almost all those studies ask lie catchers to view a 1-minute video clip of an individual, with no background or other information about the person and often no individual or situational baseline. This technique may be an even more impoverished judgment task than we stated in Chapter 6. It further suggests that maybe our laboratory situations seriously underestimate the abilities of professionals to detect lies, as they damage the fourth condition for judgmental accuracy—the proper interpretation (see Chapter 6 on the Realistic Accuracy Model's four conditions for accuracy—relevance, availability, detection, and interpretation). Our lab science may have removed the environmental background and thus removed a key variable empowering proper *interpretation* of the behavioral clues.

Finally, Maccario also clarifies the goal of his nonverbal observational techniques—to identify which individuals to approach and gather more information. Note that he does not mention that he arrests anyone on the basis of his or her verbal or nonverbal behavior. He also notes that he and his officers know that there are no 100% perfect signs or signals that indicate someone has malfeasant intentions and that they all realize other innocent factors may generate those behavioral markers. So part of his job is to try to assess why that individual has shown those behaviors (what he called "human alarm resolution"). This strikes us as a very responsible use of nonverbal communication. If he cannot find an innocent reason for the behaviors, then that individual is simply put into the security lane where he or she receives additional screening. Airport security will be doing additional screening on randomly selected individuals anyhow, and thus if the science supports what he is doing, then it makes sense to use what we know to be one factor—the science of behavior—along with other factors to determine who should receive extra scrutiny.

Chapter 8—A Cop's Nonverbal Journey: From Gut to Mind

Ennett provides very useful information concerning how he developed his nonverbal skills. Starting with his military experience, moving to his local police officer experience, and then to his federal agent experience, he nicely describes how he came about his advanced knowledge of nonverbal communication, including a key factor or two that helped him unlock those abilities. Along the way, he raises an issue that scientists would question.

The issue is Ennett's description of "gut" level instincts about individuals. One consistent finding in the research literature is that one's confidence in his or her ability to spot liars is uncorrelated with one's actual abilities (see Chapter 6). Thus, someone who thinks he or she is really good at spotting lies tells us nothing about whether that person is actually good. The individual may in fact be excellent, but he or she is just as likely to be average or even terrible. Misplaced confidence can be toxic. We know people who are often wrong but never in doubt (to paraphrase the late psychologist Amos Tversky), who seem to create much collateral distress amongst all those they interact with, be they friends, colleagues, or suspects. Our guts may be filled with knowledge, but they are also filled with unfounded biases. Examining the relationship of, and distinguishing between, the two is a goal of science—but if individuals cannot articulate why they have the gut impression, our task is even harder.

However, Ennett also provides enough description to help us understand how someone *might* develop a good gut instinct for understanding people. Like Maccario's (Chapter 7) contribution on aviation security, Ennett too describes the process of developing knowledge about the environmental norms of the situations and people of his particular district. Thus, day in, day out, encountering the same people, and the same situations, will likely create a particular norm or set of base rates for behavior that one can readily use—consciously or subconsciously—to compare the current behaviors one sees. This seems equivalent to Maccario's description of the typical airport environment. If this base rate knowledge is subconscious, then we think this might be the "gut" to which Ennett refers. This experience base that he builds, from interview to interview, then becomes his unspoken, unarticulated "norm" upon which deviations are detected. We are not aware of any study that directly addresses this in the emotion and deception judgment literature. However, there is a long research history on judgment differences between experts and novices, and the transition from novice to expert involves much practice (10,000 hours according to Malcolm Gladwell's popular book [2008] on experts and excellence called *Outliers*), but it also involves reorganizing and recategorizing information to allow the proper weighting of information (e.g., Chi, Glaser, & Farr, 1988). When we do the math, 10,000 hours comes to around 5-and-a-half years' work experience. This seems right around the timetable that Ennett describes in his contribution. Again, we cannot determine that definitively, but it is interesting how that matches his progress.

The other concept that Ennett introduces is how his subconscious understanding of nonverbal communication was unlocked and made even more available to him through training. He describes how training clarified the concepts that previously had been floating in his mind at a more subconscious level and how by bringing it to consciousness helped him understand it all the better. It also allowed him to understand the limits of his knowledge.

Ennett suggested that what turned his initial gut reactions to something he was able to articulate was training that helped unlock the fact that he was comparing the consistency between a person's verbal and nonverbal expression. This is not really taught or studied in science, where instead scientists simply count specific clues—but do not look at them in context. Our research teams have done that, and it was interesting to note that Ennett was subconsciously doing the same. Thus, it is not the presence of fear that betrays deception; it is the presence of fear that does not fit the story line. Fear can in fact be a sign of truth if the person is describing a scary experience. This is a different approach in that typical scientists will simply count signs of fear and not put them into verbal context. This is then a good example of that symbiotic relationship where a real-world practitioner had noted something that the laboratory then confirmed, and then that confirmation could be fed back to other real-world practitioners.

Ennett also introduces us to nonverbal communication beyond deception—identifying aggression. He notes how various body and facial clues tipped him off to impending violence. He notes how he used that knowledge to change tactics to cool things down, thus avoiding the situation in the first place.

Finally, Ennett, like other contributors, recognizes that there are no guaranteed signs of deception in the nonverbal behaviors of anyone. He also recognizes that the interpersonal context in which the nonverbal is assessed is critical to its interpretation. He understood, in his story about the bank teller who showed fear even though she was not the target of the investigation, that simply asking accusatory questions can generate signals that a less informed person might erroneously infer were caused by deception.

Chapter 9—Anomalies and Nonverbal Behavior

Moskal's chapter also recognized the role of anomalies in behavior. Again, this concept of comparing behaviors to some external or historical context has been heretofore missing in the scientific literature on deception. He describes how the nonverbal behavior of crying exhibited by the patriarch of the family—when discussing money, not the death of his family member—was anomalous and alerted him to not necessarily assume the man was lying, but to assume that there was something more hidden and that he should focus his investigative skills to resolve this discrepancy—and in the process he solved the case.

His chapter was also a good reminder of the dangers of overconfidence in one's abilities to read others. He describes a story where he stumbled into catching a bank robber, but only through luck, and notes that it was his overconfidence in his abilities to read people that caused him to miss obvious clues to the behavior of the other person that would have been apparent if he entered the situation with a more open mind. This is a common reason why people miss detecting lies—they get so focused on one particular explanation, theory, or observation that they only pursue evidence consistent with that theory and thus avoid looking closely at anything not directly related to it. Scientists can make the same mistakes—and thus may miss some interesting phenomenon because of a too-narrow focus on only the one specific hypothesis. And other science has shown that initial pieces of information disproportionately affect final judgments (what are called primacy effects; Anderson, 1965)—that is, these pieces of information help establish the hypothesis, and then all ensuing data is interpreted in light of the first pieces of evidence. In fact, we may not know which of the pieces of evidence is most important until we have them all, but unfortunately the randomness of discovery can bias the ensuing search for truth.

Moskal's chapter also serves as a reminder that accurate nonverbal communication is dependent upon not only noticing signals but interpreting them properly. He noted the signals in both stories he told—but he did not bother to interpret them in the first story about the bank robbers, in which he stumbled into the truth, whereas he accurately interpreted them in the second story about the Ponzi scheme.

Chapter 10—Understanding Body Language and the Polygraph

Baxter's chapter provides some insight into what we think is typical of most experienced police officers—that they do not receive much if any training on nonverbal communication. In fact, the training he observed involved tricking people into confessions. He observed the power of certainty and threats. But he did not get any formal training in nonverbal communication.

When he did learn of some potentially useful phenomena, it was stuff like this: "that when people fold their arms or they raise their foot so the investigator can see the sole of the shoe, then they are using blocking mechanisms. Also, if someone touches his or her nose while the officer is talking, then the person believes that the investigator's story or statement 'stinks'" (see Chapter 10, p. 174). However, we emphasize the word *potentially* useful, not *actually* useful, because there are no published research studies demonstrating any of this. These are the sorts of observations that often come from popular magazines or books but do not have any sound scientific backing. Or, as we found later, they may come from single case studies, as in Hirsch and Wolf's (2001) case study of former president Clinton's nose touching when allegedly lying.

It is interesting then to note that his first formal training came a few years later, and one key concept emphasized in this training was to look for changes in the baseline behaviors of individuals. Specifically, he was taught to look for nonverbal behavioral patterns when asking nonthreatening questions and to use those as a baseline for their truthful behavior. But that was all in service to better conducting a polygraph examination.

What Baxter then notes is that nonverbal communication shifted the order of investigation during polygraph examinations. Originally, he would conduct the polygraph and then, depending upon the results, conduct an interrogation to clarify deceptive responses or to obtain confessions. The newfound knowledge of nonverbal communication moved his observation skills up in the process—so that he was now starting the investigation, including examining nonverbal communication, *before* the polygraph test, as well as after the test. This was a profound shift. Our conversations with government polygraphers in the United States and other countries suggest that they all strongly believe that nonverbal signals are a very useful adjunct to their polygraph machines. Often they can use these skills to get accurate information without giving the polygraph test at all. These accomplished individuals don't see nonverbal signs of lying as a direct competitor to the polygraph; they see nonverbal signs as one more potentially useful piece of information that can help them sharpen their observations, better construct their tests, and improve their interpretation of the posttest interaction with subjects.

This was highlighted very well in Baxter's story about the man who poisoned the soup that accidentally harmed his daughter. Rather than simply taking the man's responses at face value, Baxter noticed a nonverbal change. Even though Baxter did not know exactly what this meant, he knew at least that this topic meant something to this man. So he adopted a sympathetic but confident pose and phrased a question in a way that made it seem that he knew more than maybe he knew. Notice as well that it was Baxter's own nonverbal behavioral display that was part of what made this compelling to that man. In the research literature on detecting deception from behavior, rarely is the behavior of the interrogator even considered (Frank, 2005), and yet in this instance it was essential to the outcome, and it is likely essential to most outcomes. Given what we know about lying—that the liar knows the truth in his or her head—this likely made that man feel transparent to Baxter. And given that Baxter adopted a sympathetic but not judgmental pose, he made it psychologically safe for the man to confess.

Baxter also courageously tells us of a time when he was misled by a nonverbal behavior—the man who cried as he confessed his crime (but as it turned out, only part of his crime). The man's nonverbal display caused Baxter to feel sympathetic to the man and to thus end his investigation prematurely.

In his final story about the job applicant who was sexually abusing his stepdaughter, Baxter points out again the issue of a change in baseline behavior. He identifies this change: "his demeanor—drooping head, lowered voice, and the lack of any gestures" (see Chapter 10, p. 179). This configuration is likely a guilt or distress behavioral pattern (see Chapters 2 and 4). And notice that Baxter did not have to probe with a specific question; just asking a confident "What else?" caused this man to go from initially admitting that he might have been seen undressing by the stepdaughter to admitting to sexually assaulting another daughter.

Finally, as with Ennett, Baxter also acknowledged how the specific scientific training he received later in his career helped him unlock the subjective or informal information that guided his earlier work. It also helped him obtain the language to train his protégés in a way that combined his hard experience with the science and empowered him to state with more confidence that these behavioral clues are not perfect and are often better used to obtain more information from a subject than to draw a hard conclusion about the subject. We think this is a very responsible use of nonverbal behavior.

Chapter 11—Nonverbal Behavior in the Courtroom

Judge Brownell reiterates many of the interesting observations of others in his contribution and adds some unique ones. First, he acknowledges that nonverbal clues are a helpful adjunct to interpreting issues in court, such as gauging the credibility of a witness or other testimony. Second, he suggests a novel use—not reported in the literature—that nonverbal clues are important to help a judge understand whether a litigant who appears without an attorney truly understands what is going on, including the full repercussions of the judge's rulings. Brownell makes a compelling case that taking this extra step to note the reaction and then addressing it—despite the time pressures faced by a judge—can not only save time later (as the litigant will be less likely to return to court) but also improves the litigant's (and hence society in general) confidence in our legal system.

Brownell acknowledges, as do the previous contributors, that examining nonverbal clues in context is critical to interpreting them. Also like the previous contributors, he imports the idea of a general environmental baseline, along with a personal behavioral baseline, to deploy when assessing whether or not the nonverbal behavior "fits" the context. Thus the juvenile "Calvin" who was responsible for the burglary did not match the normal behavioral patterns of typical juveniles (general environmental baseline). Then he noted the subtle smile shown by Calvin that did not fit Calvin's specific behavioral baseline. He noted the signs of worry or distress shown by Calvin later in the interview and his leakage of these facial signals at key points in the interview. The judge noted that none of these nonverbal signs prove Calvin's guilt, but they all alerted Brownell to dig deeper by asking more questions—questions that eventually undid Calvin's lies. Parallel to this, Brownell also noted how some earlier training by our colleague Maureen O'Sullivan helped unlock many of his capabilities to detect those leakage signs in the face.

Brownell also raises the issue of the absence of behavior. This is an interesting and important part of nonverbal behavior analysis that is often forgotten. Humans are wired to notice things that happen—but we are much less wired to notice when things don't happen (Nisbett & Ross, 1980). Sherlock Holmes made famous the observation that the absence of a behavior not noticed by others—in this case, the dog that did not bark—can be as much of a clue as the presence of a clue (the absence of the bark suggested that the person who must have passed by the dog was known by the dog). Similarly, Brownell notes that the absence of signs of anxiety, nervousness, anger, or discomfort in the face of Calvin was a tip-off that got his attention. In science, we too are often not as well equipped to measure the role of the absence of behavior on a phenomenon. We determine the presence of various behaviors and then compare a subject's amount of those behaviors to his or her behaviors in some baseline period. We often do not code such behaviors by presence versus absence for each time period. Thus a 1-minute segment of behavior will log the number of nods, smiles, or whatever. It often will not log the amount of time spent not doing a given behavior.

In the story about the litigants, Judge Brownell discusses how a close examination of the nonverbal reaction of the litigants can reveal important information to the judge about whether the individuals understood what happened, the reasoning behind it, and whether it met their expectations. He nicely points out how had he not stopped and asked further questions about how the litigant reacted, he would not have discovered the new problems created by his decision. He also points out other research showing that when litigants feel like they have been heard, they feel the procedure was fair. This is interesting to us because normally when we interact with judges or attorneys they immediately want to know when people are telling lies in court. But this element of using nonverbal observation skills to ensure the clarity of the ruling, reduce future redress litigation, and so forth is novel and seems to be an excellent idea on many levels.

Finally, Brownell raises a great point about how to better exploit nonverbal skills in the courtroom by rearranging the courtroom so as to better view more of the nonverbal expressions of litigants. He suggests moving the witness box so that the judge (and/or the jury) can get a better, face-to-face view. In some of his caseload, the judge suggested asking the person who testifies to do it from the front of the jury box, so the judge can see more than just a profile of this individual. All very intriguing ideas, and it would be interesting to test the effects this might have on witness credibility. In previous Supreme Court decisions, Justice Scalia has argued that face-to-face cross-examination is essential to a defendant's legal protections because it has the power to unmask a lying witness (*Coy v. Iowa*, 1988). Maybe this would occur if the witness was face-to-face—rather than in profile—with a jury (or judge if he or she is the trier of fact). Future research will we hope address that issue.

Chapter 12—Persuasion, Negotiation, and the Law

Freshman outlines a number of ways in which an attorney can use nonverbal communication. He agrees with Brownell about the importance of spotting deception in the courtroom. And like Brownell, Freshman takes the concepts and principles of nonverbal communication further to push it into corners of the legal process in which it is often not considered, such as helping manage a client who is going through a very emotional situation or in facilitating negotiations.

Freshman also introduces us to a slight change in terminology. We had used the term "hot spot" (Chapter 6) to describe the emotion or other nonverbal behavioral clue that contradicted the words or other aspects of behavior. Freshman uses the terms "soft spots" and "sweet spots" to capture particular elements of the hot spot. He argues that these moments are "soft" and "sweet" because they can be exploited to obtain cooperation in a number of different ways. And because this implies cooperation, *hot spots* sounds too confrontational, which might work at cross-purposes to cooperation. This is a good example of how scientists are always seeking to adequately conceptualize a phenomenon. We still prefer the term "hot spots," as it can apply to confrontational situations as well as the cooperative ones. But we can understand the logic of Freshman's terminology. The term "hot spots" has been around now for some time, and we fear the introduction of these other terms may confuse individuals. However, it may be that Freshman's terminology better captures some particular situations. When are the costs and benefits of using a particular term in such proportion that it becomes worthwhile to change the term and try to update the field? We don't know, but this is an issue scientists face often.

On other issues Freshman further reinforces the science and observations of other contributors. He discusses the importance of the verbal/nonverbal discrepancy as a potentially productive source of information—one that should be mined thoroughly with additional questions to fully elucidate the nature of the discrepant behavior.

He also adds an additional role for nonverbal communication to help monitor how effective the lawyer's argument is on the other person. Are there subtle signs of resistance? Do we see subtle signs of pleasure? The detailed observation of nonverbal communication can clearly help the lawyer manage his or her line of reasoning to obtain maximal impact on the client, witness, jury, or cross-examinee. In a similar vein, he also discusses how an attorney can use detailed observation of the client while issuing options to see which ones to sweeten or withdraw. Thus, in any situation in which the attorney wants to know the feelings of any individual he or she encounters, close nonverbal behavior observation can be an effective adjunct to his or her effectiveness.

Chapter 13—Negotiation and Nonverbal Communication

Boughton's contribution on negotiation is very much geared toward almost immediate application by describing the process to deploy one's nonverbal observational skills. It is these nonverbal elements he raises that will be our focus.

First, he raises the issue of context, which is similar to the issues of baseline discussed by others. He states that the negotiation context is much simpler than a law enforcement context, as the motive for the other person in the interaction is always clear—to get the best deal. This is not always the case in law enforcement, as motives may include getting away with a crime, avoiding punishment, protecting another person, and so forth.

Given that narrow focus, he gives the reader much more of a "how to" approach to using nonverbal behaviors in negotiations. He raises a number of points that catch the eye of the scientist. First, he puts stock in the utility of the manipulators (see Chapter 4) to identify changes in the other's thinking or comfort level. As we've noted earlier (Chapter 6), manipulators have not shown a strong relationship to deception despite many beliefs about this. Likewise, he mentions fidgeting, which research shows people often believe to be associated with deception, when in fact the data suggest it is not a good clue—and actually, often the opposite pattern happens such that liars move or fidget less than truth tellers (DePaulo et al., 2003). However, as we mentioned earlier in this chapter, it may be the added emotional value of real-world situations that gives these clues diagnostic value in the real world because the lab studies are not emotionally compelling enough to provide diagnostic value in the laboratory.

Boughton also mentions a few things that apply to managing the interpersonal situation in such a way as to give us the best possible chance to identify useful and diagnostic behaviors of the other. He writes about throwing in comments to see exactly what this person's "hard no" comment looks like behaviorally. He writes about having other conversations to identify how this person reacts to things he or she likes or dislikes. In other words, he is actively generating baseline behaviors at a time of his choosing. The advantage of this approach is that he can know when he will get a look at the baseline, rather than allowing that insight to emerge spontaneously through random conversation. Thus he can prepare himself ahead of time to be ready to note carefully the behaviors that occur during these crucial segments of interaction. This aspect of situation management is almost always ignored in the research literature on nonverbal clues and lying (Frank, 2005). Yet, based on what he argues and upon what we've seen, we believe it is very important.

Boughton also introduces us to the concept of the crunch point. This is the point at which the most important information and decisions are made, leading to an opportunity to deploy fully all nonverbal observation skills to detect the meaning behind the spoken words. It is interesting to note that the crunch point is driven by the situation, as compared to hot spots, which are driven by the behavior of the individual. The crunch point is the moment at which one should turn up his or her nonverbal observation abilities to high. He also suggests that a second "spotter" can help observe the nonverbal behaviors present during negotiations, so that the main negotiator can focus a bit more on the details and/or numbers in the negotiation. This technique is used in many law enforcement agencies whenever possible, and we have had some luck in persuading agencies to do this. It takes the pressure off the individuals by allowing one of them to focus mainly on the questions, and the other to focus more on the behaviors associated with the response.

Finally, Boughton makes an interesting suggestion about how one's focus might change depending upon the nature of the negotiation. If it is a collaborative negotiation, then one might train his or her nonverbal detection focus on to the other person and the issues related to the relationship. If it is distributive, then one might look harder at nonverbal behaviors that occur as a function of the topic of discussion. This seems reasonable, and scientifically, this sort of focus change and its resultant effects on either judgment or patterns of behavioral clues has never been studied, to the best of our knowledge.

Chapter 14—Interpersonal Skills and Nonverbal Communication

Longford's contribution concerns the utility of nonverbal observation as a means to improve general interpersonal skills. One thing that stands out is his excellent description of the history of training in organizations and his identification of how bureaucratic processes may have led to a discounting of the importance of nonverbal skills through two erroneous beliefs: first, that training on technology was somehow more important and second, the fact that nonverbal training outcomes could not be measured on some clear metric—and that they were innate anyhow and thus immune from training. We still see this today, where decision makers seem to believe that if technology is involved in making judgments, then these judgments are somehow more objective and scientific than judgments made without technology. But we counter that science is the *method* of inquiry, and social science and other seemingly more wooly topics are just as amenable to the scientific method as measuring chemicals and so forth. Thus knowledge about judgments made via behavioral science is real science.

As with our other contributors, Longford reiterates the importance of noting that *when* a particular nonverbal behavior occurs is critical to its interpretation. In other words, what is happening in the words and other behaviors of the individual as this clue is being expressed?

Longford adds a number of new ideas. First, he suggests that not all nonverbal behavior is the same—that we should weigh the importance and potential informativeness of each clue by the nature of its origin. That is, a clue that is biologically driven and universal across people will be less controllable and thus potentially more informative about someone's internal states than a behavior that is subconscious or one that is clearly conscious and under the greater control of the individual. This makes a great deal of sense to us. Although issues concerning automaticity and spontaneity are not as clear-cut as one would think, the clearly controllable behavior will be the one most likely used to try to mislead or persuade others because it *can* be used to do that. Moreover, a "faked" version of a controllable behavior is likely much harder to distinguish from its spontaneous version than would be a less controllable behavior between its faked and spontaneous versions. In fact, some research does show clear and measurable appearance and timing differences between smiles that are driven by an emotional reaction versus smiles that are simply posed for social purposes (see Chapter 2). This is a topic amenable to future study.

Longford also speculates as to which types of people might be most amenable to nonverbal training. This topic of who can be trained has never been dealt with directly in the literature, although there are studies suggesting that those with higher motivations, such as professional psychologists of police officers, might be better (e.g., Ekman, O'Sullivan, & Frank, 1999; O'Sullivan, Frank, & Hurley, 2010). Longford takes this one big step forward by identifying prototypical student types that will likely apply to any group training situation. He identifies how the popularity of television shows featuring expert lie catchers or nonverbal readers has generated a number of people with such high expectations for the ability of nonverbal skill training to make them into perfect mind readers that they inevitably walk away from training disappointed. In fact, a recent study showed that avid viewers of at least one of these TV shows were poorer detectors of deception than those who did not watch (Levine, Serota, & Shulman, 2010).

The people he finds most amenable to training are those who are open to science, want to know the science behind the behaviors, and can see direct, tangible results of the training for their jobs or life circumstances. But Longford notes that what helps make them better students is that these groups will study harder and practice more, even when the training has concluded. This makes perfect sense. The effects of self-motivation have not been studied in the scientific literature in any systematic way to our knowledge (although they are addressed by Ekman et al., 1999). As mentioned earlier, others, including ourselves, have found various correlates to accuracy, but Longford suggests that the reason motivation works is because individuals will practice more often and will continue to educate themselves after the session is over. So it seems that sheer hard work, with an open (but not *empty*) mind, is the optimal combination. Again, science has not fully explored this.

Chapter 15—Nonverbal Communication in Consumer Research

Harrington's contribution takes us in a different direction again. As an accomplished scientist himself, he employs tight experimental designs to study how nonverbal clues may further inform product development and marketing. His contribution does a nice job of explaining the mind-set of typical consumers—how we are often not very self-reflective in our daily lives, and for many of our mundane tasks, we simply often are not aware why we do what we do. Thus asking people about products using entirely verbal measures can put the subject/consumer in a very awkward position of rating something he or she is not sure of.

Harrington describes how the consumer situation is different from the other interpersonal, legal, or law enforcement situations we've addressed so far. Consumers are not dealing with life and death situations; they are dealing with mundane tasks that they wish to accomplish easily and without inducing any negative feelings. Thus, he argues that consumers are more motivated to remove the negative emotions from their use of various products than they are about feeling really happy about using the product. He has shifted the focus a bit to the importance of *both* the presence and absence of negative emotional expression, and this major shift in research focus was due in some part to our collaborative work involving nonverbal behaviors.

He points out that his collaborative research with us has found many emotional expressions in product research. He found that most of them are moderate to low intensity, of brief duration, often partial in appearance, and mostly negative. The startling statistic he presents is that across almost 3,000 facial expressions noted in the studies, 39% of them were inconsistent with the verbal report issued by the consumer. This is very interesting, particularly in light of the fact that consumer preference is almost always assessed by verbal report. It is also interesting that, as he described earlier, individuals often don't have access to their preferences consciously and to see that their more "involuntary" reactions—expressed through emotions—are so strongly biased toward negativity. This suggests a very strong rethinking on the part of standard consumer researchers on how they assess consumer preference.

The other advantage of the science of nonverbal communication, as pointed out by Harrington, is that its incorporation into his work has enabled him to make more objective what had been previously subjective to his research team. His company is a world leader in consumer goods, and thus he works with very sharp and insightful colleagues, but this approach has helped him to identify measurable features in emotion expression, which in turn enabled him to teach his research team exactly what to look for, rather than speaking in vague terms about "vibes" coming off consumers.

Chapter 16—Nonverbal Communication in Medical Practice

Sheeler's contribution moves us into the world of medicine and clinical practice. He identifies a very similar issue as Longford—that within his profession, nonverbal communication almost seemed too squishy a concept to measure. This likely caused it to be ignored during physician training. Yet, Sheeler lays out many different situations in which patients may be motivated to withhold critically important information from the physician, much to the detriment of their own care. He notes how nonverbal clues are so important in tipping him off about what questions to ask, and when, and how, to help overcome the barriers to patient disclosure such as embarrassment, privacy, potential illegality, punishment, and so forth.

Like almost all of our contributors, Sheeler notes that the verbal/nonverbal mismatches are the most compelling sources of information in the clinic. And like the other contributors, he points out that these mismatches are simply clues, not answers, to the fact that something interesting is going on in the head of the patients and that he should try to identify what motivates that action. Thus he lays out a nice set of examples about how he would interpret a behavioral reaction and how he might then follow up on it to exploit it to better care for his patients. He also expands this beyond just the patient into the patient's family or caregiver to further secure their involvement in care. This issue of using nonverbal clues to help successfully manage the family of the patient has not been systematically studied by scientists, but it should be.

Sheeler also emphasizes the fact that he is not just a detector of nonverbal signals, but is a producer of them (as did Baxter in his chapter). He describes how important it is that he express the nonverbal clues that will maximize his patient's comfort but also secure his compliance. The proper displays of empathy, for example, are critical to creating the "space" that a patient might need to disclose some important piece of information that might alter the physician's course of treatment for that patient. He also realizes that his expression of nonverbal signals, and his reading of the patient's nonverbal signals, occur in a back-and-forth manner that enables enough feedback for him to know when to adjust his behavior to ensure maximum compliance by the patient. But he recognizes that he has to be in control and use his nonverbal displays in a strategic manner.

As with others, Sheeler identifies how receiving some formal training—particularly later in his career—helped him unlock many of his nonverbal observational skills and made him better at identifying nonverbal behavior. He further proposes, like Longford did, that certain people are more amenable to being trained than others. He notes that it is the individual who thinks he or she has much nonverbal skill but in fact does not who is the most difficult to train. Those who have intuitively good skills, or those who don't but know they don't, tend to be better students of nonverbal training. This observation has not been subjected to scientific testing, although groups with higher motivation tend to do better (e.g., Ekman et al., 1999; but no data on whether they can be trained more effectively).

Finally, Sheeler lists those skills he feels most important to be trained—first and foremost are nonverbal observation skills, followed by management of one's own behavior skills. Then he explains the options a physician faces once he or she recognizes some nonverbal clue or behavior that does not fit—the physician can simply recalibrate his or her approach, use it to gently probe the patient more deeply, or directly confront the patient about the topic (the latter of which he sees as the option at greatest risk to alienate the patient, but at the same time he indicates that confrontation can be transformative). This is consistent with what the other contributors have mentioned—that nonverbal clues are for more than lie catching or more than just emotion assessment. Again, there is surprisingly little science on which approach listed might be effective, which won't, and when they might be effective. However, we see that outside of his third approach—the direct confrontation—there seems to be no drastic evaluation shift as a function of noticing various behaviors.

Chapter 17—Nonverbal Behavior and Psychiatric Observation

Privitera's contribution is also practice driven. He points out that most of the training he received as a physician and psychiatrist was done informally, through interactions with his supervisor. As a psychiatrist, he is likely more prepared than a general-practice physician to make detailed nonverbal observations, as psychiatry involves identifying behaviors to diagnose the disease, whereas the rest of medicine involves identifying other things like visible marks, rashes, and other indicators to diagnose the disease.

Like other contributors, he notes the importance of both verbal and nonverbal information. What he does through his outline of the mental status examination is to peel back specific layers of observation like an onion—starting with the wider situation, moving into the static clues of the individual, and then into the dynamic behaviors of the individual.

Privitera raises a number of new sorts of nonverbal clues that haven't been discussed much in this book. He describes the role of dress and style—two nonverbal clues—as potentially diagnostic clues to understand the patient. He also introduces us to the use of odors—body odor, alcohol, gasoline—to make inferences about the inner emotional and mental states of individuals. There has been research on the role of odors in humans but mainly about how the odors may trigger various impressions of others (e.g., Schleidt, 1980). In this case, Privitera has elevated odors to a diagnostic variable.

Privitera then lists a number of interesting case studies in which nonverbal observation was the key to addressing each case. Much of the informative nonverbal clues he describes are the incongruent ones, such as sweating when it is cold, whispering, and facial expressions that are not tracking the interaction with the psychiatrist. Many of these behaviors are noted in medical diagnostic manuals and are taken as one clue, amongst the constellation of clues, to indicate various mental states. He notes, as do all our contributors in this volume, that nonverbal clues are just one piece of a larger picture; no clue is perfectly diagnostic, but in conjunction with other observations, histories, and measures, they are important to identifying and managing very difficult interpersonal encounters with mentally ill individuals.

Lessons Learned

This foray into the applied world enables us to extract some principles for scientists. There are very clear commonalities raised by all contributors, much of which is invisible in the scientific literature. Moreover, all contributors recommend some optimal ways to use their knowledge of nonverbal communication to better do their jobs, and there are commonalities as well.

Commonalities

Importance of training. This may be a selection bias, but all of our contributors believe nonverbal communication training is lacking in their jobs, yet they all believe it is essential to their optimal performance on the job. Many lamented the fact that they didn't get good scientific training until later in their careers. This raises the questions of whether training can be beneficial, and the optimal point in one's career to train an individual. Our experience is that although we think all training is helpful, individuals who have already started their careers, seen how their jobs actually function, and even encountered a few bumps or an occasional bad outcome are the most amenable to training. First, this is because they now know, as Moskal discussed in Chapter 9, that they are no longer infallible. In fact, more than one Part II contributor mentioned how it was the mistake he made that drove him to seek better information on nonverbal communication. Second, with experience they now have the practical knowledge base and a comfort level with their job such that they can do more of their job automatically, thus not taxing their cognitive capacity. This leaves more "brain space" available to incorporating new tools without confounding other elements of their job. And third, the experience base they have now developed can be a useful backdrop to help them put the information they learned in a clear context for more effective deployment on their jobs.

Importance of context in interpretation. All contributors noted that there was no perfect nonverbal indicator of deception or other internal states. And all noted that it is not simply the presence or absence of particular behaviors that is diagnostic of an individual's inner states, but that it is when and where the behaviors occur in conjunction with other (mainly verbal) behavior that is most useful. Thus it is not a sign of fear that might indicate deception; in fact, that sign of fear might indicate credibility if the individual is conveying his or her fears to a doctor. But if the context or words contradict an expression of fear, then it might be diagnostic. We discussed this in Chapter 6, but the broader research literature (outside of ourselves) has ignored this to date.

All contributors note that these changes or discrepancies in nonverbal behavior are not concrete indicators of deception but instead are likely indicators of feelings or thoughts. But they all acknowledge that they cannot know for sure why the individual might feel something or be thinking on his or her feet, so they all recommend following up with questions to try to resolve the behaviors that don't fit. Again, this is not discussed in the scientific literature.

Importance of baseline. All acknowledge the role of a baseline in assessing nonverbal communication—although some (e.g., Chapters 7, 8, 11, 13) have expanded our definitions of baseline to include not just a given person's behaviors, but that of the situation or wider environment. This is a particularly important issue for scientists, as our baselines are usually one-shot designs involving small samples of participants.

Importance of the interpersonal interaction. The contributors all acknowledge the role of the interaction itself in generating the sorts of nonverbal clues that might be useful to the practitioner. This is an often neglected element of nonverbal communication research (Frank, 2005). There is an assumption that any questions, delivered in any given way, won't have any systematic effects on a subject. But as our experienced practitioners point out, how they ask their questions, and how they manage their own demeanor, seems essential to generating clear, diagnostic behaviors. Conversely, muddled, confused questions and threatening demeanor will likely produce muddy, incomprehensible nonverbal signals.

Application

We can take the science from Part I and marry it to the practitioner accounts in Part II and generate the following mnemonic (Frank, Yarbrough, & Ekman, 2006) that will help practitioners best deploy their knowledge of nonverbal communication:

- Awareness
- Baseline
- Changes
- Discrepancies
- Engagement
- Follow-up

Awareness means that practitioners must be aware of a number of things to optimally take advantage of nonverbal communication. They must be aware of the nonverbal signals they are sending and receiving. They must be aware of various cultural norms for given groups of people that may govern their eye contact, the distance at which they stand, the amount of body and facial movements, and so forth. They even must be aware of the physical environment, the weather, time of year, and so forth. And finally, they must be aware of the power and limitations of nonverbal behavior analysis.

Baseline means that practitioners must take account of the environmental, situational, and behavioral norms of given persons and situations. They must be aware of when and where in the interaction they can generate the sorts of behaviors that they can note as examples of truth and deception so they can later compare them to the critical, crucial, or crunch points in the interaction to enable optimal comparisons for nonverbal behavior and achieve goals.

Changes refers to looking for behavioral changes in baseline—anomalies—be they environmental or individual baseline. Noticing when these changes occur in the behavioral sequence over time, and for which particular topic, is essential. These are best thought of as hot spots that signal that something internally has changed in the other person. This does not mean that the person is lying, as there can be many innocent reasons for these behaviors. But they are signs for further investigation.

Discrepancies refers to looking for those nonverbal behaviors that are discrepant from verbal or other behaviors not across time but at a given point in time. These too are hot spots, but they best represent a mismatched signal occurring amongst the different behavioral channels within an individual at one given point in time. In contrast, changes refer more to nonverbal behavioral changes in any given channel over time. Metaphorically, discrepancies refer to vertical differences across different channels at one point in time, whereas changes refer to more horizontal differences across the same behavioral channels over time for particular topics.

Engagement refers to the fact that once the changes and discrepancies are noted, the practitioner should engage the hot spots by either adjusting his or her own behavior or by asking additional questions about the topic that was being addressed once the hot spot occurred. This is often better executed, based on our experience, not at the immediate moment of the hot spot but after the individual completes his or her initial account or statement.

Follow-up refers to the fact that the issues raised during engagement need to be followed up—with other potentially corroborating information, or further questions, and so forth, to ascertain as best as possible what is going on in the mind of the other person.

Conclusion

We hope this journey through the world of scientists and practitioners was informative. Ideally, you've now developed a better sense of how to comprehend our opening example in this book:

> You are walking home late at night. You notice a man is walking toward you. He suddenly quickens his pace, body leaning forward, hands out in fists moving rhythmically with his stride. His eyebrows are drawn down in the middle. His eyes are wide. His lips are tight. He looks right at you.

We hope you'll look at that now and think that you have an angry man bearing down on you. Your gut reaction was caused by our description of nonverbal clues associated with the emotion of anger. You likely inferred that an angry man is more likely to assault you and that your reaction was likely some fear and a desire to move away from this person.

The science and the practice of nonverbal communication is at once complicated but also easy. It is easy because we have natural, biologically based expressive and detection mechanisms. Thus we need to do nothing to recognize overt nonverbal communication. But it is also complicated because living in the social world has caused us to manage, falsify, squelch, and conceal expressions when we really don't feel like expressing various nonverbal signals. Thus to be an accurate reader of others, we have to plow through all that socially expected chaff to find the kernel of wheat that is a person's true thoughts or feelings. And we must understand nonverbal communication at the moment it is expressed, not in some general accounting later where we simply count the number or amount of various behaviors. Recognizing it when it happens, interpreting it accurately, and then adjusting one's own behavior to maximally take advantage of that is difficult. That aspect of nonverbal communication has not been studied much by scientists. But our practitioners have lived in a world where their jobs, and sometimes their lives, depended upon doing that well. We hope the stories and insights they provided can give us a better perspective to understand the limits of the scientific analysis of nonverbal communication and prompt our scientists to incorporate many of the observations of the practitioners to render their scientific work more relevant to practitioners.

References

Anderson, N. (1965). Primacy effects in personality impression formation using a generalized order effect paradigm. *Journal of Personality and Social Psychology, 2*, 1–9.

Chi, M. T. H., Glaser, R., & Farr, M. J. (Eds.). (1988). *The nature of expertise.* Hillsdale, NJ: Erlbaum.

Coy v. Iowa, 108, S. Ct., 2798 (1988).

DePaulo, B. M., Lindsay, J. J., Malone, B. E., Muhlenbruck, L., Charlton, K., & Cooper, H. (2003). Cues to deception. *Psychological Bulletin, 129,* 74–118.

Ekman, P., O'Sullivan, M., & Frank, M. G. (1999). A few can catch a liar. *Psychological Science, 10,* 263–266.

Frank, M. G. (2005). Research methods in detecting deception research. In J. Harrigan, R. Rosenthal, & K. Scherer (Eds.), *The new handbook of methods in nonverbal behavior research* (pp. 341–368). New York: Oxford University Press.

Frank, M. G., Yarbrough, J. D., & Ekman, P. (2006). Improving interpersonal evaluations: Combining science and practical experience. In T. Williamson (Ed.),

Investigative interviewing: Rights, research, regulation (pp. 229–255). Portland, OR: Willan.

Gladwell, M. (2008). *Outliers: The story of success*. New York: Little, Brown.

Hirsch, A. R., & Wolf, C. J. (2001). Practical methods for detecting mendacity: A case study. *Journal of the American Academy of Psychiatry and Law, 29*, 438–444.

Levine, T. R., Serota, K. B., & Shulman, H. C. (2010). The impact of *Lie to me* on viewer's actual ability to detect deception. *Communication Research, 37*, 847–856.

Nisbett, R. E., & Ross, L. (1980). *Human inference: Strategies and shortcomings of social judgment*. Englewood Cliffs, NJ: Prentice-Hall.

O'Sullivan, M., Frank, M. G., & Hurley, C. M. (2010). Training for individual differences in lie detection accuracy. In J. G. Voeller (Ed.), *Handbook of science and technology for homeland security*. New York: Wiley.

Schleidt, M. (1980). Personal odor and nonverbal communication. *Ethology and Sociobiology, 1*, 225–231.

Author Index

Subject Index

About the Editors

David Matsumoto received his B.A. from the University of Michigan in 1981 with high honors in psychology and Japanese. He subsequently earned his M.A. (1983) and Ph.D. (1986) in psychology from the University of California at Berkeley. He is currently professor of psychology and director of the Culture and Emotion Research Laboratory at San Francisco State University, where he has been since 1989. He is also director of Humintell, LLC, a company that provides research, consultation, and training on non-verbal behavioral analysis and cross-cultural adaptation. He has studied culture, emotion, social interaction, and communication for over 30 years. His books include well-known titles such as *Culture and Psychology,* the *Cambridge Dictionary of Psychology,* and *Cross-Cultural Research Methods in Psychology.* He is the recipient of many awards and honors in the field of psychology, including being named a G. Stanley Hall lecturer by the American Psychological Association. He is the series editor for Cambridge University Press' series on *Culture and Psychology.* He is also editor in chief for the *Journal of Cross-Cultural Psychology.*

Mark G. Frank is a professor and director of the Communication Science Center at the University at Buffalo. He received his Ph.D. in social psychology from Cornell University in 1989, and afterward he received a National Research Service Award from the National Institute of Mental Health to do postdoctoral research with Paul Ekman in the Psychiatry Department at the University of California at San Francisco Medical School. He had previously been on the faculty in the School of Psychology at the University of New South Wales in Australia, as well as the Communication Department at Rutgers University in New Jersey. He has published numerous research papers on facial expressions, emotion, and interpersonal deception, with much of the work funded by the National Science Foundation, Homeland Security, and the Department of Defense. He is also the codeveloper of an automated computer system to read facial expressions. He has used these findings to lecture, consult with, and train virtually all US federal law enforcement/intelligence agencies, as well as local/state and select foreign agencies. He has also given workshops to US and foreign judges and magistrates. He has presented briefings to the National Academy of Sciences and the US Congress on deception and counterterrorism. Finally, his work has been featured in print and on radio and television, including *Time* magazine, the *New York Times, CBS Evening News,* CNN, Fox News Channel, National Public Radio, the Learning Channel, the Discovery Channel, *Oprah,* and so forth.

Hyi Sung Hwang received her M.A. from San Francisco State University and her Ph.D. from the Center for Psychological Studies of the Graduate School of Human Behavior, Berkeley, CA, 2009. She is a research scientist at Humintell, LLC, and visiting scholar at San Francisco State University. Her research interests are in emotion, nonverbal behaviors, and culture. She is an expert at the Facial Action Coding System and in the conduct of research examining facial expressions and other nonverbal behaviors. She is cocreator of many of the training tools used to teach law enforcement officers, national security personnel, and intelligence agents, as well as individuals in many other professions, how to recognize micro and subtle facial expressions of emotion. She has also coauthored numerous scientific articles and book chapters on nonverbal behavior, facial expressions, and culture and has made presentations of her research nationally and internationally.

About the Contributors

Daniel H. Baxter (Chapter 10) holds a master's degree in forensic psychology and was a police officer and detective for 14 years before becoming a Special Agent for the Department of Defense in 1987. He is currently a Technical Director for the polygraph and has been the principal investigator for several research projects involving deception detection. For the past 15 years, he has taught interviewing techniques to various national, federal, and state organizations.

Andrew Boughton (Chapter 13) is the managing partner at the Edge Negotiation Group. Prior to his consulting practice, he worked in the music industry.

Scott Brownell (Chapter 11) is a Circuit Judge, Twelfth Judicial Circuit, (1987 to date) in Bradenton, Florida. He holds a B.A. from Eckerd College (1971) and a J.D. from the University of Florida College of Law (1974). He has been a judicial education presenter at the National Judicial College, Reno, Nevada, and at judicial conferences in Florida, Georgia, Delaware, Ohio, Washington, Alaska, and Minnesota.

Joseph Ennett (Chapter 8) holds a bachelor of science degree from the American University and is currently retired from his career in law enforcement. He was a criminal investigator in the United States Army, a police officer in Virginia and Missouri, and is retired from 24 years as a Special Agent in the United States Treasury Department. He has instructed in the interviewing field for 16 years with an emphasis on nonverbal communication.

Clark Freshman (Chapter 12) is a tenured professor at University of California, Hastings College of Law, and teaches emotional intelligence, lie detection, emotion, and nonverbal communication worldwide to lawyers and negotiators. His past engagements include JAMS, the International Academy of Mediators, the Conference of Federal Administrative Law Judges, and

Harvard Law School and Business School. He has also trained negotiators at hedge funds, private equity funds, consulting firms, and at open-enrollment events. His work on negotiation, emotion, and discrimination in law and psychology has appeared in law reviews at Harvard, Stanford, Cornell, and elsewhere and has been reproduced in three major textbooks on negotiation.

Darrin J. Griffin (Chapter 3) is indigenous to Austin, Texas, and is currently a doctoral student at the Department of Communication, University at Buffalo. His research in deceptive communication occurs at the intersection of psycho-linguistics and nonverbal behavior and is designed with the goal of providing practical knowledge utilized by those working in applied settings.

Nick R. Harrington (Chapter 15) is a Principal Scientist and expert in consumer psychology at the Procter & Gamble Company in Cincinnati, Ohio. He is the technical leader of P&G's breakthrough Biometrics Group, with corporate responsibility for applying principles from psychology and the neurosciences to better understand and predict consumer behavior globally. He completed his undergraduate degree from the University of Sussex, UK, and doctorate of philosophy from the University of York, UK, in experimental psychology, specializing in the fields of learning and memory. He worked as a postdoctoral scientist in the behavioral neuroscience division at Wyeth, Cerebrus, and Vernalis Pharmaceuticals before joining P&G. He teaches psychology and advanced biometrics within P&G and has published and presented externally. In 2010 he was awarded the Marketing Research Emerging Leader Award by the American Marketing Association in recognition of his pioneering work applying psychological principles to consumer research.

Steve Longford (Chapter 14) is a former Australian police officer who attained designations of detective, senior intelligence analyst, and behavioral analyst before his resignation in 2000. He became involved in the development and deployment of intelligence and investigative management software for a private Australian organization before setting up a company dedicated to training based on science and research. He has spent the last 8 years researching and developing programs revolving around human capability, capacity, and performance. He specializes in areas of nonverbal behavior, emotions, decision making, influence, and uncertainty.

Carl Joseph Maccario (Chapter 7) is a graduate of Suffolk University in Boston, Massachusetts. He received his bachelor of science in 1982. Prior to 9/11/01, he served in the Commonwealth of Massachusetts Secretary of State's office as an investigator/auditor for the Securities Division. Subsequent to 9/11, he left his position with the state and began a career with Virgin Atlantic Airlines Security as a passenger profiler. While there, he received training in behavior pattern recognition, document ID verification, deception detection, and eliciting responses from an Israeli security firm hired by Virgin Atlantic. Shortly after the Congress created the Department of Homeland Security, he began his career with the federal government using his knowledge and security experience to help design, develop, and implement the first behavior screening program for a major international airport, one that is now being implemented in airports across the United States. During this development, he trained hundreds of security and law enforcement professionals in suspicious behavior detection, detecting deception, and eliciting responses.

Andreas Maroulis (Chapter 3) is a masters student at the Department of Communication, University at Buffalo. His research interests focus on the experimental design associated with studies in nonverbal expressions of emotion, behavior during deception and the application of both in real-world contexts.

Paul M. Moskal (Chapter 9) is a licensed attorney who has consulted in the legal, media, and security fields. He was a Special Agent with the FBI for 30 years where he worked in national and international venues on matters involving criminal violations and intelligence concerns. One of his most challenging roles was while holding the Chief Division Counsel for the Buffalo, New York, field office of the FBI. He is currently employed in the intelligence community.

Michael R. Privitera (Chapter 17) is an Associate Professor of Psychiatry at the University of Rochester Medical Center (URMC) and directs the Psychiatric Consultation/Liaison Service, which services the medical/surgical/OB-GYN service patients. He also directs the Mood and Anxiety Disorder Clinic, which services the medical community and region with consultation on difficult-to-treat mood and anxiety disorders. Through the years he has acquired clinical and administrative experience, along with the following achievements: cochairing the Department of Psychiatry Workplace Violence (WPV) Committee, membership from the URMC Workplace Safety Committee, and completing a sabbatical focusing on WPV. He has assembled national and international interdisciplinary and interprofessional experts in the WPV field, which culminated in editing and writing for the book *Workplace Violence in Mental and General Healthcare Settings* (Jones & Bartlett, 2011). He has also given international presentations on interdisciplinary and interprofessional approaches to prevention and dealing urgently with WPV issues directly before, during, and directly after violent or potentially violent events.

Robert Sheeler (Chapter 16) is a family physician at Mayo Clinic with a wide range of interests. In addition to practicing primary care medicine, he is also a board certified headache specialist. He has been involved with medical publications and teaching at Mayo Medical School. The teaching aspects of his job and his interest in better outcomes as well as the nuances of patient care have led him to an interest in teaching communications to medical professionals. He also has strong interest and background in pharmacology and in various complementary and alternative medicine practices including teaching Taiji and Qigong.

Elena Svetieva (Chapter 6) is a doctoral student at the Department of Communication, University at Buffalo. A communication scholar with a background in psychology, she mainly studies interpersonal communication processes, including nonverbal behavior in deception, social rejection, and emotion expression.

$SAGE research**methods**
The Essential Online Tool for Researchers

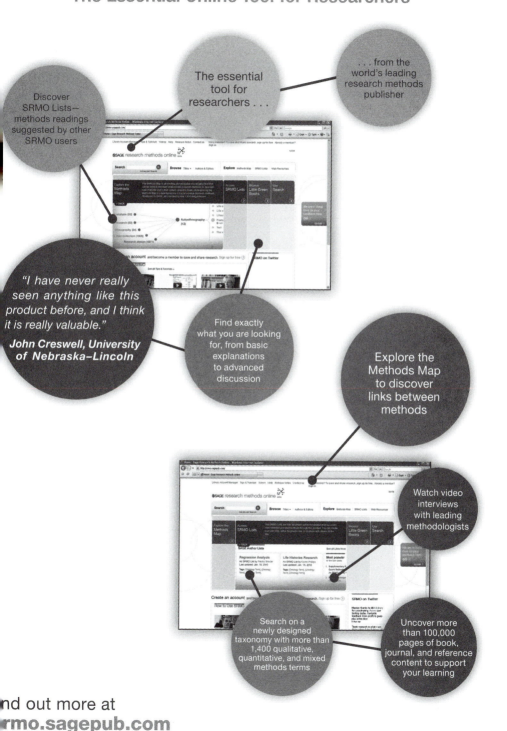

Discover SRMO Lists— methods readings suggested by other SRMO users

The essential tool for researchers . . .

. . . from the world's leading research methods publisher

"I have never really seen anything like this product before, and I think it is really valuable."

John Creswell, University of Nebraska–Lincoln

Find exactly what you are looking for, from basic explanations to advanced discussion

Explore the Methods Map to discover links between methods

Watch video interviews with leading methodologists

Search on a newly designed taxonomy with more than 1,400 qualitative, quantitative, and mixed methods terms

Uncover more than 100,000 pages of book, journal, and reference content to support your learning

nd out more at
rmo.sagepub.com